Russian Revolution of 1917

Russian Revolution of 1917

THE ESSENTIAL REFERENCE GUIDE

Sean N. Kalic and Gates M. Brown, Editors

An Imprint of ABC-CLIO, LLC
Santa Barbara, California • Denver, Colorado

Library of Congress Cataloging-in-Publication Data

Names: Kalic, Sean N., 1970- editor. | Brown, Gates M., editor.
Title: Russian Revolution of 1917 : the essential reference guide / Sean N. Kalic and
    Gates M. Brown, editors.
Description: Santa Barbara, California : ABC-CLIO, 2017. | Includes bibliographical
    references and index.
Identifiers: LCCN 2017012322 (print) | LCCN 2017013332 (ebook) |
    ISBN 9781440850936 (ebook) | ISBN 9781440850929 (alk. paper)
Subjects: LCSH: Soviet Union—History—Revolution, 1917-1921—Encyclopedias.
Classification: LCC DK265 (ebook) | LCC DK265 .R958 2017 (print) | DDC 947.084/1—dc23
LC record available at https://lccn.loc.gov/2017012322

ISBN: 978-1-4408-5092-9 (print)
       978-1-4408-5093-6 (ebook)

21 20 19 18 17   1 2 3 4 5

This book is also available as an eBook.

ABC-CLIO
An Imprint of ABC-CLIO, LLC

ABC-CLIO, LLC
130 Cremona Drive, P.O. Box 1911
Santa Barbara, California 93116-1911
www.abc-clio.com

This book is printed on acid-free paper ∞

Manufactured in the United States of America

To Marty, Anna, and Garrison, thank you for everything.
To Tracie and Katheryn, the loves of my life.

Contents

Preface

When Tsar Nicholas II abdicated his throne in February 1917, he ended over 400 years of Romanov rule in Russia. Although the abdication came suddenly, the source of discontent in Russia began long before 1917. The tsar's abdication opened an opportunity for democratic institutions to come to power in Russia. However, before 1917 ended, the Russian people were under the rule of the Bolshevik Party. This new socialist state endured for over 70 years. For many, the events of 1917 center around the Bolshevik's October Revolution of 1917. However, when the tsar stepped down and the Provisional Government began, the Bolsheviks were not even the largest socialist political party in Russia. The intent of this volume is to provide a broader understanding of the Russian Revolution and how the Bolsheviks came to solidify power in Russia, or what became the Soviet Union. Revolutions are complex events that are difficult to explain neatly. The Russian Revolution is no exception. The intent of this encyclopedia is not to provide an exhaustive explanation or analysis of the revolution. Rather, this work is an introduction to key events, figures, and documents that shaped the revolution in its broader context. In an effort to capture the complexity of the Russian Revolution and its aftermath, it is critical to understand how the events of 1917 led to the historic events that

profoundly shaped the history of Russia and its people. To provide solid historical context of the forces that shaped and ultimately produced the Russian Revolution, the scope of this work begins chronologically in 1905. Due to the realities of writing a single-volume encyclopedia, there were elements of the broader social, political, and cultural context that simply could not be discussed in this volume. For this reason, the editors focused on connecting the events of 1905 to 1917, the impact of World War I, the Provisional Government, the Bolsheviks, and the anti-Bolshevik forces that fought in the Russian Civil War. The intent is to introduce readers to the roots of the revolution and the subsequent civil war to encourage further investigation.

The entries in this volume address main actors, events, and documents in the revolution and the civil war. However, it is impossible to address the nuance of these people and events in an encyclopedic format. Therefore, contributors to this volume relied on their training in history to provide relevant analysis of facts so readers can gain the most insight given the limited space.

Although entries are the mainstay of encyclopedias, they are only one approach to understanding a topic. In order to provide readers with a greater appreciation of the events discussed, this work contains many translations of primary documents. These documents, such as Lenin's call for an uprising in 1917, give the reader the ability to read and comprehend the words and writings of the primary leaders and participants of the revolution. Each primary source document has a brief introduction to describe the context of the document and establish its connections to the events and people of the Russian Revolution. We believe that using documents provides not only a useful reference for gaining a broad understanding of the revolution and the civil war but also a chance to begin to research and go beyond the interpretations provided by the contributors to this work.

Dates are problematic when discussing the Russian Revolution. Prior to January 31, 1931, Russia used the Julian calendar. Most European countries and the United States use the Gregorian calendar, which is 10 to 14 days ahead of the Julian calendar. For example, the Bolshevik Revolution occurred in 1917 on the night of November 6–7 according to the Gregorian calendar but on October, 24–25 according to the Julian calendar. This is why it is the "The Great October Revolution" in Russia. For dates prior to January 31, 1918, the Julian dates are provided unless otherwise noted in the text.

One of the main obstacles to the study of Russian history is the language barrier. Although this volume is in English, the issue of transliteration is not straightforward. In most cases, the editors used the Library of Congress system. This renders names such as "Aleksandr" as "Alexander." There are exceptions in the case of more recognizable place-names or people.

Gates M. Brown and Sean N. Kalic
Leavenworth, KS 2017

RUSSIAN REVOLUTION AND CIVIL WAR

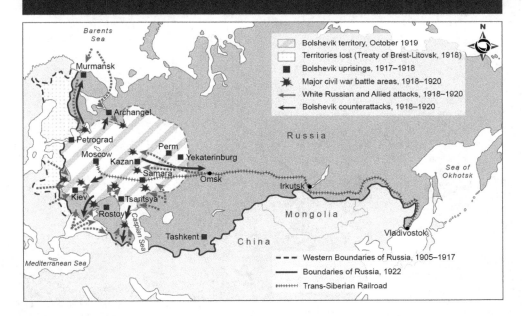

Introductory Essays

The 1905 Revolution

Though the process of discussing the events of the Russian Revolution of 1905 may not seem germane to a reference guide on the 1917 Bolshevik Revolution and the resulting Russian Civil War, the reality is that in order to understand the larger contextual undercurrent in Russia during the abdication of Tsar Nicholas II, the rise and fall of the Provisional Government, the onset of the Bolshevik Revolution, and the turbulent period of the Russian Civil War, the events of 1905 are of vital importance to building a greater understanding of the political and social issues that sparked the tumultuous change that bore the Soviet Union. Looking at the state of Russia under the leadership of Tsar Alexander III and his successor Tsar Nicholas II, the events of 1905 provide a solid context for understanding the stage that had been set for the significant events that took place across Russia in the spring and fall of 1917.

Background: Alexander III

Beginning with the assassination of his father Tsar Alexander II by the radical political organization Will of the People on March 13, 1881, his son Alexander III assumed the throne of the Russian Empire and sought to suppress the emerging revolutionary forces focused on withering the autocratic power of the tsar and his deputies. Alexander III's first act to control and suppress calls for change came with the publication of the Temporary Regulations in the summer of 1881.

Alexander III issued his Temporary Regulations as a means to assist government officials in preserving "state security and public order." In effect, the order provided the government with an expanded ability to search, arrest, imprison, exile, and try people who threatened public order. Note that these powers also applied to the press, which Alexander III saw as equally destabilizing to the regime. Though the initial issuance of the Temporary Regulations were meant to last for just three years, the reality was that Alexander III saw these measures as a means to suppress and quiet people who questioned the actions and policies of the regime. The effect of this measure according to Nicholas Riasanovsky in *A History of Russia* was that Russians lived in a "partial state of martial law."

Not just focusing on forces that questioned the power and control of the regime, Alexander III also pressed forward with counterreforms that rescinded many of his father's attempts to liberalize the bureaucratic and class systems of Russia. Alexander III sought more control and power by reemphasizing the role of the gentry, land captains, the zemstvos, and other powerful elites who traditionally had been political allies to Russia's tsars. Though the regime of Alexander III worked to suppress internal discontent for the regime, the period 1881–1894 also saw Russia wrestle with the beginnings of industrialization and the influence this socioeconomic force had on the people and the regime in Russia.

With the assistance of a string of trusted finance ministers—Nicholas Bunge (1881–1887), Ivan Vyshnegradsky (1887–1892), and Sergei Witte (1892–1903)—Russia established limitations on workdays for children ages 12 to 15. They also worked to ensure that in the textile industry children and women did not work night shifts. Finally, the regime worked to ensure that workers received regular pay without excessive fines from their employers. While these accomplishments were significant, they could not overcome the festering discontent among peasants and the proletariat class within Russia. As the regime of Alexander III passed to his son Nicholas II in 1894, the social, economic, and political conditions in Russia continued to evolve, yet the position of the tsar and their ideas about governance and rule remained fixated on an outdated concept of divine right.

Tsar Nicholas II

Traditionally, Nicholas II, the last Russian tsar, has been characterized as a strong family man and a ruler tied to outdated traditions, which served him poorly in the tumultuous years 1905 and 1917. Though he strove to maintain the power and control of his father, Nicholas had to contend with a host of social, political, and economic changes that shook Russian society to its very core. Unable to make the hard decisions necessary to navigate the increasingly chaotic political environment in Russia, Nicholas would be forced to abdicate his throne,

which was the first step in the sweeping changes that Russians had to endure between 1917 and 1921.

As a way to characterize the little real change between the regimes of Alexander III and Nicholas II, one only needs to acknowledge that Nicholas II retained his father's Temporary Regulations despite the rapidly changing social and political landscape of Russia as industrialization took hold. In addition to the political pressures that rose from the more activist proletariat class, Nicholas II also had to manage Russia within the community of nations as The Hague evolved to be an international conduit for international relations. Furthermore, one cannot discount the trials and tribulations of the Russo-Japanese War (1904–1905), which ceased with the Treaty of Portsmouth in August 1905, as the tsar and his government confronted the forces that would ultimately blossom into the 1905 revolution. Although Nicholas II had international issues that affected the regime, the forces that culminated in the politically charged events of 1905 stemmed largely from domestic issues.

The rise of increased political pressure on the regime actually started in 1891–1892, when the Russian people endured an incredible famine that affected roughly 20 million people, of whom approximately 400,000 died. This catastrophic event led to the rebirth of political activism by liberals under Alexander III. Though the powers of the Temporary Regulations served as a tamper to widespread political opposition to the regime, by the turn of the century political actors such as Peter Struve, an accomplished economist, formed the Union of Liberation, with its own journal, *Liberation* as a mouthpiece to voice concern over social, economic, and political policies of Nicholas II. By 1905, this "liberal" political organization had metamorphosed into the

Constitutional Democratic (Kadet) Party, led by historian Pavel (Paul) Miliukov. The Kadet Party catered to a wide swath of constitutional monarchs as well as republicans.

In addition to the Kadets, other more radical parties emerged seeking to alter the powers of the regime in more militant ways compared to the platform of Miliukov's Kadets. The most noteworthy party to emerge in this turbulent political and social context was the Social Democratic Party, initially led by Georgi Plekhanov. Plekhanov and other Russian Marxist intellectuals founded the party's predecessor organization, the Emancipation of Labor Group, as a means to focus on the plight of the growing proletariat in Russia. Though the party had a slow start in Russia at the twilight of the 19th century, it gained a more significant impact after its leadership held international conventions in Brussels and London in 1903. Within the emerging party that advocated the revolution of the proletariat, as established by Karl Marx, there emerged two divergent factions about how the party should move forward about organizing and advancing the revolution. The first group was led by Vladimir Ilyich Ulianov, or V. I. Lenin, within the lexicon of Russian revolutionary history. Lenin and his Bolshevik contingent argued that the ideas of Marx had to be cultivated and practiced by a professional revolutionary class that would shepherd the proletariat through the various stages of Marxism. Lenin and his Bolshevik Party believed that the vast majority of the proletariat lacked the intellectual capability and foresight to guide the revolution through the various phases, as outlined by Marx.

Therefore, Lenin built the Bolshevik wing of the Social Democratic Party as a professional revolutionary cadre that worked to foster and implement the proletarian revolution on behalf of and in conjunction with the workers of Russia and ultimately the world.

Between the turn of the 20th century and the Bolshevik Revolution, this wing of the party dealt consistently with harsh repression, imprisonment, and exile at the hands of Alexander III and, more important, Nicholas II as their advocacy for the tenets of Marxism and the ultimate end state of a communist society deeply threatened the longevity and governance of the Romanovs.

The Bolsheviks' rival faction within the Social Democrats was the Mensheviks, who also adhered to the tenets of Marxism. However, the Mensheviks differed with Lenin and his Bolsheviks over the need for a professional revolutionary class to reach Marx's projected end state. Furthermore, the Mensheviks held a more orthodox view on the proletarian revolution, as stipulated by Marx. Believing that Lenin and his Bolsheviks were accelerating Marx's formula by working with peasants and workers to foment a working-class revolution, the Mensheviks rejected this sequence by arguing that the proletarian revolution could only be cultivated and launched in the aftermath of the revolution of the bourgeois revolution. The Mensheviks argued that Marx had identified this stage as a critical and necessary step prior to the onset and development of the proletarian revolution. They did not believe that the Social Democrats should short-circuit the tenets of Marx.

Though both the Mensheviks and Bolsheviks saw the same end state for Russia, differences emerged as to the proper path the party should take to achieve the objective outlined by Marx in the middle of the 19th century. As the Social Democrats moved toward the 1917 October Revolution, this inherent difference simmered as they were on the edge of the forecasted working-class revolution.

In addition to the Bolsheviks and Mensheviks and their common Social Democratic lineage, The Socialist Revolutionary Party was yet a third force that pushed for more radical changes within tsarist Russia. The Social Revolutionaries, unlike the Social Democrats, focused on the more traditional populist movements that emerged in Russia earlier in the 19th century. The Social Revolutionaries, which advocated agricultural reform and hence a major reordering of society under the tsar, openly used violence and terrorism to push its radical agenda. Led by Victor Chernov in 1901 with the formal founding of the party, the Social Revolutionaries continued to harass the tsar as well as other political parties by using assassination and violence as a means to advance their political agenda, which seemed to parallel the objectives of the Will of the People who harassed and troubled Tsar Alexander III a generation earlier.

In the midst of the expanding political spectrum that focused on workers and peasants, Tsar Nicholas II also had to contend with the growth of Russia's middle class and the subsequent unions that emerged to represent their thoughts and ideas about how the tsar and Russia needed to adjust the government and society to the changing realities of the early 20th century and industrialization. In addition to these growing social and political pressures, Nicholas II also had to struggle with the Zemstvo Congress in 1904 that demanded a representative assembly for the people of Russia as well as increased civil liberties across the empire. Though the government made some very limited attempts to address the ideas and issues radiating from these various groups, the tried-and-true method of repression proved to be the most expedient means to stop criticism of the regime.

In January 1905 George Gapon, an Orthodox priest, launched a march to the tsar's Winter Palace, whereby Gapon and his police union planned to offer Nicholas II a petition that highlighted many of the social and political changes that zemstvos and political parties had advocated for since the turn of the century. At the same time that Gapon led his march to the Winter Palace, workers had been organizing their own march to the gates of the palace to voice their concerns for conditions in Russia, with the objective of asking Tsar Nicholas II for assistance.

The marches of Gapon and the workers coalesced into a single mass movement that placed the tsar's police on edge. Yet in both cases, the marchers were not advocating the demise of the government but instead, ironically, were asking Nicholas II to use his power to adjust the government to the changing social and economic realities in Russia. However, in the heat of the moment, the tsar's troops and police fired into the crowd as a way to stop what they perceived to be an assault on the Winter Palace.

The events of what became known as Bloody Sunday served as a significant break in the evolving political situation in Russia. Though Gapon, workers, and even the zemstvos had advocated change, for the most part they remained relatively loyal to the tsar. However, the events on Sunday, January 22, 1905, solidified opposition to the tsar and focused the energies of the Social Democrats and the Social Revolutionaries on the Left on seizing this opportunity to start the people's revolution.

The Aftermath of Bloody Sunday

In the days following the troubling events of Bloody Sunday, Nicholas II strove to mitigate the increased pressure that culminated in the public protests of January. In an attempt to demonstrate to the people of Russia that he was indeed listening to their demands, Nicholas II in March 1905 moved to pacify the people by providing some political and social concessions, though he was not willing to relinquish or alter the fundamental powers of the tsar and his government.

The primary action by Nicholas called for the development of a "consultative assembly," which had been a major point of contention between the tsar and his people. Though not willing to go so far as to allow the people a true representative assembly with real political power, Nicholas did state that he would see to the development of an assembly that could provide some venue of input from the people. However, the more radical political parties noted that this new assembly only had the power to offer insights and recommendations to the tsar. It by no means had any real political power within the context of the tsar's government.

In addition to the assembly, Nicholas also attempted to quell the discontent of his people by relaxing legislation dealing with ethnic minorities and also allowing a greater degree of religious toleration throughout his polyglot empire. Even though these were changes to the political structure of the regime, which Nicholas II believed to be significant, they were minor in the eyes of the people. The token offerings by the tsar did little to stop the growing discontent of the people throughout the Russian Empire.

One of the most significant examples of the tension within the Russian Empire can be understood by looking at the mutiny of sailors on the battleship *Potemkin* in June 1905. The events started with a seemingly simple protest by the *Potemkin*'s cook, who questioned the ship's captain and his executive officer about the quality of the meat being served to the crew. The crew believed the meat to be "rotten." The captain appealed to the ship's doctor for a final adjudication of the quality of the meat. The ship's doctor declared the meat "fit to eat."

Believing otherwise and siding with the cook, sailors on the *Potemkin* formed a delegation to make an additional appeal to the captain and his executive office about the meat's poor quality and the fact that it had worms. The delegation of sailors, led by G. M. Vakulenchuk presented their case to the executive officer of the *Potemkin,* Commander Ippolit Giliarovskii. Giliarovskii did not care for the "crude words" and manner in which Vakulenchuk presented the case about the quality of meat. Giliarovskii, having thought the matter settled and not wishing to deal further with acts of insubordination, shot and killed Vakulenchuk in a fit a rage.

The murder of Vakulenchuk led his comrades to throw Giliarovskii overboard and shoot him in the water. In the commotion, additional sailors joined the foray and killed an additional five officers, including the captain as well as the doctor, who had declared the meat fit for consumption. The mutinous sailors locked all other officers in a cabin, took control of the *Potemkin,* and hoisted the red flag of revolution. Furthermore, the sailors nominated and elected a "people's committee" to take charge of the ship. The leader elected by the sailors was a Social Democrat, A. N. Matiushenko. Beyond seizing one of the most powerful ships in the Russian Navy, Matiushenko and his comrades sought to capitalize on this opportunity and inspire other mutinies throughout the navy.

Seeing opportunity beyond the Russian Navy, Matiushenko strove to gain mass support for the actions taken by the sailors. By mid-June the *Potemkin* had set sail for Odessa, which was in the midst of strikes and open violence between revolutionaries and Cossacks. Local officials had already sent messages to the government that the strikes in Odessa had moved beyond protests and were quickly coalescing into a revolutionary uprising.

Matiushenko and the crew of the *Potemkin* arrived in Odessa at the height of this tension. Seizing the opportunity, the sailors of the *Potemkin* arrived on land with an honor guard carrying Vakulenchuk's body and laid it on the steps of the harbor with a note pinned to the body highlighting the heroic actions taken by Vakulenchuk. The note also made certain to mention that the sailors had taken the proper recourse against the captain and officers of the *Potemkin.*

Vakulenchuk's body quickly became a shrine for the strikers and revolutionaries in Odessa. When Cossacks and policemen attempted to break up the growing congregation of people around the body of Vakulenchuk, a signal was given onshore for the *Potemkin* to fire. The police and the Cossacks quickly retreated, and the ship did not fire into the city. However, the sailors on board the *Potemkin* made it known through official communications that any attempt to use violence to disperse the crowd would lead to the *Potemkin* firing into the city.

In the midst of these tense negotiations, government officials had already called for Tsar Nicholas II to impose martial law as a means to regain control of the city. Nicholas agreed and sent a telegram telling officials to "take the most decisive measures to suppress the uprising." After receiving the tsar's order, the troops, the policemen, and the Cossacks used gunfire as a means to subdue the protests. After a night of suppression the government forces had killed approximately 2,000 people and wounded an additional 3,000. The harsh means used by the tsar's forces had the intended effect and quelled the rebellion in Odessa.

Having lost the momentum of the uprising, the *Potemkin* and its revolutionary crew sailed to Constanza in Romania in an attempt to replenish much-needed supplies. The Romanian officials offered a deal to the crew of the *Potemkin* that essentially called for the peaceful surrender of the vessel. The crew of the *Potemkin* refused the offer and attempted to steam toward Feodosiia to gain coal, water, and other much-needed supplies. The landing party charged with acquiring supplies for the *Potemkin* were quickly rebuffed by government gunfire. In a hopeless situation, the crew of the *Potemkin* sailed back to Constanza, took the original offer, and surrendered the ship.

Though the mutiny and seizure of the battleship *Potemkin* did not threaten the stability of the tsar's regime, it did demonstrate that the tension that led to the marches on Bloody Sunday had not disappeared in the face of the tsar's minor political adjustments.

The October Manifesto

In the aftermath of the uprisings in Odessa and the seizure of the *Potemkin* by "revolutionaries," Tsar Nicholas II in August 1905 attempted to make an additional concession by issuing an imperial decree for an elected Duma with consultative powers. Even though the tsar moved to allow for the election of Duma representation, he still held fast on limiting the political powers granted to the assembly. His action did nothing to appease the restless demands of the people. Nicholas's offering in August provoked a massive general strike that lasted for three months and did nothing to calm the ire of the people.

Faced by this mounting tension and opposition, the tsar capitulated and on October 30, 1905, issued the October Manifesto. The essence of this important document is that the tsar announced the creation of an elected Duma with real legislative functions, which transformed the Romanov government into a constitutional monarchy. The vast majority of people affiliated with political parties hailed this change as an important and historic step in the history of Russia, which it was indeed. However, more radical factions such as Social Democrats and Social Revolutionaries saw the tsar's action as inadequate and wanted additional political and social changes for the people of Russia. The outright opposition of the Social Democrats drove the party to begin calling for revolution again through their soviets. The steadfast actions by the Social Democrats led the tsar and his government to once again crack down, arrest, and harass the Social Democrats. As 1905 came to a close it looked similar to the previous year, yet the tsar had made a major concession and allowed for the election of the Duma.

Dumas

Prior to the meeting of the First Duma, Tsar Nicholas II issued the Fundamental Laws, which outlined the framework for the new Russian political system. Though the Duma was to be elected and have limited legislative powers, the tsar via the Fundamental Laws still retained significant power for himself and his ministers, including the ability to work around the legislation of the Duma with vetoes and emergency powers to override legislation when the Duma was not in session. Furthermore, to counterbalance the elective assembly of the Duma, the tsar stipulated that the emperor still retained the right to appoint up to half of the upper house of the Duma.

Despite the recognition that these were momentous times in Russia, the first two Dumas met with little success, as they suffered from significant partisan tensions that in turn led to stalemate in the new institution. The result of the first Duma, which met on May 10, 1906, was that it was dissolved by the tsar after a turbulent and very problematic 73-day period, having made no major headway.

The Second Duma met on March 5, 1907, and fared little better than the first attempt.

Again due to tense political coalitions and vastly different competing agendas, the tsar dissolved the Second Duma after only three months.

In an attempt to provide for a more productive and fruitful political institution, Tsar Nicholas II changed the electoral laws on the very same day that he had dissolved the Second Duma, June 16, 1907. The aim of these adjustments was to produce a more cooperative Duma in order to create a political climate that would lead to a more productive and useful institution. With this new decree Nicholas II decimated the representation of peasants and workers. This action also allowed for an increase in the representation of the gentry, which was well beyond its proportion of society. The result of these unconstitutional adjustments by the tsar to the electoral laws of Russia was that the Third and Fourth Dumas functioned for full terms, even though the tension with peasants and workers continued to increase and sustain itself. The Fourth Duma served its full term from 1912 until the revolution in March 1917.

Consequences of 1905

The events of 1905 that started with Bloody Sunday and ended with the issuing of the October Manifesto provided a glimpse into the growing discontent of peasants, workers, and soldiers in Russia at the same time that Tsar Nicholas II was hesitant to alter his government and empire. For more conservative political parties such as the Octobrists, the tsar's manifesto provided a substantial and needed change in the government of the Russian Empire. However, for the Social Democrats and Socialist Revolutionaries, the October Manifesto only demonstrated that Tsar Nicholas II was unwilling to meet the demands voiced by the peasants, workers, and soldiers, who represented a far greater proportion of Russian society.

The consequences of the Russian Revolution of 1905 therefore vary depending on the political perspective. In the context of the Bolshevik Revolution of 1917, the events of 1905 demonstrated that the Social Democrats were indeed tapping into a momentous popular position that gained support with each repressive action from the tsar. The events of 1905 for the Bolsheviks and Mensheviks highlighted the need to continue work for the eventual proletarian revolution. Furthermore, interpreting events within the context of Karl Marx, minor political and social adjustments by the tsar did nothing to alter the corrupt system. Violence and revolution stood as the only means for real change in the corrupt and oppressive regime of the tsar.

The year 1905 therefore provided the Bolsheviks with keen insights and experiences from which they could learn and adapt for the eventual collapse of the tsar and his empire. Though they would suffer harsh repression and exile in the 12 years between the events of 1905 and the heady days of October 1917, the events throughout 1905 served their cause, and their agenda did indeed forever alter the regime of Tsar Nicholas II. Yet, more work had to be done in order to foster additional support throughout Russia for the Bolshevik cause. The tensions that existed in 1905 would only be magnified as Russia entered World War I, and by 1917 the conditions between March and October provided the Bolsheviks with the opportunity they had wanted in 1905: the end of the tsar's empire.

Sean N. Kalic

The 1917 Revolution

The Russian Revolution of 1917 occurred in two stages. There was the February Revolution, which overthrew the tsar's regime and resulted in the Provisional Government, and then the October Revolution, which established the Bolsheviks as the governing power over what became the Soviet Union. These two movements differed in their scale of popular support and the ideologies that drove the primary actors. The February Revolution was not a long-planned social movement. Rather, it was a spontaneous reaction to unrest. It brought together myriad political parties and classes to overthrow Tsar Nicholas II and the Romanov monarchy. Due to the differences in the political objectives of the participants, there was not a clear plan for establishing the state to follow each of these significant revolutions. Some wanted to maintain a constitutional monarchy, others sought a democratic government, and some groups aimed to leverage this into an opportunity to start a worldwide socialist revolution. These diverging hopes and political objectives frustrated efforts of the Provisional Government to build a stable base of power to unify Russia under its authority.

Background to the Revolution

Prior to the turmoil of 1917, there were several indications of unrest overlooked by the tsar. Some of these problems were vestiges of the 1905 revolution that reforms did not address. Others were new issues brought about by World War I. By February 1917, Tsar Nicholas's inability to address the concerns of his people brought a quick end to one of Europe's longest-reigning families. Before discussing the specifics of the 1917 revolution, it is important to understand the remaining problems of the 1905 revolution that Tsar Nicholas II left unaddressed.

After the violent repression of protests led by Father Gapon known as Bloody Sunday in 1905, the tsar's government granted some accommodations to the protestors. These proposed reforms, published in a document known as the October Manifesto, were not laws but rather promises of future changes that Nicholas II would make. Among them was the election of a representative body, the Duma. The Duma would allow all Russians a vote as well as expanded legal protections for citizens from the tsar's police. Although the document encouraged many participants of the 1905 revolution to cease their resistance to the tsar, it did not go far enough for the more radical groups, such as the Social Democrats and the Social Revolutionaries. The manifesto made many promises, but Tsar Nicholas II did not hold up his end of the bargain. He effectively used the promise of reform to quiet a majority of the critics and get them to stop their opposition to his government. More radical elements remembered the lack of real reform after the promises outlined in the manifesto, and this steeled their resolve when a second chance for revolution came in 1917.

When Gavrilo Princip assassinated Archduke Franz Ferdinand in Saravejo on June 28, 1914, Russia quickly began mobilizing for a possible confrontation to protect Slavic peoples against Austro-Hungarian reprisals. This mobilization, in part, drove Germany to begin mobilizations in order to be ready if war started. By the end of August 1914, the entire European continent fell into war. Initial successes on the battlefield did not translate to efficacy in subsequent campaigns. By 1916, the war was going poorly for Russia. Russian forces lost all of the gains from their initial actions.

As a result of the defeats of the Russian military in 1915 and 1916, Tsar Nicholas II personally took command of the army. He did so in order to bolster faith in the war effort and to show his dedication to victory. However, his responsibilities as commander in chief prevented him from addressing the domestic duties required of a monarch.

Nicholas looked to his wife to help run the country while he led the army. Though the military aspect of the war brought defeat, the domestic war effort did have a few positive impacts for the Russian people. One of the most important was the experience gained by establishing the Union of Zemstvos and Towns.

When the war began, there was an upsurge of support for the tsar, the military, and Russia. Many Russians wanted to help the war effort, and they struggled to find an effective outlet. In August 1914, the Union of Zemstvos and Towns pledged support to the tsar and the army. Zemstvos were similar to town councils. Tsar Alexander II granted them as a result of liberal reforms he made during his reign. They did not have a broad scope of responsibilities, and the nobles largely ruled them. However, these were the beginnings of democratic representation in Russia.

The Union of Zemstvos and Towns worked to make donations to provide medical care for soldiers and aid in the transportation of wounded soldiers to field hospitals for care. This limited scope gradually expanded during the war, as the union proved to be an effective body for organizing a broad base of support and was adept at gathering resources. Although it did not begin as an overtly political body, the act of organizing quasi-governmental work made it clear to many Russians that the union could successfully execute large-scale projects without the tsar's support.

Another problem that fomented domestic unrest was the lack of food availability in the urban areas. Due to the war, grain and agricultural produce prices rose rapidly. Farmers hoarded grain in anticipation of getting higher prices later rather than selling at a relatively cheaper price in the current market. This made it difficult for the government to move food to the cities, and the workers in the cities had to pay higher prices; however, their wages did not increase to help defray the additional costs. This made the cities a hotbed of frustration and gave revolutionaries an effective population to build their fervor. This aided the Bolsheviks, and they leveraged this discontent into political power.

The war drove unrest, which was already present in Russian society. What the state needed was an involved leader to shepherd the government through the tensions that the war and its problems inflamed. However, Russia did not have such a leader when it needed it. In an effort to turn the military situation around, Tsar Nicholas II decided to take personal command of the army. His cabinet advised against it; however, the tsarina supported his decision. Nicholas II went against the advice of his cabinet and left St. Petersburg to join the army. He left his wife, Alexandra, in charge of running the government on a day-to-day basis. She was less than sympathetic to the concerns of her people.

In January 1917, 140,000 protesters demonstrated in St. Petersburg in commemoration of Bloody Sunday. As they carried on their protest, others began to participate. Eventually the strikes grew to include other cities. Alexandra's reactions to the protests only further increased people's anger. In March 1917, tensions reached the breaking point. When officials ordered troops to fire on the protesters in St. Petersburg, many soldiers refused and joined the crowds. Upon hearing of the protests, the tsar disbanded the Duma and ordered more violent repression. Although some soldiers followed orders and killed civilians, many more mutinied and refused the orders of their tsar. Furthermore, the Duma refused to obey Nicholas's dissolution order and stayed in session, yet another significant indication of the impotence of the tsar.

Abdication of the Tsar

Protests continued in St. Petersburg, but Russia's government did not have a solution. Violence did not work, and the tsar was unwilling to make substantial civil, economic, or legal reforms to address the people's demands. After weeks of protests, officials from the Duma and the military met with Nicholas II and recommend that he abdicate. Nicholas agreed to do so both for himself and for his son; this left Russia without a head of state and without a clear government. In the immediate aftermath of the abdication, members of the Duma formed the Provisional Government. In addition to the Duma's efforts to form a government, the members of the Petrograd Soviet also planned to take advantage of the lack of a clear government. The Petrograd Soviet was one of many soviets in Russian urban areas. The soviets were assemblies of workers united by a common ideology, socialism. The Petrograd Soviet was the most influential because of its proximity to the Russian seat of power and its presence at the early stages of the protests. There were several political parties in the Petrograd Soviet. The Bolsheviks were not a majority, but they were the faction most willing to use force to secure their objectives. The Bolsheviks soon became a key opposition group against the nascent Provisional Government.

When the tsar left power, the Provisional Government assumed the responsibilities of government. However, its members did not have a mandate to assume power. Members of the Provisional Government also did not agree on what type of government should replace the tsar's. There were those, such as the Octobrists, who argued for creating a constitutional monarchy and yet others who wanted a democratic republic. Groups such as the Social Democrats their factions of Bolsheviks and Mensheviks, and the Social Revolutionaries who argued for radical changes to the state. Within the context of the Provisional Government, these more radical parties, which saw a socialist government in the future of Russia, did not have a large influence in the Provisional Government. In addition to determining the type of government to build, the Provisional Government's leaders struggled to discern the appropriate course of action for World War I. Some members advocated for continuing the war because of obligations to Russia's allies and the hope of compensation through the peace process. Others advocated for ending the war or at least beginning discussions with the Germans to see if Russia could get favorable terms.

The Provisional Government, headed by Prince Georgy Lvov, issued principles for the rule of Russia and its first set of goals for the nation. Among the more popular goals was an amnesty for many political prisoners, freedom of the press, and an abolition of class distinctions. The intent of the first Provisional Government was to address the social problems that plagued Russia under the tsar; however, the war demanded attention first.

In April 1917 Lvov published the new government's war aims to the Russian people. His declaration made it clear that Russia would uphold its obligations to its allies but would not seek to extend its borders or enrich itself at the expense of any other nation. The Provisional Government did represent the will of the people in wanting to continue the war to defeat Germany. However, there were some groups that did not want to continue the war; the most important group that militantly advocated ending the war was the Bolsheviks.

When the monarchy fell, the Bolsheviks were just one of many opposition groups. They were not even the largest socialist group. As the revolution showed, they were the most well organized and disciplined of the opposition groups, and this was the decisive element in their success. The Petrograd Soviet, of which the Bolsheviks were part, issued its Order No. 1 the day before the tsar abdicated. This order required the election of soldiers' committees, placed ownership of weapons under the committees, and required soldiers to disobey any order that contradicted orders or instructions from the Petrograd Soviet. This contradiction was part of the power struggle between the Provisional Government and the Petrograd Soviet. Although the order as written only applied to military units in Petrograd, it soon applied to all Russian military forces, to include those at the front.

In order to shore up the legitimacy of the Provisional Government, its leaders sought the approval of the Petrograd Soviet. The soviet's approval gave an air of democracy to the Provisional Government; this was important because there was no time for elections, and the leaders of the Provisional Government could not gain the former tsar's approval to allow the Duma to install a cabinet to run the country in his absence. This created an odd union between the Provisional Government and the Petrograd Soviet, as the new government relied on the soviet for its legitimacy and sought the soviet's approval for its initial legislative program. However, the soviet did not reciprocate this deference. When the soviet issued Order No. 1, it did so without clearing it through the Provisional Government. This bond between the Provisional Government and the Petrograd Soviet did not serve the new government well, as it lashed the Provisional Government to a group that had Bolsheviks as members. The Provisional Government could not move too far away from the objectives of the Petrograd Soviet, but the soviet did not have such constraints. The Bolsheviks used this to their advantage.

The Petrograd Soviet, although in a sense connected with the new government, was important as a focal point of anti–Provisional Government opposition. The Bolsheviks worked to gain control, first over the socialists' political opposition and then over all of Russia. Part of this opposition was the publication of the soviet's "Appeal to All Peoples of the World." This missive declared the soviet's war aims, which did not include support for imperial Russian allies. The document argued that defensive campaigns were legitimate and that any offensive campaign only served capitalists and was contradictory to the Petrograd Soviet's directives. The war continued to be a constant source of disagreement between the Petrograd Soviet, which was increasingly controlled by the Bolsheviks, and the Provisional Government.

Lenin Returns

In the early days of the February Revolution several Bolshevik leaders were outside of Russia, specifically Leon Trotsky and V. I. Lenin. Lenin, aided by the German government in an attempt to destabilize their enemy, entered Russia in April 1917 and soon provided political guidance to the Bolsheviks as they worked to increase control over the future of Russia. Leon Trotsky was in the United States to avoid persecution and returned in May 1917 after he heard of the political revolution. Their presence provided the needed leadership for the Bolsheviks to create what became the Soviet Union. However, before they did that, they had to overcome the Provisional Government and then the White Army.

When Lenin returned to Russia, he stressed that the Soviets needed to be the primary vehicle for political power in Russia, not the Provisional Government. One of the first things that Lenin did when he arrived in Petrograd was deliver a public address outlining his position on the war and the Provisional Government. He made clear that he and the Bolsheviks did not see the Provisional Government as a legitimate expression of the people's will; only the Soviets were true representative bodies. This tension between the Provisional Government and the Bolsheviks ultimately rendered futile any attempts at incorporating socialist parties into the government.

Although Lenin and the Bolsheviks were a vocal part of the socialist political body, they were not in the majority. Bolsheviks were a minority faction of the broader socialist movement. However, leaders such as Lenin, Trotsky, and Joseph Stalin effectively used the Petrograd Soviet and its ability to marshal large numbers of people to protest to great effect. The government under Prince Lvov struggled to build a workable coalition. Socialists' agitation was part of the problem, but a lack of consensus among the capitalist and monarchist factions also frustrated any efforts to create a viable government. Lvov did bring socialists into the government—Alexander Kerensky served as the minister of justice—but was unable to build a broad enough base to maintain power until elections provided a clear mandate.

As the Provisional Government worked to control the war effort and create a functioning state, the Bolsheviks continued to work against the government by exploiting public demonstrations in Petrograd. One of the most pivotal came in July 1917. Prior to the uprisings, the war effort took a downward turn. Kerensky, now the war minister, planned to use an offensive against the Austrians to try to unite the country. Initially successful, the offensive lost momentum when the Germans joined to help the

Austrians. After their initial success many Russian soldiers refused to attack, as they felt that they completed their duty and did not want to destroy Austria but only defend Russia. As the Germans reinforced the Austrian lines, Russian forces retreated, which was a disaster for Kerensky and his efforts to unite Russia under the Provisional Government. When the Constitutional Democratic (Kadet) Party walked out of the Provisional Government, many Russians took to the streets to protest the government. Lenin and the Bolsheviks attempted previous coups to overthrow the government in April and June, but they were unable to marshal enough support to carry the day. In July, Lenin encouraged the Bolsheviks to wait and see if the July demonstrations provided the right opportunity to change governments. As the scale of the demonstrations grew, the Bolsheviks acted.

Soldiers in the 1st Machine Gun Regiment protested their orders to move to the front in July 1917. The Bolsheviks provided education to some of the soldiers about the necessity of only fighting if the soldiers could be sure that their actions would support a revolutionary war, meaning a war ordered by a government without capitalists. This meant that the orders from the Provisional Government, which the Bolsheviks deemed infiltrated by capitalists were illegitimate. As the demonstrations grew, workers joined the soldiers in demanding the transfer of power. When the protests reached their pinnacle, Lenin was undecided as to whether to risk responding to the call for a coup, and he did not direct the Bolsheviks to act on the demand to transfer power to the soviets. If they had, then the Bolshevik Revolution, instead of occurring later in October 1917, would be the July Revolution. This lack of action allowed the Provisional Government to reclaim power. Kerensky ordered

the arrest of the Bolshevik leaders, such as Lenin and Trotsky, on charges of supporting revolution. Lenin avoided arrest by going into hiding, while Trotsky went to jail for playing a part in the failed coup.

The failure of the July coup showed the effective organization that the Bolsheviks created. Lenin's role as the center of the Bolsheviks' power was clear. Without his approval, the Bolsheviks did not move to claim power even when offered the chance by the protesters. This coordination and the ability to rally large public displays of support from a small core group of supporters served Lenin well as 1917 continued. The Bolshevik Party's ability to generate large demonstrations proved that although they were a minority political organization in the Petrograd Soviet, they were one of the more well-disciplined and well-organized groups contending for power against the Provisional Government.

One of the problems that the Provisional Government and other anti-Bolshevik groups faced was their inability to unify against the Bolsheviks. The Bolshevik Party never outnumbered its combined opposition but was effective in preventing its opposition from uniting. This continued to serve the Bolsheviks well after they successfully overthrew the Provisional Government and fought the Russian Civil War against the anti-Bolshevik forces of the White, Green, and Black Armies. These disparate groups never united, and in the case of the Greens and the Blacks, the Bolsheviks were able to co-opt them to unite against other anti-Bolshevik forces.

As 1917 continued, the Bolsheviks maintained their stance against the Provisional Government. Lenin drew attention to the failures of the Provisional Government in correcting the economy and the ongoing destruction of World War I. His platform did not call for a direct transfer of power to the Bolsheviks. Rather, he said that he wanted the soviets to maintain power. Lenin argued that the soviets were the true representatives of the people and that the Provisional Government was not a legitimate expression of the will of the people and could not rule Russia effectively. He saw the Provisional Government as more of a threat to Bolshevik power because the government, although not powerful, could rally the support of the people and appeal to their sense of nationalism. If the soviets gained political power, then Lenin was confident that the Bolsheviks could dominate the other political organizations in the soviets in the struggle for political power. Also, the soviets did not have the same possibility of appealing to a broad base of the population as the Provisional Government. So, Lenin's call for power to go to the soviets was part of a broader strategy to eliminate the most significant threat, the Provisional Government, in favor of a lesser threat, the other political organizations involved in the soviets.

Summer 1917

After the failure of the Bolshevik coup in July, the Provisional Government still struggled to create a stable base of power to build a new Russian state. As a result of the events in July, Kerensky replaced Prince Lvov as the head of the Provisional Government and began to act in a more authoritarian manner. Kerensky appointed General Lavr Kornilov as commander in chief of Russia's military forces. The relationship between the two men proved to be the undoing of the Provisional Government and provided the opportunity for the Bolsheviks to seize power.

In August 1917, Kerensky and Kornilov's relationship fractured. Kerensky accused General Kornilov of launching a coup against the Provisional Government. Kornilov denied the accusation and continued to serve Russia when no other general would replace him. This intrigue was the final undoing of the Provisional Government. It removed any support that Kerensky had from the leftist political parties, such as the Social Revolutionaries and the Mensheviks. Without this base of political support, Kerensky could not lead the Provisional Government. Kerensky looked to the Petrograd Soviet to help defend the Provisional Government. The Bolsheviks were the party responsible for the military arm of the Petrograd Soviet, making the Bolsheviks responsible for defending Kerensky's government.

The Bolshevik bid for power gained more momentum the next month when the Bolsheviks won a majority in the Workers' Section of the Petrograd Soviet. With their influence in Petrograd and in other cities such as Moscow, the Bolsheviks moved to gain greater power. They convinced the Petrograd Soviet to approve of organizing soviet members to protect Petrograd from Germans and from "domestic" enemies. This gave the Bolsheviks the political cover that allowed them to marshal the armed groups necessary to seize power. While the Bolsheviks worked to build their forces, Kerensky worried about a coup from conservative forces. Until forced from office, he continued to believe that a Bolshevik coup could open opportunities for the Provisional Government to solidify its position and was not a great threat.

The Bolsheviks started their move to gain control over Russia with a convocation of soviet delegations. They called for a meeting and called it the Congress of Soviets of the Northern Region, which began in Petrograd on October 11, 1917. The Executive Committee of the Petrograd Soviet initially did not approve of the meeting. The committee eventually approved the Bolsheviks' meeting on the condition that they delay until late October and confine their discussions to issues such as domestic concerns, the reelection of the Petrograd Soviet Executive Committee, and the upcoming elections of the Constituent Assembly. Although the Executive Committee sought to constrain the scope of the congress, the Bolsheviks had no intention of abiding by the restriction imposed on them from the Petrograd Soviet. The Bolsheviks ensured that their party had the majority in the congress by insisting on reelections for any soviet that did not approve of the Bolsheviks' call to hold a meeting. Neither the Mensheviks nor socialist parties recognized the legitimacy of the Bolsheviks' congress; however, their refusal to participate did not significantly impede the Bolsheviks' efforts.

The October Revolution

At a meeting of the Petrograd Soviet's Executive Committee, a Menshevik member moved that the Petrograd garrison prepare to defend the city from an incoming German invasion. Bolshevik leaders realized that this motion gave them an opportunity to gain control of an armed group under the umbrella of the Petrograd Soviet. Bolshevik leaders amended the motion that the armed body should prepare for both external and internal enemies. This motion in the Petrograd Soviet gave the Bolsheviks two bodies to execute their plans, the soviet Military-Revolutionary Committee and the soon to occur Second Congress of the soviets.

On October 24, 1917, the Military Revolutionary Committee began the Bolsheviks' October Revolution. The committee disconnected the telephone and telegraph lines from the Military Staff building. This prevented the Provisional Government from marshaling troops to fight the Bolsheviks. The Bolsheviks, due to their coordination with the Petrograd garrison, were able to replace guards peacefully around vital centers such as railroad stations, post offices, and bridges simply by telling the guards to go home. By the morning of October 25, the Bolsheviks gained control of most of the important lines of communication and buildings in Petrograd, leaving only the Winter Palace in the hands of the Provisional Government. After a failed attempt to attack the palace, Lenin publicized the Bolshevik takeover of Russia in the name of the Petrograd Soviet. Eventually, the Winter Palace fell because its defenders either refused to fight or left the scene when no other reinforcements arrived. The Bolsheviks dissolved the Provisional Government with an almost bloodless coup.

Although the Bolsheviks claimed to rule all of Russia, initially their power did not project much outside of Petrograd. In Moscow, the Bolsheviks struggled to gain power because their party did not have as much control over the Moscow soviet. After days of fighting progovernment forces, though, the Bolsheviks established soviet rule in the city. Bolsheviks fought for control throughout the rest of the urban areas in Russia, sometimes in concert with other socialist groups and sometimes in opposition to socialist groups. However, the majority of Russians did not realize that they had a new government.

Once the Bolsheviks claimed power in the name of the soviets, they had to fashion a government to maintain their position. This required preventing other groups from removing the Bolshevik government, mainly the Constituent Assembly, and creating an institution that could impose its order on the Russian people without fear of their rejection. The Bolsheviks needed to build a new government quickly to ensure that their position was unassailable. Although there were other socialist parties and a majority of those in the new government were not Bolsheviks, the Bolshevik Party held the most important posts and was able to dictate policies for the whole government.

In January 1918, the Bolsheviks eliminated the final political challenge to their rule. After the November election, the Socialist Revolutionary Party won a majority of votes. The Bolsheviks allowed the All-Russian Constituent Assembly to begin its meetings on January 5. However, the Bolsheviks closed the hall and locked attendees out after the first night. The members of the Constituent Assembly were unable to breach the Bolsheviks' blockade and admitted defeat. This was the last viable political opposition that the Bolsheviks faced. The rest of the opposition to Bolshevik rule mainly came from former tsarist officers, discontented peasants, and former Russian allies.

The Bolsheviks' October Coup began the Russian Civil War. The main opposition force, the White Army, was not truly an army but a disparate group united in their resistance to the Bolsheviks' government. The war was very different from the American Civil War in that there were few battles and the White forces were not a consolidated whole, as the Confederate States of America was. The main strength of the Red Army was not in its size or its military competency but rather the Red soldiers' discipline to fight as a unit and their leaders' dedication to the ideas of the revolution. The White Army forces suffered from divided loyalties. There was infighting among White Army leaders to determine what type of government would replace the Bolshevik state and the best strategy for resisting the Red Army. These divisions prevented the White Army from forming a unified front of opposition and allowed the Red Army to isolate and defeat opposition forces in detail.

When the Red Army defeated the White Army in 1922, the Bolshevik government created the Union of Soviet Socialist Republics, better known as the Soviet Union. This state ruled Russia and many of the former states of the Russian Empire for almost seven decades until the collapse of the Soviet Union in 1991. The Soviet Union, the nexus of socialist power, created the Warsaw Pact in 1955 as a balance against the North Atlantic Treaty Organization. The Soviet Union was the bedrock of socialist military strength during the Cold War.

Consequences

The Bolsheviks were successful in taking power in Russia not because of their superior numbers but because of their discipline and focus on their objective. When they began the October Revolution, they were not even a majority socialist party in the Petrograd Soviet. However, their lack of numbers did not inhibit their actions. Lenin effectively used the disjointed nature of the Provisional Government against the prime minister of the Provisional Government, Alexander Kerensky. Similarly, as the Bolsheviks were the best-organized party in the Petrograd Soviet, they leveraged their control of the Military Revolutionary Committee to neutralize any threats to the nascent government. Bolshevik leaders such as Lenin and Stalin did not hesitate to use force to solidify their position. This appeal to the use of force to subjugate people continued with the secret police force known as the Cheka as well as the Committee for State Security (KGB) that followed the Cheka and served a similar purpose during the existence of the Soviet Union.

Often the October Revolution overshadows the February Revolution of 1917 because of the success of the Bolsheviks in establishing the Soviet Union. The February Revolution is important, because the inability of the Provisional Government to institute a viable coalition allowed a minority socialist party to oust a government that had the broad but not ardent support of the Russian people. Revolutions are difficult for societies to handle. This was especially true of the February Revolution. This revolution instituted a new government but still had to fight a war, which it was losing. Added to the problems of the new government was the fact that the Allies expected Russia to fulfill its treaty obligations and continue to fight against the Central Powers, and the Provisional Government soon promised that it would. Continuing the war further inflamed many Russians, and the war effort compounded economic problems that drove workers to protest in the streets of Petrograd in the first place. Although it is convenient to see the ultimate success of the Bolsheviks as a foregone conclusion, given the inability of their opponents to mount a unified resistance, this simplifies the situation too much. Lenin and his party's audacity and tolerance for risk allowed the Bolsheviks to claim victory before their opponents even knew they were being attacked.

Gates M. Brown

The Russian Civil War (1917–1922)

Prior to seizing power, the Bolshevik Party was well known for its radical opposition to capitalism and to Russian involvement in World War I. In response to the October Revolution, numerous Russian and foreign forces therefore intervened to limit and if possible eliminate the new Bolshevik regime. Beset by attacks from all directions, that government made practical decisions that were at odds with its previous conduct and ideological beliefs. These compromises and the resulting struggle made a lasting impact on Soviet economic, political, and security policies.

First Moves

In the late fall of 1917, the Cossacks became the first to resist Bolshevik control but operated as independent groups rather than forming a unified opposition. The Don Cossacks, led by General A. M. Kaledin, rebelled openly, leading to the first deployment of armed Bolshevik revolutionaries by rail, a procedure later referred to as *eshelonnaia* (railway war). Directed by the first people's commissar for war, V. A. Antonov-Ovseyenko, the revolutionaries captured Kharkov and dispersed the Don Cossacks so thoroughly that Kaledin committed suicide in despair on February 11, 1918.

This limited Cossack resistance provided the opportunity for former Imperial Russian Army elements to assemble the nucleus of what became the major anti-Soviet or White force in the south, the Volunteer Army. Two rival generals vied for leadership: M. V. Alekseev, Tsar Nicholas's wartime chief of staff, and L. G. Kornilov, the former military commander in chief under the Kerensky government. With Kornilov as military commander, the few thousand volunteers, many of them ex-tsarist officers, fled Rostov-on-Don in February 1918 just before the city fell to Soviet railway detachments. The resulting Ice March led into the Kuban, the area between the lower Don River and the Caucasus, where local Cossacks proved no more successful against the Reds than the Don Cossacks. On April 13, guns of the newly declared Kuban Soviet Republic shelled a farmhouse containing the Volunteer Army headquarters, killing Kornilov. Alekseev died of heart failure five months later, leaving the growing Volunteer Army under the control of Kornilov's successor, Lieutenant General Anton Ivanovich Denikin.

Meanwhile, General of Division Georges Tabouis, head of the French military mission in Ukraine, encouraged the separatist

Ukrainian movement to continue the war against the Central Powers independently of the new Russian government. On January 22, 1918, the Ukrainian Rada declared independence but sued for peace with Germany and Austro-Hungary. In response, the Bolsheviks overran Ukraine, capturing Kiev on February 7.

Organizational Response

With few reliable forces at the start of the conflict, the Bolshevik regime had to create the new Red Army almost from scratch. During their long years in opposition, socialists and communists alike had come to believe that armies should be militias commanded by democratic councils, a system that the Bolsheviks had promoted to subvert discipline in the Provisional Government's Russian Army during 1917. Indeed, in December of that year the new regime abolished all military ranks and decreed that leaders would be elected by their troops. Faced with civil war, the Bolsheviks disagreed internally as to how to form an effective army.

Becoming commissar for war on March 13, 1918, Leon Trotsky immediately began to recruit former tsarist officers as "military specialists" to provide essential military skills and knowledge. In turn, commanders of various backgrounds sought to restore discipline and hierarchy. Trotsky's actions outraged other revolutionary leaders even though he assigned dedicated Bolshevik commissars with veto powers to watch over all commanders, especially restored officers. By December 1918, a compromise evolved whereby major units were commanded by military councils, each consisting of the designated commander and one or more commissars; a chief of staff was added to the council at a later date. During the remainder of its existence, the Red/Soviet Army oscillated between a unified chain of command under a commander and shared authority between commanders and commissars.

Issues of ideology and loyalty also figured in the widespread Bolshevik desire to recruit only proletarians into the ranks. To provide sufficient troops, however, Trotsky soon found himself conscripting peasants and others who did not fit the doctrinal definition of proletarians. The resulting conflict was reflected even in the official name of the new organization, Raboche-Krest'ianskaia Krasnaia Armiia (Workers' and Peasants' Red Army). The process of conscripting and supplying this army only exacerbated popular resistance to the forced food distribution and other policies of the new government. The remnants of the Russian economy struggled to meet the needs of the Bolshevik state.

Moreover, in its initial desperate search for reliable troops, the new regime acquired a sort of foreign legion. Entire formations of the former Imperial Russian Army, recruited by ethnicity from Latvia, Belorussia, and other national groups, volunteered for the Red Army. Many of these volunteers, however, hoped to gain independence from Russia as a result of the revolution.

Allied Intervention in the North

While the Bolsheviks struggled with their political allies and their Russian opponents, an even greater threat to the regime arose during 1918: foreign intervention. Quite apart from the natural antipathy of capitalists toward Marxists, Russia's erstwhile allies objected to Bolshevism because the new regime had seized power by openly promising to withdraw from the world war. Diplomats from the Western Allies had attempted to persuade the new regime to remain in the conflict but with little success.

In early 1918, German and Habsburg troops advanced steadily into the power vacuum caused by the dissolution of the tsarist army, seizing large amounts of land and munitions abandoned by retreating Russian troops. This action forced V. I. Lenin to buy time by signing the disastrous Treaty of Brest-Litovsk on March 3, 1918, withdrawing Russia from the war and making numerous concessions, including the Baltic States, to Germany and its allies. In turn, the peace agreement virtually ended Western efforts to negotiate with the Bolshevik government and instead accelerated foreign efforts to destroy the revolutionary regime.

The first stage of the Allied action was the debarkation of troops at the northern Russian ports of Murmansk and Archangel in the spring of 1918. The first company of Royal Marines landed at Murmansk in March, ostensibly to protect large stockpiles of Allied-supplied munitions. The Bolsheviks reluctantly acquiesced to this landing. The next month, however, British major general F. C. Poole, who had lobbied his government for such an intervention, arrived with a larger Allied force and much broader ideas about its mission. Poole hoped that his troops could unite with the Czechoslovak Legion in Siberia. In Poole's optimistic view, these two Allied units together would somehow overthrow the Bolshevik regime and bring Russia back into the Entente against Germany and Austria.

As the German Ludendorff Offensives created a crisis on the Western Front during the spring and summer of 1918, the clamor to get Russia back into the war increased. To this end, the Western Allies reinforced Poole with a flotilla of river-going vessels as well as British, French, Australian, and other troops. In July President Woodrow Wilson agreed to join this effort, sending the 339th Infantry Regiment (Wisconsin National Guard), reinforced with engineers and medical elements. Although Wilson apparently intended this contingent to be politically neutral, his ambassador to Russia, David R. Francis, was as anti-Bolshevik as General Poole, and the 339th, under British command, saw action around both northern ports. The total strength of the Allied northern intervention soon exceeded 13,000 troops, quite apart from local anti-Bolshevik Russian units.

The overstretched Bolshevik central regime was unable to field an effective force to counter this threat, instead choosing to destroy the telegraph lines and railway bridges connecting northern Russia with Petrograd and Moscow. In response, the exasperated Murmansk Regional Soviet, threatened by the guns of British, French, and American warships, signed a cooperation agreement with British, French, and American representatives on July 6.

Yet, the Allied expedition was slow to assemble and even slower to advance from Murmansk toward Archangel and the major Russian cities. By the time this force finally moved in the late fall, Germany had sued for peace in the West, causing many of the Allied troops in northern Russia to become disaffected with a desire to demobilize. Moreover, in an operation to seize the railroad south of Archangel, a British commander sent elements of the 339th Infantry forward without reconnaissance and then accidentally directed British artillery at his own allies.

General Poole had also irritated both local Russian socialists and his allies to the point that in September 1918, the U.S. government pressed for his replacement. Brigadier W. E. Ironside, a successful brigade commander from the Western Front (and future field marshal), replaced Poole and had some success, but by mid-October the weather impeded further Entente advances.

In January 1919, Russian general Eugene K. Miller arrived in the north and quickly recruited some 5,000 White (anti-Bolshevik)

Russian soldiers. However, these soldiers were reluctant recruits and often mutinied or refused to fight. Moreover, by the end of the month Trotsky had assembled a scratch force, grandiosely termed the "Sixth Red Army," that pushed part of the 339th Infantry back from Shenkursk, its farthest advance toward other White Russian forces in Siberia.

With the end of the Great War in France, the impetus for the northern expedition gradually collapsed. President Woodrow Wilson finally withdrew the American contingent by June 28, 1919. Despite Winston Churchill's successful recruiting of 8,000 anti-Bolshevik volunteers, Britain had also lost its enthusiasm for the operation. On September 27, 1919, the last British troops withdrew from the northern ports, leaving General Miller in charge of the White Russian forces. Without foreign support, Miller and his staff had to escape to Norway as the Red Army occupied Archangel on February 21, 1920, and Murmansk two days later.

War in the East

This resolution in the north was still far in the future in 1918, when the Bolshevik regime had to confront not only threats in the far north and south but also a much larger force, including even more numerous foreign troops, in Siberia.

The Siberian saga began with the Czechoslovak Legion. Starting in 1914, Czech nationalists including Edvard Benes and Tomáš Masaryk lobbied the Russian government to recruit expatriate Czechs and Slovaks to fight against the Habsburg Empire. After some battlefield success, the Romanov government permitted recruitment of other Czechs who had become prisoners of war. The resulting Czech Corps (also known as the Czech Legion) grew to more than 40,000 soldiers. Once the Bolshevik regime withdrew from the war against the Central Powers, it tried with some success to arm other prisoners of war to fight for the revolution, but the Czechs refused. In 1918 the legion migrated eastward along the Trans-Siberian Railway, ostensibly to circle the world and enter the war against Austria in the West.

Japan had used the occasion of World War I, when its allies were focused on Europe, to extort additional concessions from China. The chaos in Russia seemed to offer another such opportunity, this time to occupy Siberia. In April 1918, Japan and Britain had landed small troop contingents in Vladivostok to protect their citizens from riots. As soon as the first Japanese troops landed in Vladivostok, however, Trotsky stopped all rail movement for the Czechs. In May 1918 the Bolsheviks attempted to disarm the legion, which promptly mutinied at Chelyabinsk. The Czechs took control of other cities as they moved eastward along the railroad, while dissident Russian officers overthrew local Bolshevik administrations in Petropavlovsk and Omsk. On June 13, 1918, a provisional Siberian government formed in Omsk, and White forces soon controlled much of the Trans-Siberian Railway. Five months later, Admiral Alexander Vasilievich Kolchak seized control of the White government in Omsk, and other White leaders recognized him as the supreme leader of the anti-Bolshevik Russian government. Although Kolchak was a man of considerable energy and skill, he had no tolerance for the various nationalities seeking more freedom from Russia and eventually ruled as a dictator. The weak economy, difficult terrain, and the harsh climate of Siberia, combined with the advent of the influenza pandemic and other epidemic diseases, further weakened Kolchak's regime.

While the Czechs and their White counterparts took over much of the Trans-Siberian Railway, the foreign intervention in this theater grew rapidly. By November 1918, 72,000 Japanese troops had come ashore at Vladivostok and begun spreading westward along the rail line. This expansion aroused the suspicions of Japan's nominal allies, who decided to dispatch their own forces to Siberia. Many of these Allied contingents were relatively small, such as the two battalions (1,500 men) sent by Britain, 4,200 soldiers from Canada, and 1,400 men from Italy, perhaps because the end of the war in Europe made further military commitments politically unpopular.

The United States undertook a somewhat larger effort, but President Wilson insisted that his country was only acting to help evacuate the Czechs, not to become involved in the growing Russian civil conflict. Instead, he instructed Major General William S. Graves to remain neutral in the civil war while guarding the Trans-Siberian Railway and monitoring Japanese actions. Graves took two regular infantry regiments—the 27th and 31st—plus supporting troops from the Philippines to Vladivostok, landing in August–September 1918. Attempting to execute his unusual instructions, he found his 8,000 soldiers fighting low-level actions with both Bolshevik and White troops while the civil war dragged on in Siberia.

Considering the different instructions given to various Allied contingents, it is unsurprising that the Siberian expedition neither achieved a truly unified command nor intervened effectively in the civil war. General Pierre Janin, head of the French military mission in Siberia, styled himself as commander in chief and received a measure of obedience from the Czechs while coordinating with the anti-Red elements in the region.

In the spring of 1919 Kolchak's White forces had some success, advancing westward as far as the Tobol River west of Petropavlovsk and some 1,200 miles from

Moscow. Eventually, however, the Red Army proved more resilient, forcing Kolchak to retreat eastward. In the chaotic retreat that followed, Kolchak quarreled with both his generals and the Czech Legion, which handed him over to his opponents at Irkutsk on January 15, 1920. When the remnants of the White Army in Siberia attempted to rescue him, Kolchak was summarily executed on February 7.

Meanwhile, the Bolshevik regime had concluded that it could not defeat the Czech Legion and negotiated an armistice. Although the exact amounts and details are hotly disputed, the Czech military leaders reportedly traded control of a large gold reserve for safe passage eastward out of the country. When the last train left Irkutsk on March 1, 1920, the Bolsheviks took possession of this gold. The various allied contingents were already departing Siberia, followed by the last Czech elements on September 2, 1920.

Southern Russia and the Volunteer Army

The greatest threat to the Bolshevik regime came in the south. The sudden collapse of the Central Powers in October–November 1918 permitted French general Louis Franchet d'Espèrey, whose allied army was attacking northward into the Balkans, to occupy Bulgaria and portions of Hungary. This success encouraged Prime Minister Georges Clemenceau to renew French efforts in southern Russia. He dispatched General Henri Bethelot (soon succeeded by General Philippe d'Anselme) with a division of troops to occupy Odessa, which brought the French into conflict with Ukrainian separatists.

During the previous summer, opposition to the Bolshevik government had crystalized in two localities in southern Russia. By June 1918, some 40,000 Don Cossacks had taken control of the Don River region and confronted an equal number of troops, the Tenth Red Army, at Tsaritsyn (renamed Stalingrad in 1925 and then Volgograd in 1961), a transportation hub on the Volga River. The communist troops were commanded by K. E. Voroshilov (later a marshal of the Soviet Union), with Joseph Stalin as the self-appointed commissar. For this reason, subsequent Soviet accounts of the campaign tend to exaggerate the significance of their defense of Tsaritsyn, whereas in fact the battle was most noteworthy for its political controversy. On October 1, 1918, these two men attempted to remove General P. P. Sytin, a former tsarist officer, from command of the Southern Front (Army Group), the headquarters above Tenth Army. As war commissar, Trotsky was trying to build an effective national command structure and therefore backed the expert Sytin over the enthusiastic local amateurs. Trotsky persuaded Lenin to retain Sytin and reassign Stalin and later Voroshilov; although these reassignments were done tactfully, the incident contributed to the subsequent feud between Stalin and Trotsky. Meanwhile, after Tsaritsyn, Bolshevik propaganda added to the demoralization of the Don Army, which withered in the spring of 1919, permitting the Red Army to retake much of the northern Don River.

Three hundred miles farther south in the Kuban region, General Denikin had used his tiny 9,000-man Volunteer Army to seize control of the Kuban-Caucasus region, outmaneuvering a Red force almost 10 times the size of his force. As the Cossacks under Ataman P. N. Krasnov declined, the counterrevolutionary movement in southern Russia became focused on Denikin. However, like Admiral Kolchak in Siberia, Denikin espoused only a narrow form of conservative nationalism with limited local or ethnic self-government.

When the French forces landed in the Crimea at the end of 1918, local ex-tsarist leaders misinterpreted this landing as Western support for Denikin's "government." Confusion such as this impeded coordination between the Western powers and the White forces. Still, Great Britain sent extensive military aid, including a Royal Air Force squadron and British tank crews plus 1,121 artillery pieces, 198,000 rifles, and additional equipment. These weapons were particularly important, because the White elements had no industrial base of their own. British aid helped the Volunteer Army stop three Red offensives between March and May 1919, culminating with the White capture of Kharkov and Tsaritsyn in late June.

Militarily, the spring and summer of 1919 marked the high-water mark of the White cause. In addition to the Czech and Kolchak forces in Siberia, Denikin had perhaps 50,000 combat troops in May, in contrast to approximately 80,000 Reds in the Southern Front, which also had to contend with Ukrainian separatists. On July 3, 1919, General Denikin issued the so-called Moscow Directive, instructing his subordinates to move west into the Ukraine and north along the main rail lines toward Moscow. In September–October, ex-tsarist general N. N. Yudenich, with limited German and Estonian backing, led some 14,000 soldiers of the Northwest Army to briefly threaten Petrograd.

Trotsky had already appointed Colonel S. S. Kamenev, a military "specialist" who had achieved some success in the East, as overall commander of Bolshevik forces. Red Army counterattacks stalled the main White armies north of Kharkov, but in August and September Kamenev's attempt to outflank his opponents to the east failed.

By this time, however, the Bolsheviks had defeated Kolchak's army in Siberia, freeing some forces for the war in the south. In October, Trotsky personally rallied the local Bolshevik forces to halt Yudenich's advance on Petrograd; the White Northwest Army collapsed, and the Baltic States soon negotiated armistices with the Reds. Meanwhile, Denikin's forces were spread thin as they attempted to seize larger territories en route to Moscow.

Colonel A. I. Yegorov became the new commander of the Southern Front, with Stalin tightening discipline as his commissar. Then in late October 1919, Semen Mikhailovich Budenny led his Red Cavalry Corps in a series of advances that cut off the Volunteer Army's railroad supply lines. The White forces had already alienated peasants by seizing food. Denikin's emphasis on Russian nationalism had little appeal to Ukrainians, while the stereotype that Bolshevik leaders were Jewish encouraged pogroms in the Ukraine. The White leader also offended Don Cossacks by appointing a Kuban Cossack commander, S. G. Ulagai, to command them. Anarchists and others soon formed armed resistance groups behind the White lines. For all of these reasons, the hastily constructed White government and armed forces deteriorated rapidly. With the White cause weakened on all fronts, Allied aid to Denikin soon came to an end.

Budenny's corps, increased in stature to become the First Cavalry Army, led the Red pursuit of the Volunteer Army as it retreated in December 1919 and January 1920. Although the Volunteer Army rallied briefly to retake Rostov in February, Denikin's force was clearly spent. In March, the Reds trapped the Volunteers and the allied Don Army at Novorossisk; the Western navies evacuated some 34,000 White troops, but another 22,000 fell into Red hands. After ferocious internal arguments among the White leaders, Denikin resigned and went into exile in April 1920. His former subordinate and rival General P. N. Wrangel took command, but the Volunteer Army remained weak.

Polish-Soviet War (1920–1921)

Just as the Bolshevik regime achieved victory, another threat appeared. On April 24, 1920, the newly organized Polish Army invaded Ukraine and soon reached the Dnieper River. The basis of this conflict was not ethnicity but rather historical possession: for centuries, the union of Poland-Lithuania had controlled large portions of what is today Belarus and Ukraine. By 1795, however, imperial Russia had not only occupied what later became the Baltic States, Belarus, and Ukraine but also (along with Prussia and Austria) had partitioned Poland. Now, the nationalist Jozef Pilsudski, who had agitated for Polish independence under the tsars, seized the opportunity presented by the Russian Civil War to reconquer Poland's historical empire to the east.

A talented Red general, 27-year-old Mikhail Nikolaevich Tukhachevsky, promptly launched his Western Front against the flank of the Polish advance. After an initial failure, in July 1920 Tukhachevsky used the III Red Cavalry Corps and four infantry armies to repeatedly outflank the Poles, pursuing them westward at a fantastic rate. By August 1 the Red Army had reached Brest-Litovsk, having retaken all its lost territory and even occupied some areas that Poland had controlled previously.

Elated by its victory, the Politburo in Moscow rejected a British diplomatic effort to establish the Bug River as the new boundary between Poland and Russia. Instead, Moscow demanded harsh peace terms from the Warsaw government and pressed westward with hardly a pause. The Western powers sent a military mission, of whom the most prominent member was General Maxime Weygand, to advise the Polish government.

By mid-August 1920 Tukhachevsky had reached the line of the Vistula and Wierprz Rivers, with his troops therefore deployed southeast to northwest and the right wing actually northwest of Warsaw. This latter position seemed to threaten a huge encirclement of the Polish capital. However, the Western Front, redesignated the Northwestern Front, was overextended after its prolonged pursuit, and Yegorov's Southwestern Front had not yet closed up southeast of Tukhachevsky. A gap, screened only by the weak Mozyr Group of some 8,000 troops, developed between the two fronts. In the ensuing Battle of Warsaw (August 12–25, 1920), Pilsudski concentrated five of his divisions to thrust northeastward through the Mozyr Group. This decisive stroke scattered the Red forces and pushed the III Cavalry Corps into internment in East Prussia. Poland was therefore able to regain much of the territory it had previously occupied, signing an armistice on October 12, 1920, and a peace treaty the following March.

General Wrangel had attempted to exploit the Polish invasion by attacking northward in June 1920 and then entered the Ukraine in search of grain. With little allied support and declining troop strength, Wrangel withdrew into the Crimea at the time of the Polish armistice. On November 11–14, 1920, he evacuated Sevastopol in an orderly fashion. Although Bolshevik forces continued to fight opponents in remote areas of the Caucasus and Central Asia, the Battle of Warsaw marked the end of major operations in the Russian Civil War.

Consequences

The Russian Civil War and various foreign interventions almost strangled the first Marxist state at birth; not surprisingly, the conflict left both scars and a legacy.

First, the foreign interventions were proof, if any were needed, that the "capitalist" powers were the enemies of the newly created Soviet Union. Residual animosity delayed the resumption of ordinary diplomatic and economic relations with other countries, and the new leaders, especially Stalin, cited continuing foreign hostility as a principal reason for establishing and maintaining a totalitarian regime. The Polish occupation of territory that Moscow also claimed ensured a sustained conflict between the two from 1920 onward, contributing to the inability of European states to cooperate collectively against the rise of Adolf Hitler.

Second, the civil war was a pressure cooker that prompted the new regime to go to extreme measures, later termed "war communism," to maintain its existence. This accelerated both the implementation of the Proletarian Revolution and the popular resistance to that revolution. Despite Lenin's New Economic Policy, the conflict helped establish the patterns of central direction and forcible implementation of economic change.

Third, the civil war exacerbated a number of significant trends, such as independence for the Baltic States and the flight of upperclass Russians into exile.

The conflict brought some individuals to greater prominence and influence while accelerating conflict between leaders. Above all, Leon Trotsky and Joseph Stalin both proved to be indispensable for the new regime but in the process clashed repeatedly with each other. Military commanders such as Tukhachevsky and Budenny emerged as future leaders of the Red Army.

The Russian Civil War and the Polish-Soviet War also reinforced the tendency, seen already along the Eastern Front during World War I, for Russian and Soviet commanders to view warfare differently than many of their Western counterparts. On the one hand, all three of these conflicts, and especially the latter two, were characterized by much greater maneuver and mobility than the Western Front of 1914–1918. Although horse cavalry units and armored trains were the instruments of such maneuver during these conflicts, the surviving Red Army commanders welcomed and helped pioneer the kind of mechanized units and operations that dominated battlefields 20 years later. On the other hand, the inability of even large armies to achieve rapid victories prompted the Soviet state to invest extensively in heavy industry, the training of military reservists, and other elements necessary to conduct massive wars of attrition consisting of multiple offensive efforts.

Jonathan M. House

A

Alekseev, Mikhail Vasilievich (1857–1918)

Russian Army general, chief of staff of the army under Tsar Nicholas II, and commander in chief under the Provisional Government. Born on November 15, 1857, in Tver Province, Mikhail Alekseev was the son of a noncommissioned officer. Alekseev transcended his humble origins and secured admission to the Moscow School for Military Cadets. Upon graduation in 1876, he entered the army as an ensign. Alekseev's background would have destined him for an undistinguished career as a junior infantry officer had it not been for his admission to the General Staff College in 1887. There he graduated at the top of his class in 1890.

Promoted to general in 1904, Alekseev served as the quartermaster general of the Third Army in Manchuria during the 1904–1905 Russo-Japanese War. In 1905 he was posted to the Kiev Military District, where he became chief of staff in 1908 and commander of the XII Corps in 1912. While some of Alekseev's superiors (most notably Nikolai Ivanov, the prewar commander of the Kiev Military District) appreciated his talent and work ethic, his advocacy of military and political reforms did not earn him favor among conservatives at court or with War Minister Vladimir Sukhomlinov.

On the outbreak of World War I in early August 1914, Sukhomlinov secured the post of chief of staff of the army for his protégé, Nikolai Yanushkevich, although the commander in chief, Grand Duke Nikolai Nikolaevich, preferred the more able Alekseev.

Instead, Alekseev was appointed chief of staff of the Southwestern Front.

Alekseev's early offensive successes in Galicia, which nearly forced Austria-Hungary out of the war, led to his appointment as commander in chief of the Northwestern Front in March 1915. Because of his refusal to dispatch reinforcements to Southwestern Front commander General Nikolai Y. Ivanov, he bore at least some responsibility for the disastrous German breakthrough at Gorlice-Tarnów in May 1915, but Alekseev redeemed himself by organizing the Great Retreat from the Polish salient. This withdrawal, although costly, saved the Russian Army from complete destruction.

Following the Great Retreat, Tsar Nicholas II decided to assume the post of commander in chief himself, and Alekseev became his chief of staff in September 1915. The tsar's ignorance of and lack of interest in military affairs ensured Alekseev's overall control of the army. During the latter half of 1915, Alekseev and other able civil and military officials, including the energetic new war minister Alexei Polivanov, succeeded in rebuilding the army.

Despite Alekseev's considerable abilities, his failure to delegate tended to cloud his ability to appreciate the larger strategic picture. His concern for the tsar's image as commander in chief led him to adopt a cautious posture that stabilized the Eastern Front but did not produce any significant gains. Alekseev played little role in the planning or execution of General Alexei Brusilov's offensive in the summer of 1916, and Alekseev refused to commit troops to assist

Romania in 1916 until Russia's own borders were threatened.

Over time, Alekseev's dedication to the tsar waned due to mounting frustration with the incompetence of tsarist officialdom. Unable to convince Nicholas II to initiate reforms, Alekseev, who by that time was suffering from cancer and heart disease, retired in November 1916. He was recalled just in time to play an instrumental role in securing the abdication of Nicholas II during the March 1917 revolution.

Following the fall of Nicholas II, the Provisional Government appointed Alekseev commander in chief of the army. Alekseev's opposition to an offensive being planned by new war minister Alexander Kerensky (the so-called Kerensky Offensive) led to his resignation in May 1917. Alekseev was briefly recalled in September to arrange a settlement of the political dispute between Kerensky and General Lavr Kornilov, but the attempt failed, and Alekseev resigned after only 12 days. Following the Bolshevik takeover in November 1917, Kornilov and the terminally ill Alekseev formed the White (anti-Bolshevik) Volunteer Army in southern Russia. Alekseev died in Ekaterinodar (Krasnodar) on October 8, 1918.

John M. Jennings

Further Reading

Lincoln, W. Bruce. *Passage through Armageddon: The Russians in War and Revolution, 1914–1918.* New York: Simon and Schuster, 1986.

Luckett, Richard. *The White Generals: An Account of the White Movement and the Russian Civil War.* New York: Viking, 1971.

Alexandra Fyodorovna, Tsarina (1872–1918)

Last empress of Russia. Tsarina Alexandra Fyodorovna was born Princess Alix Victoria Helena Louise Beatrice of Hesse-Darmstadt in Germany on June 6, 1872, the daughter of Louis IV of Hesse-Darmstadt and Alice Maud Mary, daughter of Queen Victoria. Alix had two brothers and four sisters. Her nickname, Sunny, reflected a sparkling personality despite the loss of her brother, sister, and mother all before she was six.

Alix met her husband to be, the future tsar Nicholas II of Russia, in 1884, when she was 12. She was forced to convert from Lutheranism to the Russian Orthodox faith, and they married on November 26, 1894, three weeks after the death of Tsar Alexander III. Theirs was an unusually happy marriage. Crowned together on May 26, 1896, Nicholas II and Alexandra strongly adhered to the divine right of kings theory and ruled as autocrats, but Alexandra dominated her weak-willed husband. The two had four daughters and one son, Alexis, born in 1904. Alexis was a hemophiliac. That illness was known to originate in Alexandra's family through her grandmother, Queen Victoria. Alexandra became fanatically religious, although much of this was centered in unorthodox faith healers. Grigory Rasputin, a Siberian monk who appeared around 1905, exerted great influence. He allegedly healed Alexis on several occasions when doctors had given up hope of his recovery. Alexandra increasingly fell under Rasputin's spell, creating a poisonous atmosphere of distrust among those close to the throne. Unfounded, malicious stories soon circulated of a sexual relationship between Alexandra and Rasputin. Russia's noble elite hated Alexandra, and she in turn despised them for the problems besetting the Crown. Alexandra gradually withdrew from society and into her family circle. Despite her unpopularity, she founded schools, built hospitals, and worked to improve the conditions of the poor. During World War I, she nursed soldiers and converted the palace into an infirmary and gave money to the war effort. Her German origins and domination of her husband, however, led to untrue accusations that she was spying for Germany and betraying Russian war plans.

When in September 1915 Nicholas II ill-advisedly took command of the army at the front, he left Alexandra in charge in St. Petersburg. Not politically astute, she made grievous errors. She increasingly relied on Rasputin's advice concerning key government appointments, leading to the installation of a number of incompetents in high positions and incessant turnover.

Following the Russian Revolution of March 1917, Nicholas abdicated on March 17. Subsequently arrested by the Bolsheviks, Nicholas, Alexandra, and their entire family were held at Ekaterinburg in central Russia. There they were shot early on the morning of July 17, 1918, under orders from Vladimir Lenin in Moscow, although official Soviet accounts sought to shift responsibility for the decision to the Ural Regional Soviet. The remains were then secretly buried.

In 1998 on the 80th anniversary of the execution, the remains of Alexandra, Nicholas, and three daughters, identified through DNA, were reinterred in the St. Catherine Chapel of the Peter and Paul Cathedral of the Fortress of St. Peter and St. Paul in St. Petersburg. In 2000, the Russian Orthodox Church canonized Alexandra along with Nicholas II and their children.

Annette Richardson

Further Reading

Erickson, Carolly. *Alexandra: The Last Tsarina.* New York: St. Martin's, 2001.

Kozlov, Vladimir A., and Vladimir M. Khrustalëv. *The Last Diary of Tsaritsa Alexandra.* New Haven, CT: Yale University Press, 1997.

Massie, Robert K. *The Romanovs: The Final Chapter.* New York: Random House, 1995.

Allied Intervention in Russia (1918–1922)

Immediately upon seizing power in Petrograd in November 1917, the Bolsheviks announced that Russia was withdrawing from World War I. Russia's former allies of Britain, France, and the United States wanted to keep that country in the struggle against the Central Powers and also prevent stocks of weapons from falling into the hands of the Central Powers by reversing the political situation in Russia, but they had no coordinated plans to accomplish this end. Even after the Allied Supreme War Council decided to intervene on the side of the anti-Bolshevik (White) forces in Russia, the action was haphazard and ineffective. In part this was because the Allied governments provided only military assistance and not the economic support indispensable to victory. Throughout, the Western powers pursued short-range military goals, but they never seriously discussed the political future of a non-Bolshevik Russia.

During a conference of Allied leaders at Rapallo in November 1917 concerning military cooperation, the British and French representatives were unsuccessful in securing an agreement on a common policy toward Russia. Then on December 23, 1917, London and Paris signed a convention agreeing to enter the Russian Civil War in support of the White forces against the Reds (Bolsheviks). This gave rise to the Bolshevik charge that the Western Allies had agreed to dismember Russia.

German occupation of the strategically and economically important Ukraine triggered the Allied intervention. Also, negotiations at

ALLIED INTERVENTIONS IN WESTERN RUSSIA

Canadians
Americans

British
French
Canadians
Italians
Serbs

Murmansk

NORWAY

SWEDEN

Archangel

Shelkursk

FINLAND

Finns

Finns

Helsinki

British

ESTONIA
Latts

Petrograd

RUSSIA

Perm

LATVIA
Riga

Latts

Pskov

Kazan

Baltic
Sea

LITHUANIA

Kaluga

Moscow

Nizhni
Novgorod

GERMANY

Baltic
Germans

Minsk

Smolensk

Samara

Orenburg

Warsaw

Poles

Penza

Ural

POLAND

Tambov

Saratov

CZECHOSLOVAKIA

Dniester

Kiev

Kharkov

Don

Zhitomir

Dnieper

Poltava

HUNGARY

Yekaterinoslav

Rostov

Volga

Astrakhan

Romanians
ROMANIA
Bucharest

Odessa

Sea
of Azov

YUGOSLAVIA

Sevastopol

Novorossiysk

Maikop

Caspian
Sea

BULGARIA

French

Black   Sea

Batumi

Baku

British

GREECE

Constantinople

OTTOMAN EMPIRE

British

Tehran

PERSIA

Mediterranean
Sea

Boundary of Russian Empire, 1914
Eastern Front, Autumn 1918
Area of Soviet Territory, Mar 1921
Main locations of Bolshevik Uprisings
Attacks by Allied Powers

Trans-Siberian Railway

0   100   200 mi
0   100 200 km

Allied soldiers and sailors from the United States, France, Great Britain, Canada, Japan, China, and Italy parade in front of the Allied headquarters in Vladivostok, Russia, September 1918. (National Archives)

Brest-Litovsk between the Bolshevik government and the Germans led to concern in the Allied capitals that the Baltic States, eastern Poland, Ukraine, and part of the Caucasus would come under either German or Ottoman/Turkish control.

The French took the lead in the Allied intervention. French general of division Ferdinand Foch, later supreme Allied military commander, strongly favored intervention in Russia to keep that state in the war against Germany. His plan envisaged a multinational military force under his own command. On December 24, 1917, the Allied Supreme War Council proclaimed that the Allied powers would provide military assistance to any political faction in Russia that supported that country's participation in the war against Germany. The French government strongly supported the Czech Legion

in Russia, and between March and May 1918 during the Ludendorff Offensives (March 21–July 18) on the Western Front, France made every effort to reopen the Eastern Front and encouraged Japan to take part.

The Allied intervention in Russia began with the landing of British troops at Murmansk on March 9, 1918, although London was less concerned than Paris about a Bolshevik Russia and feared a Japanese thrust into the Russian Far East more. The British government was also far more pragmatic in its Russian policy in that it was willing to support any Russian government, including the Bolsheviks, which would guarantee British economic interests in the Russian market. In Ukraine, British economic interests met French competition; White leaders were able to use this rivalry to play the Allies against each other.

In early 1919 during the Paris Peace Conference, British prime minister David Lloyd George and U.S. president Woodrow Wilson encouraged negotiations with the Bolsheviks. Wilson suggested a conference of all factions in the Russian Civil War to begin on February 15, 1919, on Prinkipo Island in the Sea of Marmara. This effort came to naught, because leading White leaders Alexander Kolchak and Anton Denikin as well as the Bolshevik leaders sought to continue their military offensives. The Bolsheviks also feared that a peace conference under Allied auspices would necessarily favor the Whites, as they were the clients of the Western powers. Lloyd George and Wilson believed that the Whites only deserved to win, however, if they could gain the support of the Russian population. Moreover, there was no agreement between the Allies and the White leaders concerning Russia's political future after an end to the Bolshevik regime. The political values of the Western democracies and the authoritarian White generals were so different that the Allies could not be certain that a White regime in Russia would be an improvement over the Bolsheviks.

Meanwhile, the Russian Civil War continued. Although the Allies provided military equipment and advisers, they made no effort to force political change that would bring about an efficient political system on territory occupied by the Whites. Moreover, French-British and U.S.-Japanese rivalries prevented unified action in the Russian Civil War.

Following the death of Admiral Kolchak in February 1920, the Western Allies did seek a modus vivendi with the Bolshevik regime. As a first step toward that end, they lifted the economic blockade of Bolshevik Russia. At the same time, the Allied powers began their withdrawal from Russian territory. According to an official French government report of October 1919, France alone had spent more than 7 billion francs in its Russian intervention, with nothing to show for the massive outlay. There was also some sentiment among Western politicians to cultivate Bolshevik Russia as an ally against a resurgent Germany.

Japan's approach was quite different, however. Even before Japan's gains of the 1904–1905 Russo-Japanese War, that nation's leaders had sought to expand Japanese influence on the Asian mainland in Korea and Manchuria. Japanese expansionists perceived in the Russian Civil War a splendid opportunity to enhance their holdings in Russia's eastern territories. Japanese general Tanaka Giichi in Manchuria proposed the creation of an independent noncommunist Siberian state, allied with and presumably dominated by Japan. Whereas the United States sent to Siberia 9,000 soldiers, Great Britain sent 7,000, China sent 2,000, Italy sent 1,400, and France sent 1,200; Japan dispatched some 73,000 troops to eastern Siberia and the Russian Far East. In addition, Japan had 60,000 soldiers deployed in neighboring Manchuria.

Some Japanese leaders predicted that Siberia would be the site of an eventual clash between the civilizations of the "yellow" and "white" races in the Far East. Thus, the Japanese intervention into Siberia was not only directed against Russia but also was intended to forestall U.S. engagement in the region. Most White leaders, however, harbored strong patriotic and often racist suspicions of the Japanese, seeing in them only a temporarily useful force in the struggle against Bolshevism. They saw no long-term advantage in an alliance with Japan. This was one reason for the failure of Japan's intervention in Siberia. Finally, not only because of the financial strain of the enterprise but also under pressure from the United States, the Japanese were compelled to withdraw from

Siberian territory. Japan's departure was completed by the end of October 1922.

Eva-Maria Stolberg

Further Reading

Dickinson, Frederick R. *War and National Reinvention: Japan in the Great War, 1914–1919.* Cambridge, MA: Harvard University Press, 1999.

Foglesong, David S. *America's Secret War against Bolshevism: U.S. Intervention in the Russian Civil War, 1917–1920.* Chapel Hill: University of North Carolina Press, 1995.

Kennan, George F. *Soviet-American Relations, 1917–1920,* Vol. 2, *The Decision to Intervene.* Princeton, NJ: Princeton University Press, 1958.

Kettle, Michael. *Churchill and the Archangel Fiasco, November 1918–July 1919 (Russia and the Allies, 1917–1920).* 3 vols. London: Routledge, 1981–1992.

Melton, Carol Willcox. *Between War and Peace: Woodrow Wilson and the American Expeditionary Force to Siberia, 1918–1921.* Macon, GA: Mercer University Press, 2001.

Reynolds, Michael A. *Shattering Empires: The Clash and Collapse of the Ottoman and Russian Empires, 1908–1918.* Cambridge: Cambridge University Press, 2011.

Richard, Carl J. *When the United States Invaded Russia: Woodrow Wilson's Siberian Disaster.* New York: Rowman and Littlefield, 2012.

Silverlight, John. *The Victors' Dilemma: Allied Intervention in the Russian Civil War.* New York: Weybright, 1970.

American Expeditionary Force, Siberia

The American Expeditionary Force, Siberia, was a military unit sent by President Woodrow Wilson to Siberia in order to provide security for the Czech troops fighting the Bolsheviks in the Russian Civil War. This force was in addition to the American North Russia Expeditionary Force, or the Polar Bear Expedition. With either of these deployments, President Wilson was not sending an invasion force to take part in direct combat against the Red Army; he wanted the force to secure and aid the Czech Legion fighting against the Bolsheviks in Siberia. While Wilson did not support the Bolsheviks in Russia, he did not want to dedicate the United States to overthrowing them either.

What encouraged the United States and other powers to send military forces to Siberia was the success of the Czech forces in the summer of 1917. The Czech forces launched an offensive in July that surprised the Bolsheviks with its success. This spurred the Bolsheviks to redouble their efforts to build military capacity in the form of the Red Army and also encouraged foreign intervention by European powers and the United States. The success of the Czechs in 1917 gave the Allied powers the belief that they could stop the Bolsheviks with a little military support and possibly get Russia to rejoin the war under a more sympathetic government led by non-Bolsheviks. These hopes quickly died due to the infighting among anti-Bolshevik forces, the success of Trotsky's program to build the Red Army, and the lack of any other large-scale success by Czech forces.

The commander of the detachment was Major General William Graves. Graves had command of the Eighth Division and was looking forward to deploying with the division and fighting in Europe. However, on August 2, 1918, he received a coded message directing him to go to Kansas City and meet with Secretary of War Newton Baker. Baker informed Graves that his mission was to lead a force to try to influence the Russian people in Siberia. Graves learned that he had command of about 5,000 soldiers, and they had orders to go to Russia and provide some stability in order to secure and aid the Czech Legion.

Graves and his soldiers reached Vladivostok on September 1 and joined the Philippine soldiers already in the area. This combined force, commanded by Graves, numbered almost 9,000 soldiers. Graves's soldiers were not the only foreign troops in the region protecting their nation's interest. Japan had a much larger force that was several times the size of the U.S. forces deployed to Vladivostok. Farther to the west, Britain and France also had forces in Russia conducting supporting operations for the White Army.

The situation in Russia when Graves arrived was ambiguous in terms of the amount of cooperation that the foreign military forces expected. When Graves met with the Japanese commander, he learned that they expected him to turn over command of his forces to the Japanese, as the British did in Archangel. This was outside of Graves's orders, and he refused to give up authority over his unit.

The internal diplomatic situation that Graves and his force encountered was even more tumultuous. Due to the ineffectiveness of the Provisional Government to extend its power into Siberia, by the time Graves and his soldiers arrived there were already separatist groups in the area. This increased as the Provisional Government's influence declined and then dissolved due to pressure from the Bolshevik Party. In Siberia as in the rest of Russia, the Bolsheviks were in the minority. The Socialist Revolutionary Party was the group orchestrating leaving Russia due to the ineptitude of the Provisional Government. By January 1918, there was a Siberian Duma that was independent of the government in Petrograd.

When the Provisional Government dissolved in late 1917, many of its supporters fled to Siberia. This combined with the lack of support from the Marxists meant that the Siberia separatist government was increasingly non-Marxist as well as non-Leninist. An increasingly independent government in Siberia posed a problem for the nascent Bolshevik Party and the fledgling Red Army.

One of the problems that the United States and other foreign forces faced in Siberia was lack of cooperation and coordination of anti-Bolshevik forces. There were several different groups, including ones led by Cossack general Grigori Semenov and another led by Admiral Kolchak. These groups did not support the Bolshevik government, but they could not agree which of the anti-Bolshevik groups should take the lead and which were subordinate. This meant that although the White anti-Bolshevik groups outnumbered the Red forces in the region, they did not fight with a unified purpose and often fought against each other, further degrading their ability to resist the growing Red Army threat in the East.

In addition to the struggles of competing anti-Bolshevik forces, Graves also had difficulty with the increasingly large Japanese force in the area. By the end of 1918, the Japanese contingent was about 72,000 troops; this dwarfed the U.S. forces in Vladivostok. Over American objections, the Japanese took over running the railroads in Manchuria and Vladivostok. President Wilson ordered Graves to keep his forces in the Vladivostok region and not interfere in operations against the Red Army in Omsk, which was over 2,000 miles to the East. It was surprising that Wilson wanted Graves to maintain his forces in Vladivostok, given the limited strength of the U.S. forces in the region and the limited ability to supplement or reinforce them if they became critically engaged in fighting.

Peace in Europe in 1918 decreased the importance of an anti-Bolshevik government in St. Petersburg to help the Allied war effort against Germany. President Wilson deployed Graves's force but wanted to maintain neutrality among the anti-Bolshevik groups. Peace did not influence this policy. In addition, President Wilson wanted to keep Graves and his men in Siberia until after the Paris peace talks but did not want them to take an active part in the fighting in Siberia. After the Paris peace talks, there was less enthusiasm or need for an anti-Bolshevik government in Russia. Also, the increased efficacy of the Red Army and the unwillingness of the White forces to coalesce around a central government or leader made it increasingly difficult for external powers to determine which group or leader to support. The American Expeditionary Force, Siberia, returned on April 1, 1920.

Gates M. Brown

Further Reading

Ackerman, Carl. *Trailing the Bolsheviki.* New York: Scribner, 1919.

Foglesong, David. *America's Secret War against Bolshevism: U.S. Intervention in the Russian Civil War, 1917–1920.* Chapel Hill: University of North Carolina Press, 2001.

Saul, Norman. *War and Revolution: The United States and Russia: 1917–1921.* Lawrence: University Press of Kansas, 2001.

Anarchists

Anarchists are individuals who favor destroying the established order. They hold that all existing political and economic institutions must be extinguished to achieve true social and political liberty. Anarchists believe that it is only in the absence of governmental restraint that the political ideal of a society based on the cooperative and voluntary association of individuals can be achieved.

Anarchism in the early 1900s often embraced syndicalism, or the idea that business and industry—the employer class—should be overthrown so that the workers themselves could establish control over the workplace in solidarity. Anarchism in general was decidedly leftist in its varying political philosophies but did not embrace the concept of a traditional state or government. Instead, it championed the notion that governing power be invested in the people through collectivist prescriptions.

While some anarchists were pacifists, others held that war—be it an internal revolution or an international conflagration such as World War I—was only worthwhile if it would result in the demise of capitalism. Those active in the antiwar movement were to a large extent influenced by several incidents of the late 19th century and by theorists of that era. The most prominent anarchist of that period was Russian-born Mikhail Bakunin. He grounded his beliefs in the writings of 19th-century German philosopher Friedrich Hegel yet professed the need for violent overthrow of the old order to effect true liberty. The German social revolutionary Johann Most took this position further with the publication in 1885 of *The Science of Revolutionary Warfare,* which often served as a terrorist handbook among certain anarchists.

The Paris Commune of 1871, which occurred in the aftermath of the Franco-Prussian War, was short-lived but invigorated anarchist thought worldwide by seeming to prove the viability of the bottom-up formation of independent voluntary communes and associations coming out of violent struggle. French anarchism, however, never became a true mass movement, fading in popularity at the turn of the century.

Many of the more outspoken anarchists in Europe during this period immigrated to the United States. The elation inspired by the Paris Commune was tempered in 1886 with what became known as the Haymarket Affair, in which four anarchists were executed in the United States for their role in organizing workers in Chicago. This led to significant government repression of those professing anarchist sentiments.

In Russia, on the other hand, anarchists became increasingly active, the result of difficult economic and social conditions brought on by unbridled rapid industrialization and the 1904–1905 war with Japan. In the early 20th century, attempts were made at international coordination of anarchist efforts, bringing together such individuals as the Italian thinker Errico Malatesta, the German anarchist Rudolf Rocker, and Russian prince Peter Kropotkin. At the beginning of World War I in 1914, the predominant camp urged avoiding any political and military involvement in what they saw as a purely capitalist conflict, although Kropotkin urged support of France against the Germans. American anarchist groups generally opposed any U.S. military involvement in the war, including an arms buildup. Anarchist activities included the publication of antiwar materials in journals and newspapers and the staging of mass rallies.

Two of the best-known American anarchists of this period were Emma Goldman and Alexander Berkman. Although they had been involved with episodes of violence prior to the war, they later openly disavowed its use. Goldman, a Lithuanian immigrant often referred to as "Red Emma," incited peaceful opposition to involvement in the war through her passionate speeches and editorials in her journal, *Mother Earth.*

Goldman was arrested during the war, tried under the Espionage and Sedition Acts, and jailed for two years; she was also fined $10,000. In 1919 during the postwar Red Scare, she was forcibly deported to Russia.

The Russian-born Berkman, also known as "Sasha," was best known for his unsuccessful attempt in 1892 to assassinate Carnegie Steel chairman Henry Clay Frick. After serving time in prison, Berkman joined Goldman in organizing mass antiwar demonstrations. He too was arrested during the war, receiving the same sentence as Goldman. Berkman was deported in 1919.

The November 1917 Bolshevik Revolution in Russia fueled fear in Western Europe and the United States of radicals and anarchists and led to repressive legislation. In the United States, the Espionage Act of 1917, later amended by the Sedition Act of 1918, outlawed opposition to government policies and the war effort. These acts led to the closing of anarchist newspapers and other publications and caused internal splintering of anarchist organizations.

During the immediate postwar period in the United States, Attorney General Alexander Mitchell Palmer ordered raids on anarchist meetings and the arrest of those thought to be subversives. Most of the leadership of the International Workers of the World, a quasi-syndicalist labor group, was arrested, tried, and sentenced to long prison terms. Palmer was responsible for the deportation of at least 1,000 aliens espousing anarchist and antigovernment beliefs and presided over the arrests—without warrants—of several thousand other suspected radicals.

Pamela L. Bunker

Further Reading

Avrich, Paul, ed. *The Anarchists in the Russian Revolution.* Ithaca, NY: Cornell University Press, 1973.

Berkman, Alexander. *Life of an Anarchist: The Alexander Berkman Reader.* Edited by Gene Fellner. New York: Four Walls Eight Windows, 1992.

Goldman, Emma. *Living My Life.* 2 vols. 1933; reprint, New York: Dover, 1970.

Marshall, Peter. *Demanding the Impossible: A History of Anarchism.* Oakland, CA: PM Press, 2010.

Moritz, Theresa, and Albert Moritz. *The World's Most Dangerous Woman: A New Biography of Emma Goldman.* Vancouver: Subway, 2001.

Wenzer, Kenneth C. *Anarchists Adrift: Emma Goldman and Alexander Berkman.* St. James, NY: Brandywine, 1996.

Antonov-Ovseyenko, Vladimir (1883–1938)

Vladimir Antonov-Ovseyenko was the leader of the Red Army in Ukraine and southern Russia for the Soviet invasion of Ukraine. He began his involvement with revolutionary politics in 1903 by joining the Menshevik Party. In the Russian Revolution of 1905, he was instrumental in the uprising in Poland. Antonov-Ovseyenko was arrested for his involvement in the revolution and was sentenced to 20 years' hard labor. However, in 1910 he escaped and sought refuge in Paris. Ovseyenko joined the Bolshevik Party in protest of World War I and moved back to Russia to take part in the October Revolution. He continued to work for the Bolshevik Party after the revolution and served as a special minister coordinating Soviet support for the Republican forces in the Spanish Civil War. Antonov-Ovseyenko fell victim to the Great Purge in the late 1930s and was killed. Nikita Khrushchev later rehabilitated him posthumously.

After the Bolsheviks came to power in October 1917, they moved to secure their positions against attack from opposition forces. One of the first maneuvers in support of the Bolshevik government was the deployment of forces into the Donbas region to secure the railway to the Caucasus region. Antonov-Ovseyenko, already well known for his leading the arrest of the Provisional Government in the Winter Palace in Petrograd, was by December 1917 the people's commissar for war. The Council of People's Commissars, the Sovnarkom, appointed him the main commander in chief for the struggle with counterrevolution in southern Russia. This meant that Antonov-Ovseyenko had operational control and responsibility for forces in the Donbas region. He faced the ominous task of protecting the Bolshevik government from White forces but also had to help build up the Red Army forces that he would use to accomplish his mission. Although the Red Army was in its formative stages, the Cossack forces that faced the Bolshevik forces were also ill-prepared for combat.

Antonov-Ovseyenko's progress was slow in securing the region, as he did not have adequate forces to hold territory and continue the assault. Also, the Bolshevik government was in the process of demobilizing the army and negotiating a peace with the Central Powers, the Treaty of Brest-Litovsk. With the signing of the treaty in March 1918, the Bolshevik government agreed to cede its authority in Ukraine and southern Russia in order to secure peace. Although Lenin wanted Antonov-Ovseyenko to continue his operations and use Antonov-Ovseyenko's Ukrainian ethnicity to the Bolsheviks' benefit in gaining support, it was impossible for the Red forces of approximately 10,000 troops to gain any ground against the enemy troops in the region. Increasing the Soviet government's hold in Ukraine would have to wait until later in 1918.

As the Central Powers removed their troops from Ukraine, the Red forces moved in behind them to expand Soviet control of Ukraine. In January 1919, Soviet forces led by Antonov-Ovseyenko invaded Ukraine with the intent of installing a government friendly to the Bolshevik regime. The invasion forces numbered about 6,000 soldiers. In addition to the soldiers, the invading forces also had 15 planes, 6 armored trains, and 170 field artillery pieces. The Bolshevik government denied any direct involvement in the invasion and claimed that the conflict was a civil war and not Bolshevik intervention or invasion. Although this was a Bolshevik military operation, the command and control elements of the Red Army were not well established. Leon Trotsky had difficulty controlling Antonov-Ovseyenko, and Antonov-Ovseyenko similarly had trouble controlling his subordinate units. This lack of control stemmed from the fact that many of the Ukrainian forces fighting for the Bolsheviks were insurgents, not regular troops. In addition to the lack of formal control, another obstacle that Antonov-Ovseyenko faced was his focus on securing Ukraine, even at the expense of the broader revolutionary mission of expanding Soviet authority to the West.

Antonov-Ovseyenko continued to push his forces past the Dnieper River. Although he was successful, he extended his lines of communication too far and was unable to support his position when Major Nikifor Grigoriev, a leading Ukrainian Cossack commander, or ataman, defected. Grigoriev's defection meant the removal of the paramilitary forces that he commanded, which bolstered the White forces in the region. In order to consolidate their position in Ukraine, the Red Army had to stall other advances. Antonov-Ovseyenko's actions in the Ukrainian invasion were too narrowly focused on securing Ukrainian territory. This focus led to lost opportunities to support other Red Army units in the Don region. This lack of support allowed the White forces to mount a counterattack in May 1919. The success of the White offensive led to the dissolution of the Ukrainian Army Group that Antonov-Ovseyenko commanded. He would never receive another large military command. Ultimately, Soviet forces were successful in capturing Ukraine and establishing a Soviet republic in Ukraine.

After his command in the Ukrainian invasion, Antonov-Ovseyenko continued to work for the Bolshevik Party as consul for several East European countries. He worked with the Republicans in the Spanish Civil War to coordinate Red Army support for their forces. However, he fell victim to the Great Purge of Soviet officials in the late 1930s and was executed. His reputation was later rehabilitated posthumously by Nikita Khrushchev in 1956 when he absolved many of those executed in Stalin's purges.

Gates M. Brown

Further Reading

Courtois, Stéphane, Nicolas Werth, Jean-Louis Panné, Andrzej Paczkowski, Karel Bartosek, Jean-Louis Margolin, and Mark Kramer. *The Black Book of Communism: Crimes, Terror, Repression.* Cambridge, MA: Harvard University Press, 1999.

Mawdsley, Evan. *The Russian Civil War.* Winchester, MA: Allen and Unwin, 1987.

April Theses

When the February Revolution occurred, Vladimir Lenin was in Switzerland. He quickly returned to Russia, arriving on April 16 (April 3 in the Julian calendar), 1917. On arriving in Russia, he gave an address outlining the April Theses, a blueprint for how the Bolsheviks should work to gain power at the expense of the Provisional Government. The theses stressed that the Bolsheviks could not support the Provisional Government and had to work to increase the class consciousness of the proletariat in order to build the workers into a power bloc that could take power away from the bourgeoisie who, Lenin argued, made up the controlling members of the Provisional Government. He also outlined his view that a parliamentary government was counterproductive to Bolshevik goals, as the Bolsheviks needed to demand that all power go to the Soviets. In addition, Lenin argued that the Bolsheviks needed to rename their party the Communist Party and needed to have an international meeting in order to continue the worldwide revolution that Lenin believed was beginning in Russia.

When Lenin found out about the revolution in Russia, he knew that he needed to return in order to exploit the situation to the advantage of the Bolshevik Party. He traveled through Germany by train, although he was not allowed to leave the train while it was in Germany; he took a ferry to Sweden and finally took a train through Sweden and Finland to Russia. Germany eagerly supported Lenin's trip to Russia in hopes that he would instigate further political instability and lead to Russia withdrawing from the war. During the trip, Lenin took the time to sketch out his strategy for how to approach the turbulence in Russia. He ensured that his ideas communicated in the theses were attractive to more than just the Bolsheviks. Lenin wanted to gain the support of all leftist groups who felt that the Provisional Government was not the best solution for Russia.

One significant plank in Lenin's platform was the idea of unseating the Provisional Government. Traditional Bolshevism focused on Russia becoming a parliamentary state and then, after the failure of that democratic state, turning to communism. This fit well with Marxist ideology concerning the natural progression of governments from monarchy through democracy and finally to communism. This view of a truncated revolution in Russia was part of Lenin's plan to make the most of the situation in Russia. He wanted to be successful in Russia and export the revolution in Russia to other nations in order to create a worldwide revolution.

Lenin's pronouncements exposed a rift in the Bolshevik Party. Although Lenin was the leader of the party, his view expressed in the April Theses did not represent the view of those who followed him. Some Bolsheviks, such as Lev Kamenev, saw Lenin's disconnection and lack of familiarity with Russia as the reason why Lenin's ideas were so ill-formed and irrelevant to the political situation in Russia. Lenin surprised his party by calling for the end of the Provisional Government; this was a revolutionary statement considering that there was wide representation of socialists in the Provisional Government, although the Bolsheviks were a minority in the new government. Another example of the divide in the Bolshevik Party concerning Lenin's theses was that *Pravda,* the official Bolshevik newspaper, refused to print them by claiming incorrectly that their printers were not working.

However, this initial refusal to print did not deter Lenin. Days after his arrival in Petrograd, he was able to leverage his position in the party to get them published. Four days after Lenin gave his speech in Petrograd, *Pravda* printed them. Other senior Bolsheviks worried that printing Lenin's ideas would imply that the party approved of them. In order to make it clear that Lenin's article did not carry the approval of the Bolshevik Party, Lev Kamenev wrote a statement that

Lenin's positions were contrary to official Bolshevik policy. After their publication, the Kiev and Saratov Bolshevik parties also reacted negatively to Lenin's ideas.

Although the initial reaction to Lenin's ideas were negative, due to his position in the party he was able to overcome this setback and made his theses the ideological framework of the Bolshevik Party in its opposition to the Provisional Government. Lenin's theses and their call for transfer of power to the soviets fit well within the democratic nature of the February Revolution in Russia. However, Lenin also understood that if the Provisional Government allowed the soviets to gain political power, the Bolsheviks could ensure that they controlled the soviets and, by extension, wielded the real power in Russia. This was an example of how Lenin was able to couch his revolutionary policies, such as calling for the overthrow of the Provisional Government, while not overtly calling for a revolution.

The April Theses outlined Lenin's thoughts about how to gain his objective of a Bolshevik revolution in Russia. The theses made it clear that Lenin did not see the Provisional Government as a legitimate power and that he considered it a threat to a true socialist Russian state. Lenin, in his speech outlining the theses, also deviated from traditional Bolshevik revolutionary theory by calling for a rapid move to a socialist state instead of waiting for the democratic revolution to founder and a socialist state to overthrow the democratic government after the people realized its shortcomings. Many senior Bolshevik leaders and Bolshevik groups in other urban cities did not support Lenin's ideas as expressed in his April Theses speech or the *Pravda* article published days after his speech in Petrograd. Although Lenin faced initial skepticism concerning his ideas, he was able to leverage his position in the party

to force his ideas on the party and make them the foundation of Bolshevik strategy through 1917.

Gates M. Brown

Further Reading

Kingston-Mann, Esther. *Lenin and the Problem of Marxist Peasant Revolution.* New York: Oxford University Press, 1983.

Pipes, Richard. *The Russian Revolution.* New York: Vintage, 1990.

Rappaport, Helen. *Conspirator: Lenin in Exile.* New York: Basic Books, 2010.

Army, Soviet (Red Army; 1918–1991)

The Red Army was created in 1918 after the Bolshevik Revolution, renamed the Soviet Army in 1946, and formally ended with the collapse of the Soviet Union in 1991. The Russian Army was created from its remains.

Origins and the Civil War

During the Conference of Bolshevik Organizations in June–July 1917, the decision was made to abolish the tsarist army and form a new one that would serve the party and the revolution. Although the demobilization of the Imperial Russian Army continued until April 1918, the Soviet government created the Workers' and Peasants' Red Army (Raboche-Krest'ianskaia Krasnaia Armiia), recruited from the class-conscious workers and toiling peasants in January 1918. All prerevolutionary grades, ranks, orders, and titles were abolished. The name "Red Army" referred to the traditional color symbolizing the communist movement. The new force underwent its baptism of fire on February 23, 1918, fighting German troops at Narva and Pskov. This date became Soviet Army Day, still celebrated in Russia as Defender of the Fatherland Day.

Initially, the army was a small voluntary force based on the Red Guards (Krasnaya Gvardiya), formations created in major cities during 1917 by factory workers. These small militias of 100–150 men patrolling the streets grew into irregular infantry brigades of up to 1,200 partisans under the loose command of a democratically elected officer. In November 1917 the Red Guards numbered over 200,000 men, who fought in a fierce but undisciplined way. Although it was the Red Guards of Petrograd who made possible the seizure of power by the Bolsheviks, it quickly became evident that these poorly trained, ill-armed, decentralized militias could not uphold the revolution. After a breakdown in peace talks with Germany, the Bolshevik forces were defeated in the Eleven-Day War, which led to the disastrous Brest-Litovsk Treaty of March 3, 1918. Russia left World War I with tremendous territorial losses. The

German onslaught and the treaty demonstrated that the Bolsheviks needed an army able to protect their revolution.

In March 1918 Lenin assigned Leon Trotsky, the people's commissar for war, the task of creating a regular army of traditional style: tightly disciplined and with a centralized chain of command. Trotsky (re)introduced authority and harsh discipline and abolished the popular election of officers. His most controversial decision was the deployment of the former tsarist officers, termed "military specialists" (*voyenspetsy*), as a temporary solution to overcome the shortcomings of the Bolsheviks' military expertise. During the Russian Civil War, the army used over 300,000 *voyenspetsy* personnel, who proved vital in building the organizational and administrative structure of the Red Army, improving the quality of training, and introducing a military culture. Some

Red Army soldiers pass in review of Leon Trotsky during the Russian Civil War. (Library of Congress)

130,000 former noncommissioned officers, who were promoted to Red Army platoon commanders, trained new recruits and led them in combat. Two distinguished tsarist noncommissioned officers, later to become marshals of the Soviet Union, were Semen Budenny and Georgy Zhukov. In May 1918, Trotsky established the post of commander in chief of the army; the first person to hold the post was Mikhail A. Muravyev, though he was replaced in July 1918 by Ioakhim I. Vatsetis, who was followed in 1919 by Sergei S. Kamenev. All three were former tsarist colonels. The reality of war challenged the utopian communist vision of a new type of army distinct both from imperial forces and the Western military model. Bolshevik principles were gradually replaced by the rules typical of traditional armies, and the last to give way was the volunteer system. The military defeats at the hands of Cossack and Czech units in May and June 1918 demanded the introduction of a compulsory conscription, and the first drive in June– August brought about 540,000 men. The Red Army's capture of Kazan in September 1918, a turning point in the civil war, marked the end of the Bolsheviks' constant retreat and the beginning of the army's centralization and massive growth. By the end of 1918, the army had grown to 800,000 men; in 1919 it had 3 million men and increased to almost 5.5 million by October 1920.

The force was not yet strong enough, however, to export the revolution, as demonstrated by its defeat in the Battle of Warsaw in August 1920. Even at the height of its growth there were only some 2.25 million men at the front, of whom no more than 700,000 were active combatants and fewer than 500,000 were properly armed. The rest were recruits under training (2.25 million), reserve units (391,000), labor armies (159,000), and wounded, sick, or deserters.

The development of the army as a mass conscript force generated a few interrelated problems. First, the Red Army's membership initially was restricted and required a recommendation from a military body, trade union, or other organization associated with the Bolshevik Party; then it was limited to workers and poor peasants. Because there were not enough workers to fill the ranks, though, the army had to be based overwhelmingly on the peasantry. Contrary to Marxist ideology and the early Bolsheviks' intentions, the majority of servicemen (almost 80 percent of recruits in 1919) were not workers but peasants, whom the Bolsheviks did not trust. Second, the army grew much faster than the state's ability to sustain it, despite large sectors of the economy having been militarized under war communism. It was difficult to supply sufficient food, uniforms, weapons, transportation, and medicine. Trotsky captured the essence of this problem: "We have mobilized millions, but our bayonets are numbered in hundreds of thousands." It was also increasingly difficult to train the ever-growing numbers of recruits.

Third, the resulting coercive requisitions of supplies and forced conscription provoked peasant uprisings. Severe shortages in military supplies also meant poor living conditions, malnutrition, the spread of epidemics (during the war fewer people died in battle than from disease), a rise in disobedience, and chronic desertion. From June 1919 to June 1920, the Red Army lost from desertion almost as many men (2.64 million) as it recruited (2.7 million). Overall, some 3.7 million soldiers deserted during the war. As a countermeasure, in November 1918 Trotsky ordered all captured deserters executed on the spot, but the commanders rarely enforced this, usually only relocating deserters. The most effective means were the amnesty weeks; during the first one in June 1919, as many as 98,000 deserters returned in exchange for an exemption from punishment.

In 1918 the first higher-level operational structures were formed: the field armies and the fronts (or army groups). By the end of the year there were 12 field armies. The fronts created in June 1918 consisted of 2 to 5 field armies, reserve units, and detached forces. They were given geographical names—for example, the Eastern, Western, Northern, Ukrainian, or Caspian-Caucasian Front. They changed over time and were often integrated (e.g., in February 1919 the Northern Front was incorporated into the Western Front).

In March 1918 the Supreme Military Council headed by Trotsky was created; it was replaced in September by the Revolutionary Military Council of the Republic, which accommodated the Field Staff to command combat operations. The first Army Staff was formed in 1921 and was retitled the General Staff in 1935.

Despite opposition from Joseph Stalin, Kliment Voroshilov, and others who accused Trotsky of copying the Imperial Russian Army and departing from proletarian principles, Trotsky transformed the Red Army into an effective and massive fighting force. It was a new type of army to a much lesser extent than originally intended. There were significant continuities from the Imperial Russian Army, because the ex-tsarist personnel carried into the Red Army the traditional military culture.

The Party's Army

The Red Army originated as a political force as an instrument for implementing the Bolshevik Party's goals, spreading its principles, consolidating its power, defending a new regime, and building a new Soviet identity. The best representation of this integration of the party with its fighting force was the Main Political Administration, which oversaw the political loyalty of the military. To impose political control over the military and prevent a counterrevolutionary coup, the military commissar system was developed, with political officers (*politruks*) assigned to every unit. Under the policy of dual command (*dvoyenachaliye*), they had the power to abrogate commanders' decisions if they contradicted the principles of communism and the party's interests. At the regiment, brigade, and division levels, the commander shared power and responsibility with the *politruk,* and his orders were valid only when countersigned. By introducing the death penalty for military failures, Trotsky hoped to enhance combat performance and develop a terror-based mechanism of cooperation and control. (The first to be shot was the commissar, then the commander.)

In 1925 with a sufficient number of communist commanders already trained (the Bolsheviks condemned the use of the word "officer," which connoted tsarism), the system of dual leadership was lessened in favor of unity of command (*edinonachaliye*). Apart from *politruks,* the Cheka's special punitive brigades operated within the army to suppress the forces of counterrevolution, espionage, and desertion. Regular purges (*chistki*) aimed to expel undisciplined and antisocialist elements.

From its birth, the Red Army played the vital political role of molding young conscripts into "new Soviet men" endowed with a "Red" identity through indoctrination and basic education. Unsurprisingly, during 1925–1933 the number of Communist Party members among the ranks increased from 19 to 49 percent.

The Interwar Period

The demobilization that followed the end of the Russian Civil War reduced the army to a small regular force of 562,000 *krasnoarmeets*

(Red Army men) backed by a large territorial militia of part-time conscripts. For nearly two decades this mixed territorial system remained the organizational form of the armed forces. Mikhail Frunze, who in November 1924 replaced Trotsky as the head of the War Commissariat, established military districts, introduced standardization of regiments and divisions, restructured conscription, and modernized armament. Having enough Red commanders, Frunze downsized the number of *voyenspetsy,* who by the late 1920s made up only 10 percent of the officer corps. Until 1941, however, the General Staff was still headed by ex-tsarist officers Mikhail Tukhachevsky, Boris Shaposhnikov, and Alexander Yegorov. Frunze also implemented a policy of militarization aimed at strengthening the authority of commanders and weakening the power of commissars (*edinonachaliye*), which was continued by his successor, Voroshilov, in 1925. In 1936 the age of draftees was reduced from 21 to 19, and all previous restrictions on military service (e.g., the prohibition on enlisting kulaks) were abolished.

Łukasz Kamieński

Further Reading

Benvenuti, Francesco. *The Bolsheviks and the Red Army, 1918–1922.* New York: Cambridge University Press, 1988.

Dunn, Walter S., Jr. *Stalin's Key to Victory: The Rebirth of the Red Army.* Westport, CT: Praeger Security International, 2006.

Figes, Orlando. "The Red Army and Mass Mobilization during the Russian Civil War 1918–1920." *Past & Present,* no. 129 (November 1990): 168–211.

Hagen, Mark von. *Soldiers in the Proletarian Dictatorship: The Red Army and the Soviet Socialist State, 1917–1930.* Ithaca, NY: Cornell University, 1990.

Khvostov, Mikhail, and Andrei Karachtchouk. *The Russian Civil War,* Vol. 1, *The Red Army.* Oxford, UK: Osprey, 1996.

B

Bloody Sunday

On January 22, 1905, Russian troops fired on a peaceful procession of demonstrators led by Father Georgy Gapon outside the Winter Palace in St. Petersburg. This dramatic event kicked off the Russian Revolution of 1905 and set the stage for the Russian Revolution of 1917.

Before Bloody Sunday, Gapon, like hundreds of his followers, believed that labor reform could occur without revolution and that the tsar, their "Little Father," was divinely appointed and had their best interests always in mind. The union that Gapon led, in fact, was sponsored by the government, and Gapon was a government agent. Because the Gaponovites trusted Tsar Nicholas II, however, they did not join the radical workers who called for a violent revolution. Gapon and hundreds of on-strike workers nevertheless planned to march on Sunday and ask the tsar for better working conditions and higher wages. The demonstrators would begin their march to the tsar's Winter Palace from all corners of the city.

Tired of the weeklong citywide strike and fearing the more radical workers, Nicholas called additional troops to St. Petersburg on January 21. Russia was still embroiled in a war with Japan, however, and the availability of trained troops was limited. After being briefed by the director of the police and the minister of the interior, Nicholas decided not to obstruct the march. On Sunday morning, the police preceded the separate groups of demonstrators and cleared the traffic for them. A few processions were stopped by mounted troops and forced to disperse. Some demonstrators built barricades and drew swords. Near the Peter and Paul Fortress, demonstrators ignored the police and pressed forward with their march.

The largest group of marchers, led by Father Gapon, marched on, singing hymns. At the Tarakanovska River, they refused to halt for the police or the military troops behind the police. When the police heard the troops' bugler sound a firing order, the police parted and retreated. The troops fired several times into the crowd of marching workers, who ran toward them while singing hymns. Gapon was knocked off his feet and shuffled off by a radical worker.

Tsarist officials reported 130 people killed that Sunday; other sources say 1,000 people died that day or from their wounds in the days following. The events of that Sunday reverberated throughout Russia. Workers went on strike, troops were called in to control them, and Father Gapon, renouncing the tsar, now called for revolution.

Mark Schwartz

Further Reading

Ascher, Abraham. *The Revolution of 1905: A Short History.* Stanford, CA: Stanford University Press, 2004.

Gapon, Georgy. *The Story of My Life.* New York: E. P. Dutton, 1905.

Sablinsky, Walter. *The Road to Bloody Sunday: Father Gapon and the St. Petersburg Massacre of 1905.* Princeton, NJ: Princeton University Press, 1976.

Brest-Litovsk, Treaty of (March 3, 1918)

Peace treaty signed between Russia and the Central Powers in the Polish city of Brest-Litovsk on March 3, 1918, which ended Russia's participation in World War I. The Treaty of Brest-Litovsk, which was essentially forced on the Russians by Germany, was a major humiliation for the Russians. In February 1917 Tsar Nicholas II of Russia was overthrown, the result of the terrible cost of World War I to Russia. The new Provisional Government vowed to continue the war, however, which was a major miscalculation. Vladimir Lenin, leader of the revolutionary Bolshevik Party, pledged a program of "Land, Peace, and Bread," and the Bolsheviks did everything they could to undermine army morale and authority.

With the failure of the Kerensky Offensive in the summer of 1917 and the accompanying collapse of the army, on November 7 the Bolsheviks seized power in a second revolution, actually a coup d'état, and Lenin, whose party had been the beneficiary of immense amounts of German money, immediately announced that Russia would leave the war. Indeed, Lenin promised a peace that would result in no land annexations, no indemnities, self-determination, and a commitment to make public and repudiate all prior secret treaties among the Great Powers. The new Bolshevik government thus broke Russia's treaties and commitments with its former allies.

On December 3, 1917, the two sides opened truce talks behind German lines in Brest-Litovsk, and on December 17 an armistice went into effect on the Eastern Front. On December 22 the first peace conference of the war began, also at Brest-Litovsk, although meaningful talks there did not begin in earnest until January 9, 1918.

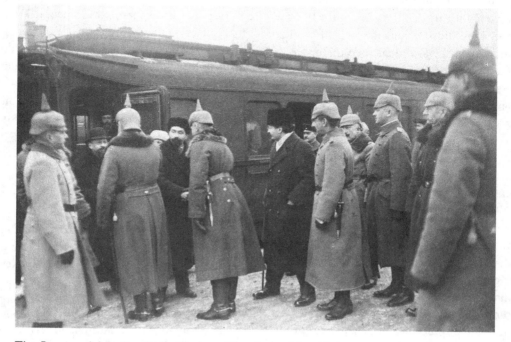

The Russian delegation, including Leon Trotsky and Lev Kamenev, arrive in Brest-Litovsk on December 27, 1917, and are greeted by the German delegation. (National Archives)

Russian commissar for foreign affairs Leon Trotsky headed the Russian delegation, and he adopted a defiant attitude. The Russian strategy was to stall the talks until an expected Bolshevik-inspired revolution swept Europe and drove Germany from the war. The Russians also naively expected the Germans to negotiate on the basis of no annexations or indemnities. But German army chief of staff in the east Major General Max Hoffmann soon disabused Trotsky of this when he presented the German demands. The German General Staff had formulated extraordinarily harsh terms that shocked even the German negotiator and career diplomat Richard von Kuhlmann.

During a brief Christmas recess, Trotsky returned to Petrograd and urged the Bolshevik leaders to pursue a policy of "no war, no peace." This was unacceptable to the Germans, although the conferees did manage to agree to extend the armistice until February 12. Two days before its expiration Trotsky proclaimed that the Russians simply considered the war at an end. An astounded Hoffmann responded by signing a separate peace with Ukraine and informing the Russian delegation on February 16 that the German Army would resume offensive military operations against Russian forces in two days.

On February 18, German troops crossed the Dvina River to capture the city of Pskov, and Trotsky returned to Petrograd for urgent consultations. Most of the Bolshevik leadership preferred continuing the war, but because they had destroyed the army in their rise to power, Russia was in no position to fight. The German Army meanwhile rolled forward in the easiest offensive of the war. It required all of Lenin's argumentative skills to convince the Bolshevik leadership to agree to peace, which the leaders accepted in a vote of seven to six. Lenin secured the narrow agreement by telling the leadership that the treaty would not last. Germany, he said, was on the brink of revolution. The most important thing was to consolidate Bolshevik power in Russia, without which there would be no hope for world revolution. Lost territory could be recovered later. The German advance continued even after the Russians had returned to the negotiating table. The Germans reached Narva, only 100 miles from Petrograd, precipitating transfer of the Russian government to Moscow.

On March 3, 1918, the Bolsheviks signed the Treaty of Brest-Litovsk. Trotsky, replaced as commissar of foreign affairs by Georgy Chicherin, refused to attend the ceremony. Russia lost Poland, Courland, and Lithuania, leaving Germany and Austria-Hungary to determine their future status. The Russians also had to evacuate Livonia, Estonia, Finland, and the Åland Islands. Russia was also forced to evacuate Ukraine and recognize the treaty between the Ukrainian People's Republic and the Central Powers. Russia had to surrender the districts of Ardahan, Kars, and Batum to Turkey as well as eastern Anatolia and had to agree to cease all Bolshevik propaganda. Finally, Russia agreed to pay Germany an indemnity the Russians estimated at from 4 billion to 5 billion gold rubles.

The treaty also forced the Russians to disarm. Their army was to be immediately demobilized, and their navy was not to venture out of Russian ports. The negotiations at Brest-Litovsk stipulated commercial ties between Russia and the Central Powers that were highly beneficial to the latter and forbade the Russians from levying export tariffs on Russian ores or lumber.

The Treaty of Brest-Litovsk virtually pushed Russia back to its pre-Petrine frontiers. Russia lost nearly 1.3 million square miles of land and 62 million people—that is, one-third of its population. The losses included approximately one-third of Russia's arable land, three-fourths of its coal and iron, one-third of its factories, and one-fourth of its railroads. In view of German protestations over the 1919 Treaty of Versailles, it is worth remembering that the Treaty of Brest-Litovsk was much harsher on the defeated power. It is a point of historical debate whether the infant Soviet regime would have collapsed had Germany refused the armistice and peace talks and continued offensive action. Some historians believe that the peace treaty saved the Bolshevik regime.

The German Reichstag accepted the treaty overwhelmingly. For the Allies, the punitive treaty helped to forge a unity of purpose hitherto lacking. The treaty also forced many Allied leaders to conclude that they would be unable to forge a reasonable peace with the Germans and that only the complete defeat of Germany would bring about an acceptable peace on their terms.

If there had been any doubts as to the future of the surrendered territories, these were laid to rest when they were immediately brought under the control of the Central Powers. In April, German troops landed in Finland, and Kaiser Wilhelm II offered the Finnish throne to his brother-in-law Prince Karl of Hesse. That same month, German and Austro-Hungarian troops occupied the Ukraine, vital for its grain production, and established a military dictatorship there under General Pavlo (Pavel) Skoropadsky. The kaiser also accepted the invitation of the Estonians to be their king, and in July Lithuania offered its throne to Prince Wilhelm of Urach, a younger member of the ruling family in Württemberg.

The treaty was of immense importance to Germany. First quartermaster general of the German Army Erich Ludendorff had already transferred perhaps half a million men to the Western Front for his great spring offensive.

He would move more men later; had he sent them initially, he might have had the victorious peace in the West that he and German Army chief of staff and field marshal Paul von Hindenburg sought. As it was, the Ludendorff Offensives failed, and in November 1918 Germany was defeated. The Treaty of Brest-Litovsk was thus voided not as Lenin had assumed by revolution in Germany but by an Allied military victory. The Paris Peace Conference failed, however, to return much of the territory to Russia, retaining it as a buffer of new states to contain Bolshevism. Not until World War II would Soviet leader Joseph Stalin regain the lost territory.

Charles M. Dobbs and Spencer C. Tucker

Further Reading

Goldstein, Erik. *The First World War Peace Settlements, 1919–1925.* New York: Longman, 2002.

Neiberg, Michael S., and Davis Jordan. *The History of World War I: The Eastern Front, 1914–1920.* London: Amber Books, 2012.

Wheeler-Bennett, John. *Brest-Litovsk: The Forgotten Peace, March 1918.* New York: Norton, 1971.

Brusilov Offensive (June 4–September 1, 1916)

When Russian forces attacked in Galicia, General Alexei A. Brusilov, only recently appointed commander of the southwestern front, opened a large-scale offensive against the Austro-Hungarians in the early hours of June 4, 1916. Almost alone among Russian commanders in believing that the army was fit for offensive action, he intended to provide relief for both the French, hard-pressed at Verdun, and the Italians, who were being pushed back in the Tyrol. As a secondary goal, Brusilov also hoped to perhaps draw

BRUSILOV OFFENSIVE, 1916

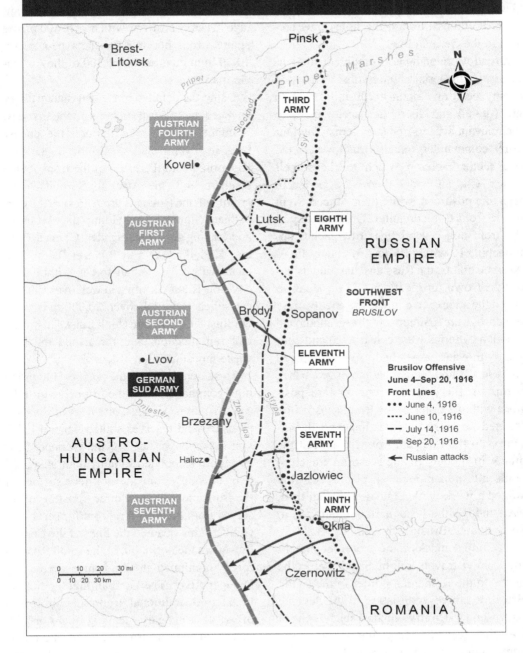

- Brest-
  Litovsk

Pinsk

Pripet   *Pripet*   M a r s h e s

Stockhod

THIRD ARMY

Syr

AUSTRIAN FOURTH ARMY

Kovel

Lutsk

EIGHTH ARMY

RUSSIAN EMPIRE

AUSTRIAN FIRST ARMY

Brody   Sopanov

SOUTHWEST FRONT
BRUSILOV

AUSTRIAN SECOND ARMY

ELEVENTH ARMY

Lvov

GERMAN SUD ARMY

Dniester

Zlota Lipa

Strypa

Brzezany

Halicz

**Brusilov Offensive
June 4–Sep 20, 1916
Front Lines**
• • • June 4, 1916
- - - June 10, 1916
— - July 14, 1916
▬▬ Sep 20, 1916
← Russian attacks

AUSTRO-HUNGARIAN EMPIRE

SEVENTH ARMY

Jazlowiec

AUSTRIAN SEVENTH ARMY

NINTH ARMY

Okna

0   10   20   30 mi
0 10 20 30 km

Czernowitz

ROMANIA

Romania in on the side of the Allies. In the overall plan, however, the Southwestern Front was merely an ancillary designed to draw off German reserves. The main Russian attacks would come in the north, where General Alexei Evert's armies would drive toward Vilnius through the holes thus created in the German line.

Brusilov nonetheless prepared meticulously. Using aerial photographs, he mapped enemy positions along a 200-mile front in great detail and distributed sector maps to the relevant officers and subalterns. The four army commanders under Brusilov selected one sector each on which to focus their attack. Chosen troops then were ferried to rear-line positions, while their officers went to the front to reconnoiter. Units already at the front dug several lines of trenches approaching to within 75 feet of enemy lines. At some points, the Russians dug tunnels under their own fortifications and obstacles to speed the attack. To confuse the enemy, false trenches were painted on the ground, and wooden batteries were constructed and constantly moved. Large dugouts were prepared for reserves and hidden behind huge earthen berms. Artillery moved into forward positions within 2 miles of the front, as Brusilov insisted on close coordination with the infantry. In the rear, the troops practiced the attack in models of the Austrian trenches. With all preparations in place, Brusilov waited a week while Stavka hesitated; then, even though the headquarters continued to voice doubts, Brusilov moved.

The initial attacks came on a front stretching from Ostrovets, on the Styr River in the north, to the Romanian border in the south. Brusilov's forces, consisting of the Seventh Army under Dmitry Shcherbechev, Alexei Kaledin's Eighth Army, the Ninth Army commanded by Pavel Lechitski, and the Eleventh Army under Vladimir V. Sakharov,

numbered over 600,000 men. Facing them were some half a million Austro-Hungarian and German troops in six armies: the First, Second, Third, Fourth, and Seventh Austrian Armies along with the mixed South Army. The Central Powers held a decided advantage in heavy artillery, with nearly 600 pieces against 165, but the Russians had nearly 1,800 light guns against 1,300 of the Austro-German forces.

Using the detailed maps, Russian artillery silenced many Austrian guns on the first day. Infantry then broke through the enemy lines in several places, pushing to the Styr River on the northern end of the front. At the southern end, the Austrian Seventh Army crumbled; the Russians drove toward the Carpathian Mountains, dividing the Austrians and leaving their commander, Colonel General Karl Freiherr von Pflanzer-Baltin, isolated with only a small force. Within three days, the Russians inflicted well over 100,000 casualties and took over 70,000 prisoners. On June 8 the Russians took Lutsk, an important rail junction, and threatened the next westernmost junction of Kovel.

To stanch the flow, the Austro-Hungarian high command halted the offensive in Italy, sent two divisions east, and begged the Germans to send reserves south. General Erich von Falkenhayn, head of the German General Staff, responded sullenly but transferred two divisions from the northern sectors of the front and withdrew three divisions of reserves from the Western Front for service in Galicia. This steadied the lines of the Central Powers in the north, but in the south Russian forces continued their advance across the Dnieper River. The German high command transferred additional troops south in aid of Austria-Hungary, leaving the northern sectors of the Eastern Front with mere battalions as reserves. The Russian plan was working; however, Evert did not attack. He claimed first that bad weather prevented a move, then that the Germans had reinforced the points he intended to assault, necessitating a change in plan. Not until June 18 did Evert move, and then he quickly halted the weak attacks his forces made against the Germans.

With his reserves exhausted and facing critical shortages of shell and ammunition and with his supply lines overextended and confronted by fresh German troops, Brusilov paused to regroup. By the time the offensive resumed on July 28, Austria-Hungary had shifted three more divisions to Galicia and shortened their front by ceding control of the sector south of Brody to Germany. Brusilov's troops overwhelmed the Austrians, pushing into the foothills of the Carpathians in the early days of August 1916.

The German General Staff, already hard-pressed on its northern sectors of the front, drew two divisions from the west to service in Galicia and created two more service divisions from reserves on both fronts. Turkey also sent two divisions to aid the Austrians, who appeared on the verge of military collapse. Unable to muster resistance at any level, the Austrians reluctantly agreed to a unified command for the Eastern Front, essentially handing control of all military operations to the Germans on August 28, one day after Romania entered the war on the Allied side.

Brusilov's offensive had by that time petered out against the stiffening resistance and mounting casualties. German forces seized control of the air and destroyed the Russian Guards Army near Kovel. Brusilov's attacks had cost the Austro-German forces over 1 million men captured, killed, or wounded and reclaimed some 250 square miles of territory. The cost in men for Russia was nearly twice that, however, and critics regarded the offensive as a failure overall.

Certainly the tremendous losses among the corps of officers and noncommissioned officers, many of them newly trained during the "quiet winter" of 1915–1916, contributed to the collapse of discipline in the Russian Army in 1917.

Had Evert attacked as planned, it is possible that Brusilov's action might have driven Austria-Hungary from the war. As it was, the Brusilov Offensive appeared to have more than fulfilled the original goals. The Italian Army had been saved when Austria was forced to withdraw its troops from Tyrol, German pressure at Verdun lessened as troops were siphoned off to reinforce the Eastern Front, and any attempt to preempt or counter the Allied attacks on the Somme was rendered null. Falkenhayn, his strategy in ruins, was replaced by Ludendorff as head of the German General Staff. Just how much of this was due to Brusilov's efforts, however, is debatable. Romania's entry into the war, though not strictly positive for the Allies, did drain German power further. Though the Brusilov Offensive may have dealt a severe blow to the Russian Army in terms of numbers and morale, it may also have saved the Allied war effort at a critical juncture. It was undoubtedly the greatest Russian military contribution in World War I and, some have argued, the first use of combined arms tactics.

Timothy C. Dowling

Further Reading

Dowling, Timothy. *The Brusilov Offensive.* Bloomington: Indiana University Press, 2008.

Hagen, Mark von. *War in a European Borderland: Occupations and Occupation Plans in Galicia and Ukraine, 1914–1918.* Seattle: University of Washington Press, 2007.

Stone, Norman. *The Eastern Front, 1914–1917.* 2nd ed. New York: Penguin, 2004.

Budenny, Semen Mikhailovich (1883–1973)

Cavalry officer, marshal of the Soviet Union, deputy commissar of defense, and commander in chief of the Soviet armies on the Southwestern Front during World War II. Semen Mikhailovich Budenny was born in Koziurin, in the Cossack district of the Don Oblast, on April 25, 1883. The son of non-Cossack peasants, he was conscripted into the Russian Army in 1903 as a private, having previously taught himself to read. He fought in the Russo-Japanese War in a cavalry regiment, eventually becoming a noncommissioned officer.

At the beginning of World War I, Budenny was still in the army; he rose to sergeant major by 1917. He actively participated in the October (Bolshevik) Revolution and in the Russian Civil War, at one point winning a guerrilla engagement against the vastly superior forces led by Anton Denikin that made him a legend of Soviet folk tales and songs. During the Russian Civil War, Budenny raised a guerrilla unit, the nucleus of the Red Army cavalry, to fight White Army forces on the Don. His unit grew to 100 men, and in the second half of 1918 he was instrumental in winning the Battle for Tsaritsyn under the leadership of Joseph Stalin, then local chairman of the military committee. Budenny was promoted quickly during 1919, commanding a cavalry division in January, a cavalry corps in June, and the First Cavalry Army in November. That same year he became a member of the Bolshevik (Communist) Party.

Budenny served during the war with Poland in 1920, relieving Kiev but being defeated by General Maxime Weygand at Warsaw. Budenny then fought in the Crimea, virtually wiping out General Pyotr Wrangel's army. Under the sponsorship of Stalin,

now chairman of the Communist Party, Budenny's career continued to flourish. In 1924 he became a member of the Executive Committee of the Soviet Union. From 1928 to 1932 he attended the Moscow Military Academy, graduating with honors, and in 1935 he became a marshal. In 1937 Budenny was appointed commander of the Moscow Military District, and in 1939 he became a member of the Central Committee of the Communist Party. At the outbreak of World War II, he commanded an army in the war against Finland. In August 1940, he was appointed deputy commissar of defense. After the German invasion, he was appointed commander in chief of the Southwest Front (army group), comprising 69 divisions, in which capacity he served from July to November 1941. He managed to escape the German encirclement at Kiev; however, as a result of this disastrous defeat, he was relieved of his command by Marshal Semen Timoshenko.

Budenny was a crack shot and an avid horseman. He remained a member of the Central Committee until 1961. He died on October 27, 1973, having been awarded the Order of Lenin several times.

Kevin S. Bemel

Further Reading

Budenny, Semyon. *The Path of Valor.* Moscow: Progress, 1972.

Montefiore, Simon. *Stalin: Court of the Red Tsar.* New York: Vintage, 2005.

Shukman, Harold. *Stalin's Generals.* New York: Grove, 1993.

Bukharin, Nikolai (1888–1938)

Russian Marxist and Bolshevik revolutionary who was an important figure in the Russian Revolution of November 1917; he was later an influential Soviet politician. Nikolai Ivanovich Bukharin was born in Moscow on October 9, 1888. Both of his parents were elementary school teachers, and Bukharin was well educated. He took an early interest in revolutionary ideas, and by age 14 he was reading literature decreed illegal by the tsarist regime. From the beginning of the Russian Revolution of 1905, Bukharin took an active role in revolutionary activities, participating in rallies and demonstrations and even organizing strikes. At that time, he also took an interest in Marxist philosophy and economic theory. He soon grew more involved in illegal activities, leading to his arrest on several occasions in 1908.

In 1911 following a brief imprisonment, Bukharin was exiled to Onega in Archangel but escaped from there to Hanover. He then went on to Krakow, where he met Bolshevik leader Vladimir Lenin, who had considerable influence on him. During Bukharin's travels, he spent time in the United States. He also wrote two books on economics, which established him as the most important Bolshevik theorist after Lenin.

The beginning of the Russian Revolution of March (February by the Russian calendar) 1917 found Bukharin in New York, and he did not reach Moscow until that May after Tsar Nicholas II had been forced to abdicate and the Provisional Government had been established. Russia remained in turmoil, however, as various political factions battled for control. Bukharin immediately joined the Bolsheviks and quickly rose to prominence as a member of the Moscow City Committee and the Central Committee of the Bolshevik Party, its highest governing body.

The Bolsheviks seized power in November (October by the Russian calendar) 1917. In the summer of 1918 Bukharin took charge of the most important party newspaper,

Nikolai Bukharin, ca. 1920. Bukharin served as a Bolshevik leader during the Revolution and was a member of the Central Committee of the Bolshevik Party and later the Communist Party. He also served as the editor of *Pravda* from 1918–1920. (Hulton Archive/Getty Images)

Pravda (Truth), remaining its chief editor until the end of the 1920s.

After the Bolshevik coup d'état, Bukharin proved his mettle as a leader. As one of the party's most radical members, he pushed for strident measures to create a true communist society. Bukharin was not reluctant to challenge anyone, including Lenin himself. Despite this, the two men remained close, and many considered Bukharin to be Lenin's favorite among the other party leaders.

During the Russian Civil War, Bukharin did not actively participate in the military campaigns but maintained his role as theorist and party leader. The fighting did cause him to modify his radical stance, however, and by the early 1920s he advocated a more gradual economic transition to a socialist state before proceeding on to communism.

Lenin died in 1924, and in the ensuing leadership struggle Bukharin and Joseph Stalin both early favored the gradual development of a Soviet state. The equanimity between the two men soon ended, as by 1928 Stalin adopted a more radical approach to the creation of a communist state. Refusing to change his own position, Bukharin quickly lost his influence and power in the party. Within a year he had been removed from the country's ruling body, the Politburo.

During the 1930s, Bukharin remained on the margin of Bolshevik society. In 1937 during the Great Purges, he was arrested on a charge of counterrevolutionary activities and placed on trial. Although the charges against him were unproven, he made a confession and was convicted. Bukharin was subsequently executed in Moscow on March 15, 1938.

David Elliott

Further Reading

Larina, Anna. *This I Cannot Forget: The Memoirs of Nikolai Bukharin's Widow.* New York: Norton, 1993.

Medvedev, Roy A. *Let History Judge: The Origins and Consequences of Stalinism.* New York: Columbia University Press, 1989.

Volkogonov, Dmitri Antonovich. *Stalin: Triumph and Tragedy.* Translated by Harold Shukman. New York: Grove Weidenfeld, 1991.

Bullitt, William C. (1891–1967)

William C. Bullitt was the first U.S. ambassador to the Soviet Union. His initial enthusiastic reception quickly turned cold as his disillusion with the Soviets' "great experiment" transformed him into a determined anticommunist. Bullitt also served as ambassador to France, where he encouraged resistance to Adolf Hitler and German expansion before World War II. During the war, Bullitt continued as a close adviser to President Franklin D. Roosevelt, though after the war his anticommunism led him to support Republican Party candidates.

Bullitt came from an old and distinguished Virginia family. He was born in Philadelphia on January 25, 1891, the son of wealthy attorney William Christian Bullitt. The younger Bullitt attended the DeLancey preparatory school before enrolling at Yale University. He graduated in 1913 and entered Harvard Law School. His legal career was cut short by his father's death, however. Bullitt returned to Philadelphia and joined the staff of the *Philadelphia Public Ledger.* He quickly rose to associate editor.

In 1914, World War I broke out in Europe. Bullitt accompanied Henry Ford's peace mission to Europe in 1915 as a reporter and traveled extensively for a year through Germany and Austria. On March 18, 1916, Bullitt married Ernesta Drinker. He returned home and in 1917 joined the State Department, where his firsthand knowledge of European conditions was important. Bullitt was appointed chief of the Bureau of Central European Information. He prepared briefings for President Woodrow Wilson and his chief aide, Colonel Edward House, especially on the Russian Revolution and subsequent events.

In December 1918, Bullitt accompanied Wilson to Paris for the Paris Peace Conference as chief of the division of current intelligence. Early in 1919, Bullitt headed a secret mission to Moscow. He met with Vladimir Lenin and other communist leaders to negotiate conditions for a peaceful settlement of the civil war in Russia. Lenin agreed to terms that included an in-place armistice, the evacuation of Allied soldiers from Russia, and Soviet recognition of imperial Russia's debt.

Disagreement between the Allied leaders led to a rejection of these terms and prevented a peaceful settlement of the war. Bullitt was disillusioned with the failure of his mission and with the Versailles Peace Treaty. He resigned from the mission and returned to the United States. In the fall of 1919 Bullitt testified before Congress against the treaty, helping to justify its nonratification.

Between 1919 and 1933, Bullitt was active in private business. He was a film story editor for Famous Players-Lasky Corporation. He and his first wife had no children and were divorced in 1923. Later that same year Bullitt married journalist Louise Bryant, widow of radical writer John Reed. In 1926 Bullitt published a novel, *It's Not Done,* a satire of high society in Philadelphia. In 1924 he met Sigmund Freud, who psychoanalyzed him in 1926. The two men collaborated on a psychobiography of Wilson, *Thomas Woodrow Wilson, Twenty-Eighth President of the United States: A Psychological Study.* Published in 1967, it received devastating reviews from historians and psychologists alike. In 1930 Bullitt and Bryant were divorced, and he gained custody of their son.

Bullitt had met Roosevelt during World War I and supported his later presidential bid. In 1933, Bullitt was appointed special assistant to Secretary of State Cordell Hull. Bullitt was a member of the American delegation at the London Monetary and Economic Conference of 1933. He was also involved in negotiations for the Roosevelt-Litvinov Agreements, which established diplomatic relations between the United States and the Soviet Union. In 1933, Roosevelt appointed Bullitt the first American ambassador to the Soviet Union.

Bullitt received an enthusiastic welcome upon his arrival in the Soviet Union in December 1933. He quickly realized, however, that Soviet leader Joseph Stalin was not keeping the terms of the Roosevelt-Litvinov Agreements and that conditions in the Soviet Union were not as proclaimed. Bullitt became increasingly critical of the communist government. Roosevelt avoided Bullitt's advice regarding relations with the Soviets, and Bullitt was more and more isolated from influencing U.S. policy.

In 1936, Bullitt was transferred to become ambassador to France. He accurately predicted Hitler's expansion into Central Europe and became Roosevelt's most important adviser regarding Europe in the late 1930s. Bullitt encouraged resistance to Hitler both in France and in the United States. With his fluent French, he developed close ties with French leaders. When war broke out in September 1939, Bullitt arranged for the French to purchase American arms.

When France fell in 1940, Bullitt returned to the United States. He advocated all-out aid short of war to Great Britain. His most important speech was published in 1940 as *Report to the American People.* Bullitt was eventually appointed ambassador-at-large to the Middle East and North Africa. His reports influenced the 1942 North Africa Campaign. After 1942, however, Bullitt was no longer employed by Roosevelt. The two had a falling out over Undersecretary of State Sumner Welles. Bullitt tried to have Welles dismissed for alleged gay sexual activity, but Roosevelt refused.

In 1944, Bullitt joined the Free French forces. After the end of the war, he spent the remainder of his life in private business while preaching against communism. He became a Republican and supported the presidential campaigns of Robert Taft and Richard

Nixon. Bullitt died of leukemia on February 15, 1967, in Neuilly, France.

Tim J. Watts

Further Reading

Brownell, Will, and Richard N. Billings. *So Close to Greatness: A Biography of William C. Bullitt.* New York: Macmillan, 1987.

Farnsworth, Beatrice. *William C. Bullitt and the Soviet Union.* Bloomington: Indiana University Press, 1967.

Nolan, Cathal J., ed. *Notable U.S. Ambassadors since 1775: A Biographical Dictionary.* Westport, CT: Greenwood, 1997.

C

Casualties, Russian Civil War (1917–1922)

Tabulating the number of deaths and injuries resulting from the struggle between the Bolshevik revolutionary government and the White Russian counterrevolutionaries is a difficult task. The Russian Civil War of 1917–1922 was a no quarter–given struggle between forces willing to take any measure, no matter how barbaric, to further their cause. Counting deaths from the actual fighting and the attendant political terror, famine, and disease, estimates range from 7 million to 13 million dead.

Best estimates for the number of military dead total about 800,000 for both sides, including losses from the Polish-Soviet War. The Red Army suffered 125,000 killed in action and 300,000 dead from disease, including cholera, typhus, and influenza. White/Polish losses included 175,000 combat deaths and 150,000 dead from disease. That more soldiers died from disease than enemy action reflects the primitive state of medical care in both armies.

An equally difficult task is arriving at an accurate figure for both the Red and White terrors. In communist-controlled areas, as many as 400,000 may have died at the hands of the Cheka and the Red Army through summary execution, prison, or during the suppression of anti-Bolshevik uprisings. White forces kept no records but executed thousands of suspected Bolsheviks in the cities they occupied and, in the countryside, shot scores of captured Red partisans and villagers they believed aided those partisans.

In the White-occupied areas of the west-central Ukraine, scores of Jews perished in pogroms during 1918–1919.

The vast majority of deaths during the Russian Civil War, however, were due to civilians suffering from famine and disease. The scale resulted from war-related shortages of medical service personnel, the lack of sanitation, and the inability to harvest and distribute vital food supplies. The Soviet government's own statistics showed almost 900,000 deaths from typhus and typhoid fever in 1919 and over 1 million dead in 1920.

These epidemics went hand in hand with the famine of 1921–1922, which hit particularly hard in the Volga region. Massive requisitions of food by the Bolshevik government under the policies of war communism brought the peasantry, particularly those living in the far eastern Ukraine, to the edge of ruin and starvation. In the Samara region on the east bank of the Volga alone, 700,000 people had died of starvation by the end of 1921.

The massive loss of life in the Russian Civil War of 1917–1922 profoundly affected Soviet society. Analysts of Soviet Russia's political, economic, and demographic development differ over whether the brutality with which both sides waged the civil war was implicit in the nature of the Russian Revolution or an inevitable projection of traditional Russian authoritarianism carried to extremes by the violence of World War I and the social upheaval of the revolution. What cannot be argued is that the civil war, with its massive losses, was the first of a series of catastrophes that has affected Russia's demographic development to this day.

Walter F. Bell

Further Reading

Figes, Orlando. *A People's Tragedy: A History of the Russian Revolution.* New York: Viking, 1996.

Lincoln, W. Bruce. *Red Victory: A History of the Russian Civil War, 1918–1921.* New York: Da Capo, 1999.

Mawdsley, Evan. *The Russian Civil War.* New York: Pegasus Books, 2007.

Cheka (Chrezvychaynaya komissiya)

The Extraordinary Commission to Combat Counter-Revolution, the first of a succession of Soviet secret police organizations and known as the Cheka, was established on December 20, 1917, and abolished on February 6, 1922, when it was succeeded by the State Political Administration (Gosudarstvennoye Politicheskoye Upravleniye).

Vladimir Lenin, the Bolshevik leader, created the Cheka in 1917. The primary role of the Cheka was to combat internal threats to the Soviet regime both in the military and in civil society; it had absolute authority over both. The Soviet government defined enemies to include former tsarist officials and officers, including family members; the clergy; the wealthy; and any individual or group suspected of harboring anti-Soviet sentiments. Such individuals might be present anywhere, including within the ranks of the Red Army. Thus, a primary mission of the Cheka was to root out subversion from within Red military formations. Cheka teams were initially formed from existing Red Guard and ex-tsarist military personnel, comprising an organization of less than 100

men. The Cheka expanded to 37,000 by 1919, growing ultimately to about 200,000 by 1921 largely because of the ongoing civil war in Russia (1917–1922). Cheka responsibilities also included administration and management of the Soviet penal labor camp system, commonly known as the Gulag (Gosudarstvennoye lageri).

The Cheka hierarchy, headed by Felix Dzerzhinski, was organized at all levels of government, with detachments at the national, province, city, or town level. This widespread deployment allowed the Cheka to enforce control even in the more remote areas of the former Russian Empire. Similarly, Chekist formations were present at all levels within the Red Army. Cheka responsibilities primarily were to root out anti-Soviet subversion and to ensure the maintenance of military and political discipline within the disparate Red Army formations.

In the summer of 1918 the Soviet government implemented war communism, a drastic utopian policy eliminating money and private property. This policy was imposed to more effectively mobilize all economic and personnel resources to fight the civil war and defeat the anti-Soviet forces. The Bolsheviks also enacted conscription, which proved unpopular in many parts of the country where support for the communists was weak. The Cheka monitored the Red Army at all command levels for suspected disloyalty or defeatism through Special Punitive Brigades.

The Special Punitive Brigades apprehended about 1 million deserters during 1918–1919. With few controls on its actions, the Cheka imposed verdicts at will. Punishments ranged from forcibly returning deserters to their units to executions. During the formation of the Red Army, ex-tsarist specialists initially comprised up to 75 percent of the Red Army officer corps, as there were not enough communists with the requisite technical skills, such as engineering and artillery. The Cheka forced these former tsarist officers to use their skills at the disposal of the Red Army by holding the officers' relatives as hostages. The Soviets continued to train more politically reliable personnel (usually ex-enlisted men and noncommissioned officers) to replace the ex-tsarist officers, but by 1922 about 80 percent of the Red Army's division and corps commanders still consisted of ex-tsarist commissioned officers.

The Cheka also pioneered new techniques to control poorly performing Red Army formations. In August 1918, Commissar for War Leon Trotsky ordered the creation of Cheka blocking detachments. These units were deployed behind suspect battalions and regiments, with orders to fire on them if they retreated. Similar detachments would be used again during World War II. The Cheka remained active throughout Russia during the civil war, but those parts of the Cheka responsible for the armed forces continued to monitor the military hierarchy and enforce Soviet policies in areas under military occupation.

The Cheka was officially dissolved in February 1922 through reorganization into a new secret police organization. Renamed the State Political Administration, the Cheka became part of the Peoples' Commissariat for Internal Affairs (Narodni Kommisariat Vnutrikh Del) and continued its primary mission of identifying, arresting, imprisoning, and/or executing those identified as foes of the Soviet government.

Tim Wilson

Further Reading

Leggett, George. *The Cheka: Lenin's Political Police.* New York: Oxford University Press, 1987.

Pipes, Richard. *The Unknown Lenin: From the Secret Archive.* Annals of Communism Series. New Haven, CT: Yale University Press, 1999.

Read, Christopher. *From Tsar to Soviets.* Oxford: Oxford University Press, 1996.

Churchill, Winston (1874–1965)

British politician, cabinet minister, and prime minister and minister of defense (1940–1945). Born at Blenheim Palace, Oxfordshire, on November 30, 1874, Winston Leonard Spencer Churchill was the eldest son of Lord Randolph Churchill, third son of the Duke of Marlborough and a rising Conservative politician, and his wife Jennie Jerome, an American heiress. Educated at Harrow and the Royal Military College, Sandhurst, from 1895 to 1899, Winston Churchill held a commission in the British Army. He visited Cuba on leave and saw active service on the Afghan frontier and in the Sudan, where he took part in the Battle of Omdurman (September 2, 1898). Captured by South African forces in 1899 while reporting on the South African War (Second Boer War, 1899–1902) as a journalist, he made a dramatic escape and won early popular fame.

Churchill won election to Parliament as a Conservative. In 1904 his party's partial conversion to protectionism caused him to join the Liberals, who, when they returned to power, made him president of the Board of Trade (1908–1910) and home secretary (1910–1911). Named first lord of the Admiralty in September 1911, Churchill enthusiastically backed the campaign of first sea lord Admiral John "Jackie" Fisher to modernize the Royal Navy with faster battleships and more efficient administration. In the latter post Churchill oversaw initial plans to convert the Royal Navy from coal to oil and helped prepare the navy for the great challenges of World War I.

Churchill headed the Admiralty for nearly three years, including the first nine months of the war, and played a central role as part of Herbert Asquith's government in Britain's early war plans and actions. Churchill kept the Royal Navy at its battle stations after completion of scheduled fleet maneuvers in late July 1914 as war appeared imminent. He also tapped Admiral Sir John Jellicoe to command the Grand Fleet.

There were serious naval setbacks early in the war, including the loss of ships and battles. Churchill's desire for taking direct action led to him briefly commanding the Royal Naval Division as it vainly sought to delay German occupation of Antwerp in October 1914.

Under growing political pressure to stem this parade of setbacks, Churchill changed his naval leadership. First Sea Lord Prince Louis Battenberg was forced to resign in October 1914, in part because of his German-sounding name. In a fateful decision, Churchill persuaded the septuagenarian former first sea lord Admiral John Fisher to return, despite King George V's initial reluctance to approve the appointment.

Tensions between Fisher and his younger superior soon arose as the cabinet considered plans to drive the Ottoman Empire from the war. Acting on an early 1915 plea from a beleaguered Russia and seeking to open a new supply route to that country and reduce the Ottoman threat to British interests in the Middle East, Churchill proposed a plan by ships alone to force entry through the narrow Dardanelles, steam to Istanbul (Constantinople), and presumably drive the Ottomans from the war. Fisher initially approved the plan but then grew steadily more pessimistic as to the outcome. Churchill believed that ships could force the Dardanelles without having to land troops, and he underestimated the effectiveness of shore artillery fire against ships.

Following the Royal Navy bombardment of the Ottoman forts protecting the Dardanelles, an attempt was made to force passage through its minefields on March 18, 1915. The loss of three battleships to mines led to a halt in the effort. Churchill had hoped that the attack would continue but agreed to support his commander on the spot. After considerable acrimony between Churchill and Secretary of War Lord Horatio Kitchener, troops were sent to occupy the Gallipoli Peninsula. The landings began on April 25, but the Ottomans had improved their defenses and held the high ground, and the attackers were unable to push to the interior. Following Fisher's stormy resignation on May 15 as a result of Churchill's plans to send more ships, Churchill's enemies united against him for having championed the Dardanelles strategy.

Churchill resigned as first lord on May 26, accepting the honorific post of chancellor of the Duchy of Lancaster. Shorn of a role in the war's direction, however, he resigned this post on November 11 to serve in France with the British Expeditionary Force (BEF). He was assigned as a major to the 2nd Battalion of the Grenadier Guards as it returned to the front at Neuve-Chapelle and spent several days in frontline trenches, barely escaping death in an artillery barrage on November 26, 1915. With the sacking of his friend BEF commander Sir John French in early December, Churchill lost any chance of a senior military post. He then took command as a lieutenant colonel of the 6th Battalion, Royal Scots Fusiliers, on January 1, 1916, at Ploegsteert (Plug Street) in Flanders.

Churchill remained with his battalion until May 1916, when he resigned his command and returned to Parliament to work to change the government's military policy. Although his Liberal colleague David Lloyd George became prime minister in December

1916, because of Tory opposition Churchill did not secure a cabinet office until he became minister of munitions on July 18, 1917. In this post he performed effectively, helping to ensure a plentiful supply of artillery shells and other munitions to the BEF.

With the postwar election, Churchill became Lloyd George's minister for war and air (1919–1922) and, as a committed anti-Bolshevik, was one of the most active supporters of Allied intervention in the Russian Civil War (1917–1922). Churchill later served as chancellor of the exchequer (1924–1929). He spent the 1930s in the political wilderness but returned as first lord of the Admiralty (1939–1940) and finally led his nation to victory as prime minister (1940–1945). He was again prime minister during 1951–1955. In 1963 Churchill became the first of only seven people to be designated an Honorary Citizen of the United States. Widely acclaimed as one of the towering figures of the 20th century, Churchill died in London on January 24, 1965.

Christopher H. Sterling

Further Reading

Churchill, Winston S. *The World Crisis*. 6 vols. New York: Scribner, 1923–1931.

Gilbert, Martin. *Winston S. Churchill,* Vols. 3 and 4. Boston: Houghton Mifflin, 1971, 1975.

Higgins, Trumbull. *Winston Churchill and the Dardanelles: A Dialogue in Ends and Means*. New York: Macmillan, 1963.

Penn, Geoffrey. *Fisher, Churchill and the Dardanelles*. Barnsley, South Yorkshire, UK: Pen and Sword, 1999.

Cossacks

The original Russian term *kazak,* which has Turkic origins, referred to groups of people who lived in the northern regions of the Black Sea and Caspian Sea basins. In the century between the 1500s and the 1600s, the term evolved from referring to independent Tatar groups to a greater immigration of freed peasants from present-day Poland, Lithuania, and Muscovy.

Often used by Polish kings as frontier guards in the Don region just north of the sea of Azov, the Cossacks gained a fierce reputation as steadfast cavalry forces that could be relied on to fight. Though committed to their independence, the Cossacks became useful tools to Polish and later Russian monarchs as the Russian Empire solidified in the traditional territory of the Cossacks. The Don, Terek, and Kuban Cossacks became trusted military forces of Russia, and in return for their military obligations, the Russian government allowed them a certain degree of autonomy.

Having defined a useful niche for themselves as a strong military force, the Cossacks expanded their territory east into Siberia. In exchange for their degree of independence, the Russian tsars and tsarinas often called on Cossack units to assist in suppressing the rebellion of groups that threatened the stability of various regions as well as the regime itself. In the turbulent period of the late 19th and early 20th centuries, the Romanovs increasingly relied on Cossacks to suppress the left-wing radicals and other revolutionary activities.

In the context of the Russian Revolution and the subsequent Russian Civil War, Don, Terek, and Kuban Cossacks served as strong and early anti-Bolshevik forces. In maintaining their traditional stance of semiautonomy, the Cossacks worked with German, Allied, and White forces during the Russian Revolution and the Russian Civil War. Though they sought to maintain control over traditional Cossack regions and even strove for a greater degree of independence, they allied with anti-Bolshevik forces, for they saw Bolshevism as a significant threat to their historical position in Russian society.

This tension stemmed from the Bolshevik Land Decree, which called for the forced redistribution of land to the peasants and workers in Russia. The Cossacks tended to live in regions that had high percentages of peasants, who often worked for Cossack landowners. The ability of Cossacks to own land had been a reward for serving the Russian regime centuries earlier. Therefore, the Cossacks in the Don and Terek regions viewed the Bolshevik call for the reapportionment of land as a direct threat to their community structure and to the stability in their regions. When the revolution happened, the Cossacks channeled their discontent with the Bolsheviks into building alliances with whomever offered the best chance to defeat the Bolsheviks.

The Don Cossacks became one of the primary Cossack factions who played a significant part in the Russian Civil War. Having been the largest Cossack contingent, with 60 cavalry regiments, in the Imperial Russian Army during World War I, the Don Cossacks figured prominently in the years of the Russian Revolution and the Russian Civil War. As the Russian Army melted away in the revolutionary period, large numbers of Cossacks returned to the Don, Terek, and Kuban regions.

In the aftermath of the Bolshevik Revolution, Imperial Russian Army general M. V. Alekseev traveled to the Don region to build a volunteer force to combat the Bolsheviks and Reds. Though he succeeded in enlisting hundreds of officers, his recruitment was lackluster because Lavr Kornilov, who had escaped prison, worked on building a competing anti-Red military structure. Alekseev and Kornilov fought over the preferred arrangement of the Volunteer Army for months. The struggle for power was only resolved when Peter Struve and Pavel (Paul) Miliukov helped broker a deal between the two that also included the assistance of the Don Cossacks, who had been allying themselves with the Germans as a means to stabilize their region.

Of importance to note is that throughout the civil war, the Don, Terek, and Kuban Cossacks largely considered themselves sovereign and therefore played a cautious and calculating game of alliances during the Russian Civil War. Their real focus and ultimate objective was maintaining their own security, which saw the Don Cossacks ally with the Germans in an attempt to establish an independent Don Republic. However, as the Germans withered in the fall and early winter of 1918, the Don Cossacks as well as the Terek and Kuban Cossacks had to adjust their aims and work with the growing volunteer and White armies in an attempt to stem the Bolsheviks' objective. Prominent Russian historian Richard Pipes in *Russia under the Bolshevik Regime* best characterized the Cossack focus as thinking in "local and regional terms," not so much on grand strategic terms.

Throughout their association with Alekseev and Kornilov, the Cossacks were not trusted allies but rather expedient partners focused on an anti-Bolshevik objective. Known for their commitment to independence, the Cossacks often robbed and took advantage of the fluid military environment to gain more power, which led to deep resentment by Kornilov, who often referred to Cossacks as "scum." Though the Don Cossacks fought valiantly under the leadership of Alexei Kaledin in the winter of 1918, they were overcome by the rising support of Bolshevism by peasants, workers, and Imperial Russian Army deserters. Facing pressure from the Reds as well as increased internal support for Bolshevism, Kaledin faced mutiny within the Don Cossacks as they questioned their affiliation with the Volunteer Army of Alekseev and Kornilov. As a result of the growing external and internal pressures, Kaledin committed suicide in February 1918 and was succeed in May 1918 by General P. N. Krasnov.

Other Cossack forces also faced similar hardships. In April 1918, the Kuban Cossacks working with Kornilov attempted to siege Ekaterinodar, the capital of the Kuban Soviet Republic. The need to enlist the assistance of the Kuban Cossacks came as a result of significant loss of approximately 3,000 combat troops during the Volunteer Army's Ice March. In attempting to capture Ekaterinador, Kuban Cossacks provided roughly 4,000 cavalry men to field a combined volunteer force of 7,000 to attack a defensive Bolshevik force of approximately 17,000. During the siege, a Bolshevik artillery shell hit the command headquarters of Kornilov, killing him and forcing General A. I. Denikin to assume command. Denikin called off the siege and retreated with the Kuban Cossacks into the Russian steppe.

The history of Cossacks in the context of the Russian Revolution and the Russian Civil War is that they initially sought to retain their historic position of semiautonomy within the regime. However, the political agenda of the Bolsheviks directly threatened this objective. As a result, the Cossacks in the Don, Terek, and Kuban regions allied with predominately White forces in an attempt to preserve their unique position within the Russian Empire. However, once the Bolsheviks succeed in winning the Russian Civil War, the Cossacks faced significant persecution and repression at the hands of the Bolsheviks. The Bolsheviks respected the military capability of the Cossacks but had to break their autonomous nature, as the military capability of the Cossacks represented a direct and continued threat to the new regime.

Sean N. Kalic

Further Reading

Burbank, Jane, Mark Von Hagen, and A. V. Remnev. *Russian Empire: Space, People, Power, 1700–1930.* Bloomington: Indiana University Press, 2002.

Julicher, Peter. *Renegades, Rebels, and Rogues under the Tsars.* Jefferson, NC: McFarland, 2003.

Khodarkovsky, Michael. *Bitter Choices: Loyalty and Betrayal in the Russian Conquest of the North Caucasus.* Ithaca, NY: Cornell University Press, 2011.

Mawdsley, Evan. *The Russian Civil War.* Edinburgh, UK: Birlinn, 2000.

McNeal, Robert H. *Tsars and Cossacks, 1885–1914.* New York: St. Martin's, 1987.

Pipes, Richard. *Russia under the Bolshevik Regime.* New York: Vintage Books, 1995.

Riasanovsky, Nicholas. *A History of Russia.* 6th ed. Oxford: Oxford University Press, 2000.

Suny, Ronald G. *The Soviet Experiment: Russia, the USSR, and the Successor States.* New York: Oxford University Press, 1998.

Czech Legion (August 1914– December 1919)

Military force that played a pivotal role in the Russian Civil War and in Allied support for an independent Czech state. At the outbreak of World War I, Czechs and Slovaks showed little enthusiasm for fighting in the Austro-Hungarian Army against their Slavic brethren, the Russians and the Serbs. Members of the Czech community living in Russia approached the Russian government about forming a unit consisting of Czech and Slovak volunteers, including Austro-Hungarian

Army prisoners of war (POWs) held by the Russians. Tomáš Masaryk, head of the Czech National Council in Paris, and the members of the council immediately saw the powerful propaganda advantage of such an entity for an independent Czechoslovak state after the war.

Formed in August 1914, the Česká Družina (Czech Brigade) ultimately numbered about 40,000 men in two divisions. Approximately one-tenth of the 100,000 Czech citizens of tsarist Russia joined the Druzina. In the years that followed, tens of thousands of additional Czechs, widely influenced by Pan-Slavism, surrendered to the Russian forces and were interned in Russia. When Tsar Nicholas II abdicated in 1917, the French government encouraged the provisional Russian government to combine the POWs and the Druzina into a Czech army. As a result, the Russians created two Czech divisions and based them at Kiev.

The Czech divisions participated effectively in the Kerensky Offensive of July 1917, but when Kerensky's government approached collapse that fall, Masaryk began negotiations to send the Czech Legion to the Western Front so it could continue to fight for the Allies. As part of the diplomatic maneuvering, France agreed to recognize the existence of a Czech state, with the Czech Legion as its army.

In January 1918, the Czech soldiers in Russia came under threat when the Ukraine declared its independence and German Army forces began to converge on Kiev. Masaryk declared war on the Central Powers, and the Czech Legion moved north and in March defeated a German force at Bakhmach. From there, the Czechs took the railway east to Moscow, destroying the tracks behind them.

The members of the Czech Legion intended to leave Russia via the Trans-Siberian Railway to Vladivostok. They seized locomotives

and rolling stock as they went. Russian commissar for war Leon Trotsky, however, ordered the legion disarmed, fearing that it would become a counterrevolutionary force following an armed clash between the legion and procommunist Hungarian POWs at Chelyabinsk on May 14.

The members of the Czech Legion, now joined by increasing numbers of their countrymen freed as POWs, feared that they would be put in a labor detachment or incorporated into the Red Army. Refusing to be disarmed or divided (the British wanted some of the Czech Legion to move north to protect Allied supplies at Archangel and Murmansk), they clashed with Red Army units at Chelyabinsk on May 25. Following Trotsky's order of the same date that armed Czechs discovered on the Trans-Siberian Railway were to be shot, the Czechs began to seize areas adjacent to the Trans-Siberian Railway. General Jan Syrový had overall command of the anti-Red forces in the area, including the Czech Legion. The well-trained and well-armed Czechs, advised by French general Maurice Janin, often acting in concert with anti-Bolshevik White forces, then began to seize control of a series of Siberian towns from Penza, southeast of Moscow, to Samara on the Volga River in south-central Russia. Indeed, the impending fall of Yekaterinburg to the Czech and White forces influenced Bolshevik leader Vladimir Lenin to order the execution of former tsar Nicholas II and his family there.

By August, Czech troops under Colonel R. Gajda had broken through opposing Red Army troops in Trans-Baikal and cleared the railroad from the Volga to Vladivostok. The capture of Kazan by the Czechs and Whites on August 7, which also gave them the imperial gold reserves, greatly aided in the formation of a provisional White government. Tomsk was the only major Soviet town in

Siberia taken by the Whites without Czech assistance. Czech military successes helped encourage the Western Allies to aid the White forces in the Russian Civil War against the Reds. The Allies subsequently supported the White Provisional Government under Alexander Kolchak. The French insisted that the Czechs abandon their plan to leave Russia in favor of securing complete control of the vital Trans-Siberian Railway. Czech forces under Rudolf Gajda also captured Trans-Baikal and took command of the Yekaterinburg Front.

The tide of battle soon turned in favor of the Reds, however. They retook Kazan on September 10, 1918, forcing exhausted Czech and White troops to withdraw. Lenin congratulated Trotsky on the "suppression of the Kazan Czechs and White Guards" as a "model of mercilessness." Thereafter, the Czech Legion restricted itself to protecting the Trans-Siberian Railway between Omsk and Irkutsk. The Czechs fought their last major battle at Ufa in November 1919. Their departure from the civil war in December, in part because of disillusionment over Kolchak's dictatorship and military weakness, greatly hurt the Whites' cause.

After the Allies approved a Czech national state during the Paris Peace Conference, the Czech Legion made plans to depart Russia. Before leaving, however, it played a role in turning over Kolchak to Bolshevik authorities and also released the Russian imperial gold reserves. The Czech evacuation was completed at Vladivostok between May and December 1919. Ships chartered by the Red Cross and American Czechs transported them to the United States. From San Francisco, the Czech Legion crossed North America and then the Atlantic Ocean, returning home to form the nucleus of the new Czechoslovak Army.

Claude R. Sasso

Further Reading

Fic, Victor M. *The Bolsheviks and the Czechoslovak Legion: The Origin of Their Armed Conflict, March–May 1918.* New Delhi: Abhinav, 1978.

Lincoln, W. Bruce. *Red Victory: A History of the Russian Civil War, 1918–1921.* New York: Simon and Schuster, 1989.

Miller, Betty. *The United States, Revolutionary Russia, and the Rise of Czechoslovakia.* College Station: Texas A&M University Press, 2000.

D

Denikin, Anton Ivanovich (1872–1947)

Lieutenant general and leader of the White Army during the Russian Civil War. Born near Warsaw (at the time part of the Russian Empire) on December 16, 1872, Anton Ivanovich Denikin joined the Russian Army at age 15. Though of humble birth, he attended the General Staff Academy in St. Petersburg. At the outbreak of the Russo-Japanese War, Denikin requested transfer from his staff job to a combat command. He distinguished himself in battle and in 1905 was promoted to colonel.

At the outbreak of World War I, Denikin was a major general and the chief of staff of the Kiev Military District. After serving briefly as deputy chief of staff to General Alexei Brusilov, in September 1914 Denikin was given command of the 4th Rifle Brigade, the "Iron Riflemen," where he again distinguished himself. In 1916 he was given command of the VIII Corps, and in August 1917, having been promoted to lieutenant general and awarded a golden St. George's sword decorated with diamonds, he was appointed commander in chief of the Southwestern Army Group.

After supporting the purported revolt of General Lavr Kornilov against the Provisional Government in August 1917, Denikin was imprisoned; however, he escaped in October 1917 and joined Kornilov's army opposing the new Bolshevik regime. In January 1919 during the Bolshevik invasion of the Caucasus, Denikin rallied the White (monarchist) counterrevolutionaries and drove out the Red Army. After General Alexei M. Kaledin committed suicide on February 11 and Kornilov was killed in action on April 13, 1918, Denikin assumed the general direction of the White armies.

Denikin launched a four-army offensive in May, recapturing Kiev on September 2. He continued to make progress through early October, when the Red Army's counteroffensive turned the tide. Denikin's army was defeated at Orel in late October, and Kiev was lost on December 17. The Whites were driven back to the Black Sea, where they evacuated on British ships on March 27, 1920. In April, Denikin resigned his command and escaped to Constantinople.

Denikin and his family lived in exile the rest of their lives. From 1921 to 1926 Denikin lived in England, Belgium, and Hungary, relocating due to financial problems. During this time he wrote his best-known book, *The Russian Turmoil,* considered to be the seminal work on the White movement in southern Russia. From 1926 to 1945 Denikin lived in France, where he continued to write and lecture. During World War II he spoke out against Nazism, and though he was glad of Soviet victories against Germany, he kept hoping that the communists would be overthrown.

In 1945 Denikin moved with his family to the United States. He died in Ann Arbor, Michigan, on August 8, 1947. In 2005 his remains were reinterred at the Donskoi Monastery in Moscow.

Kevin S. Bemel

Lieutenant General Anton Ivanovich Denikin of the Russian Imperial Army (center) with his staff. (Library of Congress)

Further Reading

Denikin, Anton Ivanovich. *The Career of a Tsarist Officer: Memoirs, 1872–1916.* Minneapolis: University of Minnesota Press, 1975.

Lehovich, Dmitry V. *White against Red: The Life of General Anton Denikin.* New York: Norton, 1974.

Duma

In the late 19th and early 20th centuries, the Russian tsars, specifically Alexander III and later Nicholas II, maintained their total control over the Russian people despite a growing social and political backlash. In fact, the tsars used the Fundamental Laws of 1832, which held that the "Emperor of all the Russias is sovereign with autocratic and unlimited powers. To obey the commands not merely from fear but according to the dictates of one's conscience is ordained by God himself." Beyond the use of the adherence to the Fundamental Laws, the use of the Okhrana (political police) further allowed the tsars to maintain control and suppress political opposition.

Though the people of Russia had some limited local self-government in the form of zemstvos, or city councils, in the second half of the 19th century, the powers of these local political organs steadily decreased as the 19th century neared to a close. In fact, as the reign of Alexander III ceded to the start of Nicholas II's regime, there was some limited hope that the new tsar would recognize the growing political tension and ease the authoritarian nature of the regime. However, Nicholas II dashed these hopes in 1894 when he stated that his intent was to "maintain the principle of autocracy just as firmly and unflinchingly as did my unforgettable father." Yet he appointed I. L. Goremykin as head of the Ministry of Internal Affairs. Goremykin, a trusted and respected bureaucrat, soon ran afoul of the regime, as he was a strong advocate for the continued use and expansion of the zemstvos. Seeing this position as a possible question of his authoritarian power, Nicholas II replaced Goremykin with D. S. Sipiagin and then V. K. Plehve. Both Sipiagin, who would be killed by a revolutionary in 1902, and Plehve believed in the use of force to maintain and enforce the totalitarian state. As a result, the revolutionary forces that had been slowly building at the end of the 19th century became a serious issue for Tsar Nicholas II at the start of the 20th century, as Plehve used the Okhrana as a means to repress the zemstvos.

The period of increased tension between the people of Russia and the regime saw the rise of political parties such as the Constitutional Democratic (Kadet) Party led by Pavel Miliukov, the Marxist Social Democratic Party led by Georgi Plekhanov, and the Socialist Revolutionary Party led by Victor Chernov. The Social Democratics in 1903 split into two parties: the Bolsheviks, led by V. I. Lenin, and the Mensheviks, who varied on their adherence to the dictums of Karl Marx and how to move forward with the class struggle.

In addition to the growth of political parties, the early 20th century saw the growth of professional labor unions. The common ground among the labor unions and the political parties was a greater political voice for and rights on behalf of the people of Russia. This tension within the Russian political system exploded on Sunday, January 22, 1905, as the Russian government shot 130 people demonstrating under the leadership of Father George Gapon. This event, know as Bloody Sunday, propelled Tsar Nicholas II to listen to growing discontent among his people.

By March 1905, Nicholas II announced that he would call for the creation of a "consultative assembly" as well as increased political toleration and repeal legislation against ethnic minorities. Though this indicated progress, the revolutionaries maintained their commitment to strikes and public protests. In August 1905, the tsar issued an imperial manifesto that created an elected Duma with consultative powers, but this failed to ease the revolutionary pressure.

In October 1905, Nicholas II issued a manifesto that guaranteed civil liberties of Russians and transformed the Duma into a legislative body that had true political powers over affairs of the Russian state. Moving beyond these announcements, in May 1906 the government of Nicholas II set forth a new outline for the Duma in the Fundamental Laws. In essence, these laws recognized the Duma but upheld many political powers for the tsar. Though the Duma was to have legislative and budgetary functions, the tsar still retained the power to assemble and disband the Duma, veto legislation passed in the Duma, and issue ukases when the Duma was not in session. On May 10, 1906, Russia saw the First Duma come into being.

As could be expected, the First Duma had significant internal political problems as well as fits of trying to define its new role within the authoritarian nature of the tsarist regime. As a result of these awkward growing pains, Nicholas II dissolved the First Duma after only 73 days.

The Second Duma convened on March 5, 1907, and much like the first, it lasted only three months. However, as a result of the lackluster performance of the First and Second Dumas, which had strong representation from peasants and workers, the tsar changed the electoral laws, which effectively decreased the representation of the radical elements of Russian society and increased disproportionately the seats of the gentry. As a result of this political ploy, the Third Duma fulfilled its full five-year term, from 1907 to 1912. Likewise, the Fourth Duma served from 1912 until the Russian Revolution of 1917.

Sean N. Kalic

Further Reading

Acton, Edward. *Rethinking the Russian Revolution.* London: Edward Arnold, 1990.

Ascher, Abraham. *The Revolution of 1905: Russia in Disarray.* Palo Alto, CA: Stanford University Press, 1988.

Hosking, Geofffrey A. *The Russian Constitutional Experiment: Government and Duma, 1907–1914.* Cambridge: Cambridge University Press, 1973.

Pipes, Richard. *Russia under the Old Regime.* New York: Scribner, 1974.

Riasanovsky, Nicholas. *A History of Russia.* 6th ed. Oxford: Oxford University Press, 2000.

Shulugin, V. V. *The Years: Memories of a Member of the Russian Duma, 1906–1917.* Hippocrane Books, 1984.

Dzerzhinsky, Felix (1877–1926)

Most known for heading the All-Russian Extraordinary Commission for Combating Counter-Revolution and Sabotage (Cheka), Felix Dzerzhinsky had a sanguine background prior to his association and commitment to the revolutionary furor of the Bolsheviks. Conflicting accounts place his birth in either Vilno or Dzerzhinovo on September 11, 1877, where he was born into a Polish family that had noble ties. Though the family had since fallen from its previous status, Dzerzhinsky was brought up in a strictly Catholic family and by the age of 16 had committed himself to studying for the priesthood. Dissuaded by his family from pursuing a career in the church, he abandoned his first career choice and instead refocused his previous commitment to religion into a fervor for revolution.

Spending time in Lithuania and Poland, where he worked with the Social Democratic parties in both countries, allowed him to build his résumé as a professional revolutionary. By most accounts, the young Dzerzhinsky had a natural ability to inspire and organize workers for labor unions, which became a primary focal point of the Left. During this formative period of his life Dzerzhinsky earned the respect of other prominent revolutionaries such as Rosa Luxemberg, Leo Jogiches, and Karl Radek. Due to his revolutionary pursuits, Dzerzhinsky frequently came to the attention of Polish and Russian authorities. Therefore, he was frequently arrested or placed in exile for his political actions. During these periods of incarceration from 1900 to 1917, Dzerzhinsky came to associate with Bolsheviks, who also suffered in circumstances similar to Dzerzhinski's. In fact, during the February Revolution of 1917 in Russia, Dzerzhinsky, who had been in prison during the events of displacing the tsar and establishing the Provisional Government, eventually came to be amnestied by Alexander Kerensky and the Provisional Government. This action was a central plank in the Provisional Government's program as it aimed to provide a more "democratic" process, which necessitated releasing political prisoners oppressed by the tsar and his regime.

Having been freed from prison, Dzerzhinsky worked with the Bolsheviks in exposing the flaws and problems associated with the Provisional Government. As such, in October

1917 he participated in the Bolshevik Revolution and became a respected member of the vanguard of the party. In December 1917 as Lenin strove to consolidate Bolshevik power and perpetuate the ideas of the Bolshevik Revolution, he was greatly afraid of a counterrevolutionary backlash against his newly established regime. To guard against such a Thermadorian reaction, Lenin and the Bolsheviks created the Cheka and appointed Dzerzhinsky as its head.

As the head of the Cheka, Dzerzhinsky had significant powers to use his secret police to root out any efforts that were deemed dangerous or counter to the ideas of the Bolsheviks. As such, he authorized the Chekists to use terror, imprisonment, and even assignation as common tools to suppress any would-be challengers to the regime. Due to his harsh methods to combat counterrevolutionaries, Dzerzhinsky earned the moniker "Iron Felix" for his cold and focused use of harsh and brutal techniques to silence political opposition.

As the Bolshevik Revolution ceded to the Russian Civil War, Lenin used the Cheka, under the direction of Dzerzhinsky, to imprison, torture, and kill tens of thousands of suspected counterrevolutionaries during a period know as the Red Terror. In the aftermath of the Russian Civil War, the Bolsheviks solidified the powers of their secret police and abolished the Cheka, a temporary committee, and in its place created the State Political Administration. Dzerzhinsky would not retain his post. Instead, he would work in various other capacities for the Bolsheviks for the next four years. His death came from a heart attack on July 20, 1926, after a heated speech before the Central Committee. Dzerzhinsky's legacy paved the way for the State Political Administration to eventually evolve into the KGB. At the headquarters of the KGB's building in Moscow, the Communist Party had a statue of Dzerzhinsky created as a testament to his steadfast commitment to the ideals of the revolution, as Dzerzhinsky came to be recognized as one of the heroes of the revolution. However, in the dramatic events of 1991 as Russia went through yet another revolution, once the anticommunist parties had solidified power and abolished the Soviet Union, the statue of "Iron Felix" was torn down by the people as a political protest of the harsh oppression and terrorism enacted by the communist regime, which can be linked back to Dzerzhinsky's actions as head of the Cheka.

Sean N. Kalic

Further Reading

Andrew, Christopher, and Vasili Mitrokhin. *The Sword and the Shield: The Mitrokhin Archive and the Secret History of the KGB.* New York: Basic Books, 1999.

Anonymous. *Felix Dzerzhinsky: A Biography.* Translated by Natalia Belskaya. Moscow: Progress, 1988.

Leggett, George. *The Cheka: Lenin's Political Police.* New York: Oxford University Press, 1981.

Service, Robert. *Spies and Commissars: Bolshevik Russia and the West.* London: Macmillan, 2011.

Shearer, David R., and Vladimir Khaustov. *Stalin and the Lubianka: A Documentary History of the Political Police and Security Organs in the Soviet Union, 1922–1953.* New Haven, CT: Yale University Press, 2015.

F

February (March) Revolution (1917)

The first of two internal Russian uprisings in 1917. The February 1917 revolution is often referred to as the March Revolution, because when it occurred Russia followed the Julian calendar, which was 13 days behind the Gregorian calendar used in the West.

After a dozen years of experimenting with a constitutional monarchy, popular support for the Russian political system had waned; in this environment, the influence of radical intellectuals grew. Adding to the burden on the population was the enormous cost of two and a half years of war, replete with military disasters, incompetent leadership, inefficient bureaucracy, arms and ammunition shortages, rampant inflation, and tremendous sacrifices in casualties. By 1917, the Russian masses had suffered enough.

Tsar Nicholas II, out of touch with his people and government and strongly influenced by his wife Alexandra, focused more on preserving the autocracy than on saving Russia. Attempts to pressure him to do otherwise only stiffened his stubborn resolve. In December 1916, conservative members of the nobility and the Duma assassinated Grigory Rasputin, who held considerable influence over the royal couple. The tsar, who had been nominally commanding the army at the front,

Revolutionary forces in Petrograd attack the tsar's police during street fighting between February 23 and March 3, 1917, on the Julian calendar, which Russia used at the time. (Edward Alsworth Ross, *The Russian Bolshevik Revolution*, 1921)

secluded himself with his family at Tsarskoye Selo, 15 miles from Petrograd, isolating himself from people and events and leaving no one at army headquarters with authority to act. Nicholas did not return to army headquarters in Mogilev until March 5, 1917.

Throughout January and February, conditions deteriorated nationwide and especially in Petrograd. Worker dissatisfaction led to periodic strikes in war industries. Inflation and food shortages because of mismanagement and an inadequate transportation network brought food riots. On January 9, 1917, some 150,000 workers in Petrograd took to the streets to commemorate the 12th anniversary of Bloody Sunday in 1905. Across Russia, other workers did likewise. This marked only the beginning of a wave of strikes across Russia in the following weeks. As conditions continued to deteriorate, the masses, especially in the capital, became more embittered.

On February 23 workers, primarily women frustrated by long hours and inadequate wages that bought little food for their families while their husbands were at the front, poured into the streets of Petrograd demanding "Bread!" As more workers joined the strikers, soon totaling 90,000, those cries were joined with shouts of "Down with the war!" and then "Down with the tsar!" By nightfall the police had restored apparent calm, but strike fever simmered through the night in the workers' quarters. The next morning, 40,000 people filled the streets. They were met initially by 500 mounted Cossacks ordered to restore calm. Facing demonstrators led by women, the Cossacks hesitated and then gave way as the strikers marched into the city center. Others joined, and by nightfall a reputed 160,000 workers had gathered in the city's center. Not since the Russian Revolution of 1905 had so many strikers converged in central Petrograd.

The police were unable to control the situation, and after three days the government ordered in regular army units to augment them. By February 25 the city had become an armed camp, with periodic gunfire erupting as police and strikers clashed. On the evening of February 25 upon returning to their barracks, soldiers of a Guards regiment mutinied and vowed not to fire on crowds again. The next morning, they refused to obey their officers' orders and joined the demonstrators in the street. Soon the entire Petrograd garrison joined the revolution.

On the afternoon of February 25, members of the Duma, which the tsar had that day ordered dissolved, elected a temporary committee to restore public order. That day in the same building the Petrograd Soviet, consisting of delegates from factories, workshops, rebelling military units, and representatives from socialist parties, established itself to take hold of the revolution and restore order. Technically neither body possessed governmental authority, although the central administration had ceased to function because the tsar was back at army headquarters, where he still controlled most of the army.

Removed from the scene, the tsar and his advisers misread the situation in the capital and underestimated its seriousness. Nicholas II first ignored pleas from his advisers to appoint a government the people could trust and instead directed military commanders to suppress the rebellion. That task force simply melted away when the soldiers came in contact with revolutionaries. On February 28 the tsar left Mogilev by train for Petrograd to take personal control, but his train was diverted to Pskov, where the army leadership, including his uncle Grand Duke Nikolai Nikolaevich, convinced him that his only option was abdication.

On March 2, the Duma Temporary Committee dissolved itself and established the

Provisional Government under Prince Georgy Lvov, a nonparty-affiliated liberal, as prime minister. Pavel Miliukov, a Duma deputy and leader of the Constitutional Democratic (Kadet) Party, became foreign minister, and Alexander Guchkov, an Octobrist Party leader, was made minister of war. Alexander Kerensky, a Socialist Revolutionary member of the Duma, became minister of justice. Kerensky was simultaneously vice chairman of the Petrograd Soviet and, given his role in both, acted as liaison between the two.

The Provisional Government's position was weak from the start because it inherited all of the problems of its predecessor, while its authority came from the Duma, from which Russian workers and peasants had been disenfranchised. It was weakened further by sharing power with the Petrograd Soviet, which had the support of the vast majority of the capital's populace and persistently second-guessed and undercut the Provisional Government's decisions.

Ominously, the leaders of the Provisional Government, responding to Allied pressure in the form of war loans, decided to continue Russia's involvement in the war, a course taken despite war weariness and the disintegration of discipline in the army. The latter was intensified by Order No. 1 issued by the Petrograd Soviet, a decree that destroyed the authority of military officers over their troops. Kerensky's dream of a great successful military offensive that would win the people's support for the government ended in military defeat, the collapse of the Russian Army, and another revolution, actually a coup d'état, carried out by the Bolsheviks.

Arthur T. Frame

Further Reading

Figes, Orlando. *A People's Tragedy: The Russian Revolution, 1891–1924.* New York: Viking Adult, 1997.

Hasegawa, Tsuyoshi. *The February Revolution: Petrograd, 1917.* Seattle: University of Washington Press, 1981.

Lincoln, W. Bruce. *Passage through Armageddon: The Russians in War and Revolution, 1914–1918.* New York: Simon and Schuster, 1986.

Wildman, Allan K. *The End of the Russian Imperial Army,* Vol. 1, *The Old Army and Soldier's Revolt (March–April 1917).* Princeton, NJ: Princeton University Press, 1980.

Frunze, Mikhail (1885–1925)

Mikhail Vasilievich Frunze was a successful leader of the Russian Civil War and one of the founders of the Russian Red Army. As a military theorist, he opposed the views of Leon Trotsky and pressed for professionalization and modernization of the armed forces.

Frunze was born in the Central Asian city of Pishpek on February 2, 1885, the son of an army medical assistant. An excellent student, he graduated from the local school with honors and went on to study at the St. Petersburg Polytechnic Institute. While in attendance, he joined the communist Bolshevik Party in 1905 and embarked on a career as a professional revolutionary.

Frunze was sent as an agitator to Ivanovo-Voznesensk, where he was arrested and sentenced to internal exile. In 1909 he was condemned to death for the murder of a policeman, but his sentence was commuted to exile in Siberia for life. Frunze assumed several false names, however, and continued his political activities throughout Irkutsk and Chita during 1914–1916. During World War I he escaped from exile, returned to Moscow, and gained appointment as head of the Bolshevik underground in Minsk just as the Russian Revolution erupted.

In May 1917, Frunze met Bolshevik leader Vladimir Lenin at the famous First Congress of the Soviet of Peasant Deputies in St. Petersburg and impressed him with his knowledge of military affairs. Frunze then assumed political responsibilities in the city of Shuya, where he also commanded a military formation, the Shuya Guards. During the October Revolution, it was Frunze's command in Moscow that stormed the Metropole Hotel and the Kremlin, putting the Bolsheviks in firm control of the city.

In consequence of his service to the Communist Party, Frunze became military commissar of Ivanovo-Voznesensk, where he crushed an anti-Bolshevik (or White) uprising in August 1918. As the Russian Civil War expanded across the country, he rose through promotion to command of the Fourth Army that December and assumed command of the Southern Group the following spring. In this capacity, Frunze enjoyed several successes against White forces under Admiral Alexander Kolchak.

Frunze then transferred to the Eastern Front, winning several important victories for the communists in the Ural Mountains. From August 1919 to September 1920, he was actively employed against White forces operating in the southern Urals and Central Asia. After capturing Bukhara in 1920, he next operated against General Pyotr Wrangel's White Army in the Crimea, defeating it decisively and concluding the civil war in a complete triumph for the communists. In recognition of his contributions, Frunze was elected to the Central Committee of the Communist Party in 1921.

After the war, Frunze continued his close association with military affairs and engaged in a long-running dispute with Trotsky, the defense minister. Soviet military doctrine was then in a state of flux and very much caught up in the revolutionary overhaul of society. Trotsky, in essence, realized the present weakness of the Soviet state and called for the creation of mass peasant armies, acting as guerrillas and led by so-called specialists who were former military officers of the Imperial Russian Army.

Frunze hotly disputed this approach, and in a series of planning papers he outlined his strategy for a "unified doctrine." This maintained that for the Soviet state to survive, military science had to be integrated into all aspects of society so it could defend itself against the inevitable invasion from the capitalist West. Frunze therefore called for the creation of national military academies and the introduction of realistic training and education for peasants and workers alike. In contrast to Trotsky's adherence to guerrilla warfare, Frunze preached the predominance of offensive tactics. Because this kind of fighting was predicated upon strategic and tactical maneuvering, army organization had to be smaller, less centralized, and less bureaucratic than prevailing political models. Finally, Frunze emphasized that former Imperial Russian Army officers constituted a threat to the Russian Revolution. The Red Army needed its own professionally trained military officers.

Trotsky, predictably, ridiculed Frunze's suggestion of a standing Red Army, but then Trotsky himself fell into disfavor. In January 1924, Frunze succeeded him as commissar for military and naval affairs and introduced universal military service for all men ages 18–40. Frunze's tenure proved brief, as in October 1925 he underwent surgery for stomach ulcers, dying in consequence on October 31, 1925. It has been speculated that the procedure had been forced on him by Soviet leader Joseph Stalin, who feared Frunze as a possible political rival and wanted him dead. Nonetheless, Frunze's reforms were ultimately implemented. From the chaos of civil war, they brought stability and structure to the Red Army and paved the way for its full-scale modernization and mechanization.

In many respects, Frunze was the "father of the Red Army," and the Frunze Military Academy was so named in his honor.

John C. Fredriksen

Further Reading

Bayer, Philip A. *The Evolution of the Soviet General Staff, 1917–1941.* New York: Garland, 1987.

Gareev, Makhmut Akhmetovich. *M. V. Frunze: Military Theorist.* Washington, DC: Pergamon-Brassey's, 1988.

Jacobs, Walter D. *Frunze: The Soviet Clausewitz, 1885–1925.* The Hague: Martinus Nijoff, 1969.

Von Hagen, Mark. *Soldiers in the Proletarian Dictatorship: The Red Army and the Soviet Socialist State.* Ithaca, NY: Cornell University Press, 1990.

G

Gapon, Father Georgy Apollonovich (1870–1906)

Georgy Gapon was born in Beliki, a small village in Poltava Province, to a family of modest means in 1870. His father was a clerk in the Volost administration, and his mother was an illiterate peasant.

By all accounts, Gapon was an intense and focused child who gravitated to religion as an intellectual pursuit. He did very well in school and continued his education at the Lower Ecclesiastical School in his home province of Poltava. After graduating from his secondary school, Gapon matriculated to the Platava seminary with the intent of being a priest. However, as indicated by historian Abraham Ascher in *The Revolution of 1905: Russia in Disarray,* Gapon quickly became disenchanted with the church due to its "religious formalism" as well as "the hypocrisy and corruption of the clergy." Around this same time period, Gapon began to take notice of people living in desperate and abject poverty. Their condition connected with Gapon and his growing sense of sympathy for the "toiling and suffering class."

Acting on his growing social consciousness, Gapon chose to leave the seminary and transfer to a university to complete his studies. Barred from entering a university due to low grades and behavior issues, Gapon secured a position in the Poltava zemstvo administration. This position allowed him to interact and work with people of the "toiling classes." While working for the Poltava zemstvo, Gapon got married, had a family, and was content in his work. His new wife

had convinced him that going back to become a priest would ultimately allow him to further his interest in working with the poor of Russia. Recognizing his wife's advice as the best means to achieve his vocational objective, Gapon worked to become an Orthodox priest and started his mission to work with the poor of Poltava.

Unfortunately, Gapon's wife died, which left him in emotional turmoil. Unable to remarry based on Orthodox Church tradition, Gapon drifted further away from the tenets of the formalized church. Seeking emotional solace in 1898, he enrolled in the St. Petersburg Theological Seminary to advance his studies while also focusing on missionary work. To alleviate his emotional trauma from his wife's death, he worked feverishly to assist the poor. His commitment and steadfast work ethic drove him to physical exhaustion and led to the resurgence of a "nervous condition" that he had wrestled with since his teen years. To recover, Gapon convalesced in the Crimea.

While in the Crimea, it appears that Gapon enjoyed the company of intellectuals with whom he debated and discussed ideas concerning the social, political, and economic conditions in Russia. These people recultivated Gapon's old concerns about the "formalism and hypocrisy" in the Orthodox Church. They encouraged him to focus on his work with the poor and move beyond the strict confines of the church.

Having recovered, Gapon returned to St. Petersburg and during 1902–1903 built his reputation as a person who cared passionately for the poor and working-class people of tsarist Russia. In 1903, Gapon learned that S. V. Zubatov, chief of the Moscow Okhrana, the secret police of the tsar, was secretly building worker organizations that supported the tsar. In many ways this was an attempt by the regime to counter the revolutionary appeal of the radical Left. Gapon and Zubatov collaborated to build a workers' union that supported the tsar, though they had different motives. Zubatov wanted support for the regime and tight police controls over the workers as a way to ensure control and support of the workers' union, whereas Gapon saw this as an opportunity to advance the cause of the working class in Russia.

In the summer of 1903, Gapon assisted in the founding of the Assembly of the Russian Factory and Mill Workers of the City of St. Petersburg. According to Ascher, in an attempt to accommodate Zubatov, Gapon ensured that the assembly focused on "dances, lectures, and other projects of self-improvement" with a low political profile. Gapon's intent was to project the image that he and his organization were law abiding and wanted to work within the present system at local, regional, and national levels to advance the cause of the working class.

Though Gapon gave the outward appearance that he was working within the system and strove to maintain an organization that did not arouse the interest of the police or government authorities, he did have a political and social agenda that went beyond the original intent of his agreement with Zubatov. With the help of several former Social Democrats in his organization, Gapon in effect set up a secret committee that focused on political matters and discussed issues that questioned the benevolence of the tsar and his regime. These actions directly contradicted the original agreement between Gapon and Zubatov.

Between the founding of his union and the events of January 22, 1905, Gapon's union had expanded to include nine branches in various regions around St. Petersburg and membership that has been estimated at between 6,000 and 20,000. By the end of 1904 as the assembly grew, Gapon expanded his base, which included radical leftist workers as well as non-Orthodox and nonethnic Russians. By all accounts, Gapon overcame the radical Left's distrust of police connections by treating them as equals and working with them as comrades.

In December 1904, four workers of a large armament and shipbuilding factory in St. Petersburg were dismissed by the plant's management, which had known hostility toward Gapon's assembly, of which the workers were members. In an attempt to peacefully quell the growing discontent of workers at the plant, Gapon sought to solve the issue amicably with the plant's management but failed. In the wake of these events, the workers of Gapon's assembly met to initiate a strike to advocate their ability to organize, even though three of the original four workers had been reinstated. By January 7, 1905, the strike had swelled to roughly two-thirds of St. Petersburg's industrial workforce.

Gapon tried to temper and convince his workers that they could still work within the tsar's system and proposed a plan by which a procession of his workers would march to the tsar's Winter Palace and present Nicholas II in person with their petition. Though the Social Democrats became increasingly impatient with Gapon's measured approach, their more radical ideas were suppressed by the majority of the assembly's workers, who sided with Gapon.

The government, having become aware of the procession and fearing the radicalization, debated the merits of stopping the procession or allowing it to proceed. In the meantime, the army and police organizations stood by to assist, while the government also made fateful decisions that led to the events that came to be known as Bloody Sunday. First, they acknowledged that Gapon would not be allowed to meet with the tsar and present his petition to Nicholas in person. Second, the tsar's government issued an order stating that "workers were not allowed to enter the city center." To deprive the workers of their ability to gather, the tsar's government ordered 9,000 infantry and 3,000 cavalry troops to stand by in St. Petersburg to quell the unauthorized gathering. Finally, by January 8, 1905, the government issued a secret arrest order for Gapon as a means to remove the head of the organization and hopefully suppress the labor unrest.

Gapon released his petition to the press as a means to demonstrate that they were not interested in violent protest but instead wanted to work with the tsar to improve the rights and conditions of workers throughout Russia. On Sunday, January 9, 1905, an estimated 50,000 to 100,000 people joined Gapon in the march to the tsar's Winter Palace. Along the way, the procession disregarded orders by the military and police to disband. As the mass of workers, including Gapon, reached the palace gates, the military and police opened fired on the workers and their procession. When the turmoil had withered, 130 people had been killed and 299 seriously wounded. Bloody Sunday ushered in a new era of revolutionary politics for Russia. Whereas Gapon and his assembly tried to work within the system of the tsar, the tragic events of Bloody Sunday propelled a more violent and radical interpretation of the changes needed in the government of Russia. On March 29, 1906, the Social Revolutionaries lured Gapon to a small cottage near the Russo-Finnish boarder and had him murdered.

Sean N. Kalic

Further Reading

Ascher, Abraham. *The Revolution of 1905: Russia in Disarray.* Stanford, CA: Stanford University Press, 1988.

Ascher, Abraham. *The Russian Revolution: A Beginner's Guide.* London: Oneworld, 2014.

Bushkovitch, Paul. *A Concise History of Russia.* Cambridge: Cambridge University Press, 2011.

Sablinsky, Walter. *The Road to Bloody Sunday: The Role of Father Gapon and the Petersburg Massacre of 1905.* Princeton, NJ: Princeton University Press, 2014.

Schwarz, Solomon M. *Russian Revolution of 1905: Worker's Movement and Formation of Bolshevism and Menshevism.* Chicago: Chicago University Press, 1967.

Golovin, Nikolai (1875–1944)

Nikolai Golovin's early life was obscure, and his military career was undistinguished; however, he has some significance as a military historian. Born in Moscow on November 22, 1875, Golovin graduated from the Corps of Pages in 1894 and from the Academy of the General Staff in 1900. He served as a professor of tactics at the General Staff Academy from 1908 to 1914. With the onset of World War I, he was given command of a Hussar regiment on the Northwestern Front. He then served as quartermaster general for the Ninth Army and in 1916 as chief of staff for the Seventh Army. Golovin also served as chief of staff on the Romanian front during 1917. With the October Revolution, he first retired to Odessa and then fled to Paris. During 1919, he traveled back to Vladivostok to join the White forces under Admiral Alexander Kolchak but found those forces already disintegrating upon his arrival. Returning immediately to Paris, Golovin set about writing on military history and military theory. His 1931 history of the Russian Army during World War I still commands attention. Golovin collaborated with the Germans during the occupation of France, earning him a death sentence from the Resistance; however, he died in Paris in 1944.

Timothy C. Dowling

Further Reading

Golovin, Nikolai. *The Russian Army in World War I.* New Haven, CT: Yale University Press, 1931.

Menning, Bruce. *Bayonets before Bullets: The Imperial Russian Army, 1861–1914.* Bloomington: Indiana University Press, 1992.

Goremykin, Ivan Logginovich (1839–1917)

Russian bureaucrat and prime minister (1906, 1914–1916). Born on November 8, 1839, in Novgorod, to a wealthy landowning family, Ivan Logginovich Goremykin entered the civil service in 1860 after graduating from law school and rose rapidly through the bureaucracy, where he was considered something of an expert on peasant affairs. In 1895, Goremykin was appointed minister of the interior. He already had a reputation for being extremely conservative and completely loyal to Tsar Nicholas II. Goremykin's term in office was largely undistinguished, and after failing in his attempt to implement organizational reform and enlarge the zemstvo program (the system of limited local government introduced by Tsar Alexander II), he retired in 1899.

In May 1906, Tsar Nicholas II made the surprising decision to appoint Goremykin prime minister just before the first session of the newly established Duma. Nicholas believed that Goremykin would faithfully

Ivan Logginovich Goremykin served as chairman of the Council of Ministers (the equivalent of prime minister) for Tsar Nicholas II from May 1906 to July 1906, and was known for his vehement opposition to the Duma. He again served the tsar from 1914–1916 as chairman of the Council of Ministers, before being asked again to retire. (Library of Congress)

defend the authority of the monarchy against the new representative body. Indeed, Goremykin had already publicly stated his complete fealty to the throne, asserting that the tsar was "the anointed one, the rightful and lone sovereign."

Nicholas was not disappointed in his appointment, as Goremykin obstinately resisted the Duma's attempts to exercise power at the tsar's expense and to implement political reforms. Nevertheless, on July 21, 1906, Nicholas forced Goremykin into retirement and replaced him with the younger and more energetic Pyotr Stolypin. By that time Goremykin's open contempt for the Duma, which he expressed by pretending to nap during its sessions, had earned him a reputation as one of the most reactionary and unyielding of the tsar's officials.

After nearly a decade in what had seemed like permanent retirement, Goremykin was again appointed prime minister by the tsar in February 1914. The elderly prime minister accomplished little in the months leading up to World War I. During the July Crisis, he was virtually invisible. As wartime prime minister, he devoted most of his energy to resisting the Duma's calls for reform, and his unquestioning devotion to the monarchy led him to support the tsar's disastrous decision to take personal command of the army in 1915. In early 1916, however, Nicholas was forced to send the by now senile Goremykin into permanent retirement.

Goremykin's replacement, the corrupt and incompetent Boris Stürmer, proved to be even more objectionable to the Russian political elites and the general public. Goremykin's extreme conservatism and unwillingness to work with the Duma and even other cabinet officials had virtually doomed his chances of political success. But those same qualities had endeared themselves to the tsar, and even Empress Alexandra had reportedly liked Goremykin.

After the March 1917 Russian Revolution Goremykin was arrested and detained, although he was soon released on orders of Alexander F. Kerensky, the erstwhile socialist prime minister. Goremykin died near his estate at Sochi in the Caucasus, according to some accounts murdered by a Bolshevik mob, on December 24, 1917, only weeks after the November 1917 revolution.

John M. Jennings

Further Reading

Crankshaw, Edward. *The Shadow of the Winter Palace: The Drift to Revolution, 1825–1917.* London: Macmillan, 1976.

Fitzpatrick, Sheila. *The Russian Revolution.* 3rd ed. New York: Oxford University Press, 2008.

Massie, Robert K. *Nicholas and Alexandra.* New York: Ballantine, 2000.

Waldron, Peter. *The End of Imperial Russia, 1855–1917.* New York: St. Martin's, 1997.

Graves, William S. (1865–1940)

U.S. Army general. Born in Mount Calm, Texas, on March 27, 1865, William Sidney Graves graduated from the U.S. Military Academy, West Point, in 1889. Commissioned in the infantry that same year, he served in various posts, including a stint with the 7th Infantry Regiment at Fort Logan, Colorado. Graves, promoted to captain in September 1899, saw service in the Philippines as a member of the 20th Infantry Regiment. There he was cited for gallantry in action during the Philippine-American War (Philippine Insurrection) of 1899–1902. He returned to the Philippines during 1905–1906. In 1909 he was assigned to the General Staff, where he earned a reputation as an able and mature staff officer. A lieutenant colonel in 1917, Graves accompanied Secretary of War Newton D. Baker to France during May–July 1917 as part of a mission to determine the supply needs and makeup of an American expeditionary force. In December 1917, Graves was promoted to brigadier general.

In July 1918, Graves was promoted to major general and given command of the 8th Division at Camp Fremont, California, thought to be about to deploy to France. In August 1918, however, Graves was summoned to Kansas City to meet with Baker, who gave him the then secret mission of commanding the American Expeditionary Force to Siberia. Graves assembled more than 9,000 troops to implement the ambiguous

U.S. policies of protecting military stores at Vladivostok, aiding the Czech Legion, and preventing Japan from expanding its influence in the region. His greatest challenge was to avoid the maelstrom of international scheming by resolutely opposing efforts by other Allied commanders to pressure him to commit his forces to aid those factions opposing the Bolsheviks in the ongoing Russian Civil War (1917–1922).

Graves returned to the United States on April 1, 1920, after 21 months of operations in Russia. He then briefly commanded Fort William McKinley in the Philippines and then the 1st Infantry Brigade (1920–1925); the 1st Division (1925); the VI Corps Area, Chicago (1925–1926); and finally the Panama Canal Division (1926–1927) and the Panama Canal Department (1927–1928). Again promoted to major general on July 11, 1925, he retired from the army on September 4, 1928. Graves died in Shrewsbury, New Jersey, on February 27, 1940.

Steven J. Rauch

Further Reading

Goldhurst, Richard. *The Midnight War: The American Intervention in Russia, 1918–1920.* New York: McGraw-Hill, 1978.

Graves, William S. *America's Siberian Adventure, 1918–1920.* New York: Cape and Smith, 1931.

Unterberger, Betty Miller. *America's Siberian Expedition, 1918–1920: A Study of National Policy.* New York: Greenwood, 1969.

Unterberger, Betty Miller. *The United States, Revolutionary Russia, and the Rise of Czechoslovakia.* Chapel Hill: University of North Carolina Press, 1989.

The Great Reforms

Tsar Alexander II, who ruled from 1855 until his assassination in 1881, instituted a series of reforms during his rule that laid the foundation of the Russian state in the 20th century. Among the most important of these reforms was liberation of the serfs. In addition to freeing the serfs, Alexander II instituted representative bodies in Russia, the zemstvos. Although the power of these bodies was far less than a parliament or a provincial government, they were an indication of the desire of the Russian people to have some form of representation in the Russian state.

One of the main reasons for the abolition of serfdom was political, not economic. In fact, just prior to its abolition, Russian nobles were able to spend more time reforming their estates because they no longer had an obligatory duty to serve the state. This increased attention made the serf agricultural system more efficient, and the years prior to its elimination were the most productive. The politics of the period demanded reform, and the main reason for the changes in the political environment was the Crimean War.

Russia's government relied on an autocratic monarch who ruled with no constitution or parliament to constrain the sovereign's power. Many in Russia who did not like the autocratic system still believed that it gave Russia the stability to have a well-run government for internal issues and that this government provided a stable foundation for the Russian military to project power externally. Many critics did not like the system but accepted it because of the success of Russia in its military campaigns against both European and Ottoman enemies. After Russia's defeat in the Crimean War, that rationale eroded, and the critics of Russia's government and economic system had a more effective argument.

When Alexander II came to the throne in 1855, Russia was already fighting the Crimean War, which it lost in 1856. The first major problem of his reign was in handling the political fallout both internally and externally of this military loss. His Great Reforms were an effort to address the ineffective economic and political policies of the Russian government that many attributed to its defeat in Crimea. Serfdom became an example of the backwardness of Russia and soon was one of the top priorities of those calling for reform in the state.

Serfdom, which tied the peasant to the land and gave the landlord authority over the peasant, had a long history in Russia dating back to the 11th century. Landlords did own their serfs, but the serfs had ties to their lands as well. Serfs had to perform labor for their landlords but could farm their own land for their own profit. The landlord could sell the serf with or without the land, since the landlord owned the land that the serf tilled. By 1861, the date of the abolition of serfdom, the system had many critics both inside and outside of Russia. However, abolition was not an easy task.

One of the problems of ending serfdom in Russia was that the state needed the serfs to remain on the land and work it. If many of the newly freed serfs abandoned their land and sought other work, Russia could face starvation. Serfs had the opportunity to buy their land. If they chose to do so, the government paid 80 percent of the cost of the land to the landlord, and the serf paid the landlord the remaining 20 percent in cash or services. The serf had 49 years to repay the debt to the government. The government ensured the loan by giving the title of the land to the commune, which the peasant could not leave, and directly to the newly freed serf.

Although Alexander II easily abolished serfdom, it was more difficult to provide an economically vibrant environment for the newly freed peasants to thrive. For one, their redemption payments to the government, in addition to the regular taxes, made it almost impossible for the serfs to maintain a livelihood. It took decades for the government to realize that it was incredibly difficult for the serfs to do well economically and be able to repay their loans to the government. In 1907, the Russian government forgave the debts of the serfs; however, the economic impacts of having to try to repay the loans was already done. Also, the decision to maintain the commune did not incentivize agricultural innovation or improvements in the land. It also meant that the hardest-working members of the commune provided support for those in the commune who could not or, worse, would not work. The final problem of the abolition of serfdom was the slow introduction of full civil rights to the newly freed serfs. This slow process did not help give them an identity as citizens of the Russian state.

Another part of the Great Reforms was the creation of the zemstvos. These elected bodies had limited authority over the provinces they represented, but their members did have the mandate of popular election, which was an important change in Russia. The zemstvo election system gave priority to the landlords and nobles, but peasants were able to participate and serve as representatives. The zemstvos gave the Russian people an introduction to popular sovereignty but also made clear the tsar's cautious and limited approach to sharing rule with his people.

The Great Reforms also gave more freedom to the press by ending the government's daily censoring of newspapers and also allowing for more freedom to publish critical books and other writings. The government could still close or seize publications deemed harmful after the fact. This freedom of the press and improvements in printing technology allowed for national newspapers. These publications created a sense among the literate of a more unified Russian state that was different from its more homogenous European counterparts. The expanded freedom to print allowed for more diverse ideas to circulate among the Russian people, including ideas detrimental to the tsar's government.

In addition to the societal reforms, Alexander II pushed for economic changes as well. He energized Russia's economy with an increase in laying railroads. These new lines allowed for more economic activity between larger urban centers and created the ability to move goods produced by the new industrial centers in Russia. Although the economic benefits of these reforms were not universal, they did help Russia improve its economic situation relative to other nations.

The reforms of Alexander II were important because they laid the foundation for Russia as it entered the 20th century. Freeing the serfs was the most well-known reform. Although well intentioned, there were serious complications in creating a system that benefitted the newly freed peasants and allowed them the ability to create an economically viable life after serfdom. In addition, the freedom of the press allowed for a broader exchange of ideas between Russians, which was positive but also created the opportunity for revolutionary ideas to spread. Alexander's reforms and the subsequent tsar's reactions to them increased the tension between those who wanted more changes in Russia and the tsars, who wanted to maintain their hold on power and keep Russia an autocracy.

Gates M. Brown

Further Reading

Eklof, Ben, ed. *Russia's Great Reforms, 1855–1881.* Bloomington: Indiana University Press, 1994.

Hosking, Geoffrey. *Russia: People and Empire.* Cambridge, MA: Harvard University Press, 1997.

Pipes, Richard. *Russia under the Old Regime.* New York: Scribner, 1974.

Greens

This lesser-known faction in the Russian Civil War was a loose conglomeration of peasants who opposed both the Whites and the Reds. Largely composed of local farming communities who violently opposed the Bolsehviks' policy of taking crops and livestock as a means to feed the workers in urban areas and the growing Red Army, the Greens were not an army per se, as they were not a cohesive entity in the traditional sense. Rather, the formation of these bands of peasants focused on protecting their communities and maintaining their traditional ways of life under the onslaught of Bolshevik-induced war communism. Though the members of the group overall agreed on the objective of stopping Bolshevism, they lacked the ability to synchronize their military efforts to their social and political objectives, which varied from band to band.

As a result of their reluctance to join and fight for the Bolshevik cause, the Reds often branded the Greens as supportors of the Whites—a propaganda tactic designed to persuade the large number of Russian peasants in the tsar's former empire, who tended to support the independent-minded Greens, to assist in suppressing the movement. As the Russian Civil War raged on, between 1918 and 1921 the Greens increasingly found themselves suffering harsh reprisals at the hands of the Bolsheviks. Though this tactic worked to suppress the Greens, it had the opposite effect on the peasants, who came to see the Reds as excessively harsh and detached from their rhetoric about a new government for the workers and peasants.

In effect the Greens were a guerrilla force that at times allied with anarchists and the Social Revolutionaries in an effort to achieve their goal of stopping the Bolsheviks. However, due to the fact that this army lacked a central command structure and tended to produce field forces that significantly varied in size from several hundred to thousands, these factions lacked a unified objective beyond stopping the Bolsheviks. The Greens typically attacked forces that were roughly equivalent in size but also tended to focus on targets such as communications stations, grain mills, and railways. The effectiveness of their attacks varied greatly due to lack of arms and critical sustainment measures that would have allowed them to capitalize on successful operations. Rather, they simply had to make do with captured weapons and volunteers from nearby towns who were at times forcibly drafted into the highly mobile guerrilla units.

Though the Greens objected to the Bolsheviks' harsh treatment of peasants, they themselves used torture, murder, and terroristic means to exact revenge on the Reds and those sympathetic to communism. As the Bolsheviks consolidated power over the Whites, they turned their attentions to the Greens in an effort to demonstrate violently that the Greens' version of opposition would not be tolerated under the new regime. The Bolsheviks greatly overestimated the size and diversity of the Green movement. Hence, they were not able to eradicate the Greens from the fluid Russian political landscape.

By the end of the civil war, the Bolsheviks had to slightly modify their stance by adjusting their agricultural policies while at the same time making sure that the Greens were harshly repressed, as Lenin did not want to leave the peasants of Russia with the slightest impression that armed insurrection was an acceptable means of political action under Bolshevik rule. The Bolsheviks' adjustment of their agricultural policies led to the withering of the central rationale of the Green movement. Hence, with this slight political accommodation, backed with military power and harsh repressions, the Bolsheviks extinguished the Green Army by 1922.

Sean N. Kalic

Further Reading

Landis, Erik. "Who Were the Greens? Rumor and Collective Identity in the Russian Civil War." *Russian Review* 69(1) (January 2010): 30–46.

Pipes, Richard. *Russia under the Bolshevik Regime.* New York: Vantage, 1995.

Radkey, Oliver H. *The Unknown Civil War in Soviet Russia: A Study of the Green Movement in the Tambov Region, 1920–1921.* Palo Alto, CA: Hoover Institution Press, 1976.

Smele, Jonathan D. *The Russian Civil Wars, 1916–1926: Ten Years That Shook the World.* New York: Oxford University Press, 2016.

Guchkov, Alexander Ivanovich (1862–1936)

Russian soldier, businessman, and politician. Born on October 14, 1862, in Moscow, to a prominent family, Alexander Ivanovich Guchkov graduated from Moscow University and also attended Berlin University. He thereafter took over and improved an already lucrative family business and also traveled extensively. Guchkov had a lifelong interest in military adventure, and he fought as a volunteer on the Boer side during the 1899–1902 South African (Second Boer) War, where he was wounded and captured. After his release he returned to Moscow via

Beijing, where he participated in the suppression of the Boxer Rebellion (Uprising) of 1899–1901. During the 1904–1905 Russo-Japanese War, Guchkov organized the Russian Red Cross, which ran the Russian Army's medical service. He was again captured, this time by the Japanese.

During the Russian Revolution of 1905, Guchkov led the conservative opposition to Tsar Nicholas II. Guchkov was the founder and leader of the conservative party called the Union of October 17, known as the Octobrists (Oktyabristy), which favored a strong central government and strong defenses. Solidly pro-Russian nationalist in outlook, it also favored industrialization along 19th-century classical liberal lines. In 1906, Guchkov formed an alliance with Prime Minister Pyotr A. Stolypin to try to modernize Russia. Guchkov supported Nicholas II's harsh repression of revolutionaries and peasant rebellions. Elected to the Third Duma (1907–1912), of which he became president in 1910, Guchkov helped secure passage of Stolypin's agrarian reform measures. He also chaired the National Defense Committee of the Duma, which urged the modernization of the Russian military. In 1909, he resigned from the Duma. He failed to win election to the Fourth Duma but was elected to the State Council (upper house of parliament).

Prior to World War I, Guchkov broke with the tsar regarding the influence of Grigory Rasputin, the royal family's close adviser. A lifelong monarchist, Guchkov gradually came to the conclusion that the tsar was the worst obstacle to the continuation of monarchical rule in Russia. When World War I began in August 1914, Guchkov first headed Russia's Red Cross and then the Central War Industries Committee to increase production and improve the distribution of war goods. He eventually became convinced that only a palace coup could save the war effort and the monarchy.

Guchkov was involved in planning such an event when the February 1917 revolution occurred. After the revolution's success, Guchkov was one of two delegates sent to Pskov to secure the tsar's abdication.

Guchkov became the first minister of war in the new Provisional Government, but he resigned following antiwar demonstrations that spring. After the November 1917 Bolshevik Revolution Guchkov went abroad, first to Berlin and then to Paris, where he became involved in various anti-Soviet activities, including sabotage and assassinations. Guchkov died in Paris on February 14, 1936.

Michael Share

Further Reading

Paxton, John. *Leaders of Russia and the Soviet Union: From the Romanov Dynasty to Vladimir Putin.* London: Routledge, 2008.

Pinchuk, Ben-Cion. *Octobrists in the Third Duma.* Seattle: University of Washington Press, 1974.

Rendle, Matthew. *Defenders of the Motherland: The Tsarist Elite in Revolutionary Russia.* New York: Oxford University Press, 2010.

Izvestia

The official name of the newspaper *Izvestia* translated from Russian is "News of the Councils of Working Peoples' Deputies of the USSR." This daily newspaper became the official media vehicle for the Soviet government in the immediate months after the October Revolution. In contrast to *Pravda,* which was the newspaper for the Communist Party, *Izvestia* became the official venue for the new government to post and distribute governmental information originating from the Supreme Soviet.

Founded in Petrograd in March 1917 by the Petrograd Soviet of Workers' and Soldiers' Deputies, this newspaper was originally a media outlet for the political views of the Mensheviks and Social Revolutionaries, both rivals of the Bolsheviks, as Vladimir Lenin tried to solidify power and provide some sense of government stability in the aftermath of the October Revolution. Though intended as a mouthpiece for the Mensheviks and Social Revolutionaries, the Bolsheviks assumed control of the paper as power stabilized in the hands of their party. Having gone through two previous name changes between March and August 1917, the newspaper by October 1917 was officially called *News of the Central Executive Committee of the Soviets of Working and Military Deputies.*

In the aftermath of the October Revolution, the Bolsheviks assumed control of *Izvestia* and quickly moved its headquarters from Petrograd to Moscow as a means to increase circulation and distribute news from the government to a wider cross section of the Russian people. After all, the Bolsheviks and their new government had to convince the people that they were the legitimate and popular government. In fact, during the Russian Civil War as the Bolsheviks sought to eradicate counterrevolutionaries, *Izvestia* became a critical venue to pass along the decrees and orders from the Central Powers. For example, in August 1918 as the Bolsheviks fought for their new government in the midst of massive desertions, questionable support, and lackluster battlefield performance, *Izvestia* became a critical media outlet for passing along orders from Trotsky and others in regard to maintaining high morale in units fighting at the front. Specifically, on August 14, 1918, *Izvestia* published an order from Trotsky "that in case of unjustified retreat, the commissar of the front was to be shot first, followed by its military field commander." As can be seen by this short quotation, *Izvestia* was at first not just a vehicle to convey dry governmental administrivia but was also a critical organ of the regime to maintain tight control over its people and the new government as they fought a civil war against counterrevolutionaries and tsarist supporters.

Izvestia's circulation grew from a high of 350,000 papers in 1924 to a staggering 1.5 million by 1932. As Joseph Stalin rapidly industrialized the Soviet Union, *Izvestia* remained a critical organ for the Soviet government to convey policies and information to its people.

After World War II and the death of Stalin, *Izvestia* under the direction of Alexei Adzhubei, the son-in-law of Soviet premier

Nikita Khrushchev, gravitated away from its original purpose and focused on becoming a "more lively and readable" newspaper. These changes included more photographs, articles, and bigger headlines. In essence, *Izvestia* adapted to the standard newspaper design and structure seen around the globe.

During the Soviet era, *Izvestia* remained a standard newpaper designed to inform the Soviet people of important news and information specifically with regard to government policy and foreign policy actions. In the aftermath of the demise of the Soviet Union in 1991, *Izvestia* became a privately owned and operated newpaper that continues to exist in the contemporary era.

Sean N. Kalic

Further Reading

Cohen, Stephen F. *Bukharin and the Bolshevik Revolution: A Political Biography, 1888–1938.* Oxford: Oxford University Press, 1980.

Pipes, Richard. *Russia under the Bolshevik Regime.* New York: Vantage, 1994.

Price, Morgan Philips. *Dispatches from the Revolution: Russia 1916–1918.* Edited by Tania Rose. Durham, NC: Duke University Press, 1997.

Tucker, Robert. *Stalin in Power: The Revolution from Above, 1928–1941.* New York: Norton, 1992.

Ulam, Adam. *The Bolsheviks: The Intellectual and Political History of the Triumph of Communism in Russia.* 2nd ed. Cambridge, MA: Harvard University Press, 1998.

J

Japanese Intervention in Siberia (1918–1922)

The Siberian Intervention was part of an Allied effort after World War I to secure Allied military stockpiles sent to the previous Russian regimes and to topple the Bolsheviks from power. The Japanese government, moreover, saw the intervention as an opportunity to further its imperialist ambitions in the region.

By early 1918, the Bolsheviks had taken Russia out of World War I. In response, the Allies sent troops to a number of places in Russia, including the Russian Far East. The intervening Allied governments publicly announced that they would respect Russian territorial integrity, would not interfere in Russian internal affairs, and would withdraw their forces as soon as the limited objectives of the intervention had been secured. Japanese leaders in Tokyo, however, saw the intervention as a golden opportunity to expand their territorial reach in East Asia. Japan already controlled Korea and had been seeking an opportunity to push northward into Manchuria and Siberia.

The United States, Britain, France, Canada, several European countries, and Japan all sent troops to Vladivostok. The largest contingents were the United States and Japanese. Each government had agreed to send 7,500 men, and while the United States did deploy that number, Japan dispatched many more. Exact figures on the Japanese forces are uncertain. The number could have been as few as 30,000 men but was probably closer to 90,000.

While Allied troops guarded military stockpiles at Vladivostok and sought to secure the vast Trans-Siberian Railway, the Japanese embarked on a grander plan. Japanese troops penetrated deep into Siberia. One force moved north from Vladivostok into the Maritime Province of eastern Siberia, while another formation headed westward from Vladivostok via the Chinese Eastern Railroad through northern Manchuria to Irkutsk, west of Lake Baikal.

In 1919, Admiral Alexander Kolchak, head of the Russian Provisional Government at Omsk, commanded the major anti-Bolshevik (White) Russian forces. In addition to Kolchak, other strong anti-Bolshevik forces were led by Grigory Semenov at Chita in the Trans-Baikal region and Ivan Kalmykov in the area around Khabarovsk in the Maritime Province. These and other anti-Bolshevik groups operated largely independently of one another. Instead of encouraging these forces to cooperate in fighting the Bolsheviks, the Japanese seemed bent on encouraging strife between the White factions. Thus, they permitted Semenov's men to interfere with railway operations and hijack quantities of arms, munitions, and other supplies intended for the Omsk government. Meanwhile, Kolchak's government at Omsk alienated many Russians by its policy of attempting to cooperate with the Japanese. Increasingly, Russian partisans carried out military operations against the Japanese occupiers, who were despised for their repressive policies. In one incident at Yufta in February 1919, partisans almost completely wiped out a unit of 300 Japanese. Perhaps in retaliation, on March 22, Japanese troops destroyed the village of Ivanovka, killing 232 inhabitants. There were other similar actions.

Following the nearly complete collapse of White forces at the end of 1919, the United States announced its intention to withdraw its forces from Siberia, an action that put great pressure on Tokyo. On February 27, 1920, the Japanese government announced a partial withdrawal from part of Siberia.

During February–May 1920 in the so-called Nikolayevsk Incident, Russian partisans executed some 700 Japanese as well as a larger number of Russians at the town of Nikolayevsk on the Amur River. On April 1 the remaining Allied forces were evacuated from Vladivostok, leaving only the Japanese as occupiers in Siberia. The Japanese military quickly established control of the Maritime Province and set up a Provisional Government of the Far Eastern Republic that declared its independence, which the Soviets recognized on May 14 in a bid to secure time. By the end of 1922 the Russian Civil War had come to an end, with the remaining White armies driven off Russian soil.

To pressure the Japanese to withdraw from Siberia, on May 31, 1921, the United States announced a policy whereby it would refuse to recognize the Japanese-supported political arrangement there. Finally, on June 10, 1922, Tokyo announced its intention to withdraw its troops. The last Japanese forces in Siberia departed Vladivostok on October 25, 1922, abandoning there some 50,000 Japanese settlers. On January 20, 1925, Tokyo signed a treaty with Moscow whereupon its troops also left north Sakhalin Island.

Andrew Jackson Waskey

Further Reading

Connaughton, Richard M. *The Republic of Ushakovka: Admiral Kolchak and the Allied Intervention in Siberia, 1918–1920.* London: Routledge, 1990.

Dickinson, Frederick R. *War and National Reinvention: Japan in the Great War, 1914–1919.* Cambridge, MA: Harvard University Press, 1999.

Morrow, John H., Jr. *The Great War: An Imperial History.* New York: Routledge, 2004.

White, John Albert. *The Siberian Intervention.* Princeton, NJ: Princeton University Press, 1950.

K

Kadets (Constitutional Democratic Party)

As a result of increased social and political activities in the aftermath of the incredible Russian famine of 1891–1892, liberal professionals in 1903 formed the Union of Liberation, and a newspaper, *Liberation,* under the direction of Peter Struve, designed to present opposition to the tsar and advance a more conservatively liberal political agenda. By 1905, they evolved into the Constitutional Democratic (Kadet) Party, an abbreviation of the Russian name of the party.

Led by historian Pavel (Paul) Miliukov, the Kadets advanced an agenda for a democratic government, a rule of law, progressive taxation, an eight-hour workday, and the distribution of land from private landlords to be paid for by the government. The question of retaining the tsar was an open point of debate for the Kadets. In the tense and traumatic times associated with the Russian Revolution of 1905, the Kadets offered a reasoned approach compared to the revolutionary platforms of the Social Democrats. The Social Revolutionaries, or even the more conservative Octobrists, who supported the monarchy. Ultimately, the Kadets' aim was to maintain a unified opposition to the tsar without the radical actions offered by the various leftist parties.

In the formation of the First Duma in the aftermath of Bloody Sunday, the Kadets emerged as the strongest party in the new assembly, with 38 percent of the deputies. As the Duma began to wrestle with its new position in the Russian government, the Kadets found it increasingly difficult to manage a coalition with either the revolutionaries or the Octobrists. With the tsar's issuance of the October Manifesto, the Kadets chose to see this edict as a move toward the development of a more democratic system, while this stance tended to alienate them from radicals and the conservatives alike.

As a result of their unique position and advocacy for democratic change, the Kadets witnessed an erosion of power in the First and Second Dumas. One of the major issues tugging at the effectiveness of the party was the fact that although it had started out as a largely professional organization, as Russia evolved in the first decade of the 20th century, the peasants and laborers became increasingly alienated from the political system and turned to more radicalized parties. The Kadets, who advocated a slower and gradual approach to a democratic system, found it increasingly difficult to influence members of their own party as well as those on the radical Left who were becoming more sympathetic to the calls for radical reforms. As a result of the growing influence of leftist radicals in the Russian political system, the Kadets watched as their power gradually diminished, yet they remained a cohesive political party through the turbulent period of 1905–1917.

In the Provisional Government of March 1917, Miliukov served as minister of foreign affairs, alongside Octobrist Guchkov as minister of war and of the navy, and Kerensky as the minister of justice. This new government saw a slight increase in "progressive support" for the Kadets' agenda between March and July 1917. However, as the Provisional Government eroded under pressure from the Left, which saw the new government as ineffective and accommodating to traditional conservative elements in Russian society, the Kadets' progressive reforms, once seen as a cautious and forward path for Russia's people, collapsed under the weight of the radical agenda from the revolutionary Left. The success of the Bolshevik Revolution left no place for the Kadets.

Sean N. Kalic

Further Reading

Chamberlin, William H. *The Russian Revolution,* Vol. I, *1917–1918: From Overthrow of the Tsar to the Assumption of Power by the Bolsheviks.* Princeton, NJ: Princeton University Press, 2014.

Kaiser, Daniel H. *The Workers' Revolution in Russia 1917: The View from Below.* Cambridge: Cambridge University Press, 1987.

Rosenberg, William G. *Liberals in the Russian Revolution: The Constitutional Democratic Party, 1917–1921.* Princeton, NJ: Princeton University Press, 1974.

Kaledin, Alexei Maximovich (1861–1918)

Born the son of a Don Cossack officer on October 24, 1861, Alexei Kaledin graduated from the Voronezh Military School in 1880, the Artillery School in St. Petersburg in 1882, and the General Staff Academy in 1889. During 1903–1906, he was head of the Novocherkassk Military Academy; he then served as assistant chief of staff for the Don Army, a Cossack cavalry force.

During World War I, Kaledin commanded a cavalry division in the Eighth Army under General Alexei Brusilov on the Southwestern Front. Brusilov praised Kaledin as one of his best commanders, particularly after his performance in the Battle of Lutsk in June 1916. Unlike Brusilov, though, Kaledin refused to accept the orders of the Provisional Government following the February Revolution; Kaledin was therefore relieved of his command.

Kaledin returned to Voronezh and was elected ataman (hetman) of the Don Cossack Army and head of a putative Cossack government. During August 1917, he traveled to Moscow to discuss a military coup with conservative army leaders, perhaps at the behest of former army chief of staff Mikhail Alekseev. Local authorities attempted to arrest Kaledin upon his return to Voronezh, having been informed by the leader of the Provisional Government, Alexander Kerensky, that Kaledin had been removed as leader of the Cossacks. Other Cossack leaders protected him, however, and Kaledin continued to work against the Provisional Government and, after the October Revolution, the Bolshevik regime.

During October–December 1917, Kaledin led a fierce and often brutal anti-Bolshevik rebellion in the Don region. His forces inflicted severe casualties but never managed to defeat the Reds; when the Cossacks lost control of Rostov-on-Don and were forced to retreat in horrible weather conditions, Kaledin lost hope and committed suicide on February 11, 1918.

Timothy C. Dowling

Further Reading

Brusilov, Aleksei. *A Soldier's Notebook.* New York: Macmillan, 1930.

Figes, Orlando. *Peasant Russia Civil War: The Volga Countryside in Revolution, 1917–1921.* London: Phoenix, 2001.

Kamenev, Lev (1883–1936)

A key player in the Russian Revolution of 1917, Lev Kamenev was a close associate of Vladimir Lenin. Kamemev later held high office in the newly created Soviet Union but eventually fell victim to Joseph Stalin's lust for power and was executed during the Great Purge.

The son of a Russian Orthodox mother and a Jewish father, Kamenev was born Lev Borisovich Rozenfeld on July 18, 1883, in Moscow. His early education occurred in Vilnius and Tiflis. Rather than following his father into engineering, Kamenev opted for a legal career, attending the University of Moscow's Faculty of Law beginning in 1901. His education was interrupted in March 1902, however, when he was arrested for his association with radicals and his participation in a demonstration. Expelled from the university, Kamenev went abroad, meeting Lenin in London and Olga Davidovna Bronstein (the sister of Leon Trotsky) in Paris. Kamenev and Bronstein eventually married and had two children.

In the fall of 1903, Kamenev returned to Russia to continue his radical activities. He organized a conference of Georgian Bolsheviks in November 1904, at which he was elected a representative to the Third Russian Social Democratic Party Congress in 1905. That same year, he aided Lenin in creating a new Bolshevik Party newspaper and continued his radical work until the spring of 1908, when he was once again arrested.

Kamenev fled the country and found himself appointed one of the directors of a number of party newspapers in exile. By 1909 he was one of Lenin's closest associates, along with Grigory Zinoviev. The three found accommodations for themselves and their

Lev Kamenev reading *Pravda*, which he oversaw while a top Bolshevik in Petrograd between January and August, 1914. (Edward Alsworth Ross, *The Russian Bolshevik Revolution*, 1921)

families in close proximity to one another in a variety of European cities as they continued to agitate for revolution in Russia from abroad. Lenin entrusted important offices to Kamenev, including the representation of the Bolshevik faction at the International Socialist Bureau. The Bolshevik leader eventually sent Kamenev back to Russia in early 1914 to oversee *Pravda*, the Bolshevik newspaper in St. Petersburg, and to take up one of the Bolsheviks' six seats in the Duma, Russia's (largely powerless) parliament.

A few months after the outbreak of World War I in August 1914, Kamenev and his fellow Bolshevik members of the Duma were arrested for antiwar activities. He spent the next two years in Siberian exile, returning to the Russian capital just after an uprising in February 1917. While the Provisional Government ruled Russia under the guise of liberal democracy, Kamenev, in conjunction with Stalin, assumed control of the Bolshevik movement in Petrograd (the former St. Petersburg). The two men pursued an agenda considerably to the right of that advocated by Lenin from Switzerland. They recognized the legitimacy of the Provisional Government and expressed a willingness to work with the Mensheviks, the long-standing opponents of the Bolsheviks within the Russian Social Democratic Party. In addition, Kamenev rejected Lenin's idea that Russia could skip over the capitalist phase of development in Marxism and immediately establish a socialist society. Following several days of upheaval in the city in July, the Provisional Government arrested only Kamenev of the nine members of the party's Central Committee, a testament to both Kamenev's prominence and the government's inability to make fine distinctions with respect to socialist ideology (since Kamenev was a relative moderate).

Kamenev was released after only a month, in time to play a central role in the events of September and October as the Bolsheviks seized power in Russia. He returned to his positions at *Pravda* and on the party's Central Committee, where he stood against Lenin's rush to armed insurrection. Kamenev (with Zinoviev's support) argued that Russia's peasants, the vast bulk of the population, would not support a revolution at this time. In addition, the working classes of foreign countries might not come to the Russian workers' aid, as Lenin and Trotsky so confidently expected. Kamenev and Zinoviev suggested that the party wait a few months and attend the Constituent Assembly, a democratically elected body to be convened by the Provisional Government. At that time the Bolsheviks could enter a coalition with other socialist parties, participating in a government with a broad base of support.

Dismissing these views, the party followed Lenin and Trotsky's plan to seize power, and Kamenev resigned from the Central Committee. Within a few days, however, as the Bolshevik coup d'état took shape, Kamenev returned to the fold, caught up in the excitement of the revolutionary moment. His role at the Smolny Institute (Bolshevik headquarters) was to help coordinate defensive actions against the forces of the Provisional Government. Once the Bolsheviks were in power, Kamenev was appointed to chair the Soviets' Central Executive Committee, making him the nominal head of the new regime. (Lenin held the real power as leader of the party.) Kamenev did not retain this position long, however, for once again he urged the party to share power with non-Bolsheviks. By November 4, 1917, he had been forced to resign from his office and once again from the Central Committee. Lenin removed him from the fulcrum of the revolutionary movement for the next two years, posting him abroad as a representative of the regime—a thankless job that entailed expulsion from various European countries on a number of occasions and even imprisonment in Finland for a time.

Returning to the center of events in March 1919, Kamenev took up a seat in the Politburo, the party's elite policy-making body. The following year, he also assumed the chairmanship of the Moscow soviet. Respected for his administrative talents, by the end of 1922 he had been entrusted with deputy chairmanships on the Council of Labor and the Council of People's Commissars. To this Lenin added the trusteeship of his personal papers at the Lenin Institute.

This last position aided Kamenev in the struggles for power that followed Lenin's strokes and ultimately his death in 1924. Kamenev had formed a three-man alliance with Zinoviev and Stalin in 1922 in order to keep Trotsky at bay. Kamenev had even been the one to nominate Stalin for the leadership of the party. To secure Stalin's position, Kamenev concealed Lenin's "Testament," in which the revered leader had criticized Stalin in no uncertain terms. In helping Stalin to oust Trotsky and his supporters, however, Kamenev and Zinoviev left themselves exposed to Stalin's unchecked power. Stalin turned on them as soon as Trotsky had been exiled. They attempted to form a new alliance with Lenin's widow but found this inadequate in the face of Stalin's position within the party.

In December 1925, Kamenev spoke at length at the Fourteenth Party Congress, condemning autocracy within the party. In reprisal, Stalin ousted Kamenev from the Council of Labor and the Council of People's Commissars. In April 1926, Kamenev even turned to his old adversary Trotsky in a desperate effort on both their parts to counter Stalin. This unlikely alliance gave Stalin the excuse to dislodge Kamenev from his remaining posts. The following year, Kamenev

was expelled from the Communist Party but managed to be readmitted once he denounced his former views. The year 1932 saw his second expulsion from the party, combined with exile to the Urals. A second recantation allowed him to work briefly at the publishing arm of the Academy of Sciences.

The 1934 assassination of S. M. Kirov, a party leader in Leningrad, touched off a wave of purges to which Kamenev fell victim. Once again he was expelled from the party, but this time he was sentenced to 10 years in prison. Worse still, in 1936 he was trotted out to confess his "crimes" as a terrorist with "Trotskyite-Zinovievite" allegiances. This case was Stalin's first show trial, at which Kamenev and 15 other long-time Bolsheviks were accused of plotting to assassinate virtually every member of the Politburo. Once convicted, Kamenev was put to death on August 24, 1936.

Daniel Siegel

Further Reading

Carmichael, Joel. *Stalin's Masterpiece: The Show Trials and Purges of the Thirties, the Consolidation of the Bolshevik Dictatorship.* New York: St. Martin's, 1976.

Haupt, Georges, and Jean-Jacques Marie. *Makers of the Russian Revolution: Biographies of Bolshevik Leaders.* Translated by C. I. P. Ferdinand and D. M. Bellos. Ithaca, NY: Cornell University Press, 1974.

Wieczynski, Joseph L., ed. *The Modern Encyclopedia of Russian and Soviet History.* 60 vols. Gulf Breeze, FL: 1976–2000.

Kanin, Vasily Aleksandrovich (1862–1927)

Russian Navy admiral. Born on December 23, 1862, Vasily Aleksandrovich Kanin graduated from the Russian Navy School in 1882 as a midshipman. He attended the Mine Officers' Class in 1891 and became a specialist in that field. He served in the Baltic Fleet and in the Pacific, participating in the suppression of the Boxer Uprising (Boxer Rebellion) in 1900–1901. He then served in the Black Sea Fleet, reaching the rank of captain first rank in 1908.

Kanin returned to the Baltic Fleet in 1911 as chief of the 4th Destroyer Flotilla. He was promoted to rear admiral on December 19, 1913, and appointed to command the mine-laying detachment. Kanin's force laid the first of the defensive minefields at the entrance to the Gulf of Finland on July 31, 1914. In early 1915, Kanin was appointed chief of the mine defenses, a post that brought together the minelayers and the light forces intended for the direct defense of the minefields. He also led a minelaying operation into German waters on January 12–14, 1915, when his force carried out the operation even though radio intelligence indicated that German vessels were nearby. Kanin was awarded the Order of St. George for this operation; in fact, reportedly he had wanted to break off the operation but was dissuaded from doing so by Captain First Rank Alexander V. Kolchak.

On February 22, 1915, Kanin was promoted to vice admiral. When Admiral Nikolai von Essen, commander of the Baltic Fleet, died on May 20, Kanin was appointed his successor. Kanin retained this post for 16 months and was promoted to admiral on April 23, 1916. He did not prove to be an outstanding fleet commander. Although several successful operations were carried out during his tenure, most notably the defense of the Gulf of Riga in August 1915, Admiral Alexander I. Rusin, chief of the Naval Field Staff at Stavka, felt that Kanin was not active enough and that under his leadership, discipline had grown lax.

In September 1916, Rusin and naval minister Admiral Ivan K. Grigorovich strongly pressed Tsar Nicholas II to replace Kanin. Nicholas reluctantly agreed, appointing Vice Admiral Adrian I. Nepenin as the new Baltic Fleet commander. Kanin was appointed to the State Council, and in January 1917 he was made a member of the Admiralty Council and served as an assistant to the naval minister for shipbuilding affairs. He retired in December 1917.

By this time the Bolsheviks had seized power, and Kanin joined the White forces in southern Russia during the ensuing Russian Civil War. In November 1918, General Anton I. Denikin appointed Kanin commander of the Volunteer Army's largely nonexistent Black Sea naval forces, but he was replaced by Admiral M. P. Sablin in early 1919. In November 1920 Kanin left Russia, settling in France. He died at Marseilles on June 17, 1927.

Stephen McLaughlin

Further Reading

Berezovskii, N. Iu., V. D. Dotsenko, and V. P. Tiurin. *Rossiiskii imperatorskii flot, 1696–1917: Voenno-istorichesskii spravochnik* [The Imperial Russian Fleet, 1696–1917: A Military-Historical Dictionary]. Moscow: Russky mir, 1993.

Saul, Norman E. *Sailors in Revolt: The Russian Baltic Fleet in 1917.* Lawrence: Regents Press of Kansas, 1978.

White, D. Fedotoff. *Survival through War and Revolution in Russia.* Philadelphia: University of Pennsylvania Press, 1939.

Kazakov, Alexander Aleksandrovich (1889–1919)

Imperial Russian Air Force aviator and top-scoring Russian ace of World War I. Born in Kherson Province on January 15, 1889,

Alexander Kazakov attended Russian military schools before joining the army as a cavalry officer in 1908. He transferred to aviation in 1913 and was assigned to the IV Corps Flight Detachment in Poland, where he flew reconnaissance and bombing missions in a Morane "G" monoplane. Kazakov brought down his first enemy aircraft in March 1915 when he rammed it with an anchor trailed behind his aircraft to damage the enemy's control surfaces.

In 1916, Kazakov assumed command of the XIX Corps Flight Detachment and participated in air operations supporting the Brusilov Offensive that June. Flying French-designed Nieuport 11 and 17 fighters, Kazakov shot down five enemy aircraft between June and December 1916. In August 1916 he took command of the 1st Combat Air Group, an elite formation. He continued to serve primarily in the southern part of the Russian lines near Tarnów (modern-day southeastern Poland). Kazakov shot down one more enemy aircraft in December 1916 despite increasingly poor weather.

Romania entered the war on the Entente side in August 1916, and Russia deployed troops and aircraft to support Romanian operations. The 1st Combat Air Group went to Romania in February 1917, where Kazakov scored 8 more victories. That March Tsar Nicholas II abdicated, succeeded by the Provisional Government of Alexander Kerensky. Russia remained in the war, however, and the 1st Combat Air Group continued operations. Kazakov was wounded in action in June 1917 but returned to service in July, running his victory total to 17 by August 1917. Between August and October, he scored his final 3 victories. In November 1917, the Bolsheviks seized power and subsequently withdrew from the war.

Despite Kazakov's prominence as an imperial officer, the Bolsheviks requested that he command the 7th Air Division on the condition that it could not fly combat missions. Kazakov, dispirited and exhausted, resigned his commission in January 1918. He then joined the anti-Bolshevik forces serving with the British at Murmansk. Kazakov commanded the Slavo-British air detachment until he was wounded in January 1919. As the British prepared to leave Russia, they offered to take Kazakov with them. Kazakov declined and was killed in a crash on August 1, 1919, while performing low-level acrobatics. One observer, Royal Air Force ace Ira "Taffy" Jones, speculated that the crash was intentional; Kazakov had been increasingly depressed by flagging anti-Bolshevik fortunes and the impending withdrawal of British support.

Kazakov's tally of German and Austrian aircraft stood at 20 confirmed kills at the time of his death, although it may have been as high as 32, as he claimed additional unconfirmed victories.

Tim Wilson

Further Reading

Durkota, Alan, Victor Kulikov, and Alan Darcy. *The Imperial Russian Air Service: Famous Pilots and Aircraft of World War I.* Boulder, CO: Flying Machines, 1996.

Franks, Norman. *Nieuport Aces of World War I.* London: Osprey, 2000.

Greenwood, John, Von Hardesty, and Robin Higham. *Russian Aviation and Airpower in the Twentieth Century.* Studies in Air-Power. New York: Routledge, 1998.

Kerensky, Alexander Fyodorovich (1881–1970)

Russian socialist and political leader. Born in Simbirsk, Russia, on May 2, 1881, Alexander Kerensky studied law at the University of

St. Petersburg and quickly established a radical reputation by representing defendants accused of political crimes. He was considered by some to be a moderate socialist, having joined the Russian Socialist Revolutionary Party and becoming the successor to the defunct revolutionary populist movement Narodnia Volia (People's Will). In 1912, Kerensky was elected to the Russian Duma (national parliament).

A powerful orator, Kerensky developed a strong following among industrial workers. When World War I began, he was one of the relatively few in the Duma who opposed Russia's entry. He became a critic of the tsarist government's prosecution of the war and an opponent of the regime. In late 1915, serious illness forced him to reduce his

Alexander Fyodorovich Kerensky served as head of the Provisional Government prior to the Bolshevik Revolution. (Edward Alsworth Ross, *The Russian Bolshevik Revolution*, 1921)

political activity; however, on his return to Petrograd (as St. Petersburg was then called) in the summer of 1916, his vocal attacks directed at the tsar increased in fervor. By then Kerensky was committed to the war as an opponent of German militarism, but he also believed that the tsar's personal command of the army had weakened the Russian effort.

Toward the end of 1916, Kerensky became a prominent voice calling for the abdication of the tsar and the dissolution of autocracy. When conditions sparked strikes and food riots in Petrograd, inducing the tsar's abdication and the revolution of March 1917, Kerensky obtained two significant appointments. He became vice chairman of the influential Petrograd Soviet (a council patterned after the Soviets of the Russian Revolution of 1905 and mirroring the national government), and he was appointed minister of justice in the Provisional Government headed by Prince Georgy Lvov. Because of his position in both bodies, Kerensky acted as liaison between the two, boosting public awareness of him.

Appointed minister of war in May 1917, Kerensky was determined that Russia should continue in the war to victory so that it could realize its war aims. He staked all on a great 1917 summer offensive, the so-called Kerensky Offensive, and he visited major army units to promote it. The offensive soon ground to a halt, however. It was in fact the final straw for the Russian Army, bringing about its collapse as well as that of the Provisional Government under Lvov in July. As Lvov's successor as prime minister that same month, Kerensky's policies vacillated between the Left and the Right and led to his increased isolation.

Although Kerensky increased socialist representation on his cabinet in August 1917, the fall of Riga to the Germans brought unrest in the capital, and he ordered Russian Army commander General Lavr Kornilov to Petrograd to restore order. Upon learning of Kornilov's intent to seize control by military coup, Kerensky issued a recall and dismissed Kornilov. When Kornilov continued to march on the capital, Kerensky sought the help of the Bolsheviks, issuing them arms. The Bolsheviks then organized a defense of Petrograd.

Kerensky declared Russia to be a socialist republic on September 14, 1917, and assigned a majority of seats to the socialists in his new cabinet, announced on October 8. His government collapsed, however, when Kerensky ordered the arrest of the leaders of the Bolshevik revolutionary committee on November 5, 1917. This action incited an uprising that forced him to flee from Petrograd. Gathering a core of loyal troops, Kerensky tried to march on Petrograd to reverse the Bolshevik Revolution, but he was forced to retreat when confronted by armed revolutionaries on November 12.

Fleeing Russia shortly thereafter, Kerensky went into exile and spent most of the remainder of his life in the United States, where he taught at the university level and wrote numerous articles and books. He died in New York City on June 11, 1970.

Arthur T. Frame

Further Reading

Abraham, Richard. *Alexander Kerensky: The First Love of the Revolution.* New York: Columbia University Press, 1987.

Bainton, Roy. *A Brief History of 1917.* London: Carroll and Graf, 2005.

Kerensky, Alexander F. *Russia and History's Turning Point.* New York: Duell, Sloan and Pierce, 1965.

Wade, Rex. *The Russian Revolution, 1917.* Cambridge: Cambridge University Press, 2000.

Kerensky Offensive (July 1–19, 1917)

Russian offensive on the Eastern Front during the summer of 1917 that led to the near total collapse of the Russian Army. After the March 1917 revolution brought about the fall of the autocracy and replaced it with the Provisional Government appointed by the State Duma, the shadow government of the Petrograd Soviet, bent on gaining the support of the army rank and file, unilaterally issued instructions to soldiers that became known as Order No. 1. This order essentially removed control of the armed forces from their officers.

The Bolshevik Party had gone on record as favoring an immediate end to Russian participation in the war, and its leaders were active in stirring up unrest among the troops. Exhausted by three years of war, often without sufficient means to sustain the fight and suffering horrific casualties, Russian soldiers began to vote for peace with their feet by fleeing the trenches. Commander of the Russian armed forces General Mikhail Alekseev and his senior commanders petitioned representatives of the Provisional Government, telling them that Russia's survival was threatened and asking them to take action to reinstate discipline and order.

By the end of April 1917, a commission established by the Petrograd Soviet had drafted a declaration of soldiers' rights that mirrored the provisions of Order No. 1. When the new regulation was presented to War and Navy Minister Alexander Guchkov, he resigned on May 1, 1917, rather than sign. Alexander Kerensky, the Provisional Government's minister of justice, then replaced Guchkov and issued the "Declaration of Soldiers' Rights" 10 days later. It provided that only elected organizations, committees, and courts, rather than officers, could discipline

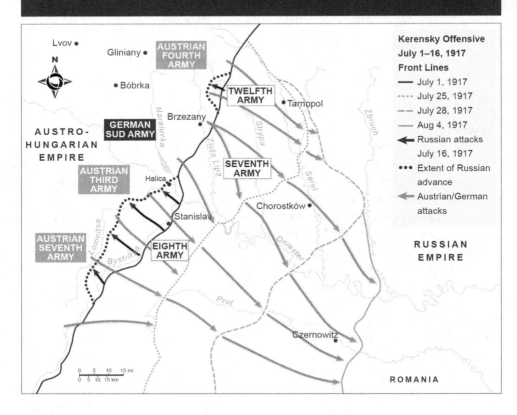

KERENSKY OFFENSIVE

Lvov

Gliniany

Bóbrka

AUSTRIAN FOURTH ARMY

TWELFTH ARMY

Tarnopol

Brzezany

GERMAN SUD ARMY

AUSTRO-HUNGARIAN EMPIRE

AUSTRIAN THIRD ARMY

Halica

SEVENTH ARMY

Stanislav

Chorostków

AUSTRIAN SEVENTH ARMY

EIGHTH ARMY

Czernowitz

RUSSIAN EMPIRE

ROMANIA

0 5 10 15 mi
0 5 10 15 km

**Kerensky Offensive
July 1–16, 1917
Front Lines**
— July 1, 1917
---- July 25, 1917
-- July 28, 1917
— Aug 4, 1917
← Russian attacks July 16, 1917
••• Extent of Russian advance
← Austrian/German attacks

soldiers except for cases of direct insubordination in combat.

At the time, Russia's Western allies were hard-pressed and requested that Russia undertake offensive action. Kerensky responded by planning a major offensive for the summer of 1917 in Galicia, where Russia faced weaker Austro-Hungarian forces. A brilliant orator, Kerensky had gone to the front to speak to the troops and rally them to fight for the defense of the motherland. He believed that the war was a means for Russia to realize its historical territorial ambitions. The soldiers enthusiastically cheered Kerensky's pleas and promised fidelity. In fact, they continued to reject the war, abetted in this by Bolshevik "truth squads" that

followed Kerensky and told the soldiers to refuse to fight. Based on his tour of the front, however, Kerensky thought that the soldiers supported the war effort as well.

To further that support, Kerensky made a number of command changes. He replaced Alekseev with General Alexei Brusilov, previously commander of the Southwestern Front and more accepting of the revolution. Only three weeks before the planned offensive, however, Kerensky also replaced the commanders of both the Southwestern and Western Fronts with those who would make the main military effort. He also replaced several army commanders only five days prior to the planned attack. All of this produced considerable confusion.

The offensive began early on the morning of July 1, 1917. Brusilov sent two armies, the Russian Eleventh and Seventh Armies, consisting of 31 divisions, to strike the combined South Army of eight divisions (three Austrian, four German, and one Turkish) and push toward Lemberg (Lvov or L'viv). Kerensky, following the offensive's progress from Seventh Army headquarters, was confident. Initial reports from the front reinforced that confidence.

On July 5, the 13 divisions of the Russian Eighth Army attacked farther to the south along the Dniester and the Carpathian foothills in the direction of Halicz and Dolina against the Austro-Hungarian Third Army, which was considerably weaker than the South Army. The Russian forces outnumbered the defending Central Powers' forces in Galicia three to one, and thanks to arms shipments from the Allies and increased Russian domestic production, the Russians had adequate artillery and shells to support the attack. Russian artillery pieces reportedly stood less than 30 yards apart along a 60-mile stretch of the front. Russian heavy guns outnumbered those of the defenders by more than five to one. The Austro-Hungarians and Germans had been forewarned by defectors of the broad outlines of the Russian plan and its timing, but the assaulting Russians nonetheless opened a breach in the enemy lines some 20 miles deep, threatening the oil wells of Drohobycz. At the same time, Brusilov ordered supporting attacks on the Northern Front.

Russia's commanders and ministers were elated by what appeared to be a major victory. Outside observers, however, detected disturbing signs in the Russian ranks that portended ill. Unit committees had held meetings to discuss the attack orders, and some refused to obey. Large numbers of soldiers deserted and returned only when they were hungry or thought the fighting had stopped. Other units moved to attack across three lines of trenches as if on parade and then withdrew to their own trenches. Many of the early gains, it seemed, had been either temporary or simply false.

The Germans shifted resources south, and when the Austrians and Germans counterattacked on July 19, Russian units voluntarily evacuated their positions without waiting for the enemy to approach. Some even killed officers who tried to persuade them to return to duty. Even the commissars assigned by the soviet to invigorate the soldiers in defense of revolutionary gains could not hold back the tide of fleeing soldiers. From the Baltic to Romania, the collapse of the Russian Army was total. All that stayed the Central Powers' advance on the Eastern Front was a greater interest in events in France. Their counteroffensive stalled temporarily just east of the prewar Russian frontier.

Meanwhile, in mid-July some units of the Petrograd garrison, fearing that they would be sent to the front, rose in revolt. The Bolsheviks took advantage of the rioting and attempted to seize power in the capital. Battles took place during July 16–18 between the rioters, joined by sailors from the nearby Kronstadt navy base, and units loyal to the government. Eventually the uprising was quelled but not before several hundred people were killed. The government ordered the arrest of Bolshevik leaders, but Vladimir Lenin escaped to Finland.

Recriminations followed the failed July offensive, creating even greater tension between the civilian government and military leadership. Brusilov was made the scapegoat and was relieved of command. Prime Minister Prince Georgy Lvov resigned, allowing Kerensky to assume the post. Kerensky replaced Brusilov with General Lavr Kornilov, who until then had been commander of the

Southwestern Front. Kornilov was a national hero, and Kerensky believed that Kornilov could rally the soldiers. Instead, a confrontation between the two led to the final collapse of the Provisional Government and the Bolshevik seizure of power in November (October in the Julian calendar) 1917.

Arthur T. Frame

Further Reading

Lincoln, W. Bruce. *Passage through Armageddon: The Russians in War and Revolution, 1914–1918.* New York: Simon and Schuster, 1986.

Wade, Rex. *The Russian Revolution, 1917.* Cambridge: Cambridge University Press, 2005.

Wildman, Allan K. *The End of the Russian Imperial Army.* 2 vols. Princeton, NJ: Princeton University Press, 1980, 1987.

Kolchak, Alexander Vasilievich (1874–1920)

Russian Army general and leader of the White forces in the Russian Civil War. Born on November 16, 1874, in St. Petersburg, Alexander Kolchak served 28 years in the Imperial Russian Navy. Kolchak's father had been a major general in the marine artillery, and he himself was educated for a naval career. He completed the Naval College in 1894 and commanded a destroyer in the 1904–1905 Russo-Japanese War. He also participated in two polar expeditions.

On the outbreak of World War I, Kolchak was chief of operations of the Baltic Fleet. Aggressive and capable, he also commanded a destroyer flotilla in the November 1915 Windau operation that drove German picket lines away from Russian bases. Promoted to rear admiral in April 1916, Kolchak took command of the Destroyer Division of the Baltic Fleet. That June, he participated in an operation in the Gulf of Norrkoping against a German convoy from Sweden. His destroyers sank a German auxiliary cruiser and a number of ships in the convoy, but Kolchak's poor tactics allowed most of the convoy to escape. Despite this, Kolchak was advanced to vice admiral and took command of the Black Sea Fleet in July 1916.

Kolchak proved to be a capable fleet commander. His aggressive tactics soon secured Russian dominance of the Black Sea. His ships conducted mining operations and coastal sweeps and shelled Turkish coastal installations. Following the March 1917 abdication of Tsar Nicholas II, however, revolutionary sailors of the Black Sea Fleet forced Kolchak to resign in June 1917. The Russian Provisional Government then sent him on a mission to Washington; he returned from the mission in the midst of the Bolshevik seizure of power.

Kolchak was determined that Russia should remain in the war against Germany. Supported by the British, he formed an anti-Bolshevik government in Siberia that was recognized by the Allies as the legitimate government of Russia. Unfortunately, Kolchak had little interest in politics and lacked revolutionary leadership qualities. His initial military offensive began well, thanks in large part to the well-organized Czech Legion, but Kolchak was unable to link his forces with those of General Anton Denikin, who was leading White forces in southern Russia and Ukraine.

Kolchak never won the popular support necessary for victory, in part because he never articulated a reform platform. His call for a more representative government did not come until the end of 1919, when his armies had already been defeated. Kolchak himself ascribed his failure to a number of causes, including constant battle, inadequate supply, poor officer leadership, and effective enemy propaganda. Although Kolchak was an honorable man, many of his subordinates were not, and his failure to curb their excesses and harsh treatment of their own soldiers drove many Siberians into Red hands.

By January 1920, with Russia having lost an estimated 1 million people to disease, famine, and fighting, on the retreat to Irkutsk Kolchak was forced to step aside as leader of White forces in favor of the more successful Denikin. Shortly thereafter, Kolchak was arrested by the Irkutsk government. Tried by a tribunal dominated by Bolsheviks, he was executed by firing squad outside Irkutsk on February 7, 1920.

Claude R. Sasso and Spencer C. Tucker

Further Reading

Bisher, Jamie. *White Terror: Cossack Warlords of the Trans-Siberian.* New York: Routledge, 2005.

Connaughton, Richard M. *The Republic of Ushakovka: Admiral Kolchak and the Allied Intervention in Siberia, 1918–1920.* London: Routledge, 1990.

Luckett, Richard. *The White Generals: An Account of the White Movement and the Russian Civil War.* New York: Viking, 1971.

Smele, Jonathan D. *Civil War in Siberia: The Anti-Bolshevik Government of Admiral Kolchak, 1918–1920.* New York: Cambridge University Press, 1996.

Kornilov, Lavr Georgievich (1870–1918)

Russian Army general and commander of the army under the Provisional Government. Born on August 30, 1870, in Ust-Kamengorsk in western Siberia, Lavr Kornilov was a retired officer's son and thus had the right to a free education in a Siberian Cadet Corps school, a kind of secondary school with military discipline. After graduating with distinction, he attended the Mikhailovski Artillery Training Corps for Officers. Commissioned in 1892, Kornilov joined the Turkistan Artillery Brigade. In 1895 he attended the General Staff Academy in St. Petersburg, and following graduation and a short period of service in the Warsaw Military District, he returned to duty in Turkestan.

Assigned to intelligence duties in connection with expeditions into eastern Persia, Kornilov became fluent in several Central Asian languages and published articles on eastern Persia, India, and Baluchistan. During the Russo-Japanese War of 1904–1905, he was chief of staff of the 1st Fusilier

General Lavr Georgievich Kornilov was appointed commander in chief of Russia's Army by Alexander Kerensky and served in this capacity from July–August 1917, before he ran afoul of Kerensky and the Provisional Government. General Kornilov is seen here with his staff. (Edward Alsworth Ross, *The Russian Bolshevik Revolution*, 1921)

Brigade and earned the Cross of St. George. At war's end, he was assigned to the central offices of the General Staff and served in Turkistan, the Caucasus, and western Russia. From 1907 to 1911, he was the military attaché to China and undertook some horseback treks through China and Mongolia.

Kornilov rose rapidly through the officer ranks. Already a general when World War I erupted, he first commanded the 49th Infantry Division and then the 48th Infantry Division on the Southwestern Front. In April 1915, his division spearheaded the Russian offensive thrusting through the Carpathians into the Austrian plains. When the army suddenly found itself short of arms and ammunition, particularly artillery, Kornilov's unit was forced to retreat. He was wounded and taken prisoner at Przemyśl by the Austrians. In 1916, Kornilov escaped from captivity and crossed through Romania to rejoin the Russian Army. News of his escape and repatriation made headlines and made him a hero. He was given command of the XXV Corps, again on the Southwestern Front then commanded by General Alexei Brusilov. When the imperial government fell and was replaced by the Provisional Government in March 1917, Kornilov became commander of the Petrograd garrison. Instructed to restore order and discipline but frustrated by the lack of government support, he was allowed to resign the post and return to the front lines as commander of the Eighth Army. Here he had some success in the opening assaults of the so-called Kerensky Offensive before the German counteroffensive drove the Russians back in disarray. Kornilov's attempts to restore order and discipline among his troops were also frustrated.

In August 1917, new prime minister Alexander Kerensky appointed Kornilov commander of the Russian Army. When the fall of Riga to the Germans brought unrest in the capital, Kerensky ordered Kornilov to Petrograd to restore order. When Kornilov called for the government to resign and pass control to him as commander in chief of the army, Kerensky dismissed Kornilov and ordered his return to the capital.

Defying Kerensky, Kornilov ordered forces under General Alexander Krymov, consisting of the elite III Cavalry Corps and the renowned Savage Division of north Caucasian mountain warriors, to march on Petrograd. Kerensky called on Bolshevik leader Vladimir Lenin for assistance, and massed railroad workers along with some soldiers and sailors blocked Kornilov's path. Discussions between Kornilov's troops and the radical workers convinced his forces to disperse, and the threat to Kerensky's government subsided.

Kornilov was arrested on September 1, 1917, at army headquarters and imprisoned at Bykhov. He later escaped and joined anti-Bolshevik White forces in the Don region. Kornilov was killed by a shell explosion during an engagement with Bolshevik forces at Ekaterinodar on April 13, 1918.

Arthur T. Frame

Further Reading

Katkov, George. *The Kornilov Affair: Kerensky and the Break-Up of the Russian Army.* London: Longman, 1980.

Kerensky, Alexander F. *The Prelude to Bolshevism: The Kornilov Rebellion.* New York: Haskell House, 1972.

Wade, Rex. *The Russian Revolution, 1917.* Cambridge: Cambridge University Press, 2005.

Kornilov Rebellion (1917)

Putative uprising by troops under General Lavr Kornilov to install him as dictator of Russia. The Provisional Government established upon the abdication of Tsar Nicholas II in February (March) 1917 was plagued by weakness. Originally composed of members of the Third Duma, it had limited popular support and thus from the outset had to share power with the Petrograd Soviet, a much more radical body. The Provisional Government also favored a continuing role for Russia in World War I, arguing that the state was obliged to fight by treaty. When it tried to stage an offensive in June 1917, however, the soldiers simply refused to fight. The more radical elements in St. Petersburg, including the Bolshevik Party led by Vladimir Lenin and the First Machine Gun Regiment, took advantage of the protests and chaos that the so-called Kerensky Offensive stirred up to stage a coup, the July Days. The government, led by Alexander Kerensky, barely managed to suppress the poorly organized uprising. Many military officers, including General Lavr Kornilov, whose Eighth Army had fought well in the recent offensive, now became more strident in their call for a return to traditional discipline—including corporal punishment and the death penalty—in the military. Kerensky, seeing an opportunity to stabilize his government, appointed Kornilov as commander in chief on July 12, 1917.

There is some evidence that Kornilov viewed his role as tantamount to dictator from the beginning. This tendency certainly was reinforced by the August 24 visit of Vladimir Lvov, former procurator of the Holy Synod, to Kornilov's headquarters at Mogilev. Claiming, probably falsely, that he had been sent by Kerensky, Lvov asked Kornilov whether he saw a dictatorship under Kerensky, an authoritarian government in which he and Kerensky shared power, or a military dictatorship with Kornilov at its head as the best solution to Russia's dilemma. Kornilov replied that he favored the last option, which Lvov reported to Kerensky the following day.

Kerensky, either alarmed by Kornilov's intentions or having manipulated Kornilov into revealing his intentions (it is unclear whether Lvov and Kerensky were cooperating), confronted Kornilov indirectly, using a Hughes teleprinter. Without revealing his identity, Kerensky asked Kornilov to confirm that he aimed at a military dictatorship, which Kornilov essentially did. Though the entire exchange was vague, Kerensky took the opportunity to accuse Kornilov of plotting against him and removed him as commander in chief. When he could not find a replacement, however, Kerensky reinstated Kornilov only hours later.

Kornilov assumed that this back-and-forth indicated that Kerensky was hostage, at least politically, to the radical factions within the Petrograd Soviet and wanted his assistance against them, possibly with an eye to establishing the military dictatorship they had discussed. Kornilov ordered his III Cavalry Corps to march against St. Petersburg to suppress the radicals and restore order. Panicked, Kerensky called on the Petrograd Soviet to defend the government; he released the political prisoners from the July Days and gave the Bolshevik Red Guards arms to aid in the effort. Before Kornilov's troops reached St. Petersburg, however, they were sidetracked and dissuaded by Bolshevik railway workers. The coup, if there ever was one, fizzled; Kerensky again removed Kornilov as commander in chief and jailed him, along with 30 other officers. The Provisional Government was saved, but Kerensky had armed a more dangerous opponent in the Bolsheviks.

Timothy C. Dowling

Further Reading

Kerensky, Alexander. *Kornilov Revolt: Prelude to Bolshevism.* Reprint ed. Charleston, SC: Nabu, 2012.

Munck, J. L. *The Kornilov Revolt: A Critical Examination of Sources and Research.* Aarhus: Aarhus University Press, 1987.

Wade, Rex. *The Russian Revolution, 1917.* Cambridge: Cambridge University Press, 2005.

Krylenko, Nikolai Vasilievich (1885–1938)

Born on May 2, 1885, near Smolensk, Nikolai Krylenko was the son of a populist revolutionary, a heritage he followed faithfully. Nikolai joined the Social Democratic Labor Party as a university student in St. Petersburg during 1904 and served as a member of the Petersburg Soviet during the Russian Revolution of 1905. He fled Russia in the aftermath of the revolution and was arrested almost immediately upon his return in 1907 and forced into exile in Poland.

Krylenko returned to St. Petersburg to finish his degree in 1909 and was drafted in 1912. He was discharged in 1913 as a second lieutenant and went to work as an editor for the Bolshevik newspaper *Pravda.* Krylenko was arrested again in 1913 and sent into exile at Kharkov, where he earned a law degree. Fearing further punishment, he fled to Austria in 1914, and when World War I erupted that August he continued on to Switzerland.

In 1915, Krylenko returned to Russia as an emissary of Bolshevik leader Vladimir Lenin. Krylenko's mission was to rebuild the Bolshevik underground, but he was arrested in Moscow in November and sent to the Southwestern Front just in time to participate in the Brusilov Offensive of June 1916.

Krylenko survived the massive casualties of that offensive and, following the February Revolution, was elected chairman of his regimental, divisional, and army soviets. He had to resign these posts in May 1917, however, as few soldiers supported the Bolshevik position of complete opposition to the Provisional Government that he advocated.

In June 1917, Krylenko became a member of the Bolshevik Military Organization and a representative to the All-Russia Congress of Soviets. He was arrested by the Provisional Government in the aftermath of the Bolsheviks' abortive July Days uprising but was released to help defend Petrograd against the putative coup of General Lavr Kornilov in August. During the October Revolution, Krylenko helped secure the support of the Petrograd garrison and played a leading role in the Bolshevik takeover in that city.

Following the revolution, Krylenko became part of a triumvirate responsible for military affairs in the nascent Bolshevik regime. When army chief of staff General Nikolai Dukhonin refused to obey Lenin's directive to open peace negotiations with the Germans in early November, Lenin announced that he had appointed Krylenko as the last head of the Russian Army.

Krylenko was also the first head of the Red Army, which was established in January 1918. He implemented radical Bolshevik policies, such as the election of all officers, but was unable to prevent the German Army's crushing victories in February 1918. Lenin and Trotsky therefore established the Supreme Military Council, to be headed by Mikhail Bonch Bruevich, which led Krylenko to resign in early March 1918. He was reassigned to the People's Commissariat for Justice, where he became chair of the Revolutionary Tribunal.

Krylenko proved to be an enthusiastic advocate of revolutionary justice and advocated terror as an instrument of the revolution. In 1922, he was appointed deputy commissar of justice and assistant prosecutor general. He led the show trial of the Russian Roman Catholic leadership in 1923, and in 1931 he became commissar of justice and prosecutor general. Krylenko retired as a prosecutor in 1932, however, and became head of the Soviet chess, checkers, and mountain climbing associations. He was removed as commissar for justice in January 1938 and arrested by the Peoples' Commissariat for Internal Affairs (Narodni Kommisariat Vnutrikh Del, or secret police). Krylenko was tried on July 29, having confessed in prison to "wrecking" and opposing Lenin at every turn. At his trial, which lasted 20 minutes, Krylenko recanted; he was found guilty nevertheless and shot that day.

Timothy C. Dowling

Further Reading

Conquest, Robert. *The Great Terror: A Reassessment.* Oxford: Oxford University Press, 1990.

Reese, Roger. *The Soviet Military Experience: A History of the Soviet Army, 1917–1991.* London: Routledge, 2000.

L

Labor Unions

Labor unions have a surprising history in imperial Russia. In the 19th century, the tsar's government outlawed labor unions and other political organizations. The reason for this was that Tsar Alexander III ruled Russia alone, and there was no need to form political or quasi-political groups. Such groups could pave the way for the people to believe that such groups were necessary at the national level, and this conflicted with the tsar's role as autocrat of Russia. However, in 1898 S. V. Zubatov presented an idea to Interior Minister Viacheslav Plehve concerning how to address the burgeoning working class in Petrograd. Zubatov argued that the best way to understand what was going on with the working class was to give them a place to organize and discuss their grievances or plans. He argued for creating police-run labor unions.

One of the main obstacles to forming unions in late 19th-century Russia was that such groups ran afoul of the law. Even if the members of the union only had economic goals, they were not allowed to gather and advocate as a union. Zubatov thought that this needlessly criminalized people who had no political aspirations but only wanted to better their economic condition. Although Plehve was skeptical of the plan, Tsar Nicholas II agreed to allow the police to sponsor the formation of some labor unions in order to see how they performed.

Workers flocked to the police-run labor unions. As a show of the success of these new unions, 50,000 Moscow workers took part in a parade to Alexander II's monument. Although the workers excitedly joined these unions, their enthusiasm slackened when the government chose the side of employers when workers in Odessa struck. The government's lack of support for the workers in their dispute against Odessa employers made it clear that the police were on the side of the employers even if the police supported the creation of labor unions.

In 1903 due the workers' strike in Odessa, Plehve fired Zubatov. Even though the police unions' sponsor was no longer working for the Interior Ministry, Plehve did not disband the police unions. Although he was not a great supporter of the police unions, he did authorize the creation of several new police unions, specifically one in Petrograd led by Father George Gapon. Father Gapon's union, the Assembly of Russian Factory and Plant Workers, focused on bettering the spiritual life of the workers, and he only allowed Christians into the union. Gapon did not create his union in order to agitate for improved economic conditions or contracts for the workers and other quality of life issues.

Gapon founded his union in February 1904, and by the end of the year he opened several new branches in the city and had approximately 11,000 members and 8,000 associate members. His union's success concerned the police. Gapon tried, without authorization, to open branches of his union in Moscow and Kiev. He also was not completely subordinate to the police. He genuinely cared for the workers and was not one who only participated in the union in order to feed information back to the police. As he became more independent, he drew more attention from the police. Gapon did not hide his association with the police and the government. Governor Vladimir Alexandrovich Fullon attended some gatherings of the meetings.

As the members of Gapon's union grew, he realized that he could not ignore the political agitation in Russia. The Zemstvo Congress, which published a call for a constitution, and the national banquet campaign that spread the congress's platform increased the calls for political reform in Russia. Gapon tried to join his group to the Social Democrats, but they rebuffed him; however, the Petrograd delegation of the Union of Liberation accepted his call for cooperation. Gapon agreed to present the platform of the Zemstvo Congress and provide the Union of Liberation's literature to his members. When Gapon led his members to present these petitions to the government at the Winter Palace, the government's reactionary firing on the protesters came to be known as Bloody Sunday and was the beginning of the Russian Revolution of 1905.

As a result of the 1905 revolution, the labor unions received official sanction and were able to form, although the government still had to approve them officially. From 1905 through the October Revolution of 1917, trade unions continued to exist but did not have the politically crucial role that they did in the 1905 revolution. Labor unions and the soviets were different. Although the soviets focused on workers' concerns, they were political organizations formed to advocate for socialists objectives.

When the Bolsheviks came to power, one of their earliest pieces of legislation outlawed labor unions. Bolshevik leaders argued that since the workers controlled the state and the state controlled the economy, the workers and their employers were one and the same. Under the socialist regime, Bolshevik leaders rationalized, the workers had no need for separate groups to advocate for their needs, as the state, which was made up of workers, always knew what was best for workers and worked to provide it. Similarly, if workers did strike against the government, they were only harming themselves, since workers, in theory, owned the government and controlled the industry that the striking workers claimed harmed them.

Labor unions in imperial Russia began as a way for the Russian police to observe the actions of workers and ensure that they did not foment political unrest. Although Father Gapon began his labor union purely as a religious organization, he soon expanded the group's focus to push for political reforms. His union's actions and the government reactions to them began the 1905 revolution that laid the foundation for the 1917 revolutions. Once the Bolsheviks came to power, they outlawed labor unions in order to prevent similar problems that the tsarist regime had faced, with its officially sanctioned police unions.

Gates M. Brown

Further Reading

Marot, John Eric. *The October Revolution in Prospect and Retrospect: Interventions in Russian and Soviet History.* Boston: Brill, 2012.

Pipes, Richard. *A Concise History of the Russian Revolution.* New York: Knopf, 1996.

Pipes, Richard. *The Russian Revolution.* New York: Knopf, 1990.

Lenin, Vladimir (1870–1924)

Russian revolutionary and political leader, author of the political doctrine known as Bolshevism, and founder of the Bolshevik faction of the Russian Social Democratic Labor Party (RSDLP) that seized control of Russia via the November 1917 revolution. Born in Simbirsk, Russia, on April 22, 1870, Vladimir Ilyich Ulyanov, who later changed his name to Vladimir Lenin, was the third of six children. The pseudonym "Nikolai Lenin" he also used probably came from his paternal grandfather's first name and the Lena River of Siberia where he was later exiled for revolutionary activity. His paternal grandfather probably rose from the peasantry to lower-middle-class town dweller. His maternal grandfather, a physician of either German or Jewish descent, practiced medicine in St. Petersburg and became a serf-owning member of the landed nobility, a fact often suppressed in official Soviet histories. A year after Lenin's birth, his father was appointed inspector of public schools for the Simbirsk District.

The Ulyanovs encouraged discipline, hard work, and diligence in school; all of their children were excellent students, including Vladimir, who was an energetic and active youth. As a young man he had no interest in politics or economics, instead favoring Russian literature, Latin, Greek, history, and geography. Lenin started down the revolutionary path only after his older brother Alexander, a member of the terrorist wing of the revolutionary populist movement Narodnaia Volia (People's Will), was executed in 1887 for participating in a plot to assassinate Tsar Alexander III.

Lenin idolized his older brother and, attempting to comprehend his motivations, abandoned the works of Russian novelist Ivan Turgenev for those of Nikolai Chernyshevsky, the leading radical Russian publicist of his time. Lenin also read Karl Marx's *Das Kapital* for the first time in 1889. By then Lenin had been expelled from Kazan University, arrested, and exiled for participation in

Vladimir Ilyich Lenin led the Bolshevik Revolution of 1917 and oversaw the establishment of the Soviet state, which remained an active world power until its demise in 1991. (Library of Congress)

radical organizations and in a student demonstration. In 1891, he was permitted to take the law exam at St. Petersburg University as an external student; he passed the exam, earning his law degree with honors, and was admitted to the bar.

Steeped in the Jacobin traditions of the Narodnaia Volia movement, in 1892 Lenin began to seriously contemplate Marxism and the feasibility of social democracy in Russia. Introduced to the writings of Georgi Plekhanov, considered the father of Russian Marxism, Lenin made his final separation from populism. He absorbed all he could from Plekhanov's writings and applied to go abroad, telling the authorities this was for health reasons to study with the master (who was in exile in Switzerland), but his request was denied.

In 1893, Lenin moved to St. Petersburg and immersed himself in the debate between the two rival varieties of socialism, Marxism and populism, through involvement in workingmen's literacy groups and Marxist study circles. He entered the debate on the correct path for Russia to enter socialist society by writing handprinted pamphlets and leaflets and circulating them among workers and by writing reviews of other Marxists' writings. This intellectual activity helped him forge his own concept of socialism in Russia and gained him local attention as a gifted Marxist theoretician.

After a severe bout with pneumonia in 1895, Lenin received permission to travel abroad for his health. He spent four months during the spring and summer in Western Europe traveling to Germany, France, and Switzerland. Lenin learned much about German social democracy and read a great deal of its literature. In Switzerland, he met and conversed with exiled Russian Marxists, including Plekhanov, and leaders of the Group for the Emancipation of Labor. Returning to Russia, Lenin visited Moscow, Vilnius, and other towns, making contacts for the exiled group and establishing the organization Petersburg League of Struggle for the Emancipation of the Working Class. He even arranged to publish an underground newspaper, the *Workers' Cause.*

Ready to go to press in December, the paper died at birth, seized by the police who arrested Lenin along with nearly all of his contacts in the newfound Petersburg League. Lenin was sent to prison for a year and then into Siberian exile for three more years, where the state allowed his continued scholarly pursuits. He wrote and published a major theoretical work, *The Development of Capitalism in Russia,* during that time.

In exile, Lenin began developing his theory that the proletariat would not achieve revolutionary consciousness naturally, as Marx had believed. Lenin concluded that workers, particularly Russians, would not go beyond unionizing but would require a core of dedicated revolutionary intellectuals to guide them to socialism. For Lenin, the model social democratic party was the German Social Democrats of the 1890s, rigidly disciplined and centrally hierarchical. In 1900 he began working to unify Russian social democracy under one banner, waging a war of words against those who sought to moderate the movement. In doing so, in 1902 he published his most famous political treatise, *Chto Delat?* (What Is to Be Done?), which not only served as a critique of evolutionary socialism but also provided the blueprint for the party organization that would provide the political structure of Soviet Russia.

When words failed to unite the party under his direction, in 1903 at the RSDLP's Second Congress, Lenin split the party into two factions. Having managed to get his followers elected as the majority of the party's Central Committee, he took the title "Bolshevik" (meaning "majority"). In reality, the Mensheviks (minority) had the majority of followers, but Lenin had controlled the voting.

Lenin spent the years between 1903 and 1917 as an émigré in Western Europe and patiently built up a Bolshevik following in Russia. Ever the pragmatist, he briefly returned to Russia after the Russian Revolution of 1905 to find Bolsheviks unprepared, but even he failed to develop a coherent program to take advantage of the revolutionary ferment. It was the Menshevik faction that made the running, with Leon Trotsky as its most prominent representative. Over the next 12 years, he focused on preventing the reunification of the RSDLP and preparing for a revolution that he never expected to see.

Living abroad in Switzerland, Lenin was again surprised in March 1917 when spontaneous strikes over food and rising inflation touched off revolution in Russia. Growing apprehensive over his ability to influence events, he gained German approval to transit Germany, Sweden, and Finland to Russia, arriving on April 16, 1917. In two speeches later known as the April Theses, he rejected cooperation with the Provisional Government, urged an end to the "predatory war," and surprised his own followers by calling for "all power to the soviets," which had been the Mensheviks' rallying cry in 1905. At the same time, however, the Bolsheviks benefitted from considerable sums of money secretly dispensed by the German government to foment revolution in Russia and bring an end to the war.

After a failed Bolshevik coup attempt in July 1917 (the July Days), Lenin went into hiding in Finland from where he tried to direct Bolshevik affairs, urging the Central Committee to act. When the growing disintegration of the empire under the increasingly feeble Provisional Government reached a critical point, the Bolsheviks, practically prepared by Lenin's surprising new collaborator Leon Trotsky, simply occupied the most strategic points in the capital and seized power on November 7, 1917. Lenin had only returned to Russia the night before. His role in the revolutionary takeover was to order it.

Once in power, Lenin promised peace to the war weary, land to the peasants, and control of production to workers. Initially, the Bolsheviks refused to negotiate with Germany for an end to the war, following Trotsky's slogan of "no peace, no war," but Russian soldiers voted against the war by abandoning their positions when facing German advances. In March 1918, Commissar for Foreign Affairs Trotsky negotiated the Treaty of Brest-Litovsk, which deprived the Bolsheviks of vast stretches of land and populations, including some of the most fertile regions of the former empire.

Lenin's regime survived the tumult of revolution in the midst of war, war communism, a civil war during 1918–1922, and foreign intervention through little more than his personal stature and reliance on the Bolshevik Party. As chairman of the Council of People's Commissars, he eclipsed all other Bolshevik leaders except perhaps Trotsky. And in fulfillment of Trotsky's earlier prophesy, Lenin stated that "the organization of the party [took] the place of the party itself; the central committee [took] the place of the party organization; and finally the dictator [took] the place of the central committee." Economic chaos forced Lenin to order a retreat from pure communism (war communism) in his 1921 New Economic Policy, although he also initiated all the instruments of Bolshevik (Red) terror and had a hand in ordering the execution of former tsar Nicholas II and his family. Lenin kept control of the new Soviet state until a series of debilitating strokes in 1922, and an incapacitating stroke in 1923 wrested it from his grasp. He died in Moscow on January 21, 1924.

Arthur T. Frame

Further Reading

Service, Robert. *Lenin: A Biography.* New York: Macmillan, 2000.

Volkogonov, Dmitri. *Lenin: A New Biography.* Translated by Harold Shukman. New York: Free Press, 1994.

White, James D. *Lenin: The Practice and Theory of Revolution.* New York: Palgrave, 2001.

Litvinov, Maxim Maximovich (1876–1951)

Soviet foreign minister and diplomat. Maxim Maximovich Litvinov was born Meer Genokh

Moisevich Vallakh on July 17, 1876, in Bialystok in the Jewish Pale of Settlement in what is now Poland. Litvinov joined the Russian Army in 1893 and was there exposed to Marxism. In 1898 he refused to fire on strikers at a factory in Baku, and while this insubordination was covered up, he was soon dismissed for other violations of army regulations. That same year, Litvinov joined the Russian Social Democratic Party. He eventually settled in Kiev, where he managed a sugar factory by day and worked for the underground Social Democratic Party at night. Arrested in 1901, he was sentenced to two years in prison but escaped and fled to Berlin and then to Britain. In 1903 when the Social Democratic Party split into the Mensheviks and Bolsheviks, Litvinov sided with the Bolsheviks and worked to promote revolution in Russia.

In November 1917 the Bolsheviks seized power in Russia, and Litvinov, who had been living in Britain for a decade, became the Russian diplomatic representative in London. Expelled from Britain in 1919, he returned to Russia and began working in the Commissariat for Foreign Affairs. During the Russian Civil War, Litvinov was the Russian government's only official diplomat. He became commissar for foreign affairs in July 1930, and in February 1932 he led the Russian delegation to the World Disarmament Conference in Geneva, where he proposed general and complete disarmament.

When Adolf Hitler came to power in Germany in 1933, Litvinov championed ties with Western Europe and collective security. Diplomatic relations were also established with the United States in November 1933. In 1935, Litvinov signed mutual assistance pacts with both France and Czechoslovakia directed against Germany.

Following the appeasement of Germany over Czechoslovakia by Britain and France at the September 1938 Munich Conference,

Joseph Stalin began to reverse Russian foreign policy in an effort to secure time to rearm. Litvinov was dropped as foreign minister in May 1939, replaced by hard-liner Vyacheslav Molotov. Hitler said that this step of dropping an internationalist and a Jew helped convince him that Stalin was serious about a rapprochement. On August 23 in Moscow, the Soviet Union and Germany concluded a nonaggression pact that also secretly partitioned much of Eastern Europe between them.

Following the German invasion of the Soviet Union in Operation BARBAROSSA on June 22, 1941, Stalin appointed Litvinov Soviet ambassador to the United States. Litvinov held this post from November 1941 to August 1943 and greatly assisted in the inclusion of the Soviet Union in Lend-Lease assistance.

Litvinov then returned to the Soviet Union to serve as deputy commissar for foreign affairs until he retired in August 1946. He died in Moscow on December 31, 1951.

Spencer C. Tucker

Further Reading

Bishop, Donald G. *The Roosevelt-Litvinov Agreements: The American View.* Syracuse, NY: Syracuse University Press, 1965.

Browder, Robert P. *The Origins of Soviet-American Diplomacy.* Princeton, NJ: Princeton University Press, 1953.

Phillips, Hugh D. *Between the Revolution and the West: A Political Biography of Maxim M. Litvinov.* Boulder, CO: Westview, 1992.

Lloyd George, David (1863–1945)

British Liberal Party leader and prime minister (1916–1922). Born on January 17, 1863, in Manchester, England, to Welsh parents, David Lloyd George grew up in Wales, where the family moved a year after his birth following the death of his father. Lloyd George began training and apprenticing as a lawyer with the Beese, Jones and Casson firm in Portmadoc and was admitted to the bar in 1884. Six years later he entered politics and was elected to the House of Commons as a member of the Liberal Party. Lloyd George became a member of the party's radical wing, and he made his reputation as an articulate opponent of the Second Boer War (1899–1902) and as a strong advocate of progressive social reform.

A brilliant politician and gifted orator, Lloyd George rose quickly within the ranks of the Liberal Party. From 1905 to 1908, he served as president of the Board of Trade under the government of Sir Henry Campbell-Bannerman. In 1908 Lloyd George was appointed chancellor of the exchequer, a position he held until 1915. In this post, he promoted a progressive reform agenda. In 1909 he submitted the People's Budget, whereby he sought to balance the budget, pay for extensive naval construction, and carry out radical social reform through sharp increases in taxes on land and a supertax on incomes above £3,000. The political struggle unleashed by the People's Budget resulted in the Parliament Act (1911) limiting the power of the House of Lords, which had attempted to block its passage.

In the July Crisis of 1914 that followed the assassination of Archduke Franz Ferdinand of Austria, Lloyd George hoped that Britain could stay out of a continental war, but he became an advocate of intervention following the German invasion of Belgium in August. From the beginning, Lloyd George realized that the war would demand a determined effort on Britain's part. Prime Minister Herbert Asquith (1908–1916) initially took a business as-usual approach to the war effort, which Lloyd George strongly criticized.

To deal with the crisis occasioned by a shortage of munitions, in May 1915 Asquith appointed Lloyd George minister of munitions. In that post Lloyd George oversaw the reorganization of Britain's war effort to meet the demands of total war. In June 1916, Lloyd George became minister of war. Increasingly dismayed by Britain's conduct of the war, he helped to bring down the Asquith government in December 1916 and bring about his own appointment as prime minister.

As prime minister, Lloyd George sought to bring the same energy and dynamism to Britain's larger war effort that he had brought to the country's war economy. He created a five-member War Cabinet to oversee the effort. Central to Lloyd George's efforts was Britain's military strategy in the war. Appalled by the horrifying losses on the Western Front, he advocated a peripheral strategy directed against Germany's allies, especially the Ottoman Empire. Such an indirect strategy, Lloyd George argued, would "knock out the props from under Germany." This strategic preference brought him into conflict with Britain's military leadership, including Field Marshal Sir Douglas Haig, commander of the British Expeditionary Force in France, and General Sir William Robertson, chief of the Imperial General Staff.

No sooner had Lloyd George assumed the premiership than he was confronted with a series of major strategic developments: Germany's resumption of unrestricted submarine warfare on February 1, 1917; revolution in Russia in March 1917; the entrance of the United States into the war on April 6, 1917; and widespread mutinies in the French Army in May and June 1917. In response to Germany's resumption of unrestricted submarine warfare, Lloyd George, supported by U.S. authorities, forced a reluctant Admiralty leadership to adopt the convoy system, thereby helping to defeat the U-boat menace.

The overall strategic situation in early 1917, coupled with the desire not to repeat the bloodletting of 1916, led Lloyd George to prefer a defensive stance on the Western Front and await the arrival of the American Expeditionary Force before launching further offensives in France. He argued that any offensive action should come against Austria-Hungary or the Ottoman Empire rather than on the Western Front. Despite this preference, Haig and Robertson persuaded him to support another major offensive on the Western Front in 1917. The result was the Third Battle of Ypres, also known as the Passchendaele Offensive (July 31–November 10, 1917), that cost Britain 400,000 casualties, a result that horrified Lloyd George and further strained his relations with Haig in particular.

On November 7, 1917, Lloyd George won a victory over his generals with the creation of the Supreme War Council to coordinate Allied strategy. Further successes at the expense of his generals followed. In February 1918 General Sir Henry Wilson replaced Robertson, and in the crisis of the 1918 German spring offensives, French general of division Ferdinand Foch became supreme Allied commander on April 14. Lloyd George concurred with the reinforcement of the Western Front, even taking forces from the Middle East, in the desperate struggle in the spring. The Allies held, and in July they went on the offensive. On November 11, Germany signed the armistice.

Victory in the war was followed by victory in the general election of December 1918. Fought in the immediate aftermath of Britain's triumph in the war and on a platform of "hanging the kaiser" and "making the Germans pay," the result was a decisive win for Lloyd George's government, which now turned its attention to the postwar peace.

Even before the 1919 Paris Peace Conference began, Great Britain had realized its major war aims: the defeat of Germany, the surrender of the bulk of the German battle fleet, the removal of Germany as a major colonial rival, and the defeat of Germany's bid for hegemony on the European continent.

At the peace conference, Lloyd George sought to consolidate Britain's victory by steering a course between Wilson's idealism and French premier Georges Clemenceau's demand for a punitive peace. On most major issues of the conference, however, Lloyd George stood with Wilson, outvoting Clemenceau two to one. The remaining years of Lloyd George's premiership were concerned with dealing with the legacy of World War I both at home and abroad. Among his most notable postwar achievements was the Government of Ireland Act of 1920, which ultimately paved the way for the creation of the Irish Free State in December 1921. Lloyd George resigned in October 1922.

Although he never again held public office, Lloyd George remained influential in the Liberal Party and in British politics. In 1940 he declined Prime Minister Winston Churchill's offer of a cabinet post. On New Year's Day 1945, Lloyd George was elevated to the peerage as Earl Lloyd George of Dwyfor, Viscount Gwynedd of Dyfor. He died in Ty Newydd, Wales, on March 26, 1945.

J. David Cameron

Further Reading

Adams, R. J. Q. *Arms and the Wizard: Lloyd George and the Ministry of Munitions, 1915–1916.* College Station: Texas A&M University Press, 1978.

Cassar, George H. *Lloyd George at War, 1916–1918.* London: Anthem, 2009.

Constantine, Stephen. *Lloyd George.* New York: Routledge, 1992.

French, David. *The Strategy of the Lloyd George Coalition, 1916–1918*. Oxford: Oxford University Press, 1995.

Gilbert, Bentley Brinckerhoff. *Lloyd George: A Political Life*. 2 vols. Columbus: Ohio State University Press, 1987, 1992.

Grigg, John. *From Peace to War: Lloyd George, 1912–1916*. Los Angeles: University of California Press, 1985.

Grigg, John. *Lloyd George: War Leader, 1916–1918*. New York: Penguin, 2003.

Guinn, Paul. *British Strategy and Politics, 1914 to 1918*. Oxford: Oxford University Press, 1965.

Lloyd George, David. *War Memoirs*. 6 vols. Boston: Little, Brown, 1933–1937.

Morgan, Kenneth O. *Consensus and Disunity: The Lloyd George Coalition Government, 1918–1922*. New York: Oxford University Press, 1979.

Mowat, Charles L. *Lloyd George*. London: Oxford University Press, 1964.

Rothwell, V. H. *British War Aims and Peace Diplomacy, 1914–1918*. New York: Oxford University Press, 1971.

Woodward, David R. *Lloyd George and the Generals*. London: Associated University Presses, 1983.

Lvov, Prince Georgy Yevgenievich (1861–1925)

Russian political leader and head of the Provisional Government in Russia in 1917. Born in Dresden, Saxony, on November 2, 1861, Georgy Yevgenievich returned to Russia with his family soon after his birth. The family owned large estates in Tula Province. After graduation from Moscow University in 1885, Lvov worked to make his land profitable. Drawn into politics by the ineptitude of the tsarist government, he was elected to the local zemstvo (district assembly). During the 1904–1905 Russo-Japanese War, he

was active in organizing a chapter of the Union of Zemstvos and Towns to aid sick and wounded soldiers. Lvov became a reluctant member of the Constitutional Democratic (Kadet) Party and as such was elected to the Russian Duma (parliament) in 1906 and 1907.

With the beginning of World War I, Lvov resumed his relief work, and Tsar Nicholas II authorized the creation of an All-Russian Zemstvo Union for Aid to Sick and Wounded Soldiers under Lvov's leadership. This organization proved far superior in supplying aid to the soldiers than the government's own General Headquarters Medical Division. Lvov also became a leader in the Union of Towns and in the Central War Industry Committee. In 1917, the Zemstvo Union and the Union of Towns combined into the so-called Zemgor.

Lvov was a reluctant politician, drawn by the increasing importance of the Zemstvo Union and its involvement in munitions manufacture and the provisioning of troops, at which it was more successful than the government agencies. Lvov's constant criticism of the government's war efforts was taken by progressives within the Duma to mean that he shared their political goals.

Following the abdication of Nicholas II on March 15, 1917, Lvov became both head of the Provisional Government and minister of the interior. He headed a state that now lapsed into near anarchy as the grievances of centuries broke to the surface. Revolutionary elements controlled large areas of the country, the peasants began seizing land from the nobles, workers in the cities struck for better conditions, and discipline broke down in the army.

Under pressure from the Allies and to realize Russia's war aims for which so much had already been sacrificed, the Provisional Government took the fatal step of continuing

Russia in the war. The government also deferred the tough decisions on reform, especially in land ownership. Lvov's appeal to the peasants to wait until a future constituent assembly could decide this issue fell on deaf ears.

Lvov's commitment to a defensive war without territorial annexations and indemnities saved him riots in May 1917 resulting from revelations that the government sought to acquire the Turkish Straits and other areas. Lvov accepted Foreign Minister Pavel Miliukov's resignation and reshuffled the cabinet to include Alexander Kerensky and four socialists.

Following the failure of Kerensky's great July military offensive, riots occurred in Petrograd, and on July 21, 1917, Lvov resigned, succeeded by Kerensky. Lvov had been unwilling to crack down on the shadow government of the soviet or accept socialist demands for a radical agrarian solution and a republic. Lvov remarked that "To save the situation it was necessary to dissolve the soviets and fire at the people. I could not do it. But Kerensky can."

Arrested by the Bolsheviks after their seizure of power in November, Lvov escaped and made his way to Paris, where he sat on the Russian Political Conference organized to support Admiral Alexander Kolchak during the Russian Civil War. Lvov died in Paris on March 6, 1925.

Claude R. Sasso and Spencer C. Tucker

Further Reading

Abraham, Richard. *Alexander Kerensky: The First Love of the Revolution.* New York: Columbia University Press, 1987.

Wade, Rex. *The Russian Revolution, 1917.* 2nd ed. Cambridge: Cambridge University Press, 2005.

Williams, Beryl. *Lenin.* New York: Longman, 2000.

M

Makhno, Nestor Ivanovich (1889–1935)

Ukrainian anarchist and guerrilla leader. Nestor Makhno was born to a peasant family in Ukraine on October 27, 1889. He worked as a farm laborer for most of his youth but joined an anarchist group at age 17 following the abortive Russian Revolution of 1905. He was arrested for terrorism in 1908 and sentenced to death; the sentence was later commuted, although Makhno was kept in solitary confinement for some time. He was released in the aftermath of the February Revolution.

Makhno immediately returned to Ukraine and resumed his political activities. In August 1917 he was elected as chairman of the local soviet, which busied itself with seizing the property of local landowners. Many of his ideas, rooted in the Russian anarchism of Mikhail Bakunin and Prince Pyotr Kropotkin, approached the Bolshevik political program, and Makhno occasionally coordinated with Red Army units but was not affiliated with the Bolsheviks.

When German Army forces entered Ukraine following the Treaty of Brest-Litovsk, however, Makhno first attempted to resist and fight for an independent Ukraine. His forces could not match German strength, though, and Makhno fled to Moscow, where he met Vladimir Lenin but found no support.

Returning to Ukraine, Makhno organized a guerrilla war against the German puppet regime headed by Pavel (Pavlo) Skoropadsky. Makhno's forces carried the black flag of anarchism prominently during their raids, and Makhno became something of a legend; in September 1918, he led Ukrainian guerrillas to a stunning victory over a large Habsburg occupation force at Dibrivki. When German and Austrian troops departed at the end of that year, Makhno's forces, with the aid of the Red Army, overthrew the remaining government and established an independent anarcho-communist Ukraine.

Makhno then signed an agreement with the Bolshevik regime for joint action against the regional White forces commanded by Anton Denikin. The Bolsheviks double-crossed Makhno, however, sending assassins after him and ordering troops into Ukraine to dissolve the communes he had established. Caught between Red and White forces, Makhno fought gamely through 1919 and most of 1920. The Bolsheviks briefly made a truce with Makhno when it appeared White forces might take Ukraine, but once the danger had passed, they again turned on the anarchists.

In 1921, Red Army units wiped out most of Makhno's forces. Wounded, Makhno fled into Romania, where he was immediately arrested. He soon escaped to Poland, only to be arrested again. He was eventually released and settled in Paris. Makhno continued to work for an independent Ukraine and published several anarchist tracts before his death on July 6, 1935.

Timothy C. Dowling

Further Reading

Fedyshyn, Oleg. *Germany's Drive to the East and the Ukranian Revolution, 1917–1918.*

New Brunswick, NJ: Rutgers University Press, 1971.

Hunczak, Taras, ed. *Ukraine, 1917–1921: A Study in Revolution.* Cambridge, MA: Harvard University Press, 1977.

Makhnovites

This anarchist based band of peasants fought against General Denikin's White Forces in Ukraine during the Russian Civil War. Even though they fought with tacit support of the Bolsheviks, the Makhnovites had their own agenda for Ukraine under the leadership of their commander, Nestor I. Makhno. Throughout their fight for an autonomous section of southern Ukraine, the Makhnovites had to contend with the Whites as well as the Reds, as Red leaders such as Trotsky had a deep distrust for the Makhnovites because he believed that they lacked discipline and good order and thought that their reckless adventurism was ill-focused. Only after Makhno and his army assisted in defeating the Whites and helped to secure the Bolshevik victory did Lenin and the party turn on Makhno and his army, forcing them out of the country in late 1921.

Makhno was born in Gulyay Pole in 1888 to a peasant family. Though he lost his father at a very young age (10 months old), his mother and older siblings tried to make sure that the youngest Makhno child had an education. However, by the age of 12 Makhno had quit school and began working a series of jobs as a farmhand, an apprentice painter, and an ironworker. Throughout his working life, he became interested and involved in revolutionary politics against the harsh treatment of workers and peasants by the tsar.

As a result of what he believed to be the terrorist oppression of workers by the agents of the tsar during the 1905 revolution, Makhno joined the anarchist party in 1906. For the next four years because of his anarchist affiliation, he consistently ran afoul of the tsar's government and was in and out of prison on various charges. By 1910, Makhno had been convicted in an anarchist attack that killed several people and was sentenced to death, though his sentence was commuted due to his young age. Makhno remained in prison until February 1917, when the Provisional Government announced an amnesty for political prisoners convicted at the hands of the tsar and his harsh regime.

After being released from prison, Makhno organized a peasants' union with the objective of redistributing land from large estates, much like the ones he worked on as a child, to the peasants of Ukraine. In March 1918, he traveled to Moscow and met with V. I. Lenin. Lenin assisted Makhno in getting back to the Ukraine, as the Bolsheviks had concluded the Brest-Litovsk Treaty with the Germans and Austo-Hungarians, who retained control of the Ukrainian territory.

Once back in Ukraine, Makhno worked to build an army that cut an independent path between the Whites and the Reds. Capitalizing on massive political unrest and rebellions against occupation, Makhno built a Black army by pulling together peasant bands that were satisfied neither with the Whites, the Reds, or the Germans.

By 1919 Makhno had built a sizable army that Bolsheviks consistently kept an eye on; though they were violently anti-White, they could also be anti-Bolshevik. High-level Bolshevik leaders such as Lev Kamenev met with Makhno in an attempt to solidify the Black army's support for the fight against the Whites. Makhno assured Kamenev that he was indeed a friend of the Bolsheviks by showing him a tree where he himself had just hanged a White colonel. Though Kamenev may have believed that Makhno was an ally, Leon Trotsky and other Bolshevik leaders questioned his ability to control this band of peasants. In the context of the civil war, they needed to rely on Makhno as a force to assist in defeating the Whites.

Though the record of the Makhnovite Army was spotty at best, it did assist in pushing White forces out of parts of Ukraine, which assisted the ultimate Bolshevik cause. However, with the end of the civil war, the Bolsheviks could not allow Makhno and his army to remain in what would eventually become the Soviet Union, as they were a great liability for the regime. As a result, the Bolsheviks eventually used military force to break the Black army and send its remnants out of the country. Makhno fled to Romaina, Poland, and Germany and eventually settled on Paris. He died in Paris in July 1934.

The legacy of the Makhnovites in Russian history is an interesting sidenote, especially in the context of the Russian Civil War. However, the Makhnovites also had a strong anti-Semitic stance that led to their enaction of pogroms across Ukraine. In an effort to downplay their reliance on Makhno and his Black army, the Bolsheviks and later the Soviet Union consistently highlighted this fiercely anti-Jewish tenet as a key objective of the Makhnovites as they strove for independence from the Bolshevik agenda.

Sean N. Kalic

Further Reading

Carr, E. H. *The Bolshevik Revolution, 1917–1923,* Vol 1. New York: Norton, 1985.

Malet, Michael. *Nestor Makhno in the Russian Civil War.* New York: Palgrave Macmillan, 1982.

Peters, Victor. *Nestor Makhno.* Winnipeg, Canada: Echo Books, 1971.

Marx, Karl (1818–1883)

Karl Heinrich Marx is widely recognized as the most influential philosopher of the modern age. He and his friend and associate Friedrich Engels provided the intellectual basis of modern socialism and communism. The two developed a theory of history that postulated that changes in human social and cultural structures result from the evolution of economic activity.

Marx was born on May 5, 1818, the youngest child (and only son) of a middle-class family in the Prussian city of Treves. His father was a respected lawyer and was very interested in the intellectual development of his son. Purportedly in order to further the father's career, the family converted from Judaism to Christianity and became Lutherans in 1824, when Marx was 6 years old. In 1835, Marx left Treves to study law at the University of Bonn but found that he preferred literature and philosophy. As is often the case, the 17-year-old Marx behaved irresponsibly when away from parental oversight for the first time, incurring substantial debts, brawling, and finally winding up in jail for drunkenness and disorderly behavior. While in Bonn, his one constructive act was to propose marriage to Jenny von Westphalen, although they did not marry until June 1843. She was the daughter of a family friend, Baron von Westphalen, who seems to have been fond of Marx. It was the baron who interested the young man in both politics and romantic literature.

At the beginning of Marx's second year at university, his father removed him from Bonn and sent him to the more staid University of Berlin, hoping that the change of location would improve his habits. Either the new atmosphere or the betrothal transformed the young man into a serious scholar. At Berlin, Marx studied history and philosophy and became an active member of a group known as the Young Hegelians. The group was an association of students who were influenced by Friedrich Hegel's theory of the historic dialectic, the proposition that progress is achieved through the conflict between opposing forces—thesis and antithesis—until their proponents develop a synthesis combining the best qualities of both. Hegel's notion of progress through conflict made a deep impression on Marx. The students were also committed to social action and political resistance to the disruptions and dislocations brought about by the movement to an industrialized economy.

Marx finished his formal education in 1841, earning a doctoral degree after submitting a dissertation on Greek philosophy. He became the editor of a short-lived radical newspaper, the *Rheinische Zeitung* in Cologne, where he met Friedrich Engels. When the paper was closed, Marx married Jenny and moved to Paris. Although Marx is generally associated with the founding of modern European communism, there were active groups existing in Paris before his arrival. It was in Paris that Marx became a communist, but he did not definitively form his views of history until he joined Engels in England.

Engels and Marx formed a strong working relationship in London, collaborating on such works as the *Communist Manifesto*. Marx once remarked that it was impossible for him to determine a division between Engels's thought and his own. Engels, the son of a German textile manufacturer, helped support the Marx family through the years. Engels managed a factory in Manchester, England, for a time, and in 1845 he published an exposé of working and living conditions among the British working poor titled *The Condition of the Working Class in England*. The fervor with which Marx and Engels wrote can best be understood in

the context of the social disruptions of the Industrial Revolution.

In England, Marx developed a philosophy of history based on the assertion that changes over time were the result of material factors such as modifications in the modes of production (slave labor, serfdom, manufacturing, etc.). All other cultural structures were outgrowths of the economic relationships. Changes in productive activities proceeded in a "dialectical" fashion, provoking tensions and reactions that could only be resolved through syntheses, which led to new relationships. The tensions in the classical worlds of Greece and Rome had been between master and slave, and in the medieval period tensions had been between serf and lord. In the industrialized world, tensions were between the proletariat (workers) and capitalists (factory owners, financiers, etc.). Caught up in the struggles of industrialization, Marx and Engels predicted that eventually the proletariat would organize and seize control of production, bringing about a condition of true equality and prosperity.

Class consciousness had been growing in Great Britain since the acceleration of industrialization. Organizations of workers, such as the Chartists, were becoming increasingly confrontational during the time Marx had been in London. Centuries earlier, John Locke had postulated that ownership arose through labor; Marx developed the theory further, developing the labor theory of value. He believed that the value of objects arose from the labor that was expended for their production. Profits arose from surplus value, the amount over the cost of raw materials. Those who owned the land or other natural resources that were transformed into commodities kept their profits high by paying workers less than the value their labor contributed to the end price of the merchandise. By enriching themselves at workers' expense, the industrial capitalists were creating an atmosphere of oppression and hostility that would eventually result in class warfare.

In 1848, the year that Engels and Marx published the *Communist Manifesto,* there were over 50 revolutions in Europe, including Paris, Berlin, Frankfort, three cities in Austria, and a two cities in Hungary. A petition for workers' rights, signed by nearly 2 million people, was presented to the British Parliament. None of these movements were immediately successful, but armed with the logic of the *Communist Manifesto,* over the next decades laborers were able to gradually improve their working conditions and pay rates. Marx himself lived most of his adult life in poverty. He died, intestate

and penniless, on March 13, 1883. Engels and Marx's surviving daughter sifted through his only assets—his papers—and donated them to the German Social Democrats and the Moscow communists.

Marx was an excellent critic of the evils of early industrial capitalism and remains one of the only social scientists ever to comprehensively theorize the operation and function of capital economies. Many feel that his prognostications were not accurate, however. In the second half of the 19th century, the industrial workers of Western Europe were able to win concessions for improved conditions and ultimately the right to vote within the democratic societies. When the communists did come to power, it was by a coup d'état in Russia, the least industrialized of the Great Powers.

Carolyn Neel

Further Reading

Huaco, George A. *Marx and Sociobiology.* Lanham, MD: University Press of America, 1999.

Nimtz, August H. *Marx and Engels: Their Contribution to the Democratic Breakthrough.* Albany: State University of New York Press, 2000.

Rigby, S. H. *Marxism and History: A Critical Introduction.* 2nd ed. New York: Manchester University Press, 1998.

Wheen, Francis. *Karl Marx: A Life.* New York: Norton, 2000.

Karl Marx, founder of modern communism, was a significant philosopher and political commentator in the middle of the nineteenth century. His ideas and theories provided the foundation for Vladimir Lenin and the Bolsheviks to build their revolution. (Carl Schurz, *Reminiscences of Carl Schurz,* 1907)

Mensheviks

The Mensheviks were the more moderate faction of the Russian Social Democratic Workers' Party who in 1903 split with their more radical counterparts, Vladimir Lenin's Bolsheviks, over the question of party membership and ultimately over revolutionary strategy. While both factions believed that revolution was necessary, they differed on the question of how to bring about that revolution and as such how their party should be organized.

In the period 1903–1917 the Mensheviks, despite their name meaning "minority," typically held the majority of votes over their Bolshevik (majority) counterparts. Under the leadership of Julius Martov, the Mensheviks called for a more socially inclusive party and legalistic way of toppling the tsarist regime, as opposed to the Bolshevik strategy of a relatively small corps of professional revolutionaries who would topple the regime through armed insurrection. During this period the Mensheviks gained considerable support from the Social Democrats, who would prove to be one of the linchpins of their support bases in the 1917 revolutions. This exemplified Martov's calling for a mass party modeled on the same principles as those of the West European social democratic parties.

World War I brought a split to the Menshevik Party, with most opposing the war but some favoring it for "national defense." With most of the Bolsheviks in exile at the time, the Mensheviks played a more important role in the February Revolution and the immediate aftermath in terms of organizing and leading through the Provisional Government. In March when Bolsheviks such as Lev Kamenev and Joseph Stalin began returning from exile, both sides began entertaining the view of combining their parties at a national level to lead the country toward revolution. However, when Lenin and Grigory Zinoviev returned to Russia in April and regained leadership of the Bolshevik Party, they again took the party in a much more radical direction, and any thoughts of joining parties were dropped. From March until it was overthrown in October, the Mensheviks favored supporting the Provisional Government in order to further the revolution through legal means. The Bolsheviks, on the other hand, wanted to end Russian involvement in World War I and redistribute land to the peasants and, as the Provisional Government was not moving forward on either of these counts, wanted to overthrow it through armed insurrection. With little middle ground, Bolsheviks, Mensheviks, Social Revolutionaries, and nonfactional Social Democrats were forced to take sides.

The lack of a clear party platform splintered the Menshevik Party. Many supported its ideals but opposed the war. Some, such as Leon Trotsky, joined a nonfactional Petrograd-based antiwar group that would later merge with the Bolsheviks. As a result of this splintering, in the November All-Russian Constituent Assembly the Mensheviks received less than 35 percent of the vote.

After the Bolsheviks seized power in the October Revolution, the right wing of the Menshevik Party disagreed with the system that had replaced the Provisional Government and vehemently disagreed with the Treaty of Brest-Litovsk that ended Russian involvement in World War I. With the beginning of the Russian Civil War the Menshevik Party was truly splintered, with the right wing of the party fighting for the White armies and the left wing, by now the majority, fighting for the Bolsheviks. After the Kronstadt Rebellion in 1921 and the subsequent Bolshevik suppression, Menshevism was declared illegal. Disillusioned with the direction in which the revolution was heading, many Mensheviks emigrated after this date.

Andrew McCormick

Further Reading

Brovkin, Vladimir. *The Mensheviks after October: Socialist Opposition and the Rise of the Bolshevik Dictatorship*. Ithaca, NY: Cornell University Press, 1987.

Haimson, Leopold. *The Mensheviks from the Revolution of 1917 to the Second World War.* Chicago: University of Chicago Press, 1974.

Pipes, Richard. *The Russian Revolution.* New York: Knopf, 1990.

Trotsky, Leon. *History of the Russian Revolution.* Chicago: Haymarket Books, 2008.

Mikhail Alexandrovich, Grand Duke (1878–1918)

Born at the Anichkov Palace in St. Petersburg on December 8, 1878, Mikhail (Michael) Romanov was the third son of Tsar Alexander III of Russia and Princess Dagmar (Marie Fyodorovna) of Denmark. After the death of his elder brother Georgy in 1899, Mikhail was heir to the throne and, following the birth of Nicholas II's son Alexei in 1904, a potential regent. Mikhail served in the Horse Guards and, after 1902, as squadron commander of his mother's elite Chernigov Hussars (Blue Cuirassiers). After several unsuitable romantic entanglements, Mikhail eloped with twice-divorced Nathalia Wulfert with whom he had a son, George, in 1910. Their October 1912 marriage by a Serbian Orthodox priest in Vienna enraged the imperial family. Mikhail was banished, and all of his property was put into trusteeship.

Mikhail lived in exile in rural England and Paris from 1912 until the outbreak of World War I in August 1914, when he was recalled and given command as a major general of a new division, the Caucasian Native Cavalry, composed of volunteer Muslim Caucasian horsemen, that quickly won the sobriquet "Savage Division" for its fighting on the Galician front in November 1914 and in the Carpathian Mountains during January–March 1915. In February 1916, Mikhail was given command of the II Corps in the Seventh Army, which took part in the June 1–September 4, 1916, Brusilov Offensive.

Despite Mikhail's popularity and his military experience, Tsar Nicholas II and Alexandra refused to consider naming him as regent during the February 1917 crisis, a move that might have stabilized the throne. On Nicholas II's abdication on March 2, 1917, Mikhail, then technically the tsar, issued a manifesto refusing the throne unless it was offered by a future Constituent Assembly and pledging his support to the Provisional Government. Mikhail was discharged from the army on April 5, 1917. He then lived as a private citizen, although he fell under intense suspicion because of the Savage Division's participation in the Kornilov Plot to overthrow the government.

In November 1917 as the Bolsheviks seized power, Mikhail helped smuggle Alexander Kerensky out of the country under a Danish passport obtained from his royal relatives. The Cheka (Bolshevik secret police) arrested Mikhail on March 7, 1918, and exiled him to Perm, from which he was kidnapped on orders of the Ural Soviet and murdered in the woods outside the city on June 12. His wife and family had him declared legally dead by a London court in 1924. There was no official Russian confirmation of his death until 1989.

Margaret Sankey

Further Reading

Crawford, Rosemary, and Donald Crawford. *Michael and Natasha.* New York: Scribner, 1997.

Gray, Pauline. *The Grand Duke's Woman: The Story of the Morganatic Marriage of Michael Romanoff, the Tsar Nicholas II's Brother and Nathalia Cheremerevskaya.* London: Macdonald and Jane's, 1976.

Stone, Norman. *The Eastern Front, 1914–1917.* 2nd ed. New York: Penguin, 2004.

Miliukov, Pavel Nikolaevich (1859–1943)

Russian statesman. Born on January 27, 1859, in Moscow, Pavel Miliukov was a historian by training. He taught at the University of Moscow and wrote a number of important works on Russian history, including *Studies in the History of Russian Culture*. Miliukov's political views, which were liberal democratic, led to his dismissal from the university and exile. He spent most of the next decade abroad.

Miliukov was lecturing at the University of Chicago when the Russian Revolution of 1905 occurred. Believing that the autocratic tsarist regime was about to give way to democracy, he returned to Russia. Miliukov was promptly jailed for one month, but upon his release he played a major role in founding the Constitutional Democrat (Kadet) Party. He was elected to the Third and Fourth Dumas, in which he was instrumental in forging a coalition of center-left political parties known as the Progressive Bloc.

Miliukov supported Russia's entry into the Great War despite his opposition to the government. As the war dragged on and Russian military disasters multiplied, his support turned to increasingly vehement criticism of the government's incompetence and corruption. Miliukov and other members of the Progressive Bloc called for the establishment of a government of public confidence to take control of the war effort from inept and corrupt tsarist bureaucrats such as Ivan Goremykin and Boris Stürmer. Those calls, however, were rejected by reactionary elements at court around the fanatically autocratic Tsarina Alexandra. On November 1, 1916, Miliukov voiced his mounting frustration in a pivotal speech before the Duma. This speech, in which he listed the regime's many failings and inquired rhetorically whether those shortcomings were the result of treason or stupidity, electrified the opposition and signaled the beginning of the end of the tsarist regime. Following the March 1917 revolution, Miliukov became the foreign minister of the Provisional Government. Finding himself politically to the right in the new government, he publicly reiterated Russia's continuing commitment to the war and pursuit of tsarist war aims, including the annexation of the Dardanelles. Such pronouncements not only put him at odds with the new government, which had proclaimed a policy of "peace without indemnities," but also aroused the wrath of the increasingly powerful Petrograd Soviet, which was suspicious of Miliukov's moderate politics. Nor were his politics popular with the war-weary public, and in the wake of demonstrations in Petrograd, Miliukov resigned on May 2, 1917.

Following the November 1917 revolution, Miliukov made his way to southern Russia and assisted in the formation of the anti-Bolshevik Volunteer Army. After the collapse of the White (anti-Bolshevik) effort in the Russian Civil War (1917–1922), Miliukov returned to exile. He then became a journalist and writer in France until his death in Paris on March 31, 1943.

John M. Jennings

Further Reading

Hasegawa, Tsuyoshi. *The February Revolution: Petrograd, 1917.* Seattle: University of Washington Press, 1981.

Lincoln, W. Bruce. *Passage through Armageddon: The Russians in War and Revolution, 1914–1918.* New York: Simon and Schuster, 1986.

Riha, Thomas. *A Russian European: Paul Miliukov in Russian Politics.* South Bend, IN: Notre Dame University Press, 1989.

Stockdale, Melissa Kirschke. *Paul Miliukov and the Quest for a Liberal Russia, 1880–1918.* Ithaca, NY: Cornell University Press, 1996.

Molotov, Vyacheslav (1890–1986)

Soviet foreign minister from 1939 to 1949. Born Vyacheslav Skriabin in the village of Kukarka, Viatsk Province, Russia, on March 9, 1890, Molotov attended secondary school in Kazan. He became involved in underground revolutionary activities, and in 1906 he joined Vladimir Lenin's Bolshevik faction of the Social Democratic Party. In 1909, Molotov was arrested and exiled. On completion of his sentence in 1911 he moved to St. Petersburg, where he joined the staff of the Bolshevik journal *Pravda.* While there he met Joseph Stalin, who was one of the editors. By the time of the Bolshevik Revolution in November 1917, Molotov had become one of Stalin's most loyal followers, and as Stalin's star ascended in the 1920s, so did that of Molotov.

In 1926 Molotov became a full member of the Politburo, where he led attacks on Stalin's political adversaries, such as Leon Trotsky. During the 1930s Molotov faithfully assisted Stalin in carrying out agricultural collectivization and the massive purges of the party and armed forces, for which Stalin rewarded his diligent henchman with a succession of increasingly important positions.

In May 1939, Molotov replaced the internationalist Maksim Litvinov as foreign minister. Although Molotov had no diplomatic experience, his appointment served as a signal that Stalin was seeking to reach accommodation with Nazi Germany. Accordingly, on August 23, 1939, Molotov and German foreign minister Joachim von Ribbentrop signed the German-Soviet Non-Aggression Pact in Moscow. In November 1940, Molotov went

Vyacheslav Mikhailovich Molotov joined the Bolsheviks in the aftermath of the 1905 Revolution and formed a close relationship with Joseph Stalin. Once Stalin assumed power in the wake of Vladimir Lenin's death, Molotov had a series of government positions that ultimately found him as foreign minister of the Soviet Union from 1939 to 1949 and again from 1953 to 1956. The photograph is of Molotov during his second tenure as foreign minister, ca. 1955. (Library of Congress)

to Berlin to confer with Adolf Hitler about further defining German and Soviet spheres of influence, but the negotiations failed, and Hitler decided to attack the Soviet Union.

When the German invasion commenced on June 22, 1941, it was Molotov, not Stalin, who informed the nation in a radio broadcast; Stalin apparently was incapacitated by shock. During the war, Molotov dealt extensively with the Soviets' Western allies, but by the end of the war his stubborn pursuit of Soviet goals and disagreeable demeanor made him one of the symbols of the emerging Cold War.

After World War II, Molotov went into political eclipse. He stepped down as foreign minister in 1949 and was expelled from the Communist Party in 1962 following a dispute with Nikita Khrushchev. Rehabilitated in 1984 after spending two decades in political obscurity, Molotov died in Moscow on November 8, 1986.

John M. Jennings

Further Reading

Chuev, Felix, and Albert Resis, eds. *Molotov Remembers: Inside Kremlin Politics.* Chicago: Ivan R. Dee, 1993.

Conquest, Robert. Stalin: *Breaker of Nations.* London: Weidenfeld and Nicolson, 1991.

Watson, Derek. *Molotov and Soviet Government: Sovnarkom, 1930–41.* New York: St. Martin's, 1996.

N

Narva, Battle of (1918)

First battle of the Estonian War for Independence. Although the Soviet Union won the battle, it could not prevent the spread of Estonian nationalism. Narva remained one of the key positions of the entire conflict, situated as it was on the border between the Soviet Union and the newly proclaimed nation. It was the site of several more clashes before the Soviets recognized Estonian independence in 1920.

On March 3, 1918, German and Soviet negotiators concluded the Treaty of Brest-Litovsk, ending World War I on the Eastern Front. When Germany concluded an armistice with the Western Allies on November 11, 1918, the prevailing assumption was that Germany must give up any wartime conquests. Before the Treaty of Versailles could be completed, several states took advantage of the chaos by proclaiming their independence, seeking to present a fait accompli to the negotiators in France. Although the Soviets had officially proclaimed the right of people to self-determination, they saw the burgeoning independence movements as a bourgeois attempt at counterrevolution and immediately invaded, ostensibly to guarantee the rights of workers in the newly independent areas.

On November 28, 1918, barely two weeks after the German Army had begun to evacuate Estonia, the Soviet 6th Rifle Division attacked the city of Narva. Its defenders included the 4,000 untrained and poorly armed members of the Estonian Defence League as well as a German regiment that had not completed its withdrawal. After only one day of fighting, the Soviet division assumed control over the city.

As the departure point for a full-scale invasion, Narva quickly became a key logistical position for the Red Army. Narva also attracted Estonian Bolsheviks who wished to side with the Soviet occupiers.

Foreign intervention propped up Estonian efforts to secure their independence, providing much-needed arms and advisers. On January 17, 1919, Estonian forces landed 1,000 troops near Utria, behind the Soviet front lines. This cut off the occupiers in Narva, who were forced to abandon the city. For the remainder of the war the Narva River became a fairly stable front, with the numerically superior Red Army of 120,000 troops unable to drive out the dogged 40,000 Estonian defenders. The Soviets indiscriminately shelled the city but could not recapture it. After a year of combat, the Red Army had made inching progress at a cost of 35,000 casualties, exhausting itself for little gain. On February 2, 1920, the Soviets agreed to a peace treaty and accepted Estonian independence, with the border drawn at the Narva River.

Paul J. Springer

Further Reading

Parrott, Andrew. "The Baltic States from 1914 to 1923: The First World War and the Wars of Independence." *Baltic Defence Review* 2(8) (2002): 131–158.

Taagepera, Rein. *Estonia: Return to Independence.* Boulder, CO: Westview, 1993.

Nicholas II, Tsar (1868–1918)

Last tsar of Russia. Born the son of Tsar Alexander III and Empress Marie Fyodorovna, daughter of King Christian of Denmark, on May 6, 1868, Nicholas was the eldest of three boys and two girls. He grew up in the Anichkov Palace in St. Petersburg and at Gatchina, just outside the city. Alexander's imposing personality overwhelmed young Nicholas. Yet, Nicholas became a firm believer in autocracy and the idea of divine right, which he inherited from his father.

While Nicholas proved to be proficient in languages, his training in politics was woefully deficient. Alexander, whom most people expected to have a long life, did not allow Nicholas to have any experience in the affairs of state. When Nicholas turned 21, however, Alexander appointed him to the State Council and to the Committee of Ministers, both of which were purely ceremonial but nonetheless had the potential to inform Nicholas on the social and political issues of the day. Overall, the appointments did not give Nicholas the political experience necessary for the role he was expected to fulfill.

Tsar Alexander III died on October 20, 1894, at the surprisingly young age of 49. His death suddenly elevated Nicholas from tsarevich to "Tsar of All the Russias," a post for which his father had given him little preparation. During the period of mourning Nicholas married Princess Alix, the daughter of the grand duke of Hesse-Darmstadt, on November 14, 1894. Despite her ambivalence throughout their courtship, she then converted to the Orthodox Church and was baptized with the name Alexandra Feodorovna. Throughout his reign, Nicholas was devoted to Alexandra and their children, Marie, Olga, Tatiana, Anastasia, and Alexei, who suffered from hemophilia. Nicholas's qualities as husband and father, however good, did not qualify him for the role of tsar.

Upon his accession, Nicholas declared that he would continue to uphold the principles of autocracy as his father had, which dashed hopes of political reform among Russian liberals; Nicholas discounted such hopes as "senseless dreams" in an 1895 address. The entire government served at his pleasure. There were some capable ministers, notably Sergei Witte and Pyotr Stolypin, who made solid efforts to modernize Russia's economy. The Okhrana, or secret police, enforced the policy of autocracy, which brutally suppressed any dissent. Russification was imposed on the various nationalities of

Tsar Nicholas II assumed leadership of the Russian Empire from his father Tsar Alexander III in 1894. Plagued by social and political unrest during his time in power, Nicholas was forced to abdicate the throne on March 15, 1917, and was eventually murdered along with his family by order of the Bolsheviks. (Library of Congress)

the Russian Empire, most notably the Poles and the Finns. Overall, the imperial bureaucracy was slow and inefficient in meeting the needs of its subjects both in the cities and in the fields, which sowed the seeds for revolution.

Because of his inexperience and political naïveté, Nicholas proved obtuse to the changes overtaking the world. A faction of expansionists, particularly A. M. Bezobrazov and V. M. Vonliarliarsky, induced Nicholas to support the Russo-Japanese War in 1904, with the purpose of extending Russia's influence into Asia and to rally popular support for the government. Instead, a string of humiliating defeats at the hands of the Japanese triggered a domestic crisis. Nevertheless, the majority of the Russian people still saw Nicholas as a father figure and protector and hoped that reforms might save them and Russia.

On January 9, 1905, however, that image was shattered on what has come to be known as Bloody Sunday, when about 150,000 peaceful protesters were fired upon by troops outside the Winter Palace. The massacre precipitated waves of civil unrest throughout Russia. Defeats at Mukden and in the naval Battle of Tsushima forced a reluctant Nicholas to negotiate peace in the Treaty of Portsmouth of August 1905 and limited his ability to suppress the unrest. After much resistance, he therefore issued the October Manifesto, promising for the first time in Russian history "freedom of conscience, speech, assembly, and association" and the creation of a Duma, or parliament.

Nicholas did not relish his role as a constitutional monarch, which clashed with his belief in pure autocracy. He therefore undermined the Duma's independence, since he had final approval over all decision making. He repeatedly dissolved assemblies he disagreed with and increasingly restricted the franchise. Social tensions heightened further when Stolypin, whose reforms might have stabilized Russia's peasantry, was assassinated in 1911.

Nicholas's reign unraveled with the coming of World War I. Russia's involvement was part of the spiral of events that followed the assassination of Archduke Franz Ferdinand of Austria-Hungary, and Nicholas demonstrated his characteristic indecisiveness in dealing with them. Of the major belligerents, Russia was perhaps the least prepared to fight a modern war, and the early battles exposed Russian inefficiency both at home and at the front, yet Nicholas refused to allow reforms that might have improved the condition of the military. His fatal mistake though, was taking personal command of the Russian Army in August 1915, leaving Alexandra to rule in his stead. Alexandra's German heritage and rumors of her involvement with the mystic Grigory Rasputin made her a target for criticism from all levels of society. Political and social leaders soon lost what little faith they had in the tsar, and by the winter of 1916 unrest was spreading both in the army and on the home front.

Amid the bread riots and the breakdown of social order in the March Revolution of 1917, Nicholas abdicated as tsar under pressure from his generals. He also abdicated for Alexei because doctors predicted that the tsarevich would not survive in his condition if he were to be separated from his family. Nicholas and his family became virtual prisoners of the Provisional Government and later on by the Bolsheviks. As long as they were alive, they continued to be a rallying point for anti-Bolshevik forces during the Russian Civil War. Therefore, on July 18, 1918, at Ekaterinburg, Nicholas and his family were executed by their Bolshevik captors under the command of Yakov Yurovsky.

Dino E. Buenviaje

Further Reading

King, Greg. *The Court of the Last Tsar: Pomp, Power, and Pageantry in the Reign of Nicholas II.* Hoboken, NJ: Wiley, 2006.

Lieven, Dominic. *Nicholas II: Twilight of the Empire.* New York: St. Martin's, 1993.

Warth, Robert D. *Nicholas II: The Life and Reign of Russia's Last Monarch.* Westport, CT: Praeger, 1997.

Nikolai Nikolaevich, Grand Duke (1856–1929)

Russian Army general and commander of the Russian Army during the early stages of World War I. Born in St. Petersburg on November 18, 1856, Nikolai Nikolaevich (the Younger) was a member of the Russian imperial family and received the customary Russian military education. He completed the Nikolaevsky Engineering School in 1873 and graduated from the General Staff Academy in 1886.

During the 1877–1878 Russo-Turkish War, Nikolai Nikolaevich served first as an aide to the Russian field commander, his father, Grand Duke Nikolai Nikolaevich (the Elder) and then in the Guards Cavalry. A major general by 1885, during 1895–1905 Nikolai the Younger served as the army's inspector general of cavalry.

In 1901 during the reign of his nephew, Tsar Nicholas II, Grand Duke Nikolai was promoted to general of cavalry. Four years later during the Russian Revolution of 1905, he enhanced his reputation as a political liberal by refusing to suppress unrest and pushing the tsar toward constitutional reform.

The grand duke gained a reputation as a military reformer during the period after the 1904–1905 Russo-Japanese War. He headed the Council of State Defense during 1905–1908, coordinating the operational tasks of the army and navy. In response to unjust criticism from the Duma, he resigned from the Council on State Defense in 1908 and became inspector general of cavalry and commander of the St. Petersburg Military District.

On August 2, 1914, during the Russian mobilization for war, Tsar Nicholas II appointed his uncle commander in chief of the army. This came as a surprise in military circles because of the grand duke's lack of combat experience and of the operational and administrative skills required in this post. Grand Duke Nikolai ordered a series of offensives that proved to be his primary contribution to the 1914 campaign, but he did not control daily operations. Continued military reversals, although hardly the fault of the grand duke, led Tsar Nicholas II to remove his uncle on August 21, 1915, and take command of the army himself. The grand duke then became the head of the Caucasus Military Region.

During the February 1917 revolution, Grand Duke Nikolai urged his nephew to abdicate. Nikolai then retired and moved to the Crimea. In March 1919 he went abroad, living out his final years in Italy and France. Nikolai died in Antibes, France, on January 5, 1929.

Joseph D. Montagna

Further Reading

Ferro, Marc. *Nicholas II: Last of the Tsars.* Translated by Brian Pearce. New York: Oxford University Press, 1993.

Root, G. Irving. *Battles East: A History of the Eastern Front of the First World War.* New York: PublishAmerica, 2007.

Wildman, Allan K. *The End of the Russian Imperial Army.* 2 vols. Princeton, NJ: Princeton University Press, 1980–1987.

October (November) Revolution (1917)

The second of two internal uprisings in 1917 in Russia. Led by the Bolshevik Party, this revolution (really a coup d'état) resulted in Russia's withdrawal from World War I and the transformation of the Russian government and society. It is often referred to as the October Revolution because at the time Russia followed the Julian calendar, 13 days behind the Gregorian calendar of the West, or as the Bolshevik Revolution.

Spontaneous uprisings in February 1917 led to the collapse of the imperial government and the abdication of Tsar Nicholas II. Two self-appointed governing bodies—the Provisional Government and the Petrograd Soviet—sought to fill the vacuum. On the one hand, the Provisional Government lacked the allegiance of the masses of the people, especially in the capital, because its authority theoretically derived from the Duma (legislative council), which the tsar had tried to dissolve. On the other hand, the Petrograd Soviet had limited popular support because it was elected by workers and soldiers in the capital only. It hesitated to lead, fearful of being tainted by the "bourgeois" nature of the revolution. Instead, its leaders second-guessed and undercut Provisional Government decisions. Thus, from February to October 1917 Russia had two governing bodies, one claiming formal authority without power and the other with power but no authority.

An example of the cross purposes at which the two worked was the Petrograd Soviet's Order No. 1. It removed control and discipline in the armed forces by abolishing the death penalty, establishing political commissars at every level, and directing command by committee where privates and officers had equal votes. Spurred on by the Bolshevik Party, Russia's frontline soldiers began to fraternize with the enemy, and officers' attempts to enforce discipline encountered hostile resistance.

The revolution in February 1917 led to the return of thousands of veteran revolutionaries from internal and external exile. From Switzerland via Germany and Sweden came 38 exiles, including Vladimir Lenin, leader of the Bolsheviks. Lenin arrived in Petrograd on April 3, 1917, and presented speeches over the next two days that were later printed as the April Theses. He claimed that the revolution marked the beginning of the international revolution of the proletariat, rejected cooperation with the Provisional Government, called for all power to be with the soviets (the councils that had sprung up across Russia mirroring those of the Russian Revolution of 1905), and demanded an end to what he called the "predatory" war.

One compromise between the Provisional Government and the Petrograd Soviet was continuation of the war. The Western Allied governments insisted on this as a condition of financial loans. When the Provisional Government proclaimed support for Russia's original war aims and planned a major offensive, though, the compromise fell apart. This June 19–July 7 Kerensky Offensive, named for War Minister Alexander Kerensky, collapsed in part due to war weariness

Red Guards form a defensive line in Petrograd as the Bolsheviks work to solidify power during the Russian Revolution of 1917. (Keystone/Getty Images)

and the indiscipline prompted by Order No. 1. Some units of the Petrograd garrison, fearing that they would be sent to the front, revolted and were joined by idle workers and radical sailors from the nearby Kronstadt naval base. Eventually the uprising was quelled, though with some loss of life. Because Bolsheviks had joined the uprising, believing they would be blamed for it in any case, the Provisional Government ordered Bolshevik leaders arrested, but Lenin escaped to Finland.

On July 26, a prolonged government crisis developed following the resignation of Prince Georgy Lvov over anticipated labor and agrarian policies. Kerensky succeeded him as prime minister. Kerensky's cabinet was moderately Left-oriented, with 12 of the 16 ministers divided between the Socialist Revolutionary Party, the largest political party in Russia, and the Mensheviks, an evolutionary socialist party. Kerensky tried to placate both the Left and the Right, but fearing the Bolsheviks, he ordered recently appointed commander of the armed forces General Lavr Kornilov to prepare to march on Petrograd if the Bolsheviks stirred up an insurrection.

In early September when the German Army occupied Riga and the road to Petrograd lay open, Kornilov sent a cavalry corps toward the capital, ostensibly to protect it. His action was seen as a right-wing attempt to reverse the revolution, however. Sensing the approaching danger, the Petrograd Soviet organized to protect the revolution. The Petrograd garrison and Kronstadt sailors were joined by idle workers, all strongly influenced by Bolshevik calls for peace, land, and bread, were now mobilized to barricade and protect the capital. Kerensky appealed to the Bolsheviks to assist in defending against counterrevolution, released imprisoned leaders such as Leon Trotsky, and armed the Bolsheviks' Red Guard. Meanwhile, Bolshevik-influenced railroad workers stopped Kornilov's troops short of the capital, convincing even the most trusting soldiers that they were helping to restore the hated monarchy.

The Bolsheviks, able to claim that they had saved the revolution, now gained 50 percent of the seats in the Petrograd Soviet. In September backed by leftist Social Revolutionaries, Trotsky was elected chairman of the Petrograd Soviet. He immediately withdrew that body's support from the Provisional Government. When in September the rumor circulated that the government might move the capital to Moscow to protect it from the German Army, the Petrograd Soviet claimed full control of troop deployments in and around Petrograd. On October 14, the Petrograd Soviet appointed a Military Revolutionary Committee. Ostensibly it was to defend the capital; however, its members became the General Staff of the Bolshevik Revolution.

Lenin had slipped back into Petrograd, and although many leading Bolsheviks balked at his suggestion that the time was ripe for an armed uprising, on October 17 in a secret meeting the Central Committee of the party voted narrowly in favor of an attempt to seize power. The Provisional Government remained passive, although it was vaguely aware of Bolshevik preparations. The non-Bolshevik Executive Committee of the All-Russian Congress of Soviets postponed its meeting until October 26 and ordered a halt to all demonstrations and the issuance of arms without the committee's approval.

On October 24, the Bolsheviks sent regiments under their control to occupy strategic sites around the capital. On the evening of October 25, the Provisional Government announced a state of emergency and declared the Petrograd Soviet's Military Revolutionary Committee, controlled by Trotsky, to be illegal and ordered his arrest along with other Bolshevik leaders, including Lenin. Too late, the Provisional Government, barricaded in the Winter Palace, called for loyal troops to deal with the Bolsheviks.

On the morning of October 26, revolutionary sailors on the cruiser *Avrora,* which was anchored in the Neva River, fired blank rounds from its guns, the signal for the uprising to begin. Bolshevik forces seized almost without bloodshed key buildings and facilities in the capital and on October 27 stormed the Winter Palace, arresting 13 members of the Provisional Government. Kerensky managed to escape and fled into exile.

Lenin declared victory and announced the formation of the Soviet of People's Commissars, with himself as chairman. The Soviet era had begun. Lenin immediately announced an end to Russian participation in the war. When the Germans insisted on punitive peace terms, the government balked and attempted to follow a strategy of "neither war nor peace." This proved impossible when the German Army initiated a major offensive, forcing the Bolsheviks to conclude the punitive Treaty of Brest-Litovsk on German terms in February 1918. Lenin concluded that even yielding vast amounts of territory was preferable to renewal of the war and the possibility of the Bolsheviks in turn being driven from power. The new leadership also set aside the results of national elections, planned before their seizure of power, that had gone strongly against them.

Meanwhile, civil war had erupted between the Bolsheviks and their supporters (the Reds) and conservative counterrevolutionary forces (the Whites). This ended with the Reds victorious in 1920. At great human cost, the Bolsheviks also gradually reshaped the socioeconomic structure of the country. The ensuing Union of Soviet Specialist Republics endured until December 1991.

Arthur T. Frame

Further Reading

Figes, Orlando. *A People's Tragedy: The Russian Revolution, 1891–1924.* New York: Viking Adult, 1997.

Fitzpatrick, Sheila. *The Russian Revolution.* New York: Oxford University Press, 2008.

Pipes, Richard. *The Russian Revolution.* New York: Knopf, 1990.

Service, Robert. *The Russian Revolution, 1900–1927.* 3rd ed. New York: St. Martin's, 1999.

Octobrists

The formal name of this political party started as the Union of October 17 and was headed by Alexander I. Guchkov. The name of the party embraced the October Manifesto offered by Tsar Nicholas II as a means to provide civil liberties and the creation of the Duma based on the political pressures that resulted from the Bloody Sunday events of the Russian Revolution of 1905. In effect, the October Manifesto started the transformation of the autocratic Russian government into a constitutional monarchy, and the political party that formed in the subsequent creation of the First Duma embraced the tenets of these fundamental changes by incorporating the name of the manifesto into their organizational title.

In contrast to the Kadets, the Social Democrats, or even the Social Revolutionaries, the Octobrists could be considered to the right of these parties. Composed of a loose affiliation of people who held commercial and industrial interests in Moscow and the larger provinces, the party welcomed the government's attempt to work toward the recognition of civil rights and equality before the law but strove to maintain an allegiance to the monarchy. The Octobrists believed the tsar to be the center of national power and political authority, and hence they tended to reject the call for a constituent assembly. This set their political agenda in direct contrast to those of the Social Democrats and Social Revolutionaries as well as the more moderate Kadets.

The main planks in the platform of the Octobrsists focused on the right of workers to form unions as well as the right to strike over economic concerns. They did not embrace the concept of using labor strikes as a political tool to force the hand of the government. Hence, again the Octobrists' stance on political action pushed them away from the Social Revolutionaries and Social Democrats, who firmly saw labor strikes as political weapons to compel Tsar Nicholas II and his ministers to liberalize the government.

Radiating from this conceptual rift over the political right to use labor strikes as a political weapon, the Octobrists further embraced their support of the tsar by accepting his use of harsh and repressive measures against revolutionaries. Though the Octobrists recognized the need for the Russian government to provide better assistance to the peasants through economic adjustments, they rejected the revolutionary Left's call for the radical redistribution of private land. Instead, the Octobrists recognized that in "cases of state significance," they would grudgingly support the limited and very controlled redistribution of private land.

Moving from domestic issues, the Octobrists focused on maintaining a strong sense of nationalism in the context of the early 20th century. They opposed schemes that called for Poland to receive political autonomy as well as most agendas that sought to decentralize the powers of the monarchy and its bureaucracy, especially as applied to the Russian Empire. Oddly enough, the party and Guchkov specifically believed that Finland could retain its autonomy so long as it stayed within the empire.

A final unique element of the Octobrists that demonstrated their adherence to maintaining the status and prestige of the Russian Empire focused on rights for Jews within the empire. The members of the party, though largely anti-Semitic, favored reducing religious and educational restrictions on Jews because they believed that these actions could generate a more favorable view of Russia by the rest of the world.

Based on these tenets, the Octobrists firmly believed that they held the key to assisting in the slow transformation of the monarchy and its government. However, in the context of the period 1905–1907, they greatly underestimated the support for the Kadets, the Social Revolutionaries, and the Social Democrats. As such, the Octobrists failed to evolve into a major political party that was in a position to shape and form the new government. In the first two Dumas, between 1906 and 1907 the Octobrists struggled to solidify right-wing and moderate support. During the Third and Fourth Dumas the party had better success, as the tsar had adjusted election laws, which favored the more conservative parties. Hence, in the Third Duma the Octobrists had about 33 percent of the seats, of which they controlled 150 seats of the 160 allocated to parties on the Right. As Russia became further embroiled in World War I and inched closer to revolution, the Octobrist percentage of seats fell to 29 percent in the Fourth Duma.

The significance of the Octobrist Party is difficult to assess in the context of the revolutions of 1905 and ultimately 1917. However, historian Abraham Ascher in *The Revolution of 1905: Russia in Disarray* maintains that "by creating their own party they weakened Russian liberalism; and by strongly backing the manifesto they accorded a measure of legitimacy to the new regime."

Sean N. Kalic

Further Reading

Ascher, Abraham. *The Revolution of 1905: Russia in Disarray.* Palo Alto, CA: Stanford University Press, 1988.

Geifman, Anna. *Russia under the Last Tsar: Opposition and Subversion, 1894–1917.* Oxford, UK: Wiley-Blackwell, 1999.

Lockwood, David. *Cronies or Capitalists? The Russian Bourgeoisie and the Bourgeois Revolution from 1850 to 1917.* Cambridge: Cambridge Scholarly Publishing, 2009.

McCauley, Martin. *Octobrist to Bolshevik: Imperial Russia, 1905–1917.* London: Edward Arnold, 1984.

Pinchuk, Ben-Cion. *Octobrists in the Third Duma, 1907–12.* Seattle: University of Washington Press, 1974.

Rawson, Donald C. *Russian Rights and the Revolution of 1905.* Cambridge: Cambridge University Press, 1995.

Order No. I (March I, 1917)

March 1917 saw upheavals in Petrograd, the disintegration of tsarist authority, and the rise of the Provisional Committee of the State Duma (the Provisional Government). Fearing that the soldiers would become an unruly mob and turn against them, Executive Committee member Nikolai D. Sokolov was given the task of writing Order No. 1. Soldiers looked over his shoulder, offering suggestions as he wrote. The units were ordered to return to their barracks and obey their officers so long as they did not conflict with the Petrograd Soviet decrees.

Issued on March 1, 1917, and read to all units, including the Russian forces serving in France, the order stated that in "all companies, battalions, regiments, batteries, squadrons and separate services of various military departments and on board naval ships, committees shall be immediately elected from among the enlisted ranks." If representatives were not elected, the Petrograd Soviet would choose them; all representatives were to report to the State Duma on March 2, 1917.

Order No. 1 further stated that only the orders issued by the Military Commission of the State Duma should be carried out except when in conflict with decrees issued by the Soviet of Workers' and Soldiers' Deputies. All weapons were to be under control of the company and battalion committees, and they were under no circumstances to be issued to any officers. The order called for all soldiers to adhere to strict military discipline while on duty but to have the full rights granted to citizens otherwise. No longer would soldiers be obligated to stand at attention or salute when off duty. All officers, moreover, were now to be addressed as "Mr." instead of "Your Excellency" or "Your Honor." Any rudeness to the ranks was forbidden, and all violations were to be reported to the appropriate committees for action.

The result was a complete breakdown of discipline and numerous excesses committed against the officer corps. In an attempt to restore the situation, the government issued Order No. 2 on March 14, but the soldiers could not be brought back under the officers' authority and control. On March 15, 1917, Tsar Nicholas II abdicated. Two days later he issued a written appeal to the troops, noting that all authority had passed to the Provisional Government. He stressed the need for discipline and the fulfillment of duty as ordered by the new government and as necessary for the defeat of the German foe. For the soldiers, however, gaining land and peace was their major concern. Nicholas's plea went largely unheard, and over the next six months the Russian Army disintegrated.

Raymond D. Limbach

Further Reading

Cockfield, Jamie H. *With Snow on Their Boots: The Tragic Odyssey of the Russian Expeditionary Force in France during World War I.* New York: St. Martin's, 1998.

Erickson, John. *The Soviet High Command: A Military-Political History, 1918–1941.* 3rd ed. London: Frank Cass, 2001.

Golder, Frank Alfred. *Documents of Russian History, 1914–1917.* New York: Century, 1927.

Orel-Kursk, Battle of

The Battle of Orel-Kursk was the culmination of the Armed Forces of South Russia (AFSR) attack through the provinces of Orel and Kursk with the intention of capturing Moscow. The AFSR was a faction of the White Army and was led by General Anton Denikin. This force was proficient in fighting capability but faced a Red Army that was superior in number. The offensive was initially successful but lost momentum and stalled after the capture of the city of Orel. Once the offensive ceased to move, the numerically superior Red Army forces in the region were able to isolate the AFSR and force it to retreat, ending its push to Moscow. This Battle of Orel-Kursk and the victory of the Red Army forces over the AFSR ended the last significant military threat to Moscow.

The provinces of Orel and Kursk saw severe unrest in the immediate aftermath of the

Bolshevik Revolution. The provincial governments were unresponsive to local concerns and were inefficient in governing the provinces. The people suffered under grain and horse requisitions that came as a result of the communization of peasants. However, the most important reason for the unrest was the nature of communist rule in the provinces, which was cruel and capricious.

The communist government in Orel and Kursk Provinces alienated the peasants by demanding unreasonable grain tribute payments. This was largely because of the lack of rigor in the estimates by Bolsheviks leaders of the agricultural production capacity of the provinces. The people struggled under the requisition program, but they had no way to seek redress through the Bolshevik Party. As a result, the peasants began to revolt, and many deserted from the Red Army in the region and joined the Greens. The Greens were never a formidable military power, but the fact that the people in Orel and Kursk Provinces left the Red Army to join a resistance movement was indicative of the level of frustration and anger that Bolshevik policies generated in the region.

The White Volunteer Army was able to capitalize on the unrest in the southwestern region by launching an offensive. General Anton Denikin launched his offensive that targeted Moscow in the summer of 1919. His forces made progress and captured the city of Orel, which is about 200 miles from Moscow. Although initially successful, Denikin's forces in Orel were stretched too thin to adequately protect their supply lines, and the Red Army in coordination with anarchist forces of the Black Army forced the Whites to retreat and abandon the city and the push to Moscow. The Red Army's victory in pushing the White Army out of the city of Orel specifically and stopping the push to Moscow in general was the end of the military threat from the White Army in southwestern Russia.

Denikin's forces began the offensive that would lead to the capture of Orel in what is now eastern Ukraine. The AFSR captured the Donbas, Kharkov, and Tsaritsyn regions and moved to the northeast. On July 3, 1919, Denikin issued a directive announcing his intention to attack Moscow and enter the Soviet capital. The center of the AFSR was the main effort, and this axis of advance led through the provinces of Kursk and Orel. The AFSR made significant progress in advancing toward Moscow through the fall of 1919.

As the AFSR moved into Kursk Province, the Red Army forces were unable to mount an effective defense and retreated. The failures of Bolshevik governance in the region and the seeming inability of the Red Army to defend itself caused many Red Army units to desert and join the AFSR. As Denikin's forces moved into Orel, the situation for the Red Army continued to deteriorate.

Although successful in attacking, Denikin's forces did not have the luxury of consolidating their gains. They had to continue to move in order to maintain the momentum of the attack and also maintain support from external sources such as the United States. The inability to pause the offensive in order to consolidate its position contributed to the problem of securing the lines of communication, which was difficult given the limited number of troops available to the White forces in the region.

Gates M. Brown

Further Reading

Mawdsley, Evan. *The Russian Civil War.* Winchester, MA: Allen and Unwin, 1987.

P

Peasant Land Bank

The Peasant Land Bank began with an effort in 1882 to help Russian peasants purchase land and relieve some of the economic hardship of the peasantry. After the Russian Revolution of 1905, the Peasant Land Bank was part of the Stolypin reforms that aimed to create more economically prosperous peasants who, Prime Minister Pytor Stolypin, thought would be more loyal to the regime. The land bank acted as a lender to provide capital for peasants to purchase their own lands for agriculture production. As the agriculture section evolved after 1905 to focus more on privately held land and less on communal farms, private ownership allowed some peasants to become relatively successful economically. Soviet propaganda claimed that the Peasant Land Bank put inflationary pressure on land prices; however, this was not true. There were small increases in land prices from the end of the 19th century to the early 20th century but not a radical or devastating amount of inflation.

Creating individually owned farms was only part of the focus of the land bank. In addition to fostering private ownership of farmland, another intent was to disperse farmers into homesteads. As a condition of purchase, the peasants had to agree to build on their land. This had to consist of at least a home and an outbuilding for farming. However, there was little ability to enforce this measure of the mortgage, and the land bank program had little ability to force peasants to move from the village and live on their own property. Due to peasant resistance, there were changes to allow for group ownership of lands. Most of the farms financed by the Peasant Land Bank from 1909 through 1915 were for single-owner farms. However, 44 percent of the farms financed were for corporations formed of villagers.

In addition to fostering ownership of individual farms, the Peasant Land Bank also acted as an educational institution for peasants to learn innovative farming techniques to help increase their yields. By 1909 there were almost 2,000 instruction centers, and over 250,000 peasants received instruction from the land bank. These efforts were part of the program to increase the economic output of Russian farms and help create more economically sufficient farms. Soviet critics of the Peasant Land Bank protested that it impoverished peasants and intended to destroy the commune and also make peasant communities more bourgeois.

Gates M. Brown

Further Reading

Pallot, Judith. 1984. "Khutora and Otruba in Stolypin's Program of Farm Individualization." *Slavic Review* 43(2): 242–256.

Pipes, Richard. *The Russian Revolution.* New York: Vintage, 1990.

Petrograd Mutiny

The Petrograd Mutiny of February 1917 came after the imperial Russian forces stationed in Petrograd received orders to use force to put down protesters and strikers demonstrating in the city against the tsar's government and demanding reform. The initial protests began in commemoration of the Bloody Sunday protests led by Father George Gapon in January 1905. The demonstrations initially involved approximately 150,000 people but swelled as the protests gathered steam, and by the end of January 1917 the reactionaries were demanding the abdication of the tsar and a new Provisional Government.

In February 1917 the Russian military forces stationed in the city received orders to quell the demonstrations. This order backfired, as many of the soldiers sympathized with the civilian protesters, and when faced with the decision to support the protesters or use force to disperse them, many soldiers chose to desert the military and join the protests. The mutiny showed the weakness of the tsar's government and led to his abdication in March 1917.

By the beginning of 1917, the situation in Russia was deteriorating. There was a continuation of problems from 1916 such as the war front, and the economic situation in Russia was causing deprivation and unrest. On the anniversary of Bloody Sunday in 1917 and the strikes led by Father Gapon in January 1905, there were strikes in other cities, but it was the actions in Petrograd that would be the most detrimental to the tsar's government.

Petrograd was the capital of imperial Russia. The Duma, a group of elected and appointed representatives who proposed legislation to the tsar, met in Petrograd. Also, the Winter Palace, the official residence of the royal family, was in Petrograd. In addition to the political importance of the city, there was a large garrison in the town. This garrison contained new recruits who were preparing to leave for the front lines.

Mutinous soldiers parade through the streets of Petrograd in February 1917, as they join forces with protesters. Their sign reads, "Liberty, Equality, and Fraternity." Within a month these forces would force the tsar to abdicate. (Pictorial Press Ltd./Alamy Stock Photo)

In February 1917 after three years of war and numerous military defeats, Petrograd was a hotbed of revolutionaries. The soldiers stationed in the city were also critical of the government; they were new to the service and provided a fertile ground for indoctrination by political revolutionaries in the city. The soldiers also were vulnerable because they faced the impending dangers of life at the front. Although the city was an important seat of power, the tsar was in the city at the time. Tsar Nicholas II was personally commanding the Russian military, which he took over from his uncle, Grand Duke Nikolai, in 1915 after a series of military defeats sowed doubt about Russia's chances for success. However, the tsar did not have great success on the battlefield, and his absence left his wife, Tsarina Alexandra, in charge of running the government on a daily basis and providing reports to Nicholas II. Russians did not approve of the tsarina, and many believed that he was a German spy due to her German heritage. Her style of ruling only inflamed any suspicions that the people had. She frequently changed prime ministers and was not any more effective as a political leader than her husband.

When the strikes began, the protestors demanded a Provisional Government that would represent their interests. On International Women's Day, March 8 (February 23), a new wave of protesters joined the strikers. These new uprisings were mainly women who disagreed with the flour and bread rationing instituted by the Russian government as a result of economic problems brought on by the war. By now the protests grew to approximately 200,000 people in Petrograd. When the tsar ordered the military to suppress the demonstrations with force, many of the soldiers refused to do so.

As the soldiers flocked to join the protests, they further weakened the ability of the tsar's government to restore order and gave more legitimacy to the protesters. Due to the tsar's inability to countenance any political compromise that would introduce representative government or erode his power as the autocratic tsar, he alienated those who could best help him: the nobility, the professional class, and the military. Once the mutiny in Petrograd began, there were no other forces for the tsar to use to restore order. The mutinous soldiers gave the newly launched revolution the power to seize government buildings, capture arsenals to arm the protestors, and form a paramilitary force that could stand against the Russian military forces that the tsar ordered to deploy to Petrograd to impose order and oust the rebels.

By 1917, the Russian Army was a shell of what it was in 1914. Casualties depleted the regular officer corps, and by 1917 there were few regular officers on the active rolls. Many of the officers were wartime recruits and were ill-trained. They also did not have the same level of loyalty to the regime that the regular army officers did. Enlisted soldiers had little trust in their officers, who did not have the training or education in warfare to lead soldiers effectively. This collapse of confidence also influenced the soldiers' opinion of the government that they fought for. Thus, by 1917 the force that Nicholas II would need the most to help defend his hold on power was at its lowest point in terms of loyalty to the regime as well as its ability as a fighting force.

The tsar ordered General Khabalov to take command and fight the protesters. However, he was outnumbered by the armed resistance and could not effectively mount a defense. The loyal soldiers eventually retreated to the Admiralty building in the capital for protection. The Duma leader, Mikhail Rodzianko, asked for Nicholas to take action to restore order. However, the tsar did not give much credence to Rodzianko's report; Nicholas II preferred to believe his wife's estimate of the situation. The tsarina wrote to the tsar that the Duma was overreacting and that the protests were not that bad and there was no reason to overreact. This interpretation gave a false sense of security to Nicholas II while his rule was collapsing in the capital.

By the time Nicholas II understood the severity of the situation, it was too late. On March 15, 1917, Nicholas received two emissaries from the army pleading with him to abdicate because of the turmoil in Petrograd. He first agreed to abdicate so his son, Alexei, could rule. However, Nicholas soon changed his mind, and that same night he issued another decree stating that he would abdicate for himself and his son and allow his brother, Grand Duke Mikhail Alexandrovich, to rule.

The Petrograd mutiny was fundamental in providing support to the nascent revolution in 1917. The soldiers provided protection for the protestors, showed the inability of the tsarist government to provide order, and forced the tsar's hand to cede power. Although the strikes in Petrograd were the initial movements of the revolution, the mutiny was the catalyst that allowed unrest in the capital to topple the Romanov regime.

Gates M. Brown

Further Reading

Hickey, Michael. *Competing Voices from the Russian Revolution: Fighting Words.* Westport, CT: Greenwood, 2010.

Pipes, Richard. *The Russian Revolution.* New York: Vintage, 1990.

Pilsudski, Jozef (1867–1935)

Polish military leader, revolutionary, and political leader. Born on December 5, 1867, in Zulow in Wilno Province, Jozef Klemens

Pilsudski was educated at the Russian high school in the Lithuanian capital. At home, he grew up with Polish traditions and the belief that armed insurrection alone could free Poland from Russian domination. After an abortive attempt to study medicine in Kharkov, Pilsudski returned to Wilno in 1886. He became involved with the socialist movement, which he believed might help the Polish cause. This earned him a five-year banishment to Siberia.

On his return home in 1892, Pilsudski became a founding member of the Polish Socialist Party (Polska Partia Socjalistyczna, PPS). Again arrested in 1900 for his activities, he managed to escape to Galicia a year later. From there, Pilsudski exploited Russia's weaknesses at every turn. During the Russo-Japanese War of 1904–1905, he tried to talk the Japanese into financing a Polish uprising, and he considered cooperating with the Russian revolutionary movement in 1905.

When the PPS split in 1906, Pilsudski remained at the head of the smaller splinter group, the PPS Revolutionary Faction. When tensions rose between Russia and Austria-Hungary, Pilsudski approached the Austrian military and offered intelligence services in Russian Poland. This produced no direct results, but the Austrians tolerated the establishment of Polish riflemen's associations in Galicia. These associations received paramilitary training and became the core of a substantial Polish fighting force in the coming conflict.

With the start of World War I, Pilsudski obtained Austrian permission to mobilize detachments of riflemen, and the hastily established Polish Commission of Confederated Independence Parties empowered him to take military steps. The numerically unimpressive and ill-equipped riflemen marched on the city of Kielce in Russian Poland on August 6,

Jozef Klemens Pilsudski was a committed Polish Nationalist who worked throughout his youth to liberate Poland from Russia. In the aftermath of the Bolshevik Revolution, Pilsudski served as first chief of state of the newly independent Poland from 1918 to 1922. (Library of Congress)

1914. Rebuffed there, they failed to provoke the national insurrection that Pilsudski had sought.

After this, the Austrian Poles formed a surrogate government under the name Naczelny Komitet Narodowy (Supreme National Committee, NKN). The NKN absorbed the riflemen into the newly created Polish Legion. Pilsudski accepted temporary subordination to the NKN and was placed in charge of the Polish Legion's 1st Brigade. He tried to compensate for this setback by creating the secret Polska Organizacja Wojskowa (Polish Military Organization) for diversionary activities

in Russian Poland, thus enlarging his political and military base.

When the Central Powers occupied Russian Poland in 1915, Pilsudski struggled to demonstrate his independence from them, demanding the formation of a Polish government and the removal of non-Polish officers from the Polish Legion in 1916. When this was refused, he resigned his military position and directed the Polish Military Organization against the Germans.

The situation changed again after the Two Emperors' Proclamation of November 5, 1916. The Provisional Council of State was established, and Pilsudski became the head of its military department. When the Russian Revolution of March 1917 made the Central Powers the bigger obstacle to Polish independence, Pilsudski turned against the Central Powers and the council. The Germans then interned him in the fortress of Magdeburg in July 1917 after he had refused to incorporate the Polish Legion into a German-directed Polish army, the Polska Sia Zbrojna, and to swear an oath of allegiance to Kaiser Wilhelm II.

Pilsudski was released in the midst of the German revolutionary upheaval at the end of the war and arrived in Warsaw hailed as a national hero on November 10, 1918. A day later the Regency Council (which had replaced the Provisional Council of State) transferred military command to Pilsudski and put him at the helm of the Polish state on November 14. Other political bodies claiming representation of Poland fell in line, accepting the commander of the Polish Legion as the provisional head of state. Renowned pianist and Polish nationalist Ignacy Paderewski effected a reconciliation between Pilsudski and Roman Dmowski, head of the Polish National Committee in Paris, recognized by the Allies as the government of Poland. The new Polish parliament confirmed

Pilsudski in office in February 1919. The next year he was appointed the first field marshal of Poland, and he led the Poles to victory against the Russians in the Polish-Soviet War of 1919–1921.

In the following years, the staunch nationalist Pilsudski became disenchanted with the extreme parliamentary infighting and inattention to national problems that marked Poland's democracy. He staged a coup d'état in May 1926. While democratic institutions continued to operate and criticism of the military regime remained possible, Poland pursued an authoritarian course. Gradually the constitution was recast, placing more authority in Pilsudski's hands. Always dedicated to Poland's regeneration, Pilsudski died at Warsaw on May 12, 1935. He was followed in power by a succession of largely inept military leaders.

Pascal Trees

Further Reading

Davies, Norman. *Heart of Europe: A Short History of Poland.* Oxford, UK: Clarendon, 1984.

Garlicki, Andrzej. *Jozef Pisudski, 1867–1935.* Edited and translated by John Coutouvidis. Aldershot, UK: Scolar, 1995.

Holzer, Jerzy, and Jan Molenda. *Polska w pierwszej wojnie Swiatowej* [Poland in the First World War]. 2nd revised and augmented ed. Warsaw: Wiedza Powszechna, 1967.

Wandycz, Piotr. *The Lands of Partitioned Poland, 1795–1918.* Seattle: University of Washington Press, 1974.

Plekhanov, Georgi (1856–1918)

Georgi Valentinovich Plekhanov, a brilliant theoretician, philosopher, and historian, is known as the "father of Russian Marxism." He was the author of numerous philosophical works and devoted more than 35 years of his life to furthering the cause of socialist revolution in Russia. Although the leaders of the Russian Revolution eventually dismissed much of Plekhanov's work, his theories regarding social revolution continued to serve as the basis from which other theorists diverged.

Plekhanov was born on November 29, 1856, in Gudalovka, a small village in the central Russian province of Tambov. His father, Valentin, a severe and at times violent man, was a member of the local gentry. At the age of 10, Plekhanov entered the Voronezh Military Academy. After graduating from the academy in 1873, he enrolled in the Konstantinovskoe Military School in St. Petersburg.

During the 1875–1876 academic year, Plekhanov began to show increasing interest in socialism. By the fall of 1876, he had become completely immersed in the socialist movement. The following year, he joined and became a leading member of the group Land and Liberty, a populist organization that attempted to instigate a peasant revolution for instilling an agrarian social order in Russia. Amid Russia's growing climate of social and political unrest, Plekhanov became a prominent figure among those advocating drastic change in the country. He was the chief speaker at the Kazan Square demonstration in St. Petersburg in December 1876, one of the earliest and most important events in the Russian revolutionary movement.

Factionalism within Land and Liberty caused the organization to split in October 1879, with Plekhanov leading a minority group called the Black Repartition. Unlike the majority faction, the Black Repartition rejected the use of terrorism as the catalyst for revolution and instead promoted the dissemination of propaganda among Russia's lower orders to bring about radical social change. After the Russian authorities began to crack down on the fledgling revolutionary class in 1880, Plekhanov fled abroad to Geneva and then Paris.

From abroad, Plekhanov continued to play an active role in the European revolutionary movement and worked to refine his political thought. He began writing prolifically, producing theoretical works promoting scientific socialism. By this time Plekhanov was a devoted Marxist. His significance lies in the fact that he was the first theoretician to attempt to devise a Marxian program for Russia or a practical application for socialist revolution.

Plekhanov believed that the despotism that characterized the tsarist regime stemmed not only from the authoritarian nature of the ruling class but also from the backwardness of Russia. Industrialization had come late to Russia, and liberal reform had never come at all, despite some changes enacted during the reign of Tsar Alexander II. Plekhanov therefore maintained that socialist revolution must occur in two stages in Russia. First, the country must undergo a revolution that would propel the fledgling bourgeoisie into power. The bourgeoisie would quickly industrialize the country and enact some liberal reforms, but these reforms would in turn spur the development of an organized and powerful working class. The reign of the bourgeoisie therefore would be short-lived, as the growing proletariat would then launch a second revolution that would topple the bourgeoisie from power and install in its place a "dictatorship of the proletariat." Plekhanov added one important codicil to his theory, however. Socialists must not skip or rush the bourgeoisie stage of the revolution, for without that stage, Russia would not have the opportunity to develop either the modernity to stave off despotism or the necessary consciousness and organization among the working class to sustain socialism. The revolution therefore could establish a socialist government that

proved to be just as despotic as the tsarist regime had been.

Plekhanov developed these ideas over the course of several years and published them in multiple publications, not least of which were an introduction to the second Russian edition of Karl Marx and Friedrich Engels's *Communist Manifesto* (1882), "Socialism and Political Struggle" (1883), "Our Differences" (1884), and "On the Development of the Monist View of History" (1895). As a leader of the Russian revolutionary movement from abroad, Plekhanov through his theories brought hundreds of converts to the movement, who in turn disseminated his socialist views throughout Europe. As various factions developed among Russian socialists, Plekhanov often found himself in the middle, particularly in the ongoing battle between Mensheviks and Bolsheviks. Although he switched sides many times in the debate, he consistently maintained that socialism could not be achieved without true revolution. Reforms simply could not make the necessary alterations to the foundations of society.

One of Plekhanov's earliest followers was Vladimir Lenin. By the Russian Revolution of 1905, however, the two men's views had begun to diverge dramatically as Lenin developed his Marxist-Leninist theories. Plekhanov eventually denounced Lenin's ideas as a perversion of Marxism. At roughly the same time, Plekhanov began to lose influence within the revolutionary movement. His health took a turn for the worse, as he suffered from tuberculosis.

During the last two decades of his life, Plekhanov worked on historical, philosophical, and literary studies. His *Art and Social Life* was the first attempt to bridge Marxism with art and literature. He then began work on the multivolume work *History of Russian Social Thought,* which he would never complete.

Plekhanov finally returned to Russia on March 31, 1917, where a huge crowd greeted the ailing revolutionary. He played almost no role in the Russian Revolution, however. As his tuberculosis grew worse, Plekhanov retreated to a sanatorium in Finland, where he died on May 30, 1918.

Gates M. Brown and Sean N. Kalic

Further Reading

Baron, Samuel H. *Plekhanov: The Father of Russian Marxism.* Stanford, CA: Stanford University Press, 1963.

Haupt, Georges, and Jean-Jacques Marie. *Makers of the Russian Revolution: Biographies of Bolshevik Leaders.* Translated by C. I. P. Ferdinand and D. M. Bellos. Ithaca, NY: Cornell University Press, 1974.

Riasanovsky, Nicholas Valentine. *A History of Russia.* 5th ed. New York: Oxford University Press, 1993.

Shukman, Harold, ed. *The Blackwell Encyclopedia of the Russian Revolution.* New York: B. Blackwell, 1988.

Pravda

Pravda was the official daily newspaper of the Bolsheviks and later the Communist Party in Russia and then the Soviet Union. It officially began its publication on May 5, 1912, Karl Marx's birthday; however, *Pravda* did publish prior to this date but not in its daily format. Initially, it was not a politically oriented newspaper; it covered more social and artistic issues. Leon Trotsky began editing the paper in 1908 and was part of its shift to a hard-line Bolshevik platform. In 1912 at the Sixth Conference of the Central Committee, the Mensheviks left the party, and the Bolsheviks, now the controlling party, made *Pravda* the official publication of their political party. In 1914 the tsar's censors forced *Pravda* to cease publishing, but it simply changed its name and continued operations. It operated under eight different names from 1914 through the February Revolution of 1917, when *Pravda* again began publishing under its original name. After the Bolshevik Party seized control of Russia, *Pravda* continued to be its official newspaper. *Pravda* was the official newspaper of the Communist Party and the Soviet Union until the fall of the Soviet Union in 1991. After the fall, Russian president Boris Yeltsin sold the paper to a Greek business owner, who continued to publish the paper but not with its communist ideological perspective.

In order to begin publishing in Russia, the Bolsheviks needed a seated member of the Duma to serve as its head. Roman Malinovskii, who was a double agent working for the police, was a member of the Duma and worked with Vladimir Lenin in order to open *Pravda* in Russia in 1914. The reason the Bolsheviks needed someone in the Duma to head their newspaper was that the Duma members had limited immunity that allowed them more freedom to speak and write. This did not prevent the tsar's authorities from censoring the newspaper, but it did provide some protection from the tsar's police state for the opposition newspaper. Although Malinovskii served in the Duma as a spy for the Interior Ministry, his position was not secure. When a new interior minister took office in May 1914, Malinovskii's position in the new administration caused more problems than it solved. The new minister did not like the idea of the government directly interfering with opposition political parties, and he stopped his agency's use of secret agents planted to provide information. Malinovskii left Russia with the help of the Interior Ministry.

After the Bolsheviks seized power, Malinovskii returned to Russia. Although there is some doubt about how much Lenin knew of Malinovskii's work with the Interior Ministry in 1914 when Lenin used him to help open *Pravda* in Russia, Lenin had no use for him in 1917 after the Bolsheviks controlled Russia. Malinovskii went to trial under charges that the worked against the Bolsheviks and supported the government. Lenin attended the trail but did not participate. The court found Malinovskii guilty, and he was executed.

Pravda provided a way for the party to communicate to its supporters during the period of Provisional Government rule. Its publication set the party's policy and gave guidance to Bolsheviks across Russia. Having this organ allowed the Bolsheviks to have a more uniform message and platform, something that the White anti-Bolshevik forces never adequately addressed during the Russian Civil War.

This communication was critical in encouraging Bolshevik supporters and putting a positive interpretation on the military situation. In the early stages of the conflict, the Red Army struggled to defeat the old tsarist generals who led the White Army forces. However, as Trotsky's reforms improved the fighting capacity of the Red Army, the Red Army began to make some gains and capture White Army territory. *Pravda* was a critical tool in exporting this information to the rest of Russia and ensuring that Bolshevik supporters had the correct interpretation of the importance and context of Red Army actions. It also allowed the Bolshevik Party to mitigate or, if possible, hide any negative military turns between the armies of the Reds and Whites.

After the Bolsheviks won the civil war, *Pravda* continued to operate as the main publication of the Soviet Union. Party leaders used its pages to announce new programs or to convey the party's disapproval of people or groups. *Pravda* was an arm of the Soviet Union's propaganda and as such provided the interpretation of events that suited the party's interests.

Although *Pravda* was the official publication of the party, there were still times when it was controversial. Trotsky in 1923 published an article announcing his disagreement with Joseph Stalin and Lev Kamenev, the other members of the ruling Troika, in *Pravda*. This set the stage for Trotsky's ouster from the party and his exile from the Soviet Union. Generally, though, *Pravda*'s take on issues and government policies was not out of line. Trotsky's use of *Pravda* to advance a contradictory opinion to that of the Bolshevik Party was a unique occurrence.

Pravda continued to serve as the official newspaper until the fall of the Soviet Union in 1991. After the fall, Boris Yeltsin sold the newspaper to a Greek family who continued publication. The Communist Party in Russia continued to publish *Pravda* as of 2016 as a separate entity, although it is not affiliated with the original *Pravda* newspaper sold in 1991 after the fall of communism.

Pravda was the official newspaper of the Soviet Union and served an important role in the Russian Civil War by providing the Bolshevik Party with a way to communicate to its supporters. The newspaper also provided a means to ensure that Bolshevik supporters understood what the party wanted them to do and how best to support the party during the Russian Civil War. This message discipline was important and allowed the Bolsheviks to have a more unified front than their opponents, the White anti-Bolshevik forces.

Gates M. Brown

Further Reading

Lincoln, W. Bruce. *Red Victory: A History of the Russian Civil War*. New York: Simon and Schuster, 1989.

Pipes, Richard. *The Russian Revolution.* New York: Knopf, 1990.

Pipes, Richard. *Russia under the Bolshevik Regime.* New York: Knopf, 1993.

Prinkipo Conference

The Prinkipo Conference, also known as the Mormora Conference, was an effort coordinated by U.S. President Woodrow Wilson in 1919 to resolve the Russian Civil War. The conference was one of three peace efforts; the Bullitt Mission and the Hoover-Nansen food relief program were the other two. President Wilson wanted to use the Paris Peace Conference and the focus on the end of World War I to leverage peace talks between the Bolsheviks and the other warring factions of the Russian Civil War. The intent of the proposal was for the Bolsheviks and anti-Bolsheviks to meet at a conference held on the island of Prinkipo. The intention of the conference organizers was to get the groups together and negotiate a peaceful settlement to end the Russian conflict. However, the problem was that it was difficult, if not impossible, for the groups to consider a diplomatic end to the conflict, because this meant recognizing the legitimacy of the other groups; this was particularly true for the anti-Bolshevik groups.

President Wilson faced opposition to the conference from France in addition to the anti-Bolshevik opposition. Despite the lack of French support for the plan, the U.S. government appointed two members to its delegation, William Allen White and Professor George Davis Herron. In order to determine the feasibility of such a plan, William Bullitt, the U.S. representative for the proposed conference, met with Vladimir Lenin to determine whether the Bolsheviks intended to participate in the conference. In addition to the resistance that Franche displayed, the British government, led by David Lloyd George, also had reservations. Although George was enthusiastic about the discussions to end the conflict in Russia, the domestic politics in Great Britain demanded that he stop supporting the conference.

One of the reasons that Bullitt received the appointment to go to Russia was because Bullitt advocated for U.S. intervention to end the Russian Civil War. Colonel Edward House, a principal adviser to President Wilson, asked Bullitt if he wanted to take charge of direct discussions with Lenin after Bullitt discussed such a mission with the president and Colonel House. Bullitt formulated several conditions of the peace proposal to present to Lenin. Among the major points were an armistice between the Red and White groups, normalization of economic relations between Russia and other countries, and the removal of Allied troops from Russia. Colonel House approved of the points, but President Wilson did not see or approve of the specifics of Bullitt's peace proposal.

While Bullitt was in Russia, he provided information about the state of the conflict between the White and Red factions as well as his estimation of the Bolshevik government in the eyes of the Russian people. Bullitt claimed that the Bolsheviks had widespread popular support and that the other warring groups were in some cases more radical than the Bolshevik regime. Bullitt's assessment of the Red Terror and the violence of the Bolshevik regime overlooked the abuses of the Cheka and the arbitrary use of execution by the Bolsheviks in instituting their government. During his meeting with Lenin, Bullitt did not have many opportunities to research the conditions in Russia in an objective fashion and had to rely on Bolshevik-provided information, which influenced his report and view of the Bolshevik government.

One of the complicating factors of organizing the conference was the military situation between the Red and White forces in 1919. The military conflict was very fluid, and many Allied governments still had forces in Russia to aid the Whites. Although the Whites had difficulty in gaining significant military victory, they still had enough success to give the different groups hope that they could find better peace terms fighting than they could at the negotiating table.

Although Wilson wanted to bring the conflict in Russia to a peaceful end, the other allied nations wanted to ensure that whatever government came to Russia would honor its wartime debt. This was one of the reasons why many of the Allied governments withheld their recognition of the Bolshevik regime. When the Bolsheviks withdrew Russia from World War I, they called into question whether they would pay their wartime debts to their former allies. The White forces did not suffer from this ambiguity, since their policy was one of returning Russia to the war, and they were generally more friendly with the Allied governments than the Bolsheviks.

Wilson's desire to include Russia in the peace process was in part due to his intention to make the Paris peace accords more effective. President Wilson saw that the exclusion of Russia from the peace accords meant that the talks were not as effective as they could be. However, Wilson's condition that the fighting stop in order for the two sides to participate in the talks was a nonstarter.

Due to the lack of Allied support and the anti-Bolshevik groups' refusal to participate in the peace talks, the Prinkipo Conference never happened. The peace initiative foundered because there was no real urgency from the Bolsheviks for the peace discussions and because the anti-Bolshevik forces did not see the talks as a viable tool to gain their ends. In addition, President Wilson gave more and more attention to the Paris peace accords in 1919. This lack of attention was detrimental to the Prinkipo Conference, since the United States was the major Allied government behind the peace initiative. Without the support of the Wilson administration, the Prinkipo Conference never happened, and the Russian Civil War continued until the Bolsheviks destroyed the White army groups and gained control over Russia. In part, the hesitation of the Bolshevik government to participate in the conference and the impact of the Bolshevik antiwar policies led the United States and other members of the Allied coalition to not recognize the legitimacy of the Bolshevik government. When the Bolsheviks won the Russian Civil War, the U.S. government did not recognize the Bolshevik government or the later Soviet Union until 1933.

Gates M. Brown

Further Reading

Kennan, George F. *Russia and the West under Lenin and Stalin.* Boston: Atlantic Monthly Press, 1960.

McFadden, David. *Alternative Paths: Soviets and Americans, 1917–1920.* New York: Oxford University Press, 1993.

Provisional Government

The strikes and demonstrations in Petrograd eroded the trust that the people had in their government. When Tsar Nicholas II abdicated the throne, the Duma established the Provisional Government, which ruled until October 1917 when the Bolsheviks overthrew the Provisional Government. The Bolsheviks displaced the Provisional Government. Prince Georgy Lvov led the Provisional Government. However, he would only rule for about five months. In July 1917 Lvov resigned after a Bolshevik uprising, and Alexander Kerensky took over after Lvov and his fellow Constitutional Democrat (Kadet) Party ministers resigned.

The task that the Provisional Government took on was exceedingly difficult. There were no other legitimate groups who could rule in the tsar's place. The Romanovs ruled Russia for over 300 years prior to Nicholas II's abdication. In addition to the task of establishing a new government, the Provisional Government had to share power with the Petrograd Soviet. Not only did the members of the Provisional Government face an uphill battle by creating a new government, but they also had to try to convince the Russian people of the value of representative government.

As the Provisional Government struggled to gain legitimacy to rule Russia, the Petrograd Soviet frustrated its efforts. One thing that the Provisional Government lacked was popular support. Much of the reason for the lack of popular support for the Provisional Government was that the Duma appointed the new government, and the new ministers did not represent the people. Lacking popular support was not a problem that the Petrograd Soviet had. Since many more people supported the Petrograd Soviet than the Provisional Government, this meant that the soviet had more power than the Provisional Government.

Another problem that the Provisional Government faced was that its authority came from the Duma. Although the Duma was a quasi-legislative body, it was not actually a parliament. In the tsarist regime, the Duma was only an advisory group or a body for discussion; it did not make laws. In addition to all of these issues, perhaps the most problematic aspect of the Provisional Government's first days was its decision to stay in the war. Lvov's government chose to continue fighting World War I, which was unpopular.

While the Provisional Government struggled to gain its footing, the Petrograd Soviet issued several declarations. One of these directed the soldiers to create soldiers' committees and to assume control over their units. This proclamation, Petrograd Soviet Order No. 1, called for soldiers to dispense with the tradition of standing at attention for officers. It also required the use of formal language for all soldiers regardless of rank. Although it did not call for radical changes, such as the election of officers, it still was instrumental in eroding discipline in the Russian Army.

Lvov agreed to accept the Petrograd Soviet's eight measures in return for the soviet conceding the Provisional Government's authority to rule Russia. This power sharing showed the power of the soviet and the weakness of the new government. Once Vladimir Lenin returned to Russia in April 1917, he criticized the Bolsheviks for agreeing to recognize the Lvov government.

A defining moment in the Provisional Government's short existence was Joseph Stalin's decision to support Lenin and begin using the newspaper *Pravda* to encourage popular opposition to Lvov's government. Stalin wrote articles condemning Kerensky and others as counterrevolutionaries. This change further hamstrung the Provisional Government in efforts to gain legitimacy in the eyes of the Russian people.

Also in April 1917, a note concerning Russia's participation in World War I became public. This note, written by the Provisional Government's foreign minister, Pavel Miliukov, made clear that the new government would support the Allies. With the publication of Miliukov's note to the Allied powers, there were new demonstrations against the Provisional Government. Bolsheviks were the main instigators of these new demonstrations, and the protestors carried signs demanding the overthrow of the Provisional Government.

By the summer of 1917 Alexander Kerensky, as the Provisional Government's minister of war, ordered an offensive to turn the tide of war sentiment inside of Russia and restore the morale of the Russian troops. Unfortunately, the offensive ran out of momentum, and the German troops were able to repulse the Russian attack. The Russian Army, unable to stop the German advance, retreated about 150 miles from the front. Kerensky's failed assault brought more instability and demonstrations in Petrograd. The Bolsheviks initially supported the peaceful demonstrations; however, the protests did not stay peaceful. The armed uprising caused Lenin to go into hiding to avoid being arrested.

The failure of the Kerensky Offensive showed the disconnect between the people and their government. This separation was something that the Bolsheviks would leverage in the October Revolution. Another ramification of the failed offensive was the removal of General Brusilov and the appointment of General Kornilov as commander in chief of the Russian Army. This appointment would lead to the Kornilov Affair, which saw General Kornilov try to mass troops and gain financial support to secure Petrograd. Kerensky claimed that Kornilov was a counterrevolutionary who was going to use his power to unseat the Provisional Government. However, Kornilov claimed to be acting on Kerensky's orders.

One of the main ramifications of the Kornilov Affair was even greater instability of the Provisional Government. The Bolsheviks exploited this weakness. In another effort to bolster his position and hopefully detract from Lenin's power, Kerensky scheduled elections for a constituent assembly that would convene in January 1918. This election pushed the Bolsheviks to act, which contributed to the timing of the October Revolution in 1917.

When the Bolsheviks launched their coup, Kerensky called for support from the military to help the Provisional Government defend itself. Due to the Kornilov Affair, the Russian officers did not move to help the Provisional Government. With few forces to protect the government, the Bolsheviks were able to capture the Winter Palace, the seat of government for the Provisional Government. Once the Bolsheviks captured the Provisional Government in Petrograd, there were no other groups with the power to prevent them from assuming control of the government of Russia and forming the Soviet Union.

Gates M. Brown

Further Reading

Fitzpatrick, Sheila. *The Russian Revolution.* New York: Oxford University Press, 2008.

Pipes, Richard. *The Russian Revolution.* New York: Vintage, 1990.

R

Rasputin, Grigory Yefimovich (1864?–1916)

Siberian peasant and mystic who became an adviser and confidant to the Russian imperial family. Born near the Ural Mountains in the western Siberian village of Pokrovskoe sometime between 1864 and 1872, Grigory Yefimovich Rasputin was a precocious child who learned to read the Bible at an early age. As a young man, he ran afoul of the law for petty thievery and dalliances with young girls. Rasputin came under the influence of a religious sect known as the Khlysty (Flagellants) and became a self-declared holy man who claimed healing powers.

Rasputin was a wandering holy man, a Strannik (pilgrim) in search of God in the tradition of many Orthodox Russians. He was known alternately as a Starets (spiritual guide) and a Yurodivy (holy fool). Though he was careful not to wander too far from Orthodoxy, many of his practices were akin to those of the quasi-Christian sects, which fit his personal licentiousness.

Rasputin arrived in the capital of St. Petersburg in the first years of the new century, and in October 1905 his contacts within the religious hierarchy and among the nobility secured him access to the imperial family. The politics and ideologies of the era created a growing crisis of faith for Orthodoxy that emphasized saints, holy men, and miracle workers. This trend opened the way for Rasputin's rise to prominence. Rasputin was said to possess two miraculous powers: healing and precognition. He seemed able to "read" a person's character and quickly assess his or her strengths and weaknesses. His greatest ability, however, was to calm people in distress, which drew him to the attention of the imperial couple.

Tsar Nicholas II and Tsarina Alexandra were extremely devout members of the

Grigory Yefimovich Rasputin was a Russian mystic and self-proclaimed holy man, though he held no official position in the Russian Orthodox Church. He gained notoriety by providing some assistance to the Tsarevich Alexei, son of Tsar Nicholas II and Tsarina Alexandra, who suffered from hemophilia. During the First World War his influence over the tsarina increased, and he was eventually murdered by Russian nobles who disapproved of his influence over the royal family. (The Illustrated London News Picture Library)

Russian Orthodox Church, but they also believed in miracles and faith healing. Young tsarevich Alexei Nikolaevich, heir to the throne, suffered from hemophilia. Called to the boy's bedside on occasions of distress, Rasputin seemed able to stop the tsarevich's hemorrhaging. An explanation of Rasputin's success in controlling the bleeding, either through hypnosis or positive thinking, is elusive, but certainly his perceived success endeared him to the tsarina especially and gave him an intimacy with the royal family enjoyed by few. Soon his unfettered advice extended to state business, as he attempted to influence the tsar's decisions in ministerial and policy matters. From 1910, Rasputin is believed to have exercised considerable political power.

Rasputin's frequent affairs with women and his drunkenness are well documented. He opposed Russia's involvement in World War I, reportedly telling the tsar that if Russia went to war it "would drown in its own blood." When Tsar Nicholas II took personal command of the war effort in the fall of 1915, the tsarina came to exercise political power in St. Petersburg in his absence. Rasputin held considerable influence over her and the selection of cabinet ministers. Indeed, rumors circulated that the tsarina was Rasputin's lover. Convinced that Rasputin now threatened the very survival of the Romanov dynasty, members of the nobility and right-wing supporters of autocracy plotted his assassination.

Following a half dozen unsuccessful attempts, in the early morning hours of December 17, 1916, Prince Feliks Yusupov, son-in-law of the tsar's sister, supported by others in the imperial family and government, poisoned, shot, and finally drowned Rasputin. Upon learning of Rasputin's death, the tsar abandoned his command of the army, leaving no one in authority, and replaced every able minister of his government. Even members of the imperial family who asked for leniency for the assassins were exiled from the capital. With the breakdown of capable governance and command of the war effort as well as the widening chasm between the monarchy and the people, Russia stood on the brink of revolution. Although Rasputin did not materially affect the coming of the revolution that would sweep away the tsarist regime, he did perhaps hasten it.

Arthur T. Frame

Further Reading

Fuhrmann, Joseph J. *Rasputin: A Life*. New York: Praeger, 1990.

Moynahan, Brian. *Rasputin: The Saint Who Sinned*. New York: Random House, 1997.

Radzinsky, Edvard. *The Rasputin File*. Translated by Judson Rosengrant. New York: Nan A. Talese, 2000.

Shukman, Harold. *Rasputin*. Stroud, UK: Sutton, 1997.

Red Guards

Following the March Revolution of 1917, the Russian Empire was on the verge of collapse. Russian soldiers, weaponless, bootless, starving, and dying from exhaustion and exposure, were under a constant barrage by the German Army and were forced to retreat and abandon more and more of their motherland. People were dying in the streets of Moscow due to shortages of food and fuel. Soldiers mutinied in Petrograd. Anarchy reigned in both Moscow and Petrograd (as St. Petersburg was now called), and the state's bureaucratic machinery disintegrated. Out of this social and political chaos rose a group of armed workers and soldiers known as the Red Guards.

Despite the significant role they were destined to play during the Bolshevik

Red Guards form a firing line around an Austin armored car during street fighting in Petrograd in 1917. (Edward Alsworth Ross, *The Russian Bolshevik Revolution*, 1921)

(November) Revolution, the Red Guards did not begin as revolutionaries determined to overthrow the government and rule Russia. They were simple factory workers, women and men, who demonstrated for better working conditions, a living wage, and decent houses where they could raise their children. They were in many ways swept along like the rest of Russia in the cataclysmic events between February and October 1917, but most had been politically active prior to the revolution and joined Red Guards' units to defend and promote their beliefs. These paramilitary formations, like many others, were affiliated with both specific factories and with political parties. The largest such formations were created in Moscow and Petrograd.

After Nicholas II abdicated on March 15, 1917, the leaders of the State Duma (parliament) established a Provisional Government with the cooperation of the liberal and leftist political parties. This new regime formed its own self-defense units and people's militia and also incorporated several workers'

squadrons and committees for public safety patterned after the revolutionary bodies of 1905 and associated with factories and neighborhoods. In April 1917, however, Bolshevik leader Vladimir Lenin returned to Russia (with German assistance) and denounced cooperation with this government. The Bolsheviks resolved on April 14 to create their own Red Guards; its charter appeared in *Pravda* two weeks later.

Workers, sailors, and soldiers who had formed and supported the parallel Petrograd Soviet of Workers' and Soldiers' Deputies thus often were torn in their loyalties. For those who favored the Bolsheviks and their program of immediate withdrawal from the war, red became the color of the day, the color of revolution. Workers and soldiers marched beneath red banners and wore red armbands. Many joined the Bolshevik Party and pledged to defend the revolution. Enrollment was voluntary, and training often took place at work. By October 1917, perhaps a quarter of a million Russians belonged to Red Guard units, both infantry and mounted. The Petrograd Red Guards commanded by Konstantin Yurev numbered some 30,000.

The Red Guards played a key role in the November Revolution, controlling the streets of Petrograd and storming the Winter Palace. This was their final episode as an independent entity, though Red Guard units continued to serve in transitional functions under the new regime. On December 20, 1917, Lenin formed the Cheka, which served as Soviet state security and took over many Red Guard police functions. In January 1918, the Red Guards officially became members of the Workers' and Peasants' Red Army. Since then, the term "Red Guards" has often been used interchangeably with "Red Army."

John G. Hall

Further Reading

Lincoln, W. Bruce. *Red Victory: A History of the Russian Civil War, 1918–1924.* New York: Da Capo, 1999.

Wade, Rex. *Red Guards and Workers' Militias in the Russian Revolution.* Stanford, CA: Stanford University Press, 1984.

Ziemke, Earl F. *The Red Army, 1918–1941.* New York: Routledge, 2004.

Red Terror

After assuming power in 1918, the Soviet government used violence and oppression to solidify Bolshevik rule, known as the Red Terror. The formal period of the Red Terror was from September 1918 until October 1918; however, the large-scale violence of the Red Terror continued through 1922 with the end of the Russian Civil War. Estimates vary widely about the number of people killed during this period, from 50,000 to about 500,000. The Cheka, a security organization created in December 1917, was the main body responsible for carrying out the violence of the Red Terror. The official name of the Cheka was All-Russian Extraordinary Commission for Combating Counter-Revolution and Sabotage. The name "Cheka" is an acronym of the Cyrillic letters of the name. The proximate causes of the Red Terror were the attempted assassination of Vladimir Lenin and the successful assassination of Petrograd Cheka leader Moisei Uritsky. Although these events were the catalyst for the beginning of the terror, the Red Terror was part of Lenin's plan to use mass violence to consolidate Bolshevik power and eliminate any competition to control over Russia.

As 1918 continued, the Bolsheviks struggled to project their authority throughout Russia. Bolshevism was popular and powerful in urban areas, especially with the industrial workers in cities such as Petrograd. However, in other segments of society and more rural regions, the Bolsheviks did not enjoy the same level of support. Throughout the end of 1917 and into 1918, the actions of the Soviet government did not inspire loyalty from skeptical groups. Such actions as closing the elected Constituent Assembly in January 1918, territorial losses from the Treaty of Brest-Litovsk, and war communism introduced economic hardship and food shortages throughout Russia.

Felix Dzerzhinsky, the leader of the Cheka, led the wave of violence and repression during the official period of the Red Terror. In September 1918, there were several contributing factors that led to the Red Terror. The formation of several armed groups fighting against the Soviet government and growing opposition to grain requisitions from peasants led Lenin to plan to use violence to cut support for opposition movements. The events in Petrograd further undermined the security of the new Bolshevik state. The assassination of the Petrograd Cheka leader by a Kadet officer and the attempt on Lenin's life by Fanya Kaplan, a member of the Socialist Revolutionary Party, both happened within two weeks. During her interrogation that included torture, Kaplan told the Cheka that she wanted to kill Lenin because he shut down the Constituent Assembly. She thought that Lenin was an enemy to the purpose of the real revolution and wanted to remove him so the revolution could continue.

Lenin's injuries landed him in the hospital and brought him close to death. Although there was no broader conspiracy, the Bolshevik regime's reaction spread to all other political groups. Within a couple of months the Cheka executed over 800 Social Revolutionist Party members. However, the violence would expand to include any group that could potentially pose a threat to the revolution.

As the violence expanded, it included anyone who had connections to the old regime, spoke publicly against Lenin or the Bolsheviks, or sold food for profit. Also included in the oppression were those associated with the Russian Orthodox Church, liberals who supported the tsarist government, and foreigners. In addition to political targets, the Cheka also persecuted those peasants who did not turn enough of their grain over to the state to meet quotas. Industrial workers who did not meet their productivity goals later felt the wrath of the Red Terror as the Bolsheviks expanded the definition of who was an enemy of the state.

At the beginning of 1918, the Cheka had only a couple hundred agents. As the Red Terror grew in scale, the Cheka also expanded. At its height the organization swelled to about 200,000 in 1920. Although the Cheka's violence was exceedingly cruel, there were other tools that it used to enforce obedience to the Bolshevik regime. One of these was the revocation of rations from those deemed to be class enemies. Due to the hardships of the war, there was a food rationing system that made it illegal to purchase food outside of the ration system. These class enemies, who were excluded from the ration system, could not legally purchase food, so they were in the position of having to break the law in order to survive.

Another tool of oppression that the Cheka used was corrective labor camps, better known as gulags. Those sentenced to confinement in the concentration camps had to work in inhumane conditions and received very little food to support their hard work. The camps were in a range of different regions, including Siberia. The hard labor expected of inmates at the camps often meant that a sentence to a gulag was actually a death sentence.

Even families of those whom the Cheka targeted could find themselves punished as if they ran afoul of the regime. One of the tactics of the Cheka was to hold hostage the family members of someone or a group they wanted to arrest until the person or group turned themselves into the authorities. When there were desertions from the Red Army, the Cheka used this tactic to force soldiers to return to their units.

The Cheka was not the only tool of terror that the Bolshevik regime had. Once the Bolsheviks took over, they eliminated the tsarist legal code and legal system. In its place, the Bolsheviks instituted a system of Revolutionary Tribunals guided by the tribunal members' revolutionary conscience. This meant that there was no rule of law, with no set of legal codes that citizens could look to in order to ensure that they stayed on the right side of the law. This combined with the Red Terror and famine as a result of Bolshevik grain requisition programs brought an incredible level of anarchy and violence.

The Red Terror killed an incredible number of people and created an aura of instability and insecurity for those living under the Bolshevik regime. Officially, it was a short-lived explosion of state-sanctioned killings. However, the Red Terror continued long after the Bolshevik government ended it officially. Lenin would continue to use terror as a weapon to force the Russian population into compliance throughout the Russian Civil War.

Gates M. Brown

Further Reading

Mawdsley, Evan. *The Russian Civil War.* Winchester, MA: Allen and Unwin, 1987.

Pipes, Richard. *The Russian Revolution.* New York: Vintage, 1990.

Revolution of 1905

A series of uprisings and mutinies that erupted across Russia throughout 1905 and culminated in Tsar Nicholas II issuing the October Manifesto granting Russia a parliamentary body, the Duma.

Ever-growing discontent with the ruling autocratic system that had first emerged during the early 19th century began to boil over by the turn of the century. The long string of Russian defeats against Japan during 1904 only exacerbated the situation. Faced with increasing shortages and hardships caused by a distant and unfamiliar war, Russians became increasingly vocal. Workers at the vital Putilov steel works went on strike in early December 1904, leading to a rash of sympathy strikes. On January 9, 1905, Father Georgy Gapon (who may have been a police spy) led a demonstration of workers in front of the Winter Palace in St. Petersburg to present a petition to the tsar for better working conditions. The demonstration was met with a violent reaction from soldiers guarding the Winter Palace, which resulted in 800 deaths. This became infamously known as Bloody Sunday.

In the aftermath of Bloody Sunday, a wave of riots and general strikes erupted throughout Russia's major cities. In St. Petersburg, Moscow, and other urban centers, soviets, or councils of workers, soldiers, and sailors, arose to direct the revolution. In response to the growing crisis, Tsar Nicholas II made a public announcement on February 18 of the formation of an elected Duma that would act as an advisory body. The tsar intended to contain the situation as quickly as possible so as to be able to concentrate on the ongoing war with Japan. Yet the military situation was not favorable, and the eventual disaster of the Russian defeat would only make the situation worse.

In the wake of news of the loss of the Russian Baltic Fleet at Tsushima on May 14, another wave of general strikes and mutinies erupted across Russia. Fierce fighting occurred on the streets of Odessa throughout June. At the same time, offshore, mutiny erupted aboard the battleship *Potemkin* on June 15. Originally inspired by the lack of quality meat aboard, the mutineers soon aligned themselves with the revolutionary strikers in Odessa. Yet any attempts to win over other elements of the Black Sea Fleet as well as fully coordinate their efforts with revolutionary leaders in Odessa ended in failure. As a result, the crew of the *Potemkin* sailed toward Romania to escape.

It was around this time in June that nationalist insurrections broke out in non-Russian areas of the empire seeking independence. Textile workers in Łódź rioted on June 10, inspired by Polish nationalism. A similar uprising broke out in Georgia and temporarily succeeded in driving out Russian authorities. Another wave of nationalist uprisings occurred in the Baltic. In the end, all such attempts were suppressed by force, as Cossack police units and the military remained loyal to the tsar.

With the conclusion of the Russo-Japanese War, the Russian army was able to bring in greater numbers of soldiers to suppress internal insurrections. By the end of July, most uprisings were on the decline. It appeared that the fervor of the revolutionary moment had come and gone. By August 19 the first session of the Duma was conducted, yet little was achieved. This lack of results helped spark a surge in revolutionary fervor in September and early October as a new wave of general strikes swept across the country.

The situation had become critical for the tsarist regime. Prime Minister Sergei Witte advised Tsar Nicholas II that suppressing the uprisings through military force was no longer feasible and that certain concessions were necessary to restore order. The tsar detested Witte but had returned him to office as the only statesman capable of settling the war with Japan honorably, and he now was forced by Witte's popularity to heed his advice. On October 17, the tsar therefore agreed to the October Manifesto that granted Russia a constitution, certain civil liberties, and an elected parliament with legislative powers.

The promises of the October Manifesto helped extinguish many of the general strikes among workers and other civilians; ironically, it also fueled a series of spontaneous mutinies within the Russian Army throughout the rest of 1905. One of the first was the mutiny at the naval base at Kronstadt on October 26–27, which was suppressed when reinforcements in sufficient quantity were brought in to convince the mutineers to disperse. A few days later on October 30–31, soldiers and sailors rioted in Vladivostok. This helped spark a wave of mutinies among

reserve units stationed in Manchuria through the middle of November. Mutinies would still occur into 1906, and many were suppressed without violence.

The revolution was not without costs, however; some 13,000–15,000 people were killed during 1905–1906, and some 75,000 were imprisoned. The military measures to suppress peasant rebellions in the countryside spurred by the land hunger and mistreatment of serfs were particularly onerous. The noose used to hang peasant rebels became known as a "Stolypin necktie" after Interior Minister Pyotr Stolypin, who oversaw the campaigns. The tsar, moreover, gradually retracted the liberties he had granted under duress in 1905 and thus created a groundswell of mistrust and revolutionary sentiment. The revolutionaries vowed that they would not be so easily taken in the next time.

Stephen T. Satkiewicz

Further Reading

Bushnell, John. *Munity and Repression: Russian Soldiers in the Revolution of 1905–1906.* Bloomington: Indiana University Press, 1985.

Moorehead, Alan. *The Russian Revolution.* New York: Bantam Books, 1958.

Pipes, Richard. *A Concise History of the Russian Revolution.* New York: Vintage Books, 1996.

Revolutionary Military Council

The Revolutionary Military Council came from the combination of the Supreme Military Council and the Operative Department of the People's Commissariat for Military Affairs that occurred in September 1918. The unification put one person in charge of the entire Soviet military and provided a more streamlined bureaucracy for the

Bolshevik Party. The first chairman of the Revolutionary Military Council was Leon Trotsky, and the first commander in chief was Jukums Vacietis.

Lenin understood that the revolution needed military power if it was going to survive. By 1920, the Red Army was approximately 5 million strong. This growth in the size meant that there needed to be a more effective command structure for coordinating the actions of this large fighting force. Prior to the unification of the two bodies, the targeting of internal enemies as well as carrying out administrative duties rested with the Supreme Military Council, while the Operative Department of the People's Commissariat for Military Affairs was responsible for the operational control of Red Army forces. In addition to a more efficient structure, the combination also was indicative of the model that the Bolsheviks would use to govern other areas of society and government: one-man management as opposed to committee management.

The creation of the Revolutionary Military Council was to aid the Bolsheviks in creating the military power to carry the revolution not only throughout Russia but also to other nations. Lenin did not agree with other socialists or communists who advocated for a peaceful strategy of disarmament. Rather, he looked to the revolution in military terms and believed that the state had to have an adequate force to make the revolution successful. In Lenin's estimation, as long as capitalist nations would not let the Bolshevik state exist in peace, it had to have a military in order to fight the class enemies who would invade the nascent socialist state.

One of the important functions of the new council was to appoint "military specialists" for the Red Army. Although the Red Army initially supported the election by Soviets of officers, this did not provide the most effective military leadership. Former tsarist officials had professional experience and military education that party members did not have, making them militarily proficient but politically suspect. The council appointed vetted specialists and allowed them to control the military situation but with the oversight of a political commissar who ensured that the military specialists did not defect or issue orders that contradicted the will of the Bolshevik Party.

Another reason for the unification of the Soviet military command was the success of the Red Army in the Volga Campaign in 1918. Out of this campaign came the regular Red Army that would fight the civil war against the White forces and allow the Bolsheviks to solidify their control over Russia. Vacietis, the first commander in chief of the Red Army, gained valuable experience as a colonel in this campaign, and his success led to his promotion as head of the Red Army when the prior military bodies merged. Leon Trotsky also made the most of his success in the Volga Campaign; he was in charge of the Red Army, and his capabilities led to the position of head of the Red Army under the new high command.

Prior to the unification, the two military bureaus had different responsibilities. Joseph Stalin led the Supreme Military Council, which mainly targeted counterrevolutionaries. The Operative Department was responsible for the fighting forces. However, the Volga Campaign required fighting both counterrevolutionaries and military forces in the same fight. It was ineffective to have two commands directing operations in the same region, so combining the command into one headquarters made this coordination much more effective. However, it also put Stalin's forces under the control of Leon Trotsky. Stalin and Trotsky did not agree on the role of tsarist officers in the Red Army. Stalin did not trust the former regime officers who were fighting with the Red Army because of the record of some of them defecting and fighting for the Whites. However, Trotsky believed that he could compel the allegiance or at least the obedience of the officers by arresting their families in the event of their defection.

The role of former tsarist officers continued to cause trouble not only between Stalin and Trotsky but also in the Bolshevik Party in general. In March 1919 at the Eighth Party Conference, there were enough party members opposed to the use of tsarist officers to form a bloc called the Military Opposition. This bloc did not think that the special skills and experience of the former regime officers brought to the Red Army justified the risk that the party ran by allowing them to have control over military units. Trotsky's actions, his critics thought, made it seem that he was too sympathetic to these potential enemies of the state. In several cases, he argued for the release of military specialists under arrest by the Cheka.

This tension between Stalin and Trotsky continued to cause trouble. In the early 1920s Lenin's health declined, and he took a less active role in the party. Stalin was able to expand his own power, and in 1923 he appointed his own supporters as staff in the Revolutionary Military Council. This infuriated Trotsky, and he threatened to resign. The Central Committee did not accept his resignation but also did not try to mollify him. By this time, it was clear that Trotsky, although still head of the military committee, was losing his influence in the party.

The Revolutionary Military Council was important because of its ability to unite the command of the Red Army. Having one headquarters in charge of directing the forces of the Bolshevik state made the military

aspect of the civil war more efficient. The changes in the administration and control of the military were also part of a broader implementation of the ideal manner of control in the Bolshevik government, one-man rule rather than management by committee. The ramifications of this change also impacted the internal politics of the party in other ways. Using military officers from the tsar's government caused disagreements inside the party. Trotsky's actions made him suspect to others in the revolution, specifically Stalin.

Gates M. Brown

Further Reading

Acton, Edward, ed. *Critical Companion to the Russian Revolution, 1914–1921.* London: Arnold, 1997.

Swain, Geoff. *Trotsky and the Russian Revolution.* Seminar Studies in History. London: Routledge/Taylor and Francis Group, 2014.

Russian Civil War (1917–1922)

The Russian Civil War not only encompassed military actions but also had consequences for the international, economic, and social development of the new Russian Soviet structure.

The Russian Civil War began with the Bolshevik uprising in Moscow under the leadership of Vladimir Lenin. His forces were able to defeat General Pyotr Krasnov's Cossacks outside the city limits and ended resistance inside Moscow. Lenin immediately began setting up the Soviet (Bolshevik) state. The monarchists, or Whites, under the leadership of General Anton Denikin, General Pyotr Wrangel, and Admiral Alexander Kolchak, having fled, began forming their resistance to the Reds. The Whites did not have a unified plan, and each group followed its own agenda. Russia was now divided, still at war with the Central Powers, and faced a complete collapse of industrial and agricultural production.

The Reds formed a Military Revolutionary Committee from the sailors and soldiers, coupled with factory workers and urban proletariat, that formed the nucleus of the Red Guards. They were reinforced by the elite Latvian Rifle Division. These forces were under the control of Leon Trotsky, who built a conventional army with former tsarist officers and military commissars to countersign orders and carry out political education among the troops. From the outset of the civil war, the Bolsheviks controlled the urban centers and the railway network and had a larger force than the White armies.

As the anti-Bolshevik forces organized in Ukraine and Siberia, Lenin realized that they

could not face the Central Powers and the threat of the White movement and began negotiating a settlement with the Germans. In January 1918, the Ukrainian Rada declared independence. The Ukrainians initially formed the Green Army, later the Revolutionary Insurrectionary Army of the Ukraine, also known as the Anarchist (Black) Army, under Nestor Makhno. Makhno led his forces at first against both the Red and White forces in the area but cooperated with the Bolsheviks against the Whites when necessary. When the Bolsheviks hesitated during the negotiation process, German forces moved into the Ukraine and surrounding areas, which led the Soviets to proclaim decrees on food procurements and the beginning of what would be known as war communism, the nationalization of all production and

Bolsheviks muster forces in Petrograd in an attempt to consolidate and maintain power against the monarchists at the start of the Russian Civil War. (Edgar Allen Forbes, *Leslie's Photographic Review of the Great War*, 1919)

industry. Under such duress, the Bolsheviks signed the Treaty of Brest-Litovsk, ending Russia's involvement in World War I.

During this time the Czechoslovak Legion, made up of prisoners of war who had fought on the Russian side, now demanded their withdrawal from Russia. They allied themselves with the White movement, taking over key railroad centers. These events led to the intervention of the Allied powers in Russia. Fourteen countries sent forces to Russia to support the Whites on a limited scale. They supplied the Whites with aircraft, tanks, ammunition, and training.

The British were most active in support of the White movement. Fighting during the early stages of the civil war favored the Whites. In the north, though, the Red Army stopped the White advances, and the area remained relatively quiet for the rest of the conflict. As the White Army made significant advances in the central and south regions, it advanced on Ekaterinburg, where the royal family was held. The tsar, along with his wife and children, was executed by the Cheka on July 17, 1918. The White forces were eventually stopped at Kazan and pushed back.

The Bolsheviks condoned the Red Terror at all levels, carrying out killings, torture, and repression on a massive scale. White forces responded in kind. No quarter was given and no prisoners were taken on either side. Caught in the middle were the peasants, who generally favored neither side but saw the Bolsheviks, who were untainted by foreign support, as advocates of Russia. Casualties caused directly by the fighting or indirectly by starvation were enormous. By February 1919 the Red Army, bolstered by Trotsky's reforms, pushed the White forces almost completely out of the Ukraine. In Siberia, the Whites formed a government at Omsk called the Directory and proclaimed Alexander Kolchak supreme leader

of Russia. They advanced west and made significant gains at first but were stopped on April 26 before they reached the Volga River. The Red Army pushed Kolchak back to the east by June 9, then shifted west to halt a White offensive from Estonia against Petrograd led by Nikolai Yudenich. Taking advantage of the Bolsheviks' shifting forces, Anton Denikin began an offensive from the south. By October 1919, he had taken Orel and was approaching Moscow. The Whites had failed to coordinate their offensives, though, and taking advantage of interior lines, the Bolsheviks regrouped and began a counterattack against Denikin, recapturing Orel. By the end of 1919, Red forces had taken the Ukraine and southern Russia.

By early 1920, Red forces had by and large eliminated the White threat. Kolchak was captured in late 1919 and executed on February 7, 1920, and Denikin was bottled up in the Crimean Peninsula. Then on April 24 Poland attacked in an attempt to take the Ukraine, starting the Russo-Polish War. They quickly advanced, but regrouped Red forces met them and drove them back. By the end of July, the Bolsheviks were approaching Warsaw. The Poles stopped the Red Army there, however, and forced the Bolsheviks back. On October 12, 1920, an armistice was signed.

With the end of the Polish campaigns and the withdrawal of Allied forces from Russia, the Red forces turned their full power against the White forces in the Crimea. Denikin had stepped down after arriving in Crimea, and Wrangel took command. He rallied the White forces briefly but without reinforcements or resupply had no hope of defeating the Reds, and with his small remaining force he fled to Constantinople on November 14, ending the military portion of the civil war.

The Bolshevik forces then methodically eliminated all opposition, concentrating on the anarchist movement in Ukraine. Sporadic resistance in the Far East continued until 1922, and it took until 1924 before former Russian territories in the Caucasus and Central Asia were completely subdued. The total losses of Red Army personnel during the period 1918–1922, irrecoverable, sick, and wounded, have been stated at 6,791,783. This figure does not include partisans or the Red Guards who perished or were wounded during the uprisings in the urban and rural areas. There are no figures calculated for the White armies and their allies, but it is generally agreed that their losses were at least equal to those of the Red Army.

The Russian Civil War was a formative experience for the Bolsheviks. Key personalities such as Mikhail Frunze and Mikhail Tukhachevsky emerged who would play important roles in the development of the Red Army. The experience of war communism convinced Lenin and others that Russia needed "breathing space." The Allied intervention further solidified the Bolshevik views that "international capitalism" would use any opportunity to destroy them and allowed them to portray their regime as the defender of the Russian people.

Raymond D. Limbach

Further Reading

Connaughton, Richard. *The Republic of Ushakova: Admiral Kolchak and the Allied Intervention in Siberia, 1918–1920.* London: Routledge, 1990.

Figes, Orlando. *A People's Tragedy: The Russian Revolution, 1891–1924.* New York: Viking, 1997.

Lincoln, W. Bruce. *Red Victory: A History of the Russian Civil War, 1918–1924.* New York: Da Capo, 1999.

Wade, Rex A. *The Bolshevik Revolution and the Russian Civil War.* Westport, CT: Greenwood, 2001.

Russo-Polish War (February 1919–March 1921)

War between the reestablished Polish state and the emergent Soviet armed forces after World War I. In the aftermath of World War I, the Treaty of Versailles substantially redrew the borders of Europe, creating new states, including Poland, out of the ruins of the German, Russian, Ottoman, and Austro-Hungarian Empires. German occupation forces withdrew from the region in 1919, creating a vacuum in the border area between Poland and the emerging Soviet state. Both nations claimed the territory, and the Russian and Polish forces began low-intensity combat in 1919, which soon developed into full-scale war in April 1920.

By 1919, the Soviet (Red) forces were close to victory in the Russian Civil War, and the Soviet leaders extended peace feelers to the Poles to end the fighting on the western border where the Poles had enjoyed some success, occupying large tracts of the western Ukraine and parts of modern-day Belarus. The Polish head of state, Jozef Pilsudski, remained suspicious of Soviet intentions and rejected the peace overtures. Vladimir I. Lenin, leader of the Soviet government, wanted to regain the Russian territory lost as a result of the 1918 Treaty of Brest-Litovsk, but he and other Soviet leaders also entertained the idea of spreading communism beyond Russian soil, particularly to Germany. Senior Soviet leaders considered a socialist revolution in heavily industrialized Germany important to Soviet Russia's success. To encourage a revolution in Germany, however, Soviet armies would have to cross Polish territory.

For the Poles, Pilsudski greatly influenced Polish foreign policy and considered the acquisition of Russian border areas to be a guarantee of Polish independence and security on the eastern border. The Poles therefore struck first against the Soviet forces, which were slowly gathering in the Ukraine and Belarus. The Soviets were unprepared for a full-scale war.

Pilsudski's armies, numbering about 500,000 men, attacked farther into the Ukraine on April 25, 1920, hoping to capture Kiev. The Polish armies were a conglomeration of formations made up of Poles who had served the armies of Germany, Austria-Hungary, and imperial Russia. Pilsudski had multiple army-sized formations under his command during the campaign, though the size and composition changed often.

The Soviet forces on the Polish border consisted of two army groups, or "Fronts," one commanded by General Alexander Yegorov (Southwestern Front) of 84,000 men and the other led by General Mikhail Tukhachevsky (Western Front) numbering some 160,000. In total, Soviet forces fluctuated between 600,000 and 700,000 men during the campaign. The Soviet fronts operated independently, but their actions were to be guided and coordinated by Leon Trotsky, the Soviet commissar for war.

Yegorov's forces were in a state of disorganization when the Poles attacked and were soon retreating in front of the advancing Polish forces. The Poles captured Kiev on May 7, 1920. Tukhachevsky launched his own series of attacks into central Poland beginning in May 1920, in part to relieve the pressure on Yegorov to the south. As the Poles reacted to the new threat, the reorganized Southwestern Front counterattacked with its shock force, the First Cavalry Army (Konarmiya) commanded by General Semen Budenny. The Soviet attacks broke the Polish line in a series of battles, and by the beginning of June the Polish armies were in retreat.

The Soviets kept up the pressure. Tukhachevsky launched new attacks, led by the III Cavalry Corps commanded by General Chaia Ghai. On July 4, 1920, the Western Front took the offensive, with Ghai capturing Vilnius on July 14 and Grodno on July 20.

The Polish army continued to retreat, and the Western and Southwestern Fronts entered central Poland. Tukhachevsky intended to attack Warsaw as early as the beginning of August, but the Western Front could not do so because of logistical problems resulting from overextended and precarious Soviet supply lines.

The Polish defenses of Warsaw centered on a series of fortifications, including a bridgehead in the Praga suburb on the east bank of the Vistula River. During August 12–15 elements of the Western Front attacked Warsaw directly, while Ghai's III Cavalry Corps crossed the Vistula so as to flank the defenses from the north, circling around to attack the Polish positions. Tukhachevsky had some 24 divisions at his disposal, putting severe pressure on the Polish defenders. Initially, the attacks centered on the fortifications around Praga; the Russian Third, Fourth, and Fifteenth Armies engaged the Polish First Army, defending the city proper, and the Fifth Army, covering the area to the north around the fortress of Modlin and Wloclawek. Ghai's forces and the Soviet Fourth Army attacked the Polish Fifth Army, at one point breaking through the northern Polish defenses. European observers concluded that the Polish defense was doomed and began to evacuate their diplomats from Warsaw.

The Poles gained a respite when a Polish cavalry regiment exploited a gap in the southern sector of the Soviet line, however, and overran the Soviet Fourth Army's radio communications section. Out of contact with Tukhachevsky, the Fourth Army failed to receive orders to shift its attack to the south, disrupting the overall Soviet attack plan.

Despite the setback, the Soviet attacks on and north of Warsaw continued, and Pilsudski concluded that he would have to launch a counterattack earlier than planned.

The Poles had identified a potential weakness in the Soviet front, where the Western and Southwestern Fronts met. One advantage the Poles had was the ability to read Soviet radio traffic, as Polish cryptanalysts had broken the Soviet codes. Pilsudksi then ordered the newly formed Assault Group to attack the hinge in the Soviet lines. The Assault Group, 20,000 strong, consisted of the best troops available from the Polish Third and Fourth Armies. In addition, Pilsudski ordered the Polish First and Fifth Armies to counterattack the forces to their front, engaging the numerically superior Soviet Third, Fourth, and Fifteenth Armies during August 14–15.

On August 16, the Polish Assault Group counterattacked Tukhachevsky's southern flank near the city of Mozyr. The Soviet detachment, designated the Mozyr Group, consisted of a scant 8,000 men but was responsible for a 90-mile front and could not stop the Polish advance. Shattered, the Mozyr Group retreated and left a large gap between the two Soviet fronts. Pilsudski exploited the gap with further attacks to the northeast, widening the breach between the Soviet army groups. Pilsudski hoped to cut off and surround the majority of the Western Front's formations, with the Assault Group joining up with the Polish Fifth Army advancing eastward from Warsaw.

The Soviet high command, reacting to the Polish offensive, ordered Budenny's Konarmiya to redeploy to the north to support the Western Front, but the once formidable cavalry force had sustained heavy losses in fighting to capture the city of Lvov. At the time, Joseph Stalin was the senior political officer (commissar) present at Yegorov's headquarters and did not hold a command position. He profoundly influenced Yegorov's and Budenny's actions, however, urging them to continue the attacks on Lvov. Trotsky later claimed that Budenny disobeyed the order to redeploy the Konarmiya with Stalin's connivance, with the result that Budenny's shock troops did nothing to influence the fighting around Warsaw.

Tukhachevsky became aware of the disaster that had befallen his left flank on August 18 and ordered the Western Front to commence an orderly withdrawal. The Soviet command structure was disrupted after weeks of long campaigning, continued friction between the Front commanders, and an overextended supply line. Orders arrived either too late or not at all. Bereft of orders, Ghai's cavalry continued advancing to the west while the Third, Fourth, and Fifteenth Armies attempted to reorganize and withdraw. Unable to communicate with Front headquarters and under increasing Polish pressure, the Western Front formations began disintegrating, and by August 21, the entire front was routed, with heavy losses in killed, wounded, and prisoners. Ghai's cavalry were briefly interned in East Prussia, as their escape route was cut off by the Poles.

The Southwestern Front, its northern flank laid bare, also retreated after the Poles defeated the Konarmiya at Komarow on August 31. By September, the Soviets established a new defensive line on the Neiman River. The Poles attacked the Russian positions and established a bridgehead during September 15–20; however, both sides were exhausted, with many formations on both sides at 50 percent strength or less. In addition, Britain and France put heavy pressure on Pilsudski to make peace. The fighting stopped on October 18, 1920. The Soviets lost an estimated 60,000 killed, with 80,000–100,000 prisoners and missing, compared with Polish losses of around 48,000 killed,

100,000 wounded, and 50,000 missing or taken prisoner. The war officially ended with the ratification of the Treaty of Riga on March 18, 1921.

Tim Wilson

Further Reading

Davies, Norman. *White Eagle/Red Star: The Polish-Soviet War 1919–1920 and the "Miracle on the Vistula."* London: Pimlico, 2003.

Neiberg, Michael, and David Jordan. *The Eastern Front, 1914–1920: From Tannenberg to the Russo-Polish War.* London: Amber Books, 2008.

Zamoyski, Adam. *Warsaw 1920: Lenin's Failed Conquest of Europe.* New York: Harper, 2008.

S

Semenovites

The Semenovites were an armed White (anti-Bolshevik) raiding band that attacked the Red Army in Siberia. Grigory Semenov was the leader of the group, which the Provisional Government in August 1917 initially commissioned to recruit volunteers for the Russian Army. Although sent by the Provisional Government, the Petrograd Soviet also supported Semenov's mission prior to the October Revolution. After the Bolsheviks seized power, Semenov used his forces, which numbered about 550 volunteers, to launch raids on Red Army positions and villages in the Transbaikalia region, located in the eastern part of Russia. Semenov's actions often were counterproductive in the region and contributed to the success of the Red forces in consolidating their power over eastern Russia.

Semenov was an ataman, or leader, of a Cossack group in the Siberian region. His group fought against the Bolsheviks in the region but did not limit their violence to their stated enemies. The Semenovites were a force for destablization in a region that was important for the allies in the Russian Civil War. The region was far from Moscow but close to Japan. The region's proximity to the Pacific Ocean also meant that the United States would be able to send supplies and troops to support the White forces. If the White forces had a solid hold on the Siberian region, this could have helped in garnering support or supplies from the United States. However, consolidating power in the region would be difficult with leaders such as Semenov.

Semenov successfully built his forces after the prime minister of the Provisional Government gave him the mission. After the October Revolution, Semenov pledged to fight with the White forces in the region. He even told Admiral Alexander Kolchak that he would use his forces to help free the tsar and his family, held in Ekaterinburg. Although Kolchak pledged loyalty to the Whites, he was far more interested in working toward increasing his own power. Semenov named his forces the Special Manchurian Detachment, and this was the first armed anti-Bolshevik group in eastern Siberia. The detachment rapidly gained soldiers as demobilized members of the Transbaikal Cossack host came back to the region from their service in the Russian Army.

What made Semenov's forces successful was his use of spies and the possession of two armored trains. He had sources in the Bolsheviks' Red Army as well as sources in the White armies. He used them to coordinate his own operations in such a way as to cut off Bolshevik supply lines. He was able to do this effectively because his spies told him where the Red Army forces were going and what their objectives were. Semenov was especially successful in attacking the Red Army as it moved along the Trans-Siberian Railway. He was able to leverage his armored trains quickly to maneuver and exploit his intelligence advantage.

Japan supported the Special Manchurian Detachment with supplies and soldiers. After suffering defeats by the Soviet Red Army, the detachment held two cities, Verkhneudinsk and Chita. These two cities were close to the Manchurian border. Semenov's forces were able to capture the cities because the Japanese provided a battalion of volunteers and supplies for the assault.

As the White forces in Siberia grew, Admiral Kolchak organized them into the 6th East Siberian Army Corps. Semenov's detachment joined the corps in June 1919. The United States provided support to Kolchak's forces, and this caused tension between Semenov and the rest of the White forces. Semenov intercepted them and took them for his forces, but he refused to work with the Americans, since his support came from Japan. Due to his antagonism of U.S. support, the other White military leaders eventually excluded Semenov from the White armed forces. The divisions in the Siberian region between White forces showed the difficulty that the anti-Bolshevik forces had in building a resilient coalition to defeat the Red Army.

There was one episode that was emblematic of the tension between Semenov and the U.S. forces in the region. Colonel Charles Morrow, who commanded two battalions of the 27th Infantry Regiment, prevented Semenov from moving one of his armored trains into the American sector. Prior to U.S. involvement in the region, there were no limitations on his movements there. However, Colonel Morrow would not allow Semenov's train into his area of operations and threatened to fire on the train if it continued. The Japanese troops with Semenov tried to intervene and convince Colonel Morrow to change his mind, but he would not. Eventually, Semenov agreed to move his train away from the American sector.

When the Red Army consolidated its power in Siberia, Semenov faced the Red Army in Chita. This city was close to the Manchurian border. After the fall of the White forces in Siberia in 1920, Semenov escaped to Manchuria. Throughout the civil war, Semenov had the support of the Japanese government. This was the reason he was against U.S. support and worked to frustrate American efforts to supply and build a White armed force that could stop the Red Army, as it was against the interest of his sponsor, Japan, in the region.

While Semenov was in Manchuria, he continued to spy on the Soviet forces and harassed the Soviet Union. Throughout the interwar period, he maintained his position in Manchuria under the protection of the Kwantung Army, the Japanese forces in Manchuria. During World War II, Semenov used his spies to provide intelligence to the Japanese concerning Soviet maneuvers throughout the region. However, after the Japanese defeat in World War II in 1945, the Soviets captured Semenov. They tried him for a myriad of crimes and found him and the small band of followers they captured with him guilty. All of those in Semenov's group received death sentences and were executed.

Although Semenov fought against the Bolsheviks, he was not an effective asset to the White forces in the region. He did not cooperate with the United States and frustrated efforts at creating a unified military force to resist the Red Army. Semenov's acceptance of Japanese aid and his single-minded pursuit of his own objectives displayed the difficulties that Admiral Kolchak faced in creating a unified opposition to the Red Army out of the disparate band of revolutionaries who only agreed on one policy objective: resisting the Bolsheviks.

Gates M. Brown

Further Reading

Mawdsley, Evan. *The Russian Civil War.* Winchester, MA: Allen and Unwin, 1987.

Shchepkin, N. N. (1854–1919)

Nikolai Nikolaevich Shchepkin was a prominent member of the Constitutional Democrat (Kadet) Party. He was the son of an emancipated serf who later became a famous actor. Shchepkin was a member of the Kadets in the first State Duma. He remained active in liberal and revolutionary groups through the beginning of the 20th century. Shchepkin was an anti-Bolshevik activist; although he supported the revolution, he did not agree with Bolshevism or the violence of Vladimir Lenin's regime. Shchepkin organized several opposition groups in Moscow and even formed an armed group that planned to support the Whites whenever their forces entered Moscow. His actions led to his arrest in August 1919 and his execution by the Cheka on September 23, 1919.

After the Russian Revolution of 1905, Tsar Nicholas II issued a proclamation announcing the formation of the State Duma. This body was initially only an advisory body, but the tsar assented to giving the body some legislative capacity prior to the commencement of the first session. The body would be elected but would be subordinate to the upper legislative body, the State Council. The council was mainly controlled by nobles, half of whom the tsar appointed. In addition to the limited legislative power afforded the Duma, the tsar could dismiss the Duma and call for elections at any time.

Shchepkin's participation in national politics began with his election to the first session of the State Duma. Although the tsar disbanded the First Duma, this did not alleviate the frustration of the people. Shchepkin's work supporting the revolution started after the dissolution of the Duma. He signed the Vyborg Manifesto, which was a document explaining the Kadets' frustration with the monarchy and the end of the First Duma.

This document was the main reason that the tsar's government banned all Kadet leadership participation in subsequent Dumas.

After the fall of the monarchy in 1917, Shchepkin returned to national politics. The head of the Provisional Government, Prince Georgy Lvov, appointed him to lead the Turkestan Committee. This committee had the responsibility of establishing the Provisional Government's authority and governing structure over the Turkestan Krai, or governorship.

During the rule of the Provisional Government, Shchepkin argued for continued Russian participation in World War I. When the Bolsheviks overthrew the Provisional Government, Shchepkin did not accept Lenin's group legitimacy to rule Russia. The success of the Bolsheviks led Shchepkin to create several anti-Bolshevik groups, the first of which was The Nine. This group of activists came from the liberal center and Right of the political spectrum. The name of the group stemmed from the fact that there were three members from each of the larger organizations that formed the body: the Kadets, the Union of Public Figures, and the Commercial and Industrial Union. The initial aim of the group was to get rid of the Bolshevik Party with financial support of Moscow business leaders. As The Nine worked to achieve its goal, it expanded and evolved to be the Right Center. Eventually, Shchepkin led a splinter group that separated from the Right Center due to a difference of opinion concerning allying with Germany. This splinter group was the National Center and did not approve of coordinating with Germany for help in fighting Bolshevism.

Shchepkin led the National Center and its efforts to create an armed body that would overthrow the new Bolshevik government. Although the group had money to pay volunteer officers, they did not have enough funds to raise a sufficiently large military body. In addition, there was a difference of opinion in anti-Bolshevik circles about the best way to handle the rise of Bolshevism in the aftermath of the Brest-Litvosk Treaty. Some argued that the Allies were still the best force to help turn the tide against the Bolsheviks and that Russia should still seek to fulfill its obligations in fighting the Central Powers. However, there was a significant bloc of support for reaching out to the Central Powers, specifically Germany, to help restore order in Russia. Those who wanted German help argued that the treaty with Germany made that nation much more capable to intervene and gain the end of Bolshevik rule in Russia. Shchepkin did not agree that the Germans would be an effective ally; rather, he wanted to continue to fight the Germans with the Allies and fulfill Russia's obligations.

The National Center recruited officers to help fight with the White forces and helped transport these officers to Siberia so they could link up with Allied forces when they arrived to help fight the Bolsheviks. This was one of the problems that the National Center had to contend with: its reliance on outside groups for military support against the Red Army. The Bolsheviks had the capability of enforcing a draconian security state and compelling grain requisitions from the peasants or executing them if they did not acquiesce. Anti-Bolshevik groups did not have the manpower to protect the mass of people from the Red Army, and this meant that they had difficulty tapping into the mass of anti-Bolshevik sentiment that Lenin's harsh policies engendered.

In addition to his work with the National Center, Shchepkin worked with the Union of Regeneration. His position on continuing the fight with the Allies made accommodation with some groups difficult. The Union of Regeneration allowed center and leftist politically aligned individuals to coordinate their actions. The main goals of the union were restoring the war against Germany, creating a collegial directory to govern Russia for the duration of the war, obtaining help from the Allies in the fight against the Soviet state, and holding a Constituent Assembly after the war to democratically determine the future form of government for Russia. This broad policy allowed the union to gain supporters from a wider spectrum than other anti-Bolshevik groups that had more rigorously defined ends. Another benefit of the union was that the individuals joined on their own, not as members of their respective political parties. This allowed the union to gain support without having to create a political coalition that would require other political organizations to alter their own platforms.

As the fight against the Bolshevik government continued into 1919, many anti-Bolsheviks left Moscow to join White forces fighting in southern Russia. Shchepkin decided to stay behind in order to continue his work organizing armed resistance to the Bolsheviks. He worked with the Tactical Center and other armed groups in Moscow in an effort to create an underground armed force that would rise up when the White forces entered the city.

Shchepkin's work against the Bolsheviks ended when he was arrested by the Cheka in August of 1919. A month after his arrest, he was executed and buried in a mass grave. His efforts to overthrow the Bolshevik regime were unsuccessful but show the scale of anti-Bolshevik sentiment in Russia during the period of the Russian Civil War (1917–1922).

Gates M. Brown

Further Reading

Got'e, I. U. V. *Time of Troubles: The Diary of Iurii Vladimirovich Got'e; Moscow, July 8,*

1917 to July 23, 1922. Edited by Terence Emmons. Princeton Legacy Library. Princeton, NJ: Princeton University Press, 1988.

Mawdsley, Evan. *The Russian Civil War.* Winchester, MA: Allen and Unwin, 1987.

Pipes, Richard. *Russia under the Bolshevik Regime.* New York: Vintage, 1995.

Stalin, Joseph V. (1878–1953)

Born as Ioseb Besarionis dze Jushashvili (Georgian) or Iosif Vissrionovich Dzhugashvili (Russian) in Gori, Georgia in December 1878, his assumed name "Stalin" (meaning man of steel) became one of the most famous nom de guerres of the second half of the twentieth century.

Any biographical research on Stalin quickly runs into difficulties and contradictions. The historical record has been heavily redacted and recast by those seeking to either exalt or condemn his tenure as the supreme architect of the Soviet system, promote his image as the savior of the world from the Nazi terror, or reveal him as a "bloodthirsty cannibal." It is beyond dispute, however, that Stalin was chiefly responsible for the political and economic fates of Eastern and Central Europe after World War II and was the most powerful single person on the Eurasian landmass by 1945.

Early Life and Rebellions

One of the few things most sources agree on is that the future dictator was known as "Soso" (meaning "Little Joseph") to intimates all his life. His father, Iosif, was a shoemaker, and his mother, Ketevan, did whatever was necessary to keep the family going. Smallpox at age 7 left young Iosif's face pock-marked. At age 12, an accident or illness rendered his left arm shorter and stiffer than the other. The senior Iosif was an abusive drunk who terrorized not only his family but also the entire village. When Ketevan enrolled young Soso in the Orthodox Seminary in Gori in 1888, Iosif abandoned his family and moved to Tbilisi (Tiflis).

In 1894, Soso enrolled in the Tiflis theological seminary. He was a fervent Georgian nationalist, and by 1895 he had declared himself an atheist as well. He insisted that his peers call him "Koba," a character from a Robin Hood–like legend, and joined the (illegal) Russian Socialist Democratic Labor Party. Although an excellent student, he was expelled from the seminary in 1899, likely because of his revolutionary proselytizing. After a brief stint at the Tiflis Meteorological Observatory, he went underground, became a full-time revolutionary, and discovered the writings of Vladimir I. Lenin. Soso began to sign his articles and poems "Stalin" in about 1904.

Using protection rackets, bank robberies, terror attacks, and extortion to fund his activities, Stalin was in and out of prison and exile while he grew closer to Lenin's work and the Bolshevik (Communist) Party. In St. Petersburg (Leningrad) in 1912, Stalin turned the weekly Bolshevik paper *Zvezda* (Star) into the daily *Pravda* (Truth) that ran continuously until 1991 as the official voice of the Communist Party of the Soviet Union. As editor, he rejected numerous articles by Lenin and met secretly with prominent Mensheviks (socialists). Lenin fired Stalin but made him senior leader of the Russian Bureau of the Bolshevik Party. Stalin was conscripted in 1914 but exempted because of his crippled arm.

Revolution and Civil War

Stalin was the first major Bolshevik leader to arrive in Petrograd after the February 1917 revolution began, having spent much of World War I in jail, hiding, or in exile. Initially he felt compelled to support the

Provisional Government while protesting against the continuation of the war. After Lenin's arrival in April, Stalin and the Bolsheviks openly opposed the Provisional Government and the war. Stalin helped organize support for the Bolshevik (October) Revolution, although his role was small compared to the parts played by Leon Trotsky, Lenin, and others. Stalin was rewarded with the relatively minor post of people's commissar for nationalities' affairs.

During the subsequent Russian Civil War (1917–1922), Stalin was constantly at odds with Defense Commissar Trotsky, whom he had met in 1905 and never liked. Assigned to

As a young Bolshevik, Joseph Stalin proved himself a shrewd political operative, eventually maneuvering himself to become the successor to Lenin. As a ruthless dictator, Stalin led the Soviet Union through rapid industrialization, collectivization, the Second World War, and the onset of the Cold War. He was known for purging suspected rivals, counter-revolutionaries, and dissidents. This World War II–era image depicts him as marshal of the Soviet Union. (Library of Congress)

establish order in Tsaritsyn in May 1918, Stalin ordered scores of former tsarist officers and other "unreliables" publicly shot and ordered the burning of villages to discourage hoarding. In 1919, Stalin served as political commissar for an army attempting to capture L'viv (Lvov), while Trotsky, the commander in chief, attempted to take Warsaw during the Russo-Polish War (1919–1921). Stalin refused to support Trotsky, and both L'viv and Warsaw were lost.

The nascent Soviet Union had recognized the independence of Georgia in March 1918 as part of the Treaty of Brest-Litovsk. However, in 1922 the Red Army invaded Georgia; Stalin was in charge of the invasion and the occupation. He carried out a brutal gutting of its sovereignty, economy, and social structure. Lenin and Trotsky both disagreed with Stalin's policies, and Lenin denounced Stalin in the press. Stalin never forgot.

Lenin succumbed to a heart attack in January 1924, leaving no clear successor. Trotsky was the outstanding figure of the party and seemed the logical choice, but Stalin and the other Bolshevik leaders conspired to discredit him. Stalin then turned against his coconspirators and, ironically, worked with Trotsky to discredit them. This internal struggle ended with Stalin in power by 1928. Along the way, Stalin, using his power as party secretary, filled the ranks with his supporters or those he could bully. He forced Trotsky into exile, expelled him from the party, and finally had him killed. Other rivals and potential rivals, great and small, met similar fates.

In the Great Famine, the cult of personality, and the Great Purges, where Lenin had sought to persuade his opponents, Stalin's leadership emphasized the elimination of opposition, real or imagined. When the peasants in rural areas did not provide enough grain to support his program of industrialization in

1927, he invented the Urals-Siberia method (essentially expropriation by any means necessary) to meet his goals. He also created kulaks, supposedly a wealthier class of farmer, as class enemies to be liquidated so their land could be confiscated. Beginning in 1928, the forced collectivization of agriculture not only took peasants' land but also expropriated their agricultural products, often including the seed grain, for foreign sale. This generated capital for industrialization but starved millions.

Numbers are unclear, but most authorities agree that upwards of 10 million people starved to death between 1928 and 1934, many in the richest agricultural areas of the Soviet Union such as Ukraine. Millions more who resisted collectivization were thrown into gulags, where they provided free labor for Stalin's monumental construction works such as the White Sea Canal, the Dnieper Hydroelectric Dam, and the Moscow Metro.

By 1934, this had evolved into a full-blown program of state-sponsored terror; thousands of alleged anti-Soviet acts were punishable by hard labor or death. Anyone who questioned or failed to meet the expectations of the First Five-year Plan for the industrialization of the Soviet Union was labeled a counterrevolutionary and was arrested and executed or sent to a gulag. Millions, including some of the founding members of the Bolshevik Party and Stalin's closest collaborators, met such a fate. The Great Terror, or the Great Purges as they were known, also affected the Soviet armed forces. Allegedly unreliable officers, including many who had come up under the tsars but also some of the best and most innovative military thinkers in the Soviet Union, were eliminated. Over 60 percent of the staff officers on the register in 1934 were dead or in prison by 1938.

This bloodletting installed Stalin as the absolute and unquestioned leader of the Soviet Union by the end of 1937. Everywhere, "Comrade Stalin" was hailed as the savior of the Soviet Union, the "genius" behind the Soviet advances in industry and agriculture, and the defender and leader of world communism. The colossal, grandiose buildings so iconic of the early Soviet Union are known as Stalinist architecture, and his picture often appears in tandem with those of Karl Marx and Lenin; the other founders of communism could be seen on posters, in murals, and in paintings everywhere. Stalin's speeches (often hours long) were published in their entirety in *Pravda,* and he often wrote lengthy editorials for the paper as well. His birthday was celebrated with lavish parades, and poems, songs, and novels were created as paeans to him. Without Comrade Stalin, it was said, there would be no Soviet Union.

The Great Patriotic War

To some extent, this was certainly true. During the 1930s, Stalin had driven industrialization and militarization at a furious pace. Even as he destroyed the officer corps in 1937, he expanded the Red Army significantly, built a huge Red Air Force, and created a navy that verged on being world-class. He tested those forces in the Spanish Civil War (1936–1939), sending tanks and advisers to aid the Republicans against the Nationalist rebels, who were in turn supported by both Nazi Germany and fascist Italy. While ultimately defeated, the Red Army and Stalin learned many valuable lessons from the experience.

Certainly Stalin gained the impression that the Western democracies would not go to war in defense of their ideals. In his role as head of the Communist International (Comintern), Stalin had attempted to form a common Popular Front with the socialist parties in France and Western Europe (1934–1939) but found them internally divided and for the most part unwilling to follow his lead. The Soviet Union signed a treaty of alliance with France in 1935, but Stalin otherwise found only disappointment in his attempts to establish a regime of collective security against the rising power of Nazi Germany.

With an eye on the parts of Poland that had been a traditional Russian territory, Stalin therefore cautiously reopened communications with Germany in 1939. The Germans proved to be more than willing to offer Stalin part of Poland and more in return for Soviet neutrality. The two states signed the Molotov-Ribbentrop Pact in August 1939, establishing "spheres of influence" within Central and Eastern Europe. Stalin thus bought space and time to rebuild the defense establishment he had nearly destroyed. He did not believe that the treaty would last past 1944, nor did he think that it had to. Following the disastrous Winter War against Finland in 1940, he was told that the Red Army could be reorganized, based on German performance in the West, by 1943. Stalin's own propaganda further held that any state that attacked the Soviet Union would immediately undergo a workers' revolt, though how much of this he believed is unclear.

When the Germans invaded in June 1941, however, Stalin was caught by surprise and purportedly went into a state of shock. He was neither seen nor heard from for 10 days, even as his forces were being annihilated in huge cauldron battles. When Stalin reappeared, his response was predictable: while Soviet forces suffered about 800 deaths every minute, the policies of terror and retribution continued. Entire populations, from ethnic Germans in the Ukraine to the Tatars of Crimea, were deported to Central Asia under suspicion of treason. Alleged deserters retreating from hopeless fights were shot by

blocking forces that had better weapons and more ammunition than most assault battalions. Any soldier taken prisoner was declared a traitor, and his family was punished. Wrongdoers, real and imagined, were put into penal units that cleared mines under enemy fire. Though he improved as a commander over the course of the war and learned to trust his subordinates, Stalin remained at heart a Machiavellian dictator.

Charismatic enough to charm Winston Churchill and Franklin Roosevelt, Stalin nonetheless demanded much from them and anyone else fighting Germany and promised little in return. He knew exactly what he wanted and altered borders with the same calm dispatch and the same blue pencil checkmarks with which he had signed the death warrants of millions of his own citizens. His insistence on retaining the ill-gotten gains of 1939–1940 as a "buffer zone" led Churchill to imagine an "iron curtain" between the communist world and the rest of humanity. On one subject, however, they did agree at the Yalta Conference in February 1945: the Soviets, with more experience in urban warfare, would fight for Berlin alone.

Cold War

At Potsdam in July 1945, Stalin committed to an invasion of Japanese-held Manchuria and hinted, somewhat disingenuously, at an invasion of Japan. Through his spies, he was well aware of the Americans' atom bomb capabilities and hoped to make some easy gains in the East. The sudden collapse of Japanese resistance in mid-August 1945 denied the Soviets an occupation zone in Japan, but this only bolstered Stalin's grip on Eastern Europe. His legions gutted the industrial base in Soviet-occupied zones as "reparations," then rebuilt them in the crude Soviet pattern. After their failure to bring Austria into the Soviet orbit in 1945, Stalin generally adhered to the letter of the Yalta accord. Maintaining the spirit of the agreements was another matter, for Stalin was unwilling to brook even the facsimile of opposition in areas he considered vital to Soviet interests, especially Poland and Germany.

Relations between Stalin and the West thus gradually broke down following the end of the war. Rigged elections brought malleable, pro-Soviet governments into being in Poland, Czechoslovakia, and Hungary during 1946–1948. When the Western Allies reacted by restricting economic aid, Stalin responded in typical fashion. The Berlin Blockade (June 1948–May 1949), followed quickly as it was by the founding of two German states under Western and Soviet domination, marked the pivot from alliance to cold war. Whereas Stalin had sought to protect the Bolshevik Revolution through his doctrine of "socialism in one country" during the 1920s and 1930s, he now tried to use wartime success to build a protective socialist barrier.

His timing was shrewd or perhaps merely fortunate. He had supported nationalist forces in China throughout the 1920s and 1930s, believing that the country was not ready either economically or ideologically for communism. When the communist forces of Mao Tse-tung (Mao Zedong) nevertheless triumphed in the civil war in 1949, Stalin was there to claim the credit. The Sino-Soviet Treaty of Friendship that followed in 1950 actually cost the Soviet Union dearly in economic terms, but Stalin undoubtedly figured that the gain in prestige and security was worth it. The Korean War (1950–1953) was likewise not of Stalin's making, but as it worked to his benefit, he did nothing to stop it and did everything to encourage China and North Korea to continue fighting against the West.

Domestic Policy and Personal Life

Stalin's encouragement of China and North Korea was in keeping with his renewed hardline ideology. Whereas during the war he had encouraged nationalism and cultivated public support from the Orthodox Church, once victory was ensured, Stalin reverted to the norm. He put the population to work rebuilding under the directives of a new Five-Year Plan that retained the 48-hour workweek and emphasized heavy industry above consumer goods. Any unfavorable comparison to the West, or indeed any praise of the Soviets' former Western allies, was once again treated as treason. Hundreds of thousands of Soviet citizens suspected of collaborating with either the Nazis or the West, including the 300,000 prisoners of war the Western Allies had repatriated at Stalin's insistence, were thrown into gulags on charges of "formalism" and "bourgeois cosmopolitanism" and then put to work.

Andrei Zhdanov, the political boss of Leningrad, served as the guiding spirit of this movement, known as Zhdanovshchina (Era of Zhdanov). Zhdanov died in 1948, but Stalin continued and extended the policy, launching new purges that threatened to sweep away millions more, including a new generation of political leaders who might have challenged him. Before the so-called Doctors' Plot purge could be fully realized, however, Stalin suffered a severe stroke while at his dacha (summer house) in Kunetsovo. He died on March 5, 1953. By 1956, the Soviet Union had entered a period of de-Stalinization under Nikita S. Khrushchev, one of Stalin's protégés. The shifting nature of Stalin and his regime, with its constant tinge of terror, calls to mind the reign of Ivan the Terrible. Like Ivan, Stalin could be both charming and terrifying; both rulers produced monumental triumphs yet slaughtered multitudes. Many scholars have even speculated that as was the case with Ivan, the more horrific side of Stalin was unleashed by the death of his first wife. He married Ekaterina Svanidze in Georgia in 1906. She died of typhus (or tuberculosis) in 1907; her family was destroyed during the Great Terror. With her death, Stalin later stated, he lost what was left of his humanity. She bore him a son, Yakov Dzhugashvili, in 1907. In July 1941, he was captured by the Germans. Stalin refused to exchange him for Friedrich Paulus, the German field marshal captured at Stalingrad, and Yakov died at the Sachsenhausen concentration camp in 1943.

Stalin married Nadezhda Sergeevna Alliluyeva in 1919. She bore him two children: a son, Vasily Dzhugashvili, born in 1921, and a daughter, Svetlana Alliluyeva, born in 1926. Nadezhda was said to have been mentally unbalanced, and she frequently argued with Stalin, sometimes in public. In 1932, she died under mysterious circumstances. Some sources claim that Nadezhda had a gunshot wound to the head and a pistol in her hand; others attribute her death to a severe beating and yet others to tuberculosis. The doctors who signed her death certificate claiming acute appendicitis were liquidated during the Great Terror.

Neither of Nadezhda's children saw their father after her death until they were adults. Vasily joined the Red Air Force and was a major general by 1946. He was arrested and imprisoned soon after his father's death and only released in 1960. Vasily died of alcohol-related causes in 1962. Svetlana defected to the United States in 1967, returned to the Soviet Union in 1987, lived in Britain off and on, and then returned again to the United States before her death in 2011. In his personal life, as in his political life, Stalin left behind only tragedy. which is also reminiscent of Ivan IV.

John Beatty

Further Reading

Beatty, John D., and Lee A. Rochwerger. *What Were They Thinking? A Fresh Look at Japan at War, 1941–45*. Bennington, VT: Merriam, 2008.

Colley, Rupert. *Stalin*. New York: HarperCollins, 2012. Kindle Book.

Davies, Sarah, and James R. Harris. *Stalin*. Cambridge: Cambridge University Press, 2005.

Haugen, Brenda. *Joseph Stalin: Dictator of the Soviet Union*. Minneapolis: Compass Point Books, 2006.

Lewis, Jonathan, and Phillip Whitehead. *Stalin: A Time for Judgment*. London: Methuen, 1990.

Overy, Richard James. *Russia's War: Blood upon the Snow*. New York: TV Books, 1997.

Overy, Richard James. *Why the Allies Won*. New York: Norton, 1997.

Rieber, Alfred J. "Stalin, Man of the Borderlands." *American Historical Review* 106(5) (2001): 1651–1691.

Sebag, Montefiore Simon. *Stalin: The Court of the Red Tsar*. New York: Knopf, 2004.

Wettig, Gerhard. *Stalin and the Cold War in Europe: The Emergence and Development of East-West Conflict, 1939–1953*. Lanham, MD: Rowman and Littlefield, 2008.

Woodcock, Sandra. *Stalin*. London: Hodder and Stoughton, 1998.

Stolypin, Pyotr Arkadievich (1861–1911)

Prime minister of Russia from 1906 to 1911. Pyotr Arkadievich Stolypin was born to a noble family in Dresden, Saxony, on April 14, 1861, and died of an assassin's bullet on September 18, 1911. He was noted for his political and agricultural reforms, although the success of his reforms is still debated by historians. Stolypin started working for the state in his mid-20s, shortly after graduating from St. Petersburg University, and was the district marshal of the Kovno Province by 1889. In 1902 he was the youngest person ever appointed governor, serving in the Saratov Province. Tsar Nicholas II noticed Stolypin's success in suppressing radical elements while at the same time attempting to improve the condition of the peasants. The tsar faced similar challenges on a national scale during the Russian Revolution of 1905 and, in 1906 he therefore appointed Stolypin minister of the interior and subsequently prime minister.

In the first post Stolypin acted ruthlessly to suppress the rebellion in the provinces, so much so that a noose became known as a "Stolypin necktie." In the latter post, Stolypin enacted a series of reforms that he believed would placate the peasantry and modernize Russian agriculture. Stolypin's agricultural reforms, known as "The Wager on the Strong," allowed peasants to acquire private property and organize on a local level. He created a state land bank to extend credit for the purchase of land and agricultural equipment, encouraged agricultural education, and also encouraged smaller unproductive farmers to migrate to either Siberia, where he made land readily available, or to the cities, where they would provide cheap labor for Russia's industrialization. By creating a strong, independent peasantry, Stolypin hoped to quell unrest and create support for the government. He recognized, however, that it would take time and estimated that the reforms needed two decades to be effective.

Like the tsar, however, Stolypin was not willing to surrender much of the aristocracy's position of power and privilege. He worked with Nicholas II to roll back the concessions of the October Manifesto, dismissing the First and Second Dumas because they proved to be too liberal. Even during the period of the more conservative Third Duma, Stolypin and Nicholas ruled largely by decree. This combined with the creation of a new landowning class gave rise to a new generation of revolutionaries.

On September 14, 1911, a revolutionary—perhaps a police agent—shot Stolypin while he was attending the opera with the tsar in Kiev. Stolypin died four days later, with the majority of his reforms incomplete.

Robert J. Smith Jr.

Further Reading

Ascher, Abraham. P. A. *Stolypin: The Search for Stability in Late Imperial Russia.* Stanford, CA: Stanford University Press, 2001.

Korros, Alexandra. *A Reluctant Parliament: Stolypin, Nationalism, and the Politics of the Imperial Russian State Council, 1906–1911.* New York: Rowman and Littlefield, 2003.

Pallot, Judith. *Land Reform in Russia 1906–1917: Peasant Responses to Stolypin's Reforms.* Oxford: Oxford University Press, 1999.

T

Tambov Rebellion (1920–1922)

Peasant rebellion during the Russian Civil War. The Russian Civil War was a brutal affair. Both the Bolsheviks (Reds) and their opponents (Whites) requisitioned grain and other foodstuffs from peasants at gunpoint, impressed men and sometimes women into their fighting formations, and generally used terror as a weapon. While the entire nation suffered from the conflict, poor agricultural provinces such as Tambov, some 250 miles southeast of Moscow in the black soil belt of Russia, suffered perhaps more. More than 90 percent of the 3.5 million people who lived in Tambov Province farmed for a living and worked fewer than 15 acres, usually with wooden farm implements. Deep and abiding poverty was the rule rather than the exception in Tambov.

Nevertheless, as the war drew to a close, men flocked to Tambov Province not for its wealth or opportunities but because they were army deserters, and the eastern portion of the province was covered in thick forests that had for centuries been home to bandits and runaways. In the spring of 1918, they became so numerous that they began to form bands. Known as "Greens," they represented a fairly broad political and cultural spectrum but had no real program other than survival and opposition to the military authorities, be they Red or White. They did, however, have loose connections with the Union of the Working Peasantry backed by the old Socialist Revolutionary Party, or what was left of it, after the Bolsheviks had crushed a rising by Social Revolutionaries in July 1918.

By 1920, the Greens' ranks swelled with peasants displaced by the scorched-earth tactics of White general Anton Denikin or impoverished by the Bolshevik requisitioning detachments; the Greens had developed into a sizable force under the leadership of Alexander Antonov. Antonov, in his mid-30s, was a former Socialist Revolutionary. He had been arrested after the Russian Revolution of 1905 and sent to Siberia. During the 1917 revolutions, he aligned himself with the Bolsheviks as the more active party, but when his Social Revolutionary background came to light, he had fled to Tambov. Now in the summer of 1920 as the White forces of Pyotr Wrangel approached from the north, Antonov organized large-scale raids against the Bolsheviks.

With the bulk of the Red Army occupied by the war with Poland, Antonov's Greens roamed the countryside massacring any Bolshevik requisitioning detachments they encountered. Antonov and his men were not content simply to kill the Bolsheviks, however; they tortured them and committed many acts of unspeakable savagery. The villagers of Tambov supported the Greens, seeing them as avengers and Antonov as a modern Robin Hood. By autumn, the Greens effectively controlled much of the province.

Lenin and the Bolshevik leadership could hardly let this pass, and as forces became available in September and October, they were sent to Tambov with orders to repay the Greens in kind. Led by Vladimir Antonov-Ovseyenko, known as "Bayonet," Red forces proceeded to burn any village suspected of supporting the Greens. By spring, some

40,000 Red Army forces under the command of Mikhail Tukhachevsky were in Tambov Province sweeping the forests with machine guns, aircraft, and dozens of field guns. Even as Antonov-Ovseyenko continued to inflict collective punishment on the villagers, Tukhachevsky announced an end to grain requisitioning in favor of a tax in kind of 25 percent in an attempt to quell resistance. Anyone accepting these terms would be amnestied.

Few trusted the Bolsheviks enough to surrender, and the bitter fight dragged on through 1921 and 1922. Green forces, unable to draw on fresh supplies or reinforcements, grew steadily smaller. Antonov was reportedly killed in July 1922, though there were also reports that he had fled to Saratov Province. Regardless, the rebellion had been mercilessly crushed by the end of 1922. The fierceness with which it had been fought and the doggedness of the peasants in protecting their grain, however, had taught Lenin and the Bolsheviks a lesson. They abandoned war communism and its attendant requisitioning as a result of such resistance, though it would return in 1928 when the party had a firmer grip on power.

Timothy C. Dowling

Further Reading

Figes, Orlando. *A People's Tragedy: The Russian Revolution, 1891–1924.* New York: Viking, 1997.

Lincoln, W. Bruce. *Red Victory: A History of the Russian Civil War.* New York: Simon and Schuster, 1989.

Mawdsley, Evan. *The Russian Civil War.* Edinburgh, UK: Birlinn, 2001.

Trotsky, Leon (1879–1940)

Russian revolutionary, minister of war, and political leader. Born at Ivanovka, Ukraine, on October 26, 1879, into a well-to-do Jewish family, Leib (Lev) Davidovich Bronstein took the name Leon Trotsky after he became a revolutionary. At age 17, Trotsky completed his formal education and began his revolutionary activities by helping found the Russian Social Democratic Labor Party. An advocate of ending the monarchy and emancipating the people, he was arrested in 1898 and spent three years in Siberian exile. Trotsky soon escaped and made his way to London, where he met Vladimir Lenin in 1902 and wrote for the newspaper *Iskra* (Spark) during 1902–1905. Trotsky established an independent reputation as a revolutionary, rejecting Lenin's rigid model. Trotsky, but not Lenin, then returned to St. Petersburg to take an active part in the establishment of a soviet (council) there during the Russian Revolution of 1905. After the collapse of the revolution, Trotsky was again arrested. Again sent to Siberia, he escaped two years later to France. He spent the next decade as a writer, war correspondent, and revolutionary advocate not only in Russia but also all over Europe.

Trotsky was a war correspondent in Turkey during 1912–1913. At the beginning of World War I, his calls for working-class people throughout Europe not to fight in a rich man's war led France and later Spain to expel him. He traveled to New York and there taught school until he heard of the Russian Revolution of February 1917. He returned to Petrograd in May. He and Lenin were in full agreement that the Provisional Government must be overthrown. They both assumed that a successful Marxist revolution in Russia would soon spread to the other European industrialized nations.

Trotsky now joined cause with Lenin, and Trotsky, rather than Lenin, played the instrumental role in organizing and leading the Bolshevik Revolution on November 6–7,

A Marxist revolutionary and initial supporter of the Mensheviks, Leon Trotsky joined the Bolshevik cause just prior to the onset of the October Revolution in 1917. He quickly became the commissar of war and later founded the Red Army. (The Illustrated London News Picture Library)

1917. Trotsky became the new government's people's commissar for foreign affairs. He led the Russian delegation that negotiated with the Germans at Brest-Litovsk and opposed Lenin's policy of capitulation in order to protect the revolution, proclaiming a policy of no war, no peace. When the Germans resumed their military advance, Trotsky favored waging revolutionary war, but Lenin prevailed. Lenin believed that it was better to give in to German demands, which would not last because of worldwide communist revolution, and protect the revolution in Russia. Trotsky's policies thus led to harsher German terms in the Treaty of Brest-Litovsk on March 3, 1918.

With the outbreak of the Russian Civil War (1917–1922), Trotsky assumed the position of commissar for war with responsibility for training, equipping, and directing the Red Army against the White forces supported by the Western Allies. He used to advantage Red control of interior lines and the railroad net. His unbounded energy and brilliance as a leader helped decide the war for the Reds. During the conflict, he traveled from trouble spot to trouble spot in a heavily armed train. Trotsky also directed, on Lenin's orders, the unsuccessful Russian war with Poland (1919–1920). Trotsky favored creation of a national militia rather than a professional army.

When Lenin died in January 1924, most experts believed that Trotsky would assume power. Trotsky lost out, however, to Joseph Stalin, who established absolute control and expelled Trotsky from the party. Trotsky was exiled to Kazakhstan in 1928 and then deported to Turkey in 1929. After wandering over Europe, he and his wife eventually found safe asylum at Coyoacan, near Mexico City, in 1936. From there he worked to create an anti-Stalinist movement, which he called the Fourth International. Stalin sent agents to kill him. Trotsky escaped one assassination attempt in May 1940, but on August 21, 1940, a young man carrying a false Canadian passport, who was supposedly a family friend of the homeowner, gained entry into Trotsky's heavily guarded house, pulled a mountain climbing ax from his coat as Trotsky read his paper, and struck him in the head. The wound was mortal.

An intellectual and a revolutionary, Trotsky was also an exceptionally able minister of war who built a highly effective fighting force to win the Russian Civil War and maintain the Bolsheviks in power.

William Head

Further Reading

Service, Robert. *Trotsky: A Biography.* Cambridge, MA: Belknap, 2011.

Trotsky, Leon. *My Life.* Mineola, NY: Dover, 2007.

Volkogonov, Dimitri. *Trotsky, the Eternal Revolutionary.* Translated by Harold Shukman. New York: Free Press, 1996.

Tukhachevsky, Mikhail Nikolaevich (1893–1937)

Soviet marshal whose theories on military strategy put him in conflict with dictator Joseph Stalin. Born on the Aleksandrovskoe estate 150 miles southwest of Moscow on February 16, 1893, Mikhail Tukhachevsky was the son of a nobleman and a servant girl. Debts forced the family to sell the estate and move to Moscow in 1909. There Tukhachevsky entered the Alexandrovsky Military College, studying military thought and history. During World War I as an officer in the elite Semenovsky Guards, he fought in Poland and won six decorations before being taken prisoner in 1915. After three attempts, he managed to escape in 1917.

In 1918 Tukhachevsky joined the Red Army, and as a protégé of Leon Trotsky he became a prominent military commander during the Russian Civil War, leading the First Army and then the Eighth and Fifth Armies. Appointed commander in the west in April 1920, he led the Russian invasion of Poland. Fighting here laid the seeds for future conflicts and hatreds between Tukhachevsky, on one side, and Stalin and Kliment Voroshilov, on the other side. At one point during the 1920 Battle of Warsaw, Stalin withheld vitally needed troops from Tukhachevsky's command.

In March 1921, Tukhachevsky brutally suppressed the anticommunist uprisings at Kronstadt, leading a dramatic charge across the frozen Neva to subdue the fortress. He also commanded the forces that crushed the Tambov Rebellion later that year. Between 1922 and 1924, he headed the Military Academy. In May 1924 he became deputy to Marshal Mikhail Frunze, chief of the General Staff. Following Frunze's death, Tukhachevsky became chief of staff of the Red Army, occupying that post from 1926 to 1928.

Following disagreements with Defense Commissar Voroshilov, Tukhachevsky was commander of the Leningrad Military District between 1928 and 1931. There, he developed his theories of deep operations, the application of mechanization and armor along with air support to warfare, and the use of airborne troops, carrying out actual maneuvers with these forces. Tukhachevsky saw clearly the nature of the German threat, and he called for forward areas to be lightly held, with large formations remaining back for subsequent reaction and deep-penetration operations. Voroshilov, an old-fashioned proponent of cavalry, opposed his theories. Stalin recognized the need for an industrialized military, though, and at least temporarily supported Tukhachevsky.

Tukhachevsky returned to Moscow in 1931 as deputy commissar for military and naval affairs and chairman of the Revolutionary Military Council of the Soviet Union and director of armaments. In November 1935 he was promoted to marshal of the Soviet Union, and in January 1936 he headed the Soviet delegation at the funeral of British king George V.

In 1936, Tukhachevsky was named first deputy commissar for military naval affairs and director of the Department of Combat Training. So strong was his position that he reportedly was able to save the composer Dmitry Shostakovich, a close friend, from persecution by the Peoples' Commissariat for Internal Affairs (Narodni Kommisariat Vnutrikh Del), the Soviet secret intelligence service. Foreign observers recognized Tukhachevsky's contribution in creating the most advanced armor and airborne divisions in the world.

Tuckhachevsky strongly believed in the need to understand thoroughly the defensive aspects of war as a prerequisite for comprehending the operational level of war as a whole; Stalin with the support of Voroshilov and the commandant of the Frunze Academy, Marshal of the Soviet Union Andrei I. Yegorov, demanded unilateral adherence to the offensive in war. Tuckhachevsky also predicted that Adolf Hitler would cooperate with Japan and that Germany would invade both the West and the Soviet Union, and he argued for an end to cooperation with the Germans and a defense in depth. His meddling in such areas and the 1935 publication of these views in an article titled "The War Plans of Germany in Our Time" angered Stalin.

In April 1937, Tukhachevsky was removed from his posts and assigned to command the Volga Military District. He was arrested on May 26, 1937. Secretly tried and condemned on charges of spying for the Germans, he was executed by firing squad on the night of June 11–12 in Moscow. Tukhachevsky's wife was shot as well, and most members of his family were either executed or sent to gulags. After the denunciation of Stalin's terror by Soviet premier Nikita Khrushchev in 1956, a Soviet investigation concluded that the charges against Tukhachevsky had been fabricated, and he was formally rehabilitated. In 1989, the Soviet Politburo announced new evidence indicating that the German intelligence service may have fabricated evidence implicating Tukhachevsky in order to discredit his work. Almost all of Tukhachevsky's views were proven correct during World War II.

Michael Share and Spencer C. Tucker

Further Reading

Alexandrov, Victor. *The Tukhachevsky Affair.* Englewood Cliffs, NJ: Prentice Hall, 1963.

Butson, Thomas G. *The Tsar's Lieutenant, the Soviet Marshal.* New York: Praeger, 1984.

Montefiore, Simon Sebag. *Stalin: The Court of the Red Tsar.* New York: Knopf, 2011.

Shukman, Harold, ed. *Stalin's Generals.* New York: Grove, 1993.

Simpkin, Richard. *Deep Battle: The Brainchild of Marshal Tukhachevsky.* London: Brassey's, 1987.

V

Volunteer Army

The Volunteer Army was an anti-Bolshevik group made up of former tsarist officers and other anti-Bolshevik activists who wanted to resist the October Revolution forcefully. The first commander of the Volunteer Army was General Mikhail Alekseev, the former chief of staff to Tsar Nicholas II and the de facto commander of the Russian Army in the final days of the Romanov regime. Although the force began small, with only approximately 4,000 members, it would grow to over 100,000. This group of volunteers would be the most credible threat to the Bolsheviks in the Russian Civil War.

After the October Revolution and the ascension of the Bolsheviks to power, General Alekseev went to Novocherkassk to organize an armed resistance group that would challenge the Bolsheviks and their hold on power. General Lavr Kornilov joined the group and assumed military command of the Volunteer Army, while Alekseev took over control of the political aspect of the anti-Bolshevik movement. As the Bolsheviks moved into the area where their enemies were posted, the Volunteer Army moved to the south in an effort to establish a new base for their operations, which allowed Alekseev's forces to avoid destruction from the Bolsheviks. This move, occurring in the grips of the Russian winter through the harsh Russian steppes, was an epic in the anti-Bolshevik fight and became known as the Ice March. Survivors received a medal with a crown of thorns pierced by a sword.

During the Ice March the group tried to capture the town of Ekaterinodar, which was the capital of the Kuban Soviet Republic in southern Russia along the Black Sea. The Bolshevik forces killed General Kornilov with an artillery shell that hit the farmhouse that Kornilov used as a farmhouse. Kornilov's death removed a significant figure of the counterrevolutionary movement, and the Bolsheviks made a point of digging up the enemy general's body, taking it to the main square, and destroying it by burning it. The death of Kornilov was the end of the First Kuban Campaign. Lenin speculated that the Bolshevik victory over the Volunteer Army and the death of Kornilov was a turning point for the October Revolution. However, the Volunteer Army, now led by Anton Denikin, would continue to fight against the Soviet regime.

The Second Kuban Campaign began in the summer of 1918 after the Volunteer Army rebuilt its forces. This second campaign started on the Don River and had success in the beginning with the capture of Tikhoretskaia. This town was a vital rail center in not only the Kuban region but also the entire north Caucasus region. After the success of taking the rail center, the Volunteer Army moved to take Ekaterinodar. This was the city where General Kornilov died and the Volunteer Army met its defeat in the First Kuban Campaign. The success forced the Bolsheviks to move their capital from the city and relocate it southeast to another rail center, Piatigorsk, which was 200 miles from Ekaterinodar. By the end of World War I, the

Volunteer Army had the Red Army cornered in the middle of the north Caucasus.

The success of the Volunteer Army in mid and late 1918 brought more people to join the armed force. Although the Soviets had the Volunteer Army badly outnumbered, they had approximately 90,000 men. However, this number covered over the fragile nature of the Soviet hold on power in the region. The region did not have a great amount of support for the Soviet government. The Bolsheviks had trouble projecting power effectively in the region due to the lack of industrial and urban centers that would provide proletarian support.

During the Second Kuban Campaign, the Volunteer Army leveraged its superior military talent and battle-won experience from the First Kuban Campaign to effectively fight against the Red Army in southern Russia. In addition to its superior military personnel, the Volunteer Army also had the benefit of the people's support. Many in the region did not approve of the Soviet local government and saw it as a foreign rule being imposed on the people in the Kuban region. Denikin's forces established a center of power in the Kuban region but struggled to extend their territory.

One of the reasons that the Volunteer Army had trouble extending its success was their inability to effectively combine forces with the Cossack forces in the Don region. The Don Cossacks believed in Cossack nationalism; however, this ran counter to many of the volunteer officers, who believed in a united Russia and did not support Cossack nationalism. The issue came to a head when the Don Cossacks needed aid to continue their fight. The Don Cossack leader, Pytor Krasnov, had already asked for help from the Germans, and this made his position as leader of the Cossacks untenable when the Volunteer Army offered to provide aid. The Volunteer Army by this time already agreed to seek aid from the allies for continuing the war effort. When Krasnov left the Don Cossacks, the Volunteer Army group absorbed the Cossacks. Alhough the volunteers had authority over the Cossacks, the relationship was never easy, and the command was not completely unified under Denikin.

In January 1919, all of the anti-Bolshevik forces fell under Denikin. This force was called the Armed Forces in the South of Russia. One of the issues that Denikin continued to struggle with was his control over the troops in his command. The anti-Bolshevik forces were corrupt, and this frustrated efforts to build a broad base of support for the White forces in southern Russia. Bolshevik actions likewise alienated the population, but the Whites were unable to capitalize on Red mistakes largely because their own troops were acting out against the local population as well.

With the combined force, Denikin attempted an advance into central Russia to take Moscow in 1919. This assault, which relied on Allied war material to conduct, did not succeed. It was an almost impossible task because of the broad front of the advance. Although Denikin had about 100,000 troops to conduct the attack, the front was over 700 miles long. This caused the supply lines of the Volunteer Army to become increasingly strained. Even if the volunteers had been able to take Moscow, this would have meant that at the end of the civil war there was still Petrograd. It was an incredible task just to capture Moscow, much less Petrograd. Although the White forces had material support from the Allies and superior military training, it was not enough to overcome the Red Army's numerical advantage.

The Volunteer Army was an anti-Bolshevik armed group, one of the White forces that fought against the Bolsheviks in southern and central Russia. The Ice March solidified the group, and the First Kuban Campaign hardened them in combat. During the Second Kuban Campaign, the volunteers secured the Kuban and Don regions but were unable to deal a defeating blow to the Bolsheviks or overcome the Red Army's numerical superiority.

Gates M. Brown

Further Reading

Mawdsley, Evan. *The Russian Civil War.* Winchester, MA: Allen and Unwin, 1987.

Pipes, Richard. *Russia under the Bolshevik Regime.* New York: Vintage Books, 1995.

War Communism

War communism was an economic system that existed in Russia between 1918 and March 1921. Intended partially to function as a response to the stress brought on by the Russian Civil War, its main features included grain requisitioning, a ban on private trade, nationalization of industry, labor discipline, rationing, and the attempt to abolish money. Lenin employed the system to discredit opposition in the conflict between the Bolsheviks (Reds) and anti-Bolshevik forces, such as those supporting a restoration of the tsar, middle-class interests (Whites), or the peasants (Greens). The term was first popularized by Lev Kritzman, its most vocal spokesman. The earliest official use of the term "war communism" dates to the spring of 1921, when its policies were being abandoned for the more liberal New Economic Policy.

War communism commenced as Russia found itself in a deep economic crisis in early 1919. Industrial production had fallen dramatically due to supply and transport problems, paired with a dwindling population of urban-based workers who had fled to rural areas to appropriate land. The severe economic crisis was exacerbated by the aggregate strains of World War I and the disastrous agricultural and industrial deficits caused by the Treaty of Brest-Litovsk in March 1918. The signing of the treaty signaled the end of World War I for Russia but at the cost of vast areas of highly productive farmland such as the Ukraine, ceded to Germany.

Grain requisitioning, in which grain was taken from the peasants as an in-kind tax, had to be introduced subsequently in Russia. When the civil war started in earnest in May of that year, the Food Supplies Commissariat and the Red Army were created, and the forcible requisitioning of grain became standard policy.

Naturally, the peasants vehemently opposed both measures. At the start of 1919, another decree required all food surpluses to be handed over to requisitioning squads. This was met in part by severe civil unrest. The Tambov Rebellion, which was the most serious of the uprisings that broke out across Russia, began in July 1920.

The resulting shortages led the Bolsheviks to introduce a class-based system of rationing within war communism. Priority was given to the industrial labor force (the Bolsheviks' social and political base), along with Red Army soldiers. Smaller rations were given to civil servants and professional people such as medical doctors. The smallest rations, perhaps a quarter of those granted to workers and often barely enough to live on, were allotted to what had been the middle class (the bourgeoisie), who were referred to as "former people."

The middle class was effectively driven out of the workforce as the Bolsheviks sought to move to a "true communist economy." By June 1918 most large-scale industries had been nationalized, signaling the implementation of war communism in full. All major industry was centrally administered by the Supreme Council of National Economy (Vesenkha). In November, a decree banned

169

all private trade. By November 1920, nationalization of industry was extended to all businesses with more than five employees.

Bolshevik policies encouraged mass participation by workers in running plants through factory committees while ensuring that factories were not liquidated by their own owners. "Worker control," as the Bolsheviks called it, proved disastrously ineffective, however. Factory worker committees voted themselves huge raises, and few workers possessed the skills and experience to manage even a shift. Machinery broke down, supply chains ceased to function, and the monetary and wage systems simply ceased to function. The Bolsheviks responded by formally abolishing currency and implementing a barter economy. The workers, in turn, simply took the goods they produced in lieu of wages and traded them on the black market.

In the face of such chaos and lacking the administrative tools to cope with such dire problems, the Bolsheviks frequently resorted to terror. The Cheka (secret police) was active in the countryside, where it helped requisition brigades to collect grain from the peasants. The Bolsheviks also sent units of Red Guards and soldiers to the countryside to find grain for hard-pressed cities. Discipline was brought back to the workplace, with fines for lateness and absenteeism. Internal passports were introduced to stop people from fleeing to the countryside. Piecework rates were reestablished, accompanied by bonuses and a workbook that was required to receive rations.

Many Bolsheviks believed that while war communism was in part a necessary rejoinder to the economic issues facing Russia in 1919, their policies also were generating a true communist state. It certainly was not, however, an ideological device fully conceptualized prior to introduction.

War communism essentially was an impromptu series of measures pushed upon the Bolsheviks because of the failure of state capitalism and the onset of civil war. The system—if it can be called such—provided just enough resources to sustain the Bolsheviks in the civil war.

War communism ended in March 1921 after sailors at the Petrograd naval base in Kronstadt rebelled in protest over Bolshevik economic policies and restrictions on democracy. The sailors had been some of the most loyal supporters of the October Revolution. Lenin and the Bolsheviks therefore abandoned war communism for the New Economic Policy, which would last for seven years.

Dustin Garlitz

Further Reading

Malle, Silvana. *The Economic Organization of War Communism, 1918–1921.* Cambridge: Cambridge University Press, 1985.

Pipes, Richard. *The Russian Revolution.* New York: Vintage, 1991.

Raleigh, Donald J. "The Russian Civil War, 1917–1922." In *The Cambridge History of Russia,* Vol. 3, *The Twentieth Century,* edited by Ronald Grigor Suny, 140–167. Cambridge: Cambridge University Press, 2006.

Richman, Sheldon L. "War Communism to NEP: The Road from Serfdom." *Journal of Libertarian Studies* 5(1) (1981): 89–97.

Roberts, Paul Craig. "'War Communism': A Re-Examination." *Slavic Review* 29(2) (1970): 238–261.

Spahr, Warren. *Stalin's Lieutenants: A Study of Command under Duress.* Novato, CA: Presidio, 1997.

Stoecker, Sally. *Forging Stalin's Army: Marshal Tukhachevsky and the Politics of Military Innovation.* Boulder, CO: Westview, 1998.

Szamuely, L. "Major Features of the Economy and Ideology of War Communism." *Acta Oeconomica* 7(2) (1971): 143–160.

Webb, Jonathan. "War Communism, 1918–21." *20th Century History Review* (September 2009): 2–5.

White Armies in the Russian Civil War (1917–1922)

There was no single White Army during the Russian Civil War. Instead, various forces formed to oppose the Bolshevik seizure of power during the Russian Revolution of 1917. Some favored a restoration of the monarchy, while others favored a return to parliamentary democracy (or the promise thereof) represented by the Provisional Government. Very seldom did they agree on aims, strategies, or tactics. Supported by the French, British, and American governments, the White armies initially appeared capable of winning the Russian Civil War. With the advantage of interior lines of movement and communication, however, the more disciplined and focused Russian Red Army defeated the last White force remnants by 1922. The defeat of the White armies can be attributed in no small part to their elitism and inability to win popular support.

White armies formed around all the borders of the old Russian Empire as various ethnic groups and political movements rejected the Bolshevik government of Vladimir Lenin. Opponents included loyal tsarists, social revolutionaries, and Social Democrats as well as Cossacks, Czechs, and other ethnic minorities. The ideological heterogeneity of the White armies made leaders hesitant to declare favor for republicanism, democracy, or land reform, though. Many of the armies' military leaders were avowed tsarists who intended to restore the discredited monarchy of the Romanovs. This prevented them from gaining sympathy from many moderate workers or peasants who might have otherwise joined their forces. The White armies were also hampered by a reliance on foreign weapons, since the Red Army retained control of industrial regions; this led many Russians to suspect that the Whites were simply puppets of the Western Allies. At the same time, the corruption, elitism, and brutality of many former tsarist officers alienated Russians in the territories they occupied.

The largest White army formed in the southern territory of the Don Cossacks, while other White armies formed in Siberia, the Baltic States, and the Ukraine. The British, French, Americans, Germans, and Japanese sent troops into Russia and supplied the White armies with money and armaments. These support efforts were seriously hampered by lack of coordination and national rivalries. General Lavr Kornilov and General Anton Denikin, a former tsarist chief of staff, led the large White army in the south, but its advance on Moscow crumbled when Leon Trotsky enforced greater discipline, ruthlessness, and purpose in the Red Army.

Another White army advanced from Estonia but failed to take Petrograd from the Reds. Denikin then resigned his position and handed control over to General Pyotr Wrangel. The Red Army promptly defeated Wrangel in 1920, and his forces evacuated the southern territories. By 1922 the Red Army had captured Vladivostok, the last stronghold of the White army of Siberia led by Admiral Alexander Kolchak. The remaining White forces disintegrated, leaving supporters facing prison, execution, or exile.

Thomas Edsall

Further Reading

Lincoln, W. Bruce. *Red Victory: A History of the Russian Civil War.* New York: Simon and Schuster, 1989.

Luckett, Richard. *The White Generals: An Account of the White Movement and the Russian Civil War.* New York: Routledge and Kegan Paul, 1987.

Smele, Jonathan D. *Civil War in Siberia: The Anti-Bolshevik Government of Admiral Kolchak.* Cambridge: Cambridge University Press, 2006.

Wilson, Woodrow (1856–1924)

U.S. political leader and president of the United States during World War I. Born on December 28, 1856, in Staunton, Virginia, Thomas Woodrow Wilson grew up in Augusta, Georgia, and South Carolina. The son of an austere Presbyterian minister and seminary professor, Wilson was raised in a strict religious and academic environment. He studied history and politics at Princeton University, graduating in 1879. Wilson then studied law at the University of Virginia for a year and passed the Georgia bar examination in 1882.

Wilson practiced law for a short time in Atlanta, but he abandoned it to earn a doctorate in constitutional and political history at Johns Hopkins University in Baltimore in 1886. By then he had joined the faculty at Bryn Mawr College. In 1890 Wilson returned to Princeton, first as a professor of jurisprudence and political economy and then as president of the university in 1902. He won national acclaim for his academic reforms.

Turning to state Democratic politics, in November 1910 Wilson won election as governor of New Jersey. His success in championing Progressive Era legislation in the state led him to become the Democratic Party standard-bearer in the 1912 presidential election. The Republican Party split that year, driven by former president Theodore Roosevelt's third-party bid, and Wilson won the election in November, defeating incumbent Republican William Howard Taft as well as Roosevelt and socialist Eugene V. Debs. Although Wilson garnered just 41.8 percent of the popular vote, he bested his nearest opponent by nearly 15 percent.

As president, Wilson was preoccupied with domestic policy and his "New Freedom," the belief that government should encourage free competitive markets by breaking up business trusts and combinations and by bolstering free trade. He pushed through the Underwood Tariff that reduced import duties by about a fourth and increased the number of duty-free items.

To compensate for the loss of revenue, Wilson introduced the federal income tax. On his initiative, Congress also passed the Federal Reserve Act of 1913, which created 12 regional Federal Reserve banks supervised by a central Federal Reserve Board. Its primary duty was to regulate the volume of money in circulation in order to ensure a healthy economy and adequate credit. Wilson also secured passage in 1914 of the Federal Trade Commission Act, which brought about a new regulatory agency, the Federal Trade Commission, to ensure free and fair competition. That same year he signed into law the Clayton Anti-Trust Act, which prevented interlocking directorates and declared illegal certain monopolistic business practices. This act also provided that labor unions were not necessarily subject to injunction.

Wilson was not as successful in his foreign policy, where he sought to implement diplomacy based primarily on morality and the rule of law. He pledged that the United States would forgo territorial conquests, and he and his first secretary of state, William Jennings Bryan, worked to establish a new relationship between the United States and Latin America whereby Western Hemisphere states would guarantee each other's territorial integrity and political independence.

Despite Wilson's best intentions to avoid conflict with U.S. neighbors, his distaste for political upheaval and instability in Mexico led him to send forces to occupy Veracruz in April 1914. Incidents along the border caused him two years later to mobilize the National Guard and dispatch a regular army force into northern Mexico under Brigadier General John J. Pershing in a vain attempt to capture Mexican revolutionary Pancho Villa. Although the operation was unsuccessful in its stated intent, it did provide useful training for the army.

Wilson promptly proclaimed U.S. neutrality when World War I began in August 1914, calling on Americans to be neutral in thought as well as action. Germany's submarine warfare brought the nation to the brink of war, however. The sinking of the passenger liner *Lusitania* on May 7, 1915, which killed 128 American passengers, led Wilson to issue a series of threatening notes that compelled Germany to halt unrestricted submarine warfare.

Although Wilson won reelection in 1916 primarily on the platform of having kept the United States out of the war, he had secured passage by Congress that year of the National Defense Act, which greatly enlarged the peacetime army and the National Guard and provided for the establishment of reserve formations and the Reserve Officers' Training Corps. German acts of sabotage against the United States and publication of the Zimmermann Telegram, in which the German government proposed an alliance with Mexico, alienated American opinion. But the great blow to Wilson's efforts to keep the United States neutral came on February 1, 1917, when Germany resumed unrestricted submarine warfare. The sinking of U.S. merchant ships and the loss of American lives led Wilson to address Congress on April 2, 1917, and

request a declaration of war, which Congress approved on April 6.

The old tradition of avoiding foreign entanglements was so strong that the United States never formally joined the Allies. Wilson made it clear that the country was merely an "associated power" fighting the same enemy. He also did not want to bind the United States to an annexationist peace settlement. With no military experience of his own, Wilson deferred to his military advisers. His directive to American Expeditionary Force (AEF) commander Pershing was simply that he was "vested with all necessary authority to carry on the war vigorously." Wilson instructed Pershing to cooperate with the forces of other countries fighting Germany, "but in doing so the underlying idea must be kept in view that the forces of the United States are a separate and distinct component of the combined forces, the identity of which must be preserved."

Wilson supported Pershing in his refusal to have the Allies employ AEF units piecemeal or be embedded among European troops, but when General Ferdinand Foch became supreme Allied commander in the crisis of the spring of 1918, Wilson made it clear that Pershing was subordinate to him. Wilson's platform was to "make the world safe for democracy." He also unwisely referred to the conflict as "the war to end all wars."

But Wilson was determined to keep the United States free of advanced territorial commitments, and in January 1918 he announced his Fourteen Points as a basis of peace. These included "Open covenants openly arrived at," freedom of the seas, international disarmament, return of territory captured by the Central Powers as well as the return to France of Alsace-Lorraine, an independent Poland with access to the sea, and a league of nations. "Self-determination of peoples," which Wilson believed would bring lasting peace to Europe, was not one of the Fourteen Points. Meanwhile, the United States tipped the balance of the scales in favor of the Allies, and Wilson played this to full advantage.

Following the armistice of November 11, 1918, Wilson unwisely decided to head the U.S. delegation to the Paris Peace Conference. He traveled widely before the conference began and was lionized by the peoples of Europe. Wilson knew little of European affairs, however, and the public adulation went to his head and convinced him that the peoples of Europe wanted him to be the arbiter of the peace and that they favored a settlement based on "right" rather than on narrow national self-interest. Although Secretary of State Robert Lansing accompanied Wilson to Paris, the president largely ignored him and other advisers and diplomats. Wilson also failed to include in the delegation key Republicans.

At the Paris Peace Conference, Wilson developed a close working relationship with British prime minister David Lloyd George. The two men stood together on most key issues against French premier Georges Clemenceau. The League of Nations was based on an Anglo-American draft, and Wilson defeated French efforts to detach the Rhineland from Germany. The resulting Treaty of Versailles with Germany and general peace settlement were essentially Wilson's work, although he had been forced to make a number of concessions that betrayed his Progressive supporters.

Meanwhile at home, government efforts supported by Wilson and designed to control the home front with legislation such as the Espionage Act, the Sabotage Act, and the Sedition Act resulted in wholesale civil liberty violations and helped precipitate the postwar Red Scare. Indeed, these repressive measures, combined with postwar isolation-

ism and disillusionment, marked the effective end of the Progressive Era.

By the time Wilson returned to the United States in July 1919, popular sentiment had moved toward isolationism. The Republicans, led by Senator Henry Cabot Lodge, insisted on restricting the power of the League of Nations. Specifically, most Republicans feared the mutual defense clause, which they believed would commit the United States to another war in advance and without congressional oversight. Even some Democrats wanted amendments.

Wilson embarked on an exhausting cross-country speaking tour in an effort to sway public opinion, but he suffered a serious stroke on October 2, 1919, that left him virtually incapacitated for the remainder of his administration. When he insisted that Democrats in the U.S. Senate reject any compromises in the agreements, the Senate refused twice to ratify the Treaty of Versailles and to enter the League of Nations. The United States thus was never a participant in the league. Wilson died in Washington, D.C., on February 3, 1924.

Yoneyuki Sugita and Spencer C. Tucker

Further Reading

Ambrosius, Lloyd E. *Wilsonian Statecraft: Theory and Practice of Liberal Internationalism during World War I.* Wilmington, DE: Scholarly Resources, 1991.

Ambrosius, Lloyd E. *Woodrow Wilson and the American Diplomatic Tradition: The Treaty Fight in Perspective.* New York: Cambridge University Press, 1987.

Calhoun, Frederick S. *Power and Principle: Armed Intervention in Wilsonian Foreign Policy.* Kent, OH: Kent State University Press, 1986.

Cooper, John Milton, Jr. *Breaking the Heart of the World: Woodrow Wilson and the Fight for the League of Nations.* New York: Cambridge University Press, 2001.

Cooper, John Milton, Jr. *Woodrow Wilson: A Biography.* New York: Vintage, 2011.

Esposito, David M. *The Legacy of Woodrow Wilson: American War Aims in World War I.* Westport, CT: Praeger, 1996.

Ferrell, Robert H. *Woodrow Wilson and World War I, 1917–1921.* New York: Harper and Row, 1985.

Knock, Thomas J. *To End All Wars: Woodrow Wilson and the Quest for a New World Order.* New York: Oxford University Press, 1992.

Link, Arthur S. *Wilson.* 5 vols. Princeton, NJ: Princeton University Press, 1947–1965.

Link, Arthur S. *Woodrow Wilson and the Progressive Era, 1910–1917.* New York: Harper and Row, 1954.

MacMillan, Margaret. *Paris, 1919: Six Months That Changed the World.* New York: Random House, 2002.

Nordholt, John Willem Schulte. *Woodrow Wilson: A Life for World Peace.* Berkeley: University of California Press, 1991.

Thompson, John A. *Woodrow Wilson.* London: Longman, 2002.

Walworth, Arthur. *Wilson and His Peacemakers: American Diplomacy at the Paris Peace Conference, 1919.* New York: Norton, 1986.

Witte, Sergei Yulevich (1849–1915)

Sergei Yulevich Witte, minister of finance and chairman of the Council of Ministers for Russia, initiated a program of industrialization during the reign of Tsar Nicholas II and implemented a number of critical political reforms during the Russian Revolution of 1905. Russia's first constitutional prime minister, Witte attempted to reconcile Nicholas's authoritarian regime and industrial capitalism. Although a brilliant innovator and administrator, he proved ineffectual in modernizing Russia.

Witte was born into hereditary nobility on June 29, 1849, in the Russian province of Georgia. Until the age of 16, he lived in the Caucasus. He studied mathematics at Novorossisk University in Odessa. In 1871 after contemplating a career in academia, Witte joined the state bureaucracy. His first job was in the governor-general's chancellery in Odessa. After only a few months, he transferred to the local railway administration. Six years later, Witte left and started an independent career with the Southwestern Railway Company. He had enormous success, progressing rapidly to the directorship of the company and making important contacts with prominent political and business figures.

In the 1880s, Witte played a key role in developing legislation for Russia's railroad system. In 1889, he was appointed as the director of the new railroad department in the Ministry of Communications. Tsar Alexander III, learning of Witte's reluctance to accept the position, doubled his salary and promoted him from the ninth to the fourth rank of state service. Witte's success led to promotion as minister of communications in February 1892. In August, he was also named minister of finance.

Witte attempted to industrialize and modernize Russia's economy through a series of reforms, most notably railroad construction. He sought to improve service on Russia's existing rail lines and to expand Russia's railroads by constructing the Trans-Siberian Railway, a major addition that would boost trade. His system also emphasized protectionism and foreign investment. Witte called upon Russian merchant groups to play an instrumental role in developing the necessary infrastructure. He created a state bank, encouraged the development of private banks, helped reform company laws, and worked to ease the convertibility of the

Sergei Witte served as a trusted finance minister to both Tsar Alexander III and his son Tsar Nicholas II. During the political crisis of 1905, Witte was instrumental in establishing critical reforms which resulted in him being appointed to the First Council of Ministers, a post he held until April 1906. (Library of Congress)

ruble. He negotiated foreign loans from such countries as France, Belgium, Germany, and the United Kingdom. Witte also focused on education so that by 1905, 39 new committees had been established to assist with technical education and encourage businessmen to expand their networks.

Witte's policies were costly and unpopular with conservatives in Russia. His relationship with Nicholas II was tenuous, and the two frequently disagreed on policy. By 1899, when Russia was experiencing a severe economic depression and labor disputes spread to St. Petersburg and Moscow, Witte's critics were convinced that his policies were the cause of the unrest and the economic depression. In 1903, Nicholas II requested Witte's resignation. Witte complied and was

appointed to the honorific post of chairman of the Committee of Ministers.

Removed from a role in state affairs, Witte helplessly watched the Russian government blunder into the Russo-Japanese War. It is a mark of the respect he had abroad that he was asked to represent Russia at the ensuing peace talks, and he secured amazingly good terms for Russia. Nicholas II had no choice but to recall him.

After the Russian Revolution of 1905, Witte convinced Nicholas II to issue the October Manifesto, promising a greater degree of representative government, although Witte personally despised constitutional monarchism. Ironically, Witte then served as the first prime minister; he diligently weeded out the leaders of the revolution and worked to suppress social and political unrest in Russia. His most important contribution was to negotiate a series of desperately needed loans to stabilize Russia's economy. Nicholas II never fully trusted Witte, however, and after the immediate danger of revolution had passed, he forced Witte from office in April 1906.

In the last years of his life, Witte reorganized the State Council but no longer had his former influence over policy. When World War I started in August 1914, he urged the Russian government to stay out of the conflict but to no avail. Witte did not live to see Russia's collapse. He died on March 13, 1915.

Timothy C. Dowling

Further Reading

King, Greg. *The Court of the Last Tsar.* Hoboken, NJ: Wiley, 2006.

Verner, Andrew. *The Crisis of Russian Autocracy: Nicholas II and the 1905 Revolution.* Princeton, NJ: Princeton University Press, 1990.

Witte, Sergei. *The Memoirs of Count Witte.* Translated and edited by Abraham Yarmolinsky. New York: Doubleday, 1921.

Women's Battalions of Death (1917)

All-female fighting units formed under the Provisional Government but dissolved by the Bolsheviks. Women had a long tradition of fighting in the Russian military, but until 1917 they had always done so as individuals. Between August 1914 and March 1917, at least 49 (and probably several hundred) Russian women had served in the army, some disguised as men but many openly and with imperial dispensation. Following the March 1917 revolution, the Provisional Government mooted the idea of creating female labor battalions. In May, the Congress of Delegates of the Southwestern Front proposed forming revolutionary shock units. Maria "Yashka" Bochkareva, who had been serving in the V Corps (Second Army) since 1915, then suggested an all-female shock unit: the Women's Battalion of Death.

Duma president Mikhail Rodzianko and army chief of staff General Alexei A. Brusilov supported the idea. They hoped that the unit would inspire a wave of patriotism and support for the new regime; Bochkareva's aim was to shame Russian men into fighting. No one, however, anticipated the response Bochkareva got; over 2,000 women signed up to serve in the Women's Battalion of Death, and the movement quickly spread. Volunteers came from all regions and social classes. By mid-July, the General Staff had authorized five additional battalions of death, and at least 11 all-female units existed

Conceived by the Provisional Government as a way to boost the morale of the withering Russian Army, the Women's Battalions of Death were all-female fighting units tasked with continuing the fight on the Eastern Front in 1917. When the Bolsheviks took power they dismantled these units, claiming they'd lost their "moral significance." (George Rinhart/Corbis via Getty Images)

by November 1917. The Moscow Women's Battalion of Death enrolled over 1,000 volunteers, while Petrograd formed two Women's Battalions of Death in addition to Bochkareva's. Valentina Petrovna, a veteran of the 21st Siberian Rifles Infantry Regiment, commanded the all-female Black Hussars of Death, and there was even an all-female naval battalion of death.

While Bochkareva commanded her own unit and all medics in the units were female, the other officers were men; the government required officers in the Women's Battalions of Death to have frontline experience. In other respects, the female units were treated no differently than male units. They were paid at the same rate as male volunteers and were sent to the military academies for training as officers and noncommissioned officers, and their units were organized just like male battalions. The Moscow and Petrograd Women's Battalions of Death received at least three months' training, to include rifle drill, night maneuvers, and parade. Bochkareva's unit trained for only five weeks before deploying, but Bochkareva drove them so hard that fewer than half the women completed the course.

About half the female units served in the rear, freeing male units for frontline duty. More than 5,000 women saw combat. Their experience was less than successful. Bochkareva's unit, part of the Tenth Army, suffered 80 percent casualties in its only attack. The other female units incurred heavy casualties as well, sometimes via friendly fire from disgruntled male units. The Women's Battalions of Death were quickly withdrawn from combat; however, many continued to serve behind the lines. One unit was guarding the Winter Palace the night of the Bolshevik Revolution. Claiming that the women's volunteer movement had lost its "moral significance," the Bolsheviks

disbanded the all-female units after taking power.

Timothy C. Dowling

Further Reading

Bochkareva, Maria. *Yashka: My Life as Peasant, Officer, and Exile.* New York: Basic Books, 1919.

Lincoln, W. Bruce. *Passage through Armageddon: The Russians in War and Revolution, 1914–1918.* New York: Simon and Schuster, 1986.

Sanborn, Joshua A. *Drafting the Russian Nation: Military Conscription, Total War, and Mass Politics, 1905–1925.* DeKalb: Northern Illinois University Press, 2003.

Stites, Richard. *The Women's Liberation Movement in Russia: Feminism, Nihilism, and Bolshevism, 1860–1930.* Princeton, NJ: Princeton University Press, 1978.

Stockdale, Melissa K. "'My Death for the Motherland Is Happiness': Women, Patriotism, and Soldiering in Russia's Great War, 1914–1917." *American Historical Review* (February 2004): 78–116.

World War I, Russia in (1914–1917)

For some eight decades, objective historical assessment and perspective on the one hand and Russia and its performance in World War I on the other hand have represented something of a contradiction of terms for two reasons. First, Russia was defeated and driven from the ranks of Germany's enemies and thus had no direct part in that country's defeat in the autumn of 1918. The whole question of its role and value in dividing the resources and attention of the Central Powers between 1914 and 1917 failed to attract the historical attention it merited. Second, the Russian Revolution of November 1917, the ideological change that was embraced, and

EASTERN FRONT, 1914–1918

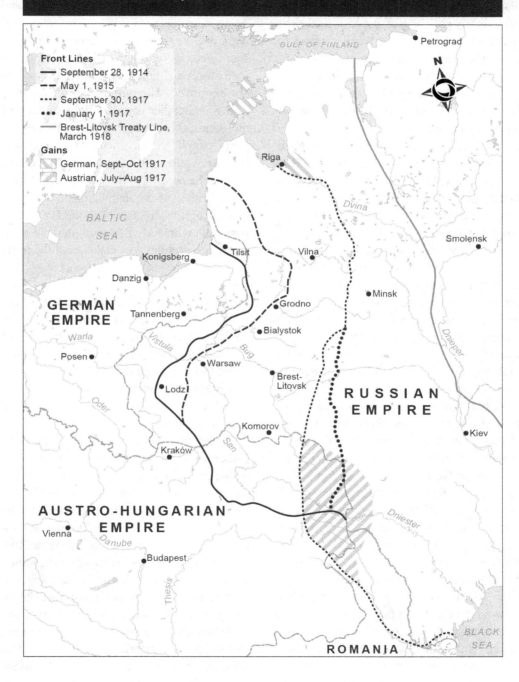

Front Lines
— September 28, 1914
-- May 1, 1915
···· September 30, 1917
••• January 1, 1917
— Brest-Litovsk Treaty Line,
   March 1918

Gains
⬚ German, Sept–Oct 1917
⬚ Austrian, July–Aug 1917

GULF OF FINLAND

Petrograd

N

Riga

Dvina

Smolensk

BALTIC
SEA

Tilsit

Vilna

Konigsberg

Danzig

Minsk

GERMAN
EMPIRE

Tannenberg

Grodno

Bialystok

Warla

Dnieper

Vistula

Bug

Posen

Warsaw

Oder

Lodz

Brest-
Litovsk

RUSSIAN
EMPIRE

Komorov

Kiev

San

Kraków

AUSTRO-HUNGARIAN
EMPIRE

Dniester

Vienna

Danube

Budapest

Thesis

BLACK
SEA

ROMANIA

this ideological impact on World War II and the Cold War had the effect of lessening the historical impact of World War I, indeed perhaps rightly so. The Russian historical experience in terms of World War I counted for little when set alongside the ordeal of the Great Patriotic War (World War II).

Russian involvement in the war was problematic from the start. While some historians have argued that Russia sought territorial gains in the Balkans and access to the Mediterranean, there was no clear strategic Russian objective. Ostensibly, Russia mobilized in defense of Serbia and Pan-Slavism. More concretely, Russia was fulfilling its treaty obligations to France, which were tied to financial considerations designed to boost the domestic economy. While most Russian military planners wanted an offensive in the southwest against Austria-Hungary, the tsar had promised an invasion of East Prussia to relieve pressure on the Western Front. This was achieved at Tannenberg, though at a cost to Russia that more than offset the early victories against Austria-Hungary.

Russia thus was crucial to the Allied cause generally in the period 1914–1917, and specifically with the Brusilov Offensive in the summer of 1916, in terms of the support it afforded its Western allies in the form of offensives specifically intended to divide enemy resources and efforts. In the general period, Russia was able to inflict upon Austria-Hungary and Turkey a series of defeats, certainly in the case of the former, from which there arguably was no recovery. In these years, Russia also put together an amphibious effort in the Black Sea that enjoyed a success that contrasted sharply with the Gallipoli failure. But no amount of success on these fronts could ever compensate for defeat at German hands, particularly the disaster of the Great Retreat in the face of the Central Powers' Gorlice-Tarnów Offensive.

In seeking to understand the basis of Russia's defeat and collapse, the events of 1915 and the enforced withdrawal across Poland possess notable significance. The withdrawal itself was for the most part orderly, but Russian forces were obliged to destroy most of their stores and equipment, since they could not be moved. The withdrawal of the army was accompanied by the flight of tens of thousands of civilian refugees to cities already unable to feed them. The result was mass starvation and what can be termed the start of the process of the unraveling of Russian morale. The problem herein, however, is that in August 1915 Tsar Nicholas II assumed personal command of an army that did rally. The Great Retreat was ended, and the army undertook the Brusilov Offensive, which regained much of the territory lost in 1915. On the eve of the Russian Revolution of February 1917, the Russian Army was better equipped than at any time since the start of the war, and one of the inescapable facts about the campaign on the Eastern Front is that half of all Russian casualties were sustained in the 12 months before the tsar took personal command of the armies.

Where the elements of defeat came together was partly in the person of the tsar. By taking direct command of the army, he was naturally tainted with and discredited by defeat. But what was equally important was the slow falling apart of Russian industry and society under the impact of war. The basic Russian problem was not inadequate production, as is often assumed, but rather problems of distribution on a transport system that simply could not move food for the cities, fuel and basic household goods for town and country, and troops and material for the army. Additionally, there was an increasingly widespread belief that the tsar, the imperial family, and the state system were the real obstacles to both the proper professionalization of the army and the successful prosecution of the war. Increasingly, it was believed throughout Russia that victory under the existing tsarist regime was impossible and that radical change was necessary for military success. As General Alexei Brusilov stated, Russia could not win the war with its existing system of government.

Such was the background to the collapse of the imperial system in March 1917. Crucial in this process was a hopelessly inadequate state administrative structure, the tsar's basic refusal to work with representatives of the Duma (which only served to strengthen organizations and individuals "outside" the basic state system), and increasingly widespread and obvious corruption and self-indulgence within government and industrial establishments. The cities of Russia experienced sharp increases in recorded crime and public disorder, and certainly by the end of 1916 there was a conscious fin de siècle extravagance that, alongside the demonization of the Romanov dynasty, pointed to a rising expectation of revolutionary change.

Hedley P. Willmott and
Timothy C. Dowling

Further Reading

Joll, James, and Gordon Martel. *The Origins of the First World War.* 3rd ed. New York: Routledge, 2006.

Lincoln, W. Bruce. *Passage through Armageddon: The Russians in War and Revolution, 1914–1918.* New York: Simon and Schuster, 1986.

Stone, Norman. *The Eastern Front, 1914–1917.* 2nd ed. New York: Penguin, 2004.

Wrangel, Pyotr Nikolaevich (1878–1928)

Pyotr Wrangel was a leading general of the White Russians, the counterrevolutionary forces that fought during the Russian Civil War, which followed the Russian Revolution of 1917. Ruthless and determined, he could not reverse the declining fortunes of his army in Russia and ended his life in exile.

Wrangel was born in St. Petersburg on August 27, 1878, into a noble family of Swedish extraction. In 1901, he graduated with a degree in mine engineering but nonetheless joined the Imperial Russian Army. Deemed good enough for the Horse Guards, Wrangel served three years before resigning to accept an engineering post in eastern Siberia. When the Russo-Japanese War commenced in 1904, he was reassigned to a Cossack regiment and fought with distinction. After the war, Wrangel was allowed to serve again in the Horse Guards and attend the General Staff Academy in 1907.

When World War I began in August 1914, Wrangel headed a Cossack regiment and saw action throughout Galicia. His good conduct resulted in his promotion to general in 1917 and command of the Seventh Cavalry Division. Though aristocratic in outlook and behavior, Wrangel was unique among contemporaries in recognizing the need for democratic reforms and better treatment of soldiers. He fought well during the ill-fated Kerensky Offensive of August 1917 but resigned from the military when his superior, General Lavr Kornilov, attempted to overthrow the Provisional Government in St. Petersburg. Because Russia was then in the throes of the communist revolution, Wrangel retired to Yalta to await the outcome of events.

By August 1918 the Bolsheviks under Vladimir Lenin had begun a brutal campaign of political and military consolidation, and many former imperial officers such as Wrangel took up arms to stop them. Given his prior military reputation, Wrangel became a lieutenant general in the counterrevolutionary army known as the Russian White Army, or Whites. Wrangel came to despise his superior, General Anton Denikin, but was nonetheless accorded command of a cavalry division and ordered to drive the Russian Red Army (of the Bolshevik government) out of the Caucasus.

Wrangel tackled the job with ruthlessness and relish. After much hard fighting at Stavropol, he was told to recruit soldiers from the 3,000 prisoners taken. Wrangel lined them up, summarily executed the officers, and warned lesser ranks of a similar fate if they did not join the White cause. In January 1919, he rose to head of the White Army once Denikin appointed himself commander of the Armed Forces of South Russia. Wrangel was then sidelined with typhus for several months but eventually recovered and scored an important victory by capturing Tsaritsyn (Volgograd) from Bolshevik forces in June 1919. The White troops under his command sustained a serious defeat at Saratov that November, and this reverse, coupled with the failure of Denikin's ambitious Moscow Campaign, spelled doom for the White Russians. Wrangel tried to reorganize his shattered army around the vicinity of Kharkov prior to launching a new offensive, but when Denikin demanded his resignation in February 1920, Wrangel complied and traveled to Constantinople (Istanbul).

As White fortunes continued to sink, Wrangel returned to Russia following Denikin's resignation in April 1920. Assuming command of the remaining White forces in Crimea, Wrangel spent several months rebuilding their offensive spirit and capability. He was assisted greatly by the Poles, who were then locked in combat with Bolshevik forces along the eastern border of Russia.

Unlike previous White leaders, Wrangel tried to attract the support of the peasantry, the Cossacks, and even the Western Allies through extensive land reforms. He eventually assembled 40,000 men, stormed into Tauride, and drove northward into the Ukraine. In August, however, his White armies suffered heavily at the hands of the Kuban Cossacks and failed to keep possession of Tauride. Wrangel withdrew back to Perekop Peninsula by November with 30,000 men, while the Red Army, 100,000 strong, slowly advanced on him. Wrangel at this juncture realized that the end was near but refused to abandon his men. With consummate skill, he organized a remarkable evacuation that transported 146,000 soldiers and dependents to safety. Wrangel himself was among the last to depart aboard the cruiser *General Kornilov* for Western Europe.

While in exile Wrangel immersed himself in refugee affairs, and in 1924 he founded the Union of Old Soldiers of Russia, which served as a focal point for anti-Bolshevik activities. He accepted work as a mining engineer in Belgium. Wrangel, one of the most effective commanders of the doomed White movement, died suddenly in Brussels on April 25, 1928.

John C. Fredriksen

Further Reading

Brinkley, George A. *The Volunteer Army and Allied Intervention in South Russia, 1917–1921: A Study in the Politics and Diplomacy of the Russian Civil War.* Notre Dame: University of Notre Dame Press, 1966.

Kenez, Peter. *Civil War in South Russia.* 2 vols. Berkeley: University of California Press, 1971–1977.

Luckett, Richard. *The White Generals: An Account of the White Movement and the Russian Civil War.* New York: Routledge and Kegan Paul, 1987.

Mawdsley, Evan. *The Russian Civil War.* Boston: Allen and Unwin, 1987.

Y

Yegorov, Alexander Ilyich (1883–1939)

Born into a peasant family near Samara on October 13, 1883, Alexander Yegorov rose to become a marshal of the Soviet Union and chief of the General Staff. He graduated from the Samara gymnasium in 1901, joined the Russian Army in 1902, and qualified as a sublieutenant in 1905, when he helped put down the Russian Revolution of 1905. Wounded five times while serving with the 132nd Infantry Battalion in World War I, he rose to the rank of lieutenant colonel.

A member of the Socialist Revolutionary Party since 1904, Yegorov fell in easily with the Bolshevik regime after the October Revolution. Promoted to colonel, he commanded the Bolshevik Tenth Army on the Southern Front from December 1918 to May 1919, when he was again wounded. Upon recovery, Yegorov took command of the Fourteenth Army and played a central role in defeating the White forces of Anton Denikin in Ukraine. Yegorov subsequently served as commander of the Kiev Military District during 1920–1921 and then the Petrograd Military District.

In September 1921, Yegorov took command of the Soviet Southwestern Front in the war against Poland. He worked closely with Mikhail Tukhachevsky, Semen Budenny, and Joseph Stalin during this campaign, which was ultimately unsuccessful. Yegorov then transferred to command of the Caucasus Red Army from February 1922 to May 1924, after which he took command of the Ukrainian Military District. During 1926–1927, he served as a military adviser in China; upon his return, he was appointed commander of the Belorussian Military District.

In June 1931, Yegorov was appointed chief of the General Staff of the Red Army and deputy commissar for defense, though he was technically still only a colonel. In September 1935, though, he was promoted to marshal of the Soviet Union when the rank was created. Two years later, he was demoted to commander and sent to the Trans-Caucasus Military District.

Yegorov was arrested in February 1938 and died in prison on February 22, 1939. He was rehabilitated in 1956, having never been charged with any crimes.

Timothy C. Dowling

Further Reading

Bayer, Philip. *The Evolution of the Soviet General Staff, 1917–1941.* New York: Garland, 1987.

Hunczak, Taras, ed. *Ukraine, 1917–1921: A Study in Revolution.* Cambridge, MA: Harvard University Press, 1977.

Parrish, Michael. *Sacrifice of the Generals: Soviet Senior Officer Losses, 1919–1953.* New York: Scarecrow, 2004.

Yudenich, Nikolai (1862–1933)

Russian Army general. Born to a noble family in Minsk Province on July 30, 1862, Nikolai Nikolaevich Yudenich graduated from the Aleksandrovsky Military College in 1881. He completed the General Staff Academy in 1887 and then served in a variety of staff assignments until 1904. During the 1904–1905 Russo-Japanese War, Yudenich commanded first an infantry regiment and then a brigade. Promoted to major general in 1905, he was posted to the Caucasus, where he was deputy chief of staff of the Caucasus Army in 1907. Advanced to chief of staff there by 1912, he was serving in that capacity at the outbreak of World War I.

Many Caucasus Army units were being relocated to other fronts at the beginning of the war when the Ottoman Third Army invaded. Yudenich resisted orders from Caucasus Army commander General Viktor Myshlaevsky that Russian forces withdraw. Instead Yudenich defended Sarikamiş, where he won a victory in late December and early January. In January 1915, Yudenich was advanced to lieutenant general and took command of the Caucasus Army. Known as a daring, resourceful commander, he defeated another Turkish advance, this one in the summer of 1915. The next year, he mounted a series of spoiling attacks that captured Erzurum, Trebizond, and Erzincan. In March 1917, Yudenich replaced Grand Duke Nikolai Nikolaevich as supreme civil and military commander of the Caucasus Front. Yudenich himself was then recalled. He remained in Petrograd until the Bolshevik seizure of power that November, when he went into hiding.

In 1919 Yudenich joined anti-Bolshevik White forces near Petrograd, and in October he became the commander of the Northwestern Front. That same month, his small White force of only some 14,000 men attacked from northeastern Estonia and reached the outskirts of Petrograd. Short of supplies and equipment, it was driven back and forced to retire into Estonia. Yudenich went into exile in 1920 and died in Nice, France, on October 5, 1933.

Claude R. Sasso and Spencer C. Tucker

Further Reading

Allen, W. E. D., and Paul Muratoff. *Caucasian Battlefields: A History of the Wars on the Turco-Caucasian Border, 1828–1921.* Cambridge: Cambridge University Press, 1953.

Drujina, Gleb. "The History of the Northwest Army of General Yudenich." Unpublished doctoral dissertation, Stanford University, 1950.

Luckett, Richard. *The White Generals: An Account of the White Movement and the Russian Civil War.* New York: Viking, 1971.

Mawdsley, Evan. *The Russian Civil War.* Boston: Unwin Hyman, 1987.

Rutherford, Ward. *The Russian Army in World War I.* London: Cremonesi, 1975.

Wildman, Allan K. *The End of the Russian Imperial Army.* 2 vols. Princeton, NJ: Princeton University Press, 1980, 1987.

Z

Zemstvo Union

The official name of the Zemstvo Union was the National Union of Zemstvos in Aid to Sick and Wounded Soldiers. This organization worked with zemstvos at the village level to provide not only aid to returning soldiers but also to help supply the army and refugees. This union partnered with the National Union of Cities. Prince Georgy Lvov led the coordination committee that provided direction for the two bodies. He would become the head of the Provisional Government after the February Revolution in 1917. The Provisional Government bolstered the zemstvo system by creating 19 regional bodies in provinces that did not have zemstvos prior to the fall of the tsar's regime. These regional groups had elected leaders chosen by popular election with universal suffrage and secret ballots. When the Bolshevik government took over, it dismissed the zemstvos and disbanded the Zemstvo Union.

Zemstvos were a system of local government that provided education, medical help, agricultural extension, and political representation to the people under its authority. Tsar Alexander III established the zemstvo system in an effort to create a more liberal state. Although there were elections for representatives to sit on the zemstvos, the nobles had an outsized presence in the bodies in relation to their share of the population. Almost 75 percent of the members of the zemstvos were nobles, while they made up less than 2 percent of the population. Although the zemstvo system provided some representation to the peasants of Russia, it was not a political system that they recognized as legitimate.

When World War I began, many peasants still looked skeptically at their local zemstvos. However, the Russian state used these organizations as a tool to explain the war to the peasants and convince them that they were a part of the broader Russian nation. The state's arguments about nationalism were largely ineffective, because peasants did not identify themselves as belonging to the Russian nation as much as they identified with their local ethnic group or region. However, peasant participation in the war did make clear the benefit of education, something that the zemstvos provided to the people. Soldiers wrote home stressing the importance of providing an education to their children, because their experiences convinced them of the importance of literacy. Similarly, their wives, who had to use officials in the zemstvos to read the letters from the front because they were illiterate, began to understand the power of reading. This increased the demand for school programs for children that soon outstripped the resources available to zemstvos.

Although the effort to convince the Russian peasants of their place in the Russian nation failed, the peasants still largely supported the war effort. They raised funds for war relief and donated food and other supplies for troops. They also provided for refugees from the war when they came to their village. The war mobilized about 40 percent of the rural male working population, so it is not surprising that the villagers held such an interest in the war. As the war continued, there was an increased demand for libraries, newspapers, and other informational programs that the zemstvos provided. Adults attended literacy classes in order to read the information about the war coming into the village.

The idea for consolidating zemstvos and town Dumas into one union to help the war effort began in Moscow in the immediate aftermath of the start of the war. The Moscow provincial government created the idea of a national union of zemstvos, and the Moscow town Duma, or city government, likewise created the idea of a national union of city governments. Although the intent of the Moscow union was to try to provide national unity, Russian political parties also saw an opportunity to strengthen their weak national power bases. The war required more participation than in peacetime, and the lack of strict restrictions about who could participate allowed many activists who were unable to participate in zemstvos or town councils to participate in the unions. This made these organizations even more important for political parties to use the unions to consolidate or build national power.

Due to the inability of the regime or the military to support the military casualties, the zemstvo unions provided trains and frontline medical support. However, this made the regime uneasy because of the politicized nature of the members of the union, but the regime had little choice due to the ability of the unions to provide the care that the soldiers needed that the government and the military were unable to produce. There were reports from the front that the Zemstvo Union's hospital trains were passing out revolutionary propaganda. The unions grew very quickly, and by 1915 every provincial zemstvo except that in Kursk was a member of the national union, and the urban counterpart had over 400 members from across the nation. Tsarist officials soon began to suspect the motives behind the unions, and some called for the unions to be constrained only to the activities that they purported to support—that is, support of the wounded and sick soldiers.

As the war continued into 1915, the problems it caused the government increased. The tsarist regime was unprepared for the length of the conflict and could not handle the multitude of problems, such as ammunition shortages, epidemics, and inflation. The unions allowed the government to delegate a vital task, medical care for soldiers, to a more capable body. However, this also provided the justification for the union leaders to be confident in their position; the government needed them, and they could take risks that previous activists could not. By 1915, the unions were calling for reforms that would introduce a government that was more responsible to the Russian people. Tsar Nicholas II rejected the unions' calls for change, and he removed his interior minister, N. B. Shcherbatov, for not being more forceful with the troublesome groups. The real problem with the tsar's rejection was that it only gave more power within the unions to the radicals who wanted more dramatic reform, while delegitimizing and silencing the moderates in the unions.

Through 1916 the political situation continued to frustrate many in the unions. The tsar grew suspicious of the unions and their role in society and politics. Public opinion began to impact the union leaders in a more forceful manner by the end of 1916. The unions began work for changes in society and the government after the war. This caused significant concern for the regime, but the government would have difficulty pulling power away from the unions. Initially, the government used propaganda to try to convince people that the Zemstvo

Union employees were draft dodgers or cowards, but this was ineffective. Later the regime forced the unions to allow police presence at meetings. As the political situation worsened, the unions called for more drastic action, such as the creation of a government responsible to the people. This caused the split between the Duma leaders and the unions to widen, as the Duma leaders called for legal reforms within the parliamentary system. By the end of 1916 the Duma leaders recognized that their call for legal reforms failed, and the union leaders, pressured from revolutionary elements within the unions, openly called for more revolutionary measures.

The unions created were emblematic of the troubling contradictions in Russian society and government prior to the collapse of the Romanov dynasty. The government was unable to provide for the economic and military aspects of the war without help from the public. However, the government was loath to recognize the importance of public support, since to do so would give credence to the importance of such organizations that would provide it. Public aid would also give legitimacy to the calls for more public participation in government affairs, since the people would be helping the government fulfill obligations that it was unable to complete on its own. The unions and the political agitation that they caused showed that the tsar's government was right to be suspicious of them, but Tsar Nicholas II provided no resolution to the contradictions that the unions exploited. When the regime fell, the head of the Provisional Government was Prince Lvov, indicative of the important role that the unions played in establishing a representative government outside of the Duma.

When the Bolsheviks took over in October 1917, they immediately stopped the zemstvo and town unions. Lenin characterized the unions as bodies that supported the bourgeois elements in Russian society. The unions, as discussed previously, were also a center for political organization and provided some level of democratic representation. Both of these were antithetical to the Bolsheviks and would present a threat to consolidating power for the nascent socialist state.

Gates M. Brown

Further Reading

George, Mark. "Liberal Opposition in Wartime Russia: A Case Study of the Town and Zemstvo Union." *Slavonic and East European Review* 65(3) (July 1987): 371–390.

Zinoviev, Grigory (1883–1936)

Grigory Yevseevich Zinoviev was an important figure in the Russian Revolution of 1917 and in the formative years of the Soviet Union. He was a favorite of Vladimir Lenin's and led the Soviet Union for a short time along with Joseph Stalin and Lev Kamenev following Lenin's death in 1924. Zinoviev was later expelled from the Bolshevik Party by Stalin, however, and eventually was a victim of the Great Purge.

Zinoviev was born in 1883 in the city of Yelisavetgrad under the name of Radomyslovsky but changed his last name to Zinoviev to hide his Jewish background. He received his education at home and worked for awhile as a clerk. In the late 1890s he became part of the Social Democratic movement but then immigrated in 1902 to Switzerland, where he studied at the University of Bern. It was there at the age of 20 that Zinoviev first met Lenin and became a member of the Bolshevik Party.

Zinoviev returned to Russia following the start of the Russian Revolution of 1905. He served as an agitator and workers' advocate

Grigory Zinoviev was an early supporter of the Bolshevik cause and a close collaborator of Vladimir Lenin. As such he was a central figure in the October Revolution and the formation of the Soviet Union. In the aftermath of Lenin's death, Zinoviev worked with Lev Kamenev and Joseph Stalin to ensure that Leon Trotsky did not assume Lenin's leadership role. Zinoviev eventually ran afoul of Stalin and was sentenced to ten years in prison in 1935, only to have a second trial in 1936, during which he was found guilty of supporting terrorist activities, and sentenced to death. He was one of the first casualties of Stalin's purges. (General Photographic Agency/Getty Images)

and was elected to the Bolshevik Party leadership in St. Petersburg. Soon he was elected to the Soviet Central Committee, the ruling committee of the Bolshevik Party. In his capacity with the party, he was arrested by the police in 1908 but was quickly released. He emigrated again and stayed abroad until the outbreak of the 1917 revolution.

During his exile, Zinoviev served the Bolshevik Party on the editorial boards of the newspaper *Proletary* (Proletarian) and the magazine *Sotsial-demokrat* (Social Democrat). Zinoviev proved to be very loyal to Lenin as well as a good propagandist and theoretician. Returning to Russia with Lenin after the outbreak of uprisings in February 1917, Zinoviev immediately resumed his role on the Central Committee. After things took a brief turn against the Bolsheviks in July 1917, Lenin again fled Russia, but Zinoviev stayed and continued to operate underground in Petrograd (the former St. Petersburg).

In October 1917, Lenin proposed an armed insurrection to seize power in Russia. Zinoviev, along with his "Bolshevik twin" Kamenev, opposed the proposal even though it was favored by a majority of the Central Committee. Zinoviev published his objections in Maxim Gorky's newspaper *Novaya zhizn* (New Life). This action would perhaps prove to be the defining moment of Zinoviev's political life. Lenin, who was enraged by Zinoviev's stance, called Zinoviev and Kamenev "traitors and strikebreakers of the revolution" and demanded their expulsion from the party. Zinoviev and Kamenev recanted, apologized for their actions, and admitted their mistake, as the Bolsheviks did indeed seize power in October 1917. They were not expelled from the party and even remained in the party's leadership. The incident proved to be an indelible stain on Zinoviev's reputation, however, and would later be used by Stalin to destroy him.

As the Russian Civil War swept across the country in 1918, Zinoviev became involved with the defense of the fledgling Bolshevik government. He was in charge of the city Petrograd, where he aggressively used terror and cruelty to defend the revolution against counterrevolutionary forces. Although a capable propagandist and an able administrator, he was not a military man, and when

Petrograd was threatened by the White Russian forces, Lenin relieved Zinoviev of command and replaced him with Leon Trotsky, who successfully defended the city. A vain and ambitious man, Zinoviev blamed Trotsky for his demotion, and the two men became enemies shortly thereafter.

Their feud became public when Zinoviev helped Stalin destroy Trotsky politically. Following the death of Lenin in 1924, Stalin, Zinoviev, and Kamenev ruled the Soviet Union as a triumvirate. After Trotsky was out of the way, however, Stalin moved to discredit Zinoviev and Kamenev so that he could assume sole control of the Soviet Union. Stalin had always considered Zinoviev and Trotsky his main rivals, as he felt that they had been closer to Lenin than he himself had been. Zinoviev had also made some poor political decisions, and as a result he quickly lost power to Stalin. By 1926, Zinoviev found himself out of office.

Zinoviev remained in the country and the party, retaining the hope that he would be returned to favor by Stalin and the Bolsheviks. Zinoviev held many second-rate jobs within the party and was even made rector of Kazan University and deputy chairman of the State Scientific Council. These positions would be short-lived, however, as Zinoviev soon found himself in Stalin's crosshairs again.

In 1934 Sergei Kirov, the Leningrad party chief, was found murdered. Stalin saw a chance to get rid of his former colleagues and rivals once and for all by blaming Zinoviev and Kamenev for the murder. The two men were arrested and charged with murdering Kirov. They pleaded for mercy and received prison sentences of 10 years. In 1936 Zinoviev and Kamenev were again brought to trial, as Stalin wanted to remove all trace of those who could remember the extent of his relationship with Lenin. In the second trial, Zinoviev and Kamenev were more compliant and confessed to the charges in exchange for Stalin's promise to spare their lives. The promise was not kept, and although the charges were never proven, Zinoviev and Kamenev, two inseparable comrades who on a personal level had been closer to Lenin than anyone, were executed on August 25, 1936, just a few hours after the trial ended for the crimes of conspiracy and murder.

David Elliott

Further Reading

Figes, Orlando. *A People's Tragedy: A History of the Russian Revolution.* New York: Viking, 1996.

Geller, Mikhail, and Aleksandr Nekrich. *Utopia in Power: The History of the Soviet Union from 1917 to the Present.* Translated by Phyllis B. Carlos. New York: Summit Books, 1986.

Medvedev, Roy A. *Let History Judge: The Origins and Consequences of Stalinism.* New York: Columbia University Press, 1989.

Volkogonov, Dmitri Antonovich. *Stalin: Triumph and Tragedy.* Translated by Harold Shukman. New York: Grove Weidenfeld, 1991.

Documents

The 1905 Revolution

The Program of the Social Democrats (1903)

The platform of the Social Democrats can be seen as a call for the tsar and his government to adjust to the changing social and political conditions of Russia. The party of the working class wanted the right to assemble and to speak freely about the issues that workers faced as Russia industrialized. Predating the events of Bloody Sunday, it is easy to see in this platform the evolving push for the tsar to loosen his power over the people of Russia and especially the workers in Russia's expanding industrial sector. The points established in this document read from a 21st-century perspective as radical but not revolutionary. However, within the context of tsarist Russia, these demands are questioning the very tenets of the tsar's control, and thus the tsar viewed them as revolutionary indeed.

[We consider] social revolution, which is the ultimate aim of all the activities of international social democracy as the class-conscious expression of the proletarian movement. By replacing private with public ownership of the means of production and exchange, by introducing planned organisation in the public process of production so that the well being and the many sided development of all members of society may be ensured, the social revolution of the proletariat will abolish the division of society into classes and thus emancipate all oppressed humanity, and will terminate all forms of exploitation of one part of society by another.

A necessary condition for this social revolution is the dictatorship of the proletariat; that is, the conquering by the proletariat of such political power as would enable it to crush any resistance offered by the exploiters. In its effort to make the proletariat capable of fulfilling its great historical mission, international social democracy organises it into an independent political party in opposition to all bourgeois parties, directs all the manifestations of its class struggle, discloses before it the irreconcilable conflict between the interests of the exploiters and those of the exploited, and clarifies for it the historical significance of the imminent social revolution and the conditions necessary for its coming. At the same time, it reveals to the other sections of the toiling and exploited masses the hopelessness of their condition in capitalist society and the need for a social revolution if they wish to be free of the capitalist yoke.

The party of the working class, the Social Democrats, calls upon all strata of the toiling and exploited population to join its ranks insofar as they accept the point of view of the proletariat. The Russian Social Democratic Labour Party therefore sets as its immediate political task the overthrow of the tsarist autocracy and its replacement by a democratic republic whose constitution would guarantee:

1. The sovereignty of the people; i.e., the concentration of the supreme power of the state in a unicameral legislative assembly composed of representatives of the people.

2. Universal, equal and direct suffrage for all citizens, male and female, who have reached the age of twenty . . . a secret ballot in these elections. . . .

3. Broad local self-government . . . [and] regional self-government for localities with special conditions of life or a particular make-up of the population.

4. Inviolability of person and dwelling.

5. Unrestricted freedom of conscience, speech, press and assembly; the right to strike and to form trade unions.

6. Freedom of movement and occupation.

7. Elimination of class privileges and the complete equality of all regardless of sex, religion, race or nationality.

8. The right of any person to obtain an education in their native language . . .; the use of the native language together with the state language in all local, public and state institutions.

9. National self-determination for all nations forming part of the state.

10. The right of every person through normal channels to prosecute before a jury any official.

11. The popular election of judges.

12. The replacement of the standing army by the general arming of the population (i.e. the formation of a people's militia).

13. Separation of church and state, and of school and church.

14. Free and compulsory general or vocational education for all children of both sexes up to the age of sixteen; provision by the state of food, clothes, and school supplies for poor children.

To protect the working class from physical and moral degradation, and also to develop its capacity for the liberation struggle; the party demands:

1. Limitation of the working day to eight hours for all hired workers. . . .

2. A complete ban on overtime work.

3. A ban on night work . . . with the exception of those (industries) which absolutely require it for technical reasons. . . .

4. The prohibition of the employment of children of school age. . . .

5. A ban on the use of female labour in occupations which are harmful to the health of women; maternity leave from four weeks prior to childbirth until six weeks after birth. . . .

6. The provision of nurseries for infants and young children in all . . . enterprises employing women.

7. State insurance for workers against old age and partial or complete disability through a special fund supported by a tax on capitalists. . . .

8. The appointment of an adequate number of factory inspectors in all branches of the economy. . . .

9. The supervision by organs of local self government, together with elected workers' representatives, of sanitary conditions in factory housing. . . .

10. The establishment of properly organised health inspection in all enterprises . . . [and] free medical services for workers at the employer's expense, with wages to be paid during time of illness.

11. Establishment of criminal responsibility of employers for violations of laws intended to protect workers.

12. The establishment in all branches of the economy of industrial tribunals made up equally of representatives of the workers and of management.

13. Imposition upon the organs of local self-government of the duty of establishing

employment agencies (labour exchanges) to deal with the hiring of local and non-local labour in all branches of industry, and participation of workers' and employers' representatives in their administration.

In order to eliminate the remnants of serfdom, which lie as an oppressive burden on the peasantry, and to further the free development of the class struggle in the countryside, the party demands above all:

1. Abolition of redemption payments and quit rents as well as all obligations which presently fall on the peasantry, the taxpaying class.

2. The repeal of all laws hampering the peasant's disposal of his own land.

3. The return to the peasants of all moneys taken from them in the form of redemption payments and quitrents; the confiscation, for this purpose, of monastic and church property as well as of lands owned by the emperor, government agencies and members of the tsar's family; the imposition of a special tax on estates of the land-owning nobility who have availed themselves of the redemption loans; the deposit of sums obtained in this way into a special fund for the cultural and charitable needs of the village communities.

4. The institution of peasant committees.

5. The granting to the courts of the right to reduce excessively high rents and to declare null and void all transactions reflecting relations of servitude.

In striving to achieve its immediate goals, the RSDRP will support any opposition or revolutionary movement directed against the existing social and political order in Russia. At the same time, it resolutely rejects all reformist projects involving any broadening or strengthening of police or bureaucratic tutelage over the toiling classes.

Source: Programme of the Social-Democratic Workers' Party, Adopted at the Second Congress of the Party (London: New Park Publications, 1978). Used by permission of Index Books.

The Program of the Social Revolutionaries (1905)

Read after the 1903 platform of the Social Democrats, the 1905 program of the more radical Social Revolutionaries provides a greater insight into the changing social and political context of Russia between 1903 and 1905. Beyond the call for universal rights, the Social Revolutionaries moved beyond the ideas of the Social Democrats in 1903 and began to argue for the redistribution of land, as well as abolition of the army. One can see how the tenets established in 1905 in this document festered between 1905 and 1917 and came into their own under the turbulent period in the summer and fall of 1917.

The Socialist Revolutionary Party of Russia views its task as an organic, component part of a universal struggle of labour against the exploitation of human dignity, against all barriers that prevent its development into social forms, and conducts it in the spirit of general interests of that struggle in ways that are determined by concrete conditions of Russian reality.

Since the process of the transformation of Russia is led by non-socialist forces, the Socialist Revolutionary Party, on the basis of the above principles will advocate, defend, and seek by its revolutionary struggle the following reforms:

In the matters of politics:

The establishment of a democratic republic with broad autonomy for oblasts and communes, both urban and rural.

Increased acceptance of federal principles in relations between various nationalities, granting them unconditional right to self-determination.

Direct, secret, equal, and universal right to vote for every citizen above 20 years of age regardless of sex, religion, or national origin.

Proportional representation; direct popular legislation (referenda and initiatives); election, removability at all times, and accountability of all officials.

Complete freedom of conscience, speech, press, meetings, strikes and unions[;] . . . complete and general civil equality inviolability of the individual and home[;] . . . complete separation of the church from the state and a declaration that religion is a private affair for every individual.

The introduction of a compulsory, general public education at government expense; equality of languages.

Abolition of permanent armies and their replacement by a people's militia.

In the matters of economics:

A reduction of the working time in order to relieve surplus labour.

Establishment of a legal maximum of working time based on norms determined by health conditions (an eight-hour working norm for most branches of industry as soon as possible, and lower norms for work which is dangerous or harmful to health).

Establishment of a minimum wage in agreement between administration and labour unions.

Complete government insurance (for accident, unemployment, sickness, old age, and so on), administered by the insured at the expense of the state and employers.

Legislative protection of labour in all branches of industry and trade, in accordance with the health conditions supervised by factory inspection commissions elected by workers (normal working conditions, hygienic conditions of buildings; prohibition of work for youngsters below sixteen years of age, limitation of work for youngsters, prohibition of female and child labour in some branches of industry and during specified periods, adequate and uninterrupted Sunday rest, and so forth).

Professional organisation of workers and their increased participation in determining internal rules in industrial enterprises.

In matters of agricultural policy:

Socialisation of all privately owned lands; that is, their transfer from private property of individual owners to public domain and administration by democratically organised communes and territorial associations of communes on the basis of equalised utilisation.

Source: V. V. Vodovozov, ed., *Sbornik programm partii v Rossii,* 1st edition, St. Petersburg, 1905, pp. 20–21. Available online at http://alphahistory.com/russianrevolution/the-political-program-of-the-socialist-revolutionaries-1905/.

The Bloody Sunday Petition to the Tsar (1905)

The petition by Father Gapon and his workers to the tsar is an important document, as it highlights the demands of workers and peasants in Russia as the country wrestled with social, political, and economic change. The demands established within this document would serve as a foundation for future political activists in Russia, especially between the spring 1917 and the Bolshevik Revolution in October 1917. It must be kept in mind that this petition was meant to be hand-delivered to the tsar, which is why Gapon and his followers marched to the tsar's winter palace. Yet the size of the group and its increased demands provoked a deadly response from the police, which only highlighted the need for political change in Russia.

Sovereign!

We, workers and inhabitants of the city of St. Petersburg, members of various sosloviia (estates of the realm), our wives, children, and helpless old parents, have come to you, Sovereign, to seek justice and protection. We are impoverished and oppressed, we are burdened with work, and insulted. We are treated not like humans [but] like slaves who must suffer a bitter fate and keep silent. And we have suffered, but we only get pushed deeper and deeper into a gulf of misery, ignorance, and lack of rights.

Despotism and arbitrariness are suffocating us, we are gasping for breath. Sovereign, we have no strength left. We have reached the limit of our patience. We have come to that terrible moment when it is better to die than to continue unbearable sufferings. And so we left our work and declared to our employers that we will not return to work until they meet our demands.

We do not ask much; we only want that without which life is hard labor and eternal suffering. Our first request was that our employers discuss our needs together with us. But they refused to do this; they denied us the right to speak about our needs, on the grounds that the law does not provide us with such a right. Also unlawful were our other requests: to reduce the working day to eight hours; for them to set wages together with us and by agreement with us; to examine our disputes with lower-level factory administrators; to increase the wages of unskilled workers and women to one ruble per day; to abolish overtime work; to provide medical care attentively and without insult; to build shops so that it is possible to work there and not face death from the awful drafts, rain and snow.

Our employers and the factory administrators considered all this to be illegal: every one of our requests was a crime, and our desire to improve our condition was slanderous insolence.

Sovereign, there are thousands of us here; outwardly we are human beings, but in reality neither we nor the Russian people as a whole are provided with any human rights, even the right to speak, to think, to assemble, to discuss our needs, or to take measure to improve our conditions. They have enslaved us and they did so under the protection of your officials, with their aid and with their cooperation. They imprison and send into exile any one of us who has the courage to speak on behalf of the interests of the working class and of the people. They punish us for a good heart and a responsive spirit as if for a crime. To pity a down-trodden and tormented person with no rights is to commit a grave crime.

The entire working people and the peasants are subjected to the proizvol (arbitrariness) of a bureaucratic administration composed of embezzlers of public funds and thieves who not only have no concern at all for the interests of the Russian people but who harm those interests. The bureaucratic administration has reduced the country to complete destitution, drawn it into a shameful war, and brings Russia ever further towards ruin. We, the workers and the people, have no voice in the expenditure of the enormous sums that are collected from us. We do not even know where the money collected from the impoverished people goes. The people are deprived of any possibility of expressing its wishes and demands, or of participating in the establishment of taxes and in their expenditure. Workers are deprived of the possibility of organising into unions to defend their interests.

Sovereign! Does all this accord with the law of God, by Whose grace you reign? And is it possible to live under such laws? Would it not be better if we, the toiling people of all Russia, died? Let the capitalists—exploiters of the working class—and the bureaucrats—embezzlers of public funds and the pillagers of the Russian people—live and enjoy themselves.

Sovereign, this is what we face and this is the reason that we have gathered before the walls of your palace. Here we seek our last salvation. Do not refuse to come to the aid of your people; lead it out of the grave of poverty, ignorance, and lack of rights; grant it the opportunity to determine its own destiny, and deliver it from them the unbearable yoke of the bureaucrats. Tear down the wall that separates you from your people and let it rule the country together with you. You have been placed [on the throne] for the happiness of the people; the bureaucrats, however, snatch this happiness out of our hands, and it never reaches us; we get only grief and humiliation.

Sovereign, examine our requests attentively and without any anger; they incline not to evil, but to the good, both for us and for you. Ours is not the voice of insolence but of the realisation that we must get out of a situation that is unbearable for everyone. Russia is too big, her needs are too diverse and many, for her to be ruled only by bureaucrats. We need popular representation; it is necessary for the people to help itself and to administer itself. After all, only the people knows its real needs. . . . Let the capitalist be there, and the worker, and the bureaucrat, and the priest, and the doctor and the teacher. Let everyone, whoever they are, elect their representatives. Let everyone be free and equal in his voting rights, and to that end order that elections to the Constituent Assembly be conducted under universal, secret and equal suffrage . . .

The following are necessary:

I. Measures against the ignorance of the Russian people and against its lack of rights

1. Immediate freedom and return home for all those who have suffered for their political and religious convictions, for strike activity, and for peasant disorders.

2. Immediate proclamation of the freedom and inviolability of the person, of freedom of speech and of the press, of freedom of assembly, and of freedom of conscience in matters of religion.

3. Universal and compulsory public education at state expense.

4. Accountability of government ministers to the people and a guarantee of lawful administration.

5. Equality of all before the law without exception.

6. Separation of church and state.

II. Measures against the poverty of the people

1. Abolition of indirect taxes and their replacement by a direct, progressive income tax.

2. Abolition of redemption payments, cheap credit, and the gradual transfer of land to the people.

3. Naval Ministry contracts should be filled in Russia, not abroad.

4. Termination of the war according to the will of the people.

II. Measures against the oppression of labor by capital

1. Abolition of the office of factory inspector.

2. Establishment in factories and plants of permanent commissions elected by the workers, which jointly with the administration are to investigate all complaints coming from individual workers. A worker cannot be fired except by a resolution of this commission.

3. Freedom for producer-consumer cooperatives and workers' trade unions, at once.

4. An eight-hour working day and regulation of overtime work.

5. Freedom for labor to struggle with capital, at once.

6. Wage regulation, at once.

7. Guaranteed participation of representatives of the working classes in drafting a law on state insurance for workers, at once.

These, sovereign, are our main needs, about which we have come to you. . . . Give the order, swear to meet these needs, and you will make Russia both happy and glorious, and your name will be fixed in our hearts and the hearts of our posterity for all time. But if you do not give the order, if you do not respond to our prayer, then we shall die here, on this square, in front of your palace. We have nowhere else to go and no reason to. There are only two roads for us, one to freedom and happiness, the other to the grave. Let our lives be sacrificed for suffering Russia. We do not regret that sacrifice, we embrace it eagerly.

Georgii Gapon, priest Ivan Vasimov, worker.

Source: George Gapon, *The Story of My Life* (London: Chapman and Hall, 1906), 257–261.

The U.S. Ambassador's Report on Bloody Sunday (1905)

The U.S. ambassador's report on the events of Bloody Sunday presents an interesting perspective. Of importance is the discussion about the "revolutionary" nature of the march as well as the character of Father Gapon and the actions of the police in their handling of him. Furthermore, it appears that the U.S. representative believed that the appearance of the tsar and his offer to receive a working group could have staved off the horrible events of 1905. This account seems to lack critical insights into the nature of the march as well as the protest.

Sir,

The changes which have come over the internal situation in Russia since my departure early in October mark distinctly the beginning of the end of the old regime and the dawn of a new era. . . .

It is now clear to every impartial observer that the [trust] . . . of the working men had been worked upon by a group of socialists

with Father Gapon, now raised by this press to the position of a demi-god—a sort of Second Savior—at its head, although he has to his record the violation of a young girl of 12 years of age. My authority for this, and he told me that he spoke with knowledge, is the Austro-Hungarian Ambassador Baron d'Aehrenthal.

The correspondent of the 'Standard', who had an interview with this renegade priest, has told me that he was a thorough-paced revolutionist, and that he had utterly deceived the working men into the belief that his sole purpose was to aid them to better their condition, and secure from their employers concessions on the lines indicated in the appeal to the Emperor, which was drawn up by him. That his own purpose went beyond the mere presentation of this appeal now seems clear, and . . . there seems little doubt that his real intention was to get possession of the person of the Emperor and hold him as a hostage.

Unfortunately the police authorities exhibited criminal weakness in dealing with this man, the Chief of Police going so far as to accompany him to the Ministry of the Interior and to Mr Witte's residence, at least to seek their cooperation in securing an audience for Gapon. Had they put him under arrest Russia might have been spared the horrible events which have aroused the anger of the outside world and thousands within the Empire, with possibilities which one shudders to contemplate.

I was in the street and inspected the crowd in the Admiralty Prospect as it worked its way towards the Place du Palais. They had not the look of revolutionists, and although there were doubtless some of the scum of the capital sprinkled in the crowd, it was my opinion that, guarded as every approach was to the Place, the Emperor might have appeared and received a committee of workmen made up of men bearing a good character with their employers, and agreed . . . to do what his latest proclamation promises, namely to investigate their grievances.

Having failed to do this, and the Chief of Police, as well as the Minister of the Interior, having proven himself unequal to the situation, and what threatened to be a dangerous crisis under the cunning leadership of Father Gapon having been allowed to develop, nothing was left but to call out the troops. Whether the situation around the Place du Palais could have been kept in hand without firing on the crowd is a matter on which opinions differ, even on the part of eye witnesses, but I have heard the assembled crowd accused of nothing worse than jeering at the troops, hustling the officers and using language to them that will not bear repetition— although they came, it is said, armed with knives, pieces of piping, sticks, and some even with revolvers.

I do know that the commanding officer of the infantry on the Place fronting the Admiralty Prospect asked . . . the crowd to disperse and twice warned them to disperse, adding that if they did not, he would be compelled to fire on them. This I have been told by a personal friend of the officer, to whom he deplored the tragedy in which he was compelled to play a part. Moreover, my private secretary stood for some time on the Place behind the troops and saw the officers moving along the front of the crowd and begging the people to disperse.

The same thing, he says, took place at all the approaches to the Place du Palais, the officers, on foot, would go right in among the people and try to reason with them, seeming to do everything in their power to persuade the people to disperse peaceably. The troopers, too, guarding the streets leading towards the Place, were invariably polite in their [warnings] . . . to the crowd to move on and in refusing them passage through the streets. But they used judgment in this, sending back the rough-looking workmen and sneering, overbearing students, while permitting those to pass who would go to them frankly and state their business and destination.

As long as it was possible, the troops kept the crowd moving and dispersed them by simply riding up against them and asking them to disperse. As the crowd grew larger and bolder, this became useless, and the troops resorted to charges with drawn [swords] . . . striking the crowds with the flat of their swords, and then, later, cutting down a few of them at each charge, the crowd always returning instantly, larger and more furious than before. My secretary adds that the mob in the centre of the Admiralty Prospect, just previous to the firing, was frantic in its demonstrations. . . .

The events of Sunday January 22nd weakened, if it did not shatter, that unswerving loyalty and deep seated reverence which has characterized the subjects of The Czar of All the Russians. I have had evidence of this from the highest to the lowest classes and it finds expression in a letter received this morning from Mr Heenan, our Consul at Odessa, who writes:

'Had I answered your enquiries about the situation here before the affair of Sunday last in your city had taken place, the views expressed would have been quite other than those I shall send you in a few days. In all the years (eighteen) I have spent in Russia, I never knew the Russian public to be so united as in their views in connection with the action of the authorities in ordering the soldiers to shoot the workmen, their wives, children and harmless spectators last Sunday in St Petersburg. All classes condemn the authorities and more particularly the Emperor. The present ruler has lost absolutely the affection of the Russian people, and whatever the future may have in store for the dynasty, the present Czar will never again be safe in the midst of his people.' . . .

I have the honor to be, Sir

Your obedient Servant
Robert S. McCormick

Source: Ambassador McCormick to the Secretary of State, telegram, January 23, 1905, summarized in U.S. Department of State, *Foreign Relations of the United States (1905)* (Washington, DC: U.S. Government Printing Office, 1905). The telegram is available online at http://alphahistory.com/russian revolution/russian-revolution-documents/.

Gapon's Eyewitness Account of Bloody Sunday (1905)

Below is Father Gapon's account of the events known as Bloody Sunday. Note that the account does not advocate the marchers' position or political agenda, but does highlight the tragedy of the event. This document needs to be read in comparison to the U.S. ambassador's account as well and V. I. Lenin's account to get a fuller understanding of how this political event was perceived in the context of revolutionary Russia.

We were not more than thirty yards from the soldiers, being separated from them only by the bridge over the Tarakanovskii Canal, which here marks the border of the city, when suddenly, without any warning and without a moment's delay, was heard the dry crack of many rifle-shots. I was informed later on that a bugle was blown, but we could not hear it above the singing, and even if we had heard it we should not have known what it meant.

Vasiliev, with whom I was walking hand in hand, suddenly left hold of my arm and sank upon the snow. One of the workmen who carried the banners fell also. Immediately one of the two police officers to whom I had referred shouted out, "What are you doing? How dare you fire upon the portrait of the Tsar?" This, of course, had no effect, and both he and the other officer were shot down—as I learned afterwards, one was killed and the other dangerously wounded.

I turned rapidly to the crowd and shouted to them to lie down, and I also stretched myself out upon the ground. As we lay thus another volley was fired, and another, and yet another, till it seemed as though the shooting was continuous. The crowd first kneeled and then lay flat down, hiding their heads from the rain of bullets, while the rear rows of the procession began to run away. The smoke of the fire lay before us like a thin cloud, and I felt it stiflingly in my throat . . . .

A little boy of ten years, who was carrying a church lantern, fell pierced by a bullet, but still held the lantern tightly and tried to rise again, when another shot struck him down. Both the smiths who had guarded me were killed, as well as all those who were carrying the icons and banners; and all these emblems now lay scattered on the snow. The soldiers were actually shooting into the courtyards of the adjoining houses, where the crowd tried to find refuge and, as I learned afterwards, bullets even struck persons inside, through the windows.

At last the firing ceased. I stood up with a few others who remained uninjured and looked down at the bodies that lay prostrate around me. I cried to them, "Stand up!" But they lay still. I could not at first understand. Why did they lie there? I looked again, and saw that their arms were stretched out lifelessly, and I saw the scarlet stain of blood upon the snow. Then I understood. It was horrible. And my Vasiliev lay dead at my feet.

Horror crept into my heart. The thought flashed through my mind, "And this is the work of our Little Father, the Tsar." Perhaps this anger saved me, for now I knew in very truth that a new chapter was opened in the book of the history of our people. I stood up, and a little group of workmen gathered round me again. Looking backward, I saw that our line, though still stretching away into the distance, was broken and that many of the people were fleeing. It was in vain that I called to them, and in a moment I stood there, the centre of a few scores of men, trembling with indignation amid the broken ruins of our movement.

Source: George Gapon, *The Story of My Life* (London: Chapman and Hall, 1906), 182–185.

Lenin's View of Bloody Sunday (1905)

As one would expect, V. I. Lenin's assessment of the events in January 1905 are much more focused on the class struggle between the tsar and the workers. Lenin's focus on the significance of the mass protest as a means to institute real change in Russia is only further focused by the violent actions of the tsar's regime. Lenin and other more radical political forces believed that indeed the events of 1905 were the beginning of the withering of the tsar and his corrupt and outdated regime. They believed that moving forward was the preferred course of action as a means to incite the revolution.

Revolt or revolution? This is the question that European journalists and reporters have been asking themselves in connection with the events in St. Petersburg, which they are reporting to the whole world and attempting to evaluate. Are they rebels or insurgents, the tens of thousands of proletarians against whom the tsarist army successfully took the field? And the foreign papers, though sooner in a position to view the events with

"detachment", with the impartiality of chroniclers, find it difficult to answer the question. They are constantly getting their terms mixed. . . .

People who witness the beginning of great and momentous events, who can obtain only very incomplete, inexact, and third-hand information of what is taking place, will not, of course, hazard a definite opinion until a better moment comes. The bourgeois papers, which continue as of old to speak of revolt, rioting, and disturbances, cannot help seeing the truly national—no, international—significance of these events.

Yet it is this significance which invests events with the character of revolution. And those who have been writing of the last days of the rioting find themselves involuntarily referring to them as the first days of the revolution. A turning point in Russia's history has been reached. This is not denied even by the most hidebound of European conservatives, however enthusiastic and sentimental they may wax over the mighty, unrestricted power of the all-Russian autocracy.

Peace between the autocracy and the people is unthinkable. Revolution is not only in the mouths of a few fearless souls, not only of "nihilists"—as Europe persists in calling the Russian revolutionaries—but of every person capable of taking any interest in world politics. . . . The Russian working-class movement has risen to a higher level in the last few days. It is developing before our very eyes into a national uprising. . . .

The government generally . . . wanted to provoke bloody reprisals under conditions most favourable to itself. . . . The government thus had its hands free to play a winning game. The demonstration, so they reckoned, would be made up of the most peaceful, least organized, and most backward workers; it would be child's play for our soldiery to handle them, and the proletariat would be taught a wholesome lesson; an excellent excuse would be furnished for shooting down anybody and everybody in the streets; at Court the victory of the reactionary parties over the liberals would be complete; the harshest repressions would follow. . . .

In reviewing the events of Bloody Sunday one is struck by the combination of naïve patriarchal faith in the tsar and the fierce armed street fighting against the tsarist rule. The first day of the Russian revolution brought the old Russia and the new face to face with startling force and showed the death agony of the peasants' age-old faith in "Our Father the Tsar", and the birth of a revolutionary people, the urban proletariat. No wonder the European bourgeois newspapers say that Russia of January 10th is no longer the Russia of January 8th.

Here, in Russia, a priest found himself at the head of the movement; one day he appealed for a march with a peaceful petition to the tsar himself, and the next day he issued a call for revolution. "Comrades, Russian workers!" Father Georgi Gapon wrote, after that bloody day, in a letter read at a meeting of liberals. "We no longer have a tsar. Today a river of blood divides him from the Russian people. It is time for the Russian workers to begin the struggle for the people's freedom without him. For today I give you my blessing. Tomorrow I shall be with you. Today I am busy working for our cause."

This is not Father Georgi Gapon speaking. This is the voice of those thousands upon thousands, of those millions upon millions of Russian workers and peasants who until now could believe naively and blindly in the Tsar Father and seek alleviation of their unbearable lot from Our Father the Tsar "himself", who put the blame for all the atrocities and outrages, the tyranny and plunder, only on the officials that were deceiving the tsar.

Reports as to the number of killed or wounded differ. Naturally, there can be no question of an exact count, and a visual estimate is very difficult. The government's report giving 96 killed and 330 wounded is obviously false, and no one believes it. According to the latest press reports, journalists handed the Minister of the Interior a list of 4,600 killed or wounded, as compiled by reporters. Of course, even this figure cannot be complete, since it would be impossible even in the day-time (let alone at night) to count all the killed and wounded in the various clashes.

The victory of the autocracy over the unarmed people took a toll no smaller than did the big battles in Manchuria. No wonder the St. Petersburg workers, according to the reports of foreign correspondents, cried out to the officers that they were more successful at fighting the Russian people than they were the Japanese.

Source: Lenin's Collected Works, Vol. 8 (Moscow: Foreign Languages Publishing House, 1962), 101–123.

The Soviet Account of Bloody Sunday from 1938

The inclusion of the Soviet Union's account of the Russian Revolution of 1905 from the perspective of 1938 provides keen insights into how the Soviet government romanticized the events of 1905 and placed the Bolsheviks in a lead position and as the primary catalyst to the events of Father Gapon and his workers. Furthermore, it is a great example of how the Soviet government wrote history in such a way to showcase the popular support and altruistic objectives of the Bolsheviks that led to the 1917 October Revolution.

On January 3rd 1905, a strike broke out at the biggest of the St. Petersburg plants, the

Putilov Works. The strike was caused by the dismissal of four workers. It grew rapidly and was joined by other St. Petersburg mills and factories. The strike became general. The movement grew formidable. The tsarist government decided to crush it in its earliest phase.

In 1904, prior to the Putilov strike, the police had used the services of an agent-provocateur, a priest by the name of Gapon, to form an organisation of the workers known as the Assembly of Russian Factory Workers. This organization had its branches in all the districts of St. Petersburg. When the strike broke out the priest Gapon at the meetings of his society put forward a treacherous plan: all the workers were to gather on January 9th and, carrying church banners and portraits of the tsar, to march in peaceful procession to the Winter Palace and present a petition to the tsar stating their needs. The tsar would appear before the people, listen to them and satisfy their demands. Gapon undertook to assist the tsarist Okhrana by providing a pretext for firing on the workers and drowning the working-class movement in blood. . . .

At these meetings the Bolsheviks explained to the workers that liberty could not be obtained by petitions to the tsar, but would have to be won by force of arms. The Bolsheviks warned the workers that they would be fired upon. But they were unable to prevent the procession to the Winter Palace. A large part of the workers still believed that the tsar would help them. The movement had taken a strong hold on the masses . . .

Early in the morning of January 9th 1905, the workers marched to the Winter Palace where the tsar was then residing. They came with their whole families—wives, children and old folk—carrying portraits of the tsar and church banners. They chanted hymns as they marched. They were unarmed. Over 140,000 persons gathered in the streets. They met with a hostile reception from Nicholas II. He gave orders to fire upon the unarmed workers. That day over a thousand workers were killed and more than two thousand wounded by the tsar's troops. The streets of St. Petersburg ran with workers' blood.

The Bolsheviks had marched with the workers. Many of them were killed or arrested. There, in the streets running with workers' blood, the Bolsheviks explained to the workers who it was that bore guilt for this heinous crime and how he was to be fought.

January 9th came to be known as 'Bloody Sunday'. On that day the workers received a bloody lesson. It was their faith in the tsar that was riddled by bullets on that day. They came to realize that they could win their rights only by struggle. That evening barricades were already being erected in the working-class districts. The workers said: "The tsar gave it to us; we'll now give it to him!"

The fearful news of the tsar's bloody crime spread far and wide. The whole working class, the whole country was stirred by indignation and abhorrence. There was not a town where the workers did not strike in protest against the tsar's villainous act and did not put forward political demands. The workers now emerged into the streets with the slogan, "Down with autocracy!" In January the number of strikers reached the immense figure of 440,000. More workers came out on strike in one month than during the whole preceding decade. The working-class movement rose to an unprecedented height. Revolution in Russia had begun.

Source: *History of the Communist Party of the Soviet Union (Bolsheviks)* (New York: International Publishers, 1939), 77–80.

The October Manifesto (1905)

The events of Bloody Sunday and the subsequent outcry and reaction across Russia as well as Europe was seen by many on the Left as the catalyst that directly led to the tsar's issuing of the October Manifesto. This was an important political document in the context of the Russian Revolution, as it showcased that the tsar could indeed be influenced to accept political action by the forces of the people. Though the October Manifesto provided some additional freedoms and changes to the overall political structure of Russia, it still retained the exalted position of the tsar and his ministers. As Tsar Nicholas II made adjustments to the system, the more radical forces of the Left argued for more pressure and the use of violence to force greater changes in the system (see Lenin's comments in the next document on the unfolding of 1905 as an example of this interpretation). These changes would have to wait for another 12 years before the conditions were right for the Bolshevik Revolution to take hold.

In the autumn of 1905, Tsar Nicholas II released his October Manifesto. Probably drafted by Witte, it promised political change and a degree of popular representation:

On the improvement of order in the state

The disturbances and unrest in St Petersburg, Moscow and in many other parts of our Empire have filled Our heart with great and profound sorrow. The welfare of the Russian Sovereign and His people is inseparable and national sorrow is His too. The present disturbances could give rise to national instability and present a threat to the unity of Our State.

The oath which We took as Tsar compels Us to use all Our strength, intelligence and power to put a speedy end to this unrest which is so dangerous for the State. The relevant authorities have been ordered to take measures to deal with direct outbreaks of disorder and violence and to protect people who only want to go about their daily business in peace.

However, in view of the need to speedily implement earlier measures to pacify the country, we have decided that the work of the government must be unified. We have therefore ordered the government to take the following measures in fulfilment of our unbending will:

1. Fundamental civil freedoms will be granted to the population, including real personal inviolability, freedom of conscience, speech, assembly and association.

2. Participation in the Duma will be granted to those classes of the population which are at present deprived of voting powers, insofar as is possible in the short period before the convocation of the Duma, and this will lead to the development of a universal franchise. There will be no delay to the Duma elect already been organised.

3. It is established as an unshakeable rule that no law can come into force without its approval by the State Duma and representatives of the people will be given the opportunity to take real part in the supervision of the legality of government bodies.

We call on all true sons of Russia to remember the homeland, to help put a stop to this unprecedented unrest and, together with this, to devote all their strength to the restoration of peace to their native land.

Nicholas II
Tsar of All the Russias

Source: U.S. Department of State, *Foreign Relations of the United States (1905)* (Washington, DC: U.S. Government Printing Office, 1905), 777–778.

Lenin on the Unfolding of the 1905 Revolution (1905)

This account by V. I. Lenin provides an insightful Bolshevik interpretation of the Russian Revolution of 1905 in the wake of these events. Of significance is the adherence to the Marxist dictum that corrupt and oppressive systems cannot be changed with political and social accommodation. According to Karl Marx, these systems can only be changed through violent revolution. Lenin noted in this work that the workers in Russia learned a valuable lesson in trying to submit reforms before the tsar in a "peaceful manner." This document provided a foundation from which the Bolsheviks continued to build and push their agenda for a more radical attempt to alter the political and social situations in Russia. The message in this document clearly foreshadowed the events that transpired in 1917.

Events of the greatest historical importance are developing in Russia. The proletariat has risen against tsarism. The proletariat was driven to revolt by the government. There can hardly be any doubt now that the government deliberately allowed the strike movement to develop and a wide demonstration to be started more or less without hindrance in order to bring matters to a point where military force could be used. Its manoeuvre was successful. Thousands of killed and wounded—such is the toll of Bloody Sunday, January 9th, in St. Petersburg. The army defeated unarmed workers, women, and children. The army vanquished the enemy by shooting prostrate workers. "We have taught them a good lesson!" the tsar's henchmen and their European flunkeys from among the conservative bourgeoisie say with consummate cynicism.

Yes, it was a great lesson, one which the Russian proletariat will not forget. The most uneducated, backward sections of the working class, who naïvely trusted the tsar and sincerely wished to put peacefully before "the tsar himself" the petition of a tormented people, were all taught a lesson by the troops led by the tsar or his uncle, the Grand Duke Vladimir. The working class has received a momentous lesson in civil war; the revolutionary education of the proletariat made more progress in one day than it could have made in months and years of drab, humdrum, wretched existence.

The slogan of the heroic St. Petersburg proletariat, "Death or freedom!" is reverberating throughout Russia. Events are developing with astonishing rapidity. The general strike in St. Petersburg is spreading. All industrial, public, and political activities are paralysed. On Monday, January 10th still more violent clashes occurred between the workers and the military. Contrary to the mendacious government reports, blood is flowing in many parts of the capital. The workers of Kolpino are rising. The proletariat is arming itself and the people. The workers are said to have seized the Sestroretsk Arsenal. They are providing themselves with revolvers, forging their tools into weapons, and procuring bombs for a desperate bid for freedom.

The general strike is spreading to the provinces. Ten thousand have already ceased work in Moscow, and a general strike has been called there for tomorrow (Thursday, January 13). An uprising has broken out in Riga. The workers are demonstrating in Lodz, an uprising is being prepared in Warsaw, proletarian demonstrations are taking place in Helsingfors. Unrest is growing among the workers and the strike is spreading in Baku, Odessa, Kiev, Kharkov, Kovno, and Vilna. In Sevastopol, the naval stores and arsenals are ablaze, and the troops refuse to shoot at the mutineers. Strikes in Revel and in Saratov. Workers and reservists clash with the troops in Radom.

The revolution is spreading. The government is beginning to lose its head. From the policy of bloody repression it is attempting to change over to economic concessions and to save itself by throwing a sop to the workers or promising the nine-hour day. But the lesson of Bloody Sunday cannot be forgotten. The demand of the insurgent St. Petersburg workers—the immediate convocation of a Constituent Assembly on the basis of universal, direct, and equal suffrage by secret ballot—must become the demand of all the striking workers. Immediate overthrow of the government—this was the slogan with which even the St. Petersburg workers who had believed in the tsar answered the massacre of January 9th. They answered through their leader, the priest Georgi Gapon, who declared after that bloody day: "We no longer have a tsar. A river of blood divides the tsar from the people. Long live the fight for freedom!"

"Long live the revolutionary proletariat!" say we.

Source: Lenin's Collected Works, Vol. 8 (Moscow: Foreign Languages Publishing House, 1962), 97–100.

The Tsar Dissolves the Second State Duma (1907)

In the aftermath of Bloody Sunday and the events of the Russian Revolution of 1905, Nicholas II issued the October Manifesto. To parties pushing for change in the government of the tsar, the manifesto was seen as a major advance, as it provided the means for the State Duma to convene. Though the tsar granted this government body and authorized it to have limited powers and representation, the October Manifesto provided very narrowly defined powers in relation to the demands of the people as well as the respective political parties vying for control of the Duma. As a result of the inherent tension in the political system, the tsar retained the right to disband the Duma. The First Duma lasted only a matter of weeks, and the Second Duma fared little better. Below is Nicholas's justification as to the need to disband the Second Duma. As a result of the failures of the first two Dumas, the tsar and his deputies adjusted the electoral laws that favored the Duma with more moderate and conservative political parties, which were more sympathetic toward maintaining the monarchy, as compared to the Social Democrats or Social Revolutionaries. Though the Third, Fourth, and Fifth Dumas served longer terms and proved more successful than the first and second attempts, the persistent problems, as seen from the Left, were only exacerbated as the nation sank deeper into World War I. The abdication of the tsar and the rise of the Provisional Government served as the last period in which the Duma functioned prior to the onset of the Bolshevik Revolution.

We proclaim to all Our faithful subjects:

Since the time of the dissolution of the first State Duma, the government has, in accord with Our orders and instructions, undertaken a consistent series of measures to bring peace to the country and establish a proper course for affairs of state. The Second State Duma, which we convened, was called upon to facilitate, in accord with Our Sovereign will, the restoration of peace to Russia: first of all, by legislative work, without which it is impossible for the state to live or for its structure to be perfected; to ensure that the economic activities of the state are being conducted correctly; and finally, by rationally exercising the right of interrogating government officials, with a view to strengthening truth and justice everywhere.

These obligations, which We entrusted to elected deputies from the population. . . . Such was Our thought and will in granting the population new foundations for the life of the state. To Our dismay, a substantial part of the membership of the Second State Duma did not justify our expectations. Many sent by the population did not undertake their work with a pure heart and with a desire to strengthen Russia and improve its institutions, but rather with a flagrant intention of increasing turmoil and encouraging the disintegration of the state. . . .

A significant part of the Duma perverted the right of interrogating the government into a means of struggle with the government and of arousing mistrust for it among wide segments of the population. . . . The judicial authorities discovered that a whole section of the State Duma was involved in a conspiracy against the state and the authority of the tsar. When our government demanded that the 55 of the Duma who were accused of this crime be suspended, pending the outcome of the trial, and that the most implicated of them be confined under custody, the State Duma did not immediately carry out this lawful demand of the authorities, which did not admit of any delay.

All of this moved Us to dissolve the Second State Duma by an ukaz [executive order] to the Senate of June 3rd; the new Duma is to be convened on November 1st of this year. . . . Since it was created to strengthen the Russian state, the State Duma should also be Russian in spirit. The other nationalities of which the population of Our realm is composed should have their spokesmen in the State Duma, but they should not and will not be there in such number as to give them the possibility of decisive influence on purely Russian questions. . . .

All these changes in the election system cannot be enacted through the ordinary legislative route, that is, through the very State Duma whose composition We have pronounced unsatisfactory. Only the authority that granted the first electoral law, the historical authority of the Russian tsar, is adequate to abolish that law and replace it with a new one. . . .

We expect our faithful subjects to follow the path We have indicated and render unanimous and ardent service to the motherland, whose sons have in all times been a solid support to her strength, grandeur and glory.

Nicholas

Source: "The Tsar Dissolves the Second State Duma (1907)," Alpha History, http://alphahistory .com/russianrevolution/tsar-dissolves-second-state -duma-1907/.

The 1917 Revolution

Abdication of Nicholas (1917)

The abdication of Nicholas II proved to be a pivotal event in the context of Russian history, especially since 1905. The fact that the political forces that had been working to depose the tsar had finally achieved their long-held objective only highlighted the tumultuous position that Russia faced as it sought to save itself from the ravages of World War I. Notice the mention of political and popular disturbances by Nicholas as forces that, compounded by the war effort, placed a severe strain on Russia, its tsar, and its people. Of significance is how the tsar continued to appeal to the people of Russia to fulfill their duties as the nation faced both internal and external threats.

Manifesto of Nicholas II
March 15, 1917

In the midst of the great struggle against a foreign foe, who has been striving for years to enslave our country, it has pleased God to lay on Russia a new and painful trial. Newly arisen popular disturbances in the interior imperil the successful continuation of the stubborn fight. The fate of Russia, the honor of our heroic army, the welfare of our people, the entire future of our dear land, call for the prosecution of the conflict, regardless of the sacrifices, to a triumphant end. The cruel foe is making his last effort and the hour is near when our brave army, together with our glorious Allies, will crush him.

In these decisive days in the life of Russia, we deem it our duty to do what we can to help our people to draw together and unite all their forces for the speedier attainment of victory. For this reason we, in agreement with the State Duma, think it best to abdicate the throne of the Russian State to lay down the Supreme Power.

Not wishing to be separated from our beloved son, we hand down our inheritance to our brother, Grand Duke Mikhail Alexandrovich, and give him our blessing on mounting the throne of the Russian Empire.

We enjoin our brother to govern in Union and harmony with the representatives of the people on such principles as they shall see fit to establish. He should bind himself to do so by an oath in the name of our beloved country.

We call on all faithful sons of the fatherland to fulfill their sacred obligations to their country by obeying the Tsar at this hour of national distress, and to help him and the representatives of the people to take Russia out of the position in which she finds herself, and lead her into the path of Victory, well-being, and glory.

May the Lord God help Russia!

Nicholas
March 15, 1917
City of Pskov

Countersigned by the Minister of the Imperial Court, Adjutant-General, Count Fredericks.

Source: Frank Alfred Golder, *Documents of Russian History, 1914–1917,* translated by Emanuel Aronsberg (New York: Century, 1927), 297–298. "Izvestiia of the Committee of Petrograd Journalists." No. 8, March 16, 1917.

Abdication of Grand Duke Mikhail Alexandrovich (1917)

In many ways Grand Duke Mikhail's abdication was more significant, as it signaled to the people of Russia that the tsar's empire had ceded to a new Provisional Government. The final sentence of the grand duke's formal notification of abdication highlighted the specific changes that the various political parties had been protesting for since the turn of the 20th century. At least in theory, democracy had come to Russia, and the Provisional Government now had to build and run the government as it fought to sustain itself on the Eastern Front of World War I.

A heavy burden has been laid on me by my brother who has passed over to me the imperial throne of Russia at a time of unprecedented war and popular disturbances.

Animated by the thought which is in the minds of all, that the good of the State is above other considerations, I have decided to accept the supreme power, only if that be the desire of our great people, expressed at a general election for their representatives to the Constituent Assembly, which should determine the form of government and lay down the fundamental laws of the Russian Empire.

With a prayer to God for His blessings, I beseech all citizens of the Empire to subject themselves to the Provisional Government, which is created by and invested with full power by the State Duma, until the summoning, at the earliest possible moment, of a Constituent Assembly, selected by universal, direct, equal, and secret ballot, which shall establish a government in accordance with the will of the people.

March 16, 1917
Mikhail, Petrograd

Source: Frank Alfred Golder, *Documents of Russian History, 1914–1917,* translated by Emanuel Aronsberg (New York: Century, 1927), 298–299. "Izvestiia of the Committee of Petrograd Journalists," No 9. March 17, 1917.

Lenin Calls for an Uprising (September 12–14, 1917)

This call to arms by Vladimir Lenin stands in direct contrast to Alexander Kerensky's letter 10 days earlier. The Bolsheviks were impatient, and Lenin wanted to ensure that Petrograd and Moscow became the two primary cities to launch the revolution against the Provisional Government. Of note is that a fissure still existed between Bolsheviks and Mensheviks at this time.

A letter to the Central Committee and the Petrograd and Moscow Committees of the RSDLP (B)

The Bolsheviks, having obtained a majority in the Soviets of Workers' and Soldiers' Deputies of both capitals, can and must take state power into their own hands.

They can do so because the active majority of revolutionary elements in the two chief cities is large enough to carry people with it, to overcome our opponents' resistance to smash them, and to gain and retain power. For the Bolsheviks, by immediately proposing a democratic peace, by immediately giving the land to the peasants and by re-establishing the democratic institutions and liberties which have been distorted and shattered by Kerensky, will form a government which nobody will be able to overthrow.

The majority of people are on our side. This was proved by the long and painful course of events from May 6 to August 31 and to September 12. We gained the majority of Soviets of the metropolitan cities because the people came over to our side. The vacillation of Socialist Revolutionaries and Mensheviks and the increase in the number of internationalists within their ranks prove the same thing.

The Democratic Conference represents not a majority of the revolutionary people, but only the compromising upper strata of the petty bourgeoisie. Let us not be deceived by the election figures; elections prove nothing. Compare the elections to the city councils of Petrograd and Moscow with the Moscow strike of August 12. Those are objectives facts regarding that majority of revolutionary elements that are leading the people.

The Democratic Conference is deceiving the peasants; it is giving them neither peace nor land.

A Bolshevik government alone will satisfy the peasants' demands.

Why must the Bolsheviks assume power at this very moment? Because the imminent surrender of Petrograd will reduce our chances a hundred times.

And it is not in our power to prevent the surrender of Petrograd while the army is headed by Kerensky and Co.

Nor can we 'wait' for the Constituent Assembly, for by surrendering Petrograd Kerensky and Co. can always obstruct its convocation. Our Party alone, by seizing power, can secure the Constituent Assembly's convocation; it will then accuse the other parties of procrastination and will be able to substantiate its accusations.

A separate peace between British and German imperialists must and can be prevented, but only if we act immediately.

The people are tired of the vacillations of the Mensheviks and Socialist Revolutionaries. It is only our victory in the metropolitan cities that will carry the peasants with us.

We are concerned now not with the 'day', or 'moment' of insurrection in the narrow sense of the word. That will only be decided by the common voice of those who are in contact with the workers and soldiers, with the masses.

The point is that now, at the Democratic Conference, our Party has virtually its own congress, and this congress (whether it wishes to or not) will decide the fate of the revolution.

The point is to make the task clear to the Party. The present task is an armed uprising in Petrograd and Moscow (with its region), the seizing of power and the overthrow of the government. We must consider how to bring this about without expressly spelling it out in the press.

We must remember and weigh Marx's words about insurrection, 'Insurrection is an art,' etc.

It would be naïve to wait until the Bolsheviks achieve a 'formal' majority. No revolution ever waits for that. Kerensky and Co. are not waiting either, and are preparing to surrender Petrograd. It is wretched vacillations of the Democratic Conference that are bound to exhaust patience of the workers of Petrograd and Moscow! History will not forgive us if we do not assume power now.

There is no apparatus? There is an apparatus—the Soviets and the democratic organizations. The international situation right now, on the eve of the conclusion of a separate peace between the British and the Germans, is in our favor. To propose peace to the nations right now means to win.

By seizing power both in Moscow and Petrograd at once (it doesn't matter which comes first, possibly Moscow), we shall win absolutely and unquestionably.

Lenin

Source: V. I. Lenin, *Collected Works,* Vol. 26 (Moscow: Progress Publishers, 1964), 19–21.

The Decree on Peace (November 8, 1917)

The Bolsheviks called for a quick and immediate end to the war and for negotiations to not be suppressed by governments. Though this plea sounds idealistic and true to the Bolshevik slogan of "bread, land, and peace," one cannot help but wonder if this was being fed by the German organs who helped the Bolsheviks come to power by providing funding. Based on the coming Russian Civil War, the Bolsheviks quickly moved beyond the need to negotiate with others who did not agree with the advance of the October Revolution.

The Workers' and Peasants' government, created by the revolution of October 24–25 and basing itself on the Soviets of Workers' Soldiers' and Peasants' Deputies, call upon all the belligerent peoples and their governments to start immediate negotiations for a just, democratic peace.

By a just or democratic peace, for which the overwhelming majority of working class and other working people of all belligerent countries, exhausted, tormented and racked by war, are craving a peace that has been most definitely and insistently demanded by the Russian workers and peasants ever since the overthrow of the Tsarist monarchy—by such a peace the government means an immediate peace without annexations (i.e. without the seizure of foreign lands, without forcible incorporation of foreign nations) and without indemnities.

The Government of Russia proposes that this kind of peace be immediately concluded by all the belligerent nations, and expresses its readiness to take all resolute measures now, without the least delay, pending the final ratification of all the terms of such a peace by authoritative assemblies of the people's representatives of all countries and all nations.

In accordance with the sense of justice of democrats in general, and of the working classes in particular, the Government conceives the annexation or seizure of foreign lands to mean every incorporation of a small or weak nation into a large or powerful state without precisely, clearly and voluntarily expressed consent and the wish of that nation, irrespective of the time which such forcible incorporation took place, irrespective also of the degree of development or backwardness of the nation forcibly annexed to the given state, or forcibly retained within its borders, and irrespective, finally, of whether this nation is in Europe or in distant, overseas countries.

If any nation whatsoever is forcibly retained within the borders of a given state, it, in spite of its expressed desire no matter whether expressed in the press, at public meetings, in the decisions of parties, or in protests and uprisings against national oppression—it is not accorded the right to decide the forms of its state existence by a free vote, taken after the complete evacuation of the troops of the incorporating or, generally, of the stronger nation and without the least pressure being brought to bear, such incorporation is annexation, i.e. seizure and violence.

The Government considers it the greatest crimes against humanity to continue this war over the issue of how to divide among the strong and rich nations the weak nationalists they have conquered, and solemnly announces its determination immediately to sign peace terms to stop this war on the terms indicated, which are equally just for all nationalities without exception.

At the same time the Government declares that it does not regard the above-mentioned peace terms as an ultimatum; in other words, it is prepared to consider any other peace terms, and insists only that they be advanced by any of the belligerent countries as speedily as possible, and that in the peace proposals there should be absolute clarity and complete absence of all ambiguity and secrecy.

The Government abolishes secret diplomacy, and for its part, announces its firm intention to conduct all negotiations quite openly in full view of the whole people. It will proceed immediately with the full publication of secret of the treaties endorsed or concluded by the government of landowners and capitalists from February to October 25, 1917. The Government proclaims the unconditional and immediate annulment of everything contained in these secret treaties in so far as it is aimed, as is mostly the case, at securing advantages and privileges for the Russian landowners and capitalists and at the retention, or extension, of the annexations made by the Great Russians.

Proposing to the governments and peoples of all countries immediately to begin open negotiations for peace, the Government, for its part, expresses its readiness to conduct these negotiations in writing, by telegraph, and by negotiations between representatives of the various countries, or at a conference of such representatives. In order to facilitate such negotiations, the Government is appointing its plenipotentiary representative to the neutral countries.

The Second All Russian Congress of Soviets

Source: Y. Akhapkin, *First Decrees of Soviet Power* (London: Lawrence and Wishart, 1970), 20–21. Used by permission of Lawrence and Wishart.

Decree on the Press (November 9, 1917)

This document is a great example of the propaganda used by the Bolsheviks to explain why they were not fulfilling the "democratic" promises of the revolution. Of special note is General Provision 1, which is ambiguous and broad, and the decision for suppression was in the hands of the Council of People's Commissars. Under Joseph Stalin, the sense of guarding against counterrevolutionaries entrenches these tenets so that "freedom of the press" never blossoms.

In the trying critical period of the revolution and the days that immediately followed it the Provisional Revolutionary Committee was compelled to take a number of measures against the counter-revolutionary press of different shades.

Immediately outcries were heard from all sides that the new socialist power had violated a fundamental principle of its program by encroaching upon the freedom of the press.

The Workers' and Peasants' Government calls the attention of the population to the fact that what this liberal façade actually conceals is freedom for the propertied classes, having taken hold of the lion's share of the entire press, to poison, unhindered, the minds and obscure the consciousness of the masses.

Everyone knows that the bourgeois press is one of the most powerful weapons of the bourgeoisie. Especially at the crucial moment when the new power, the power of the workers and peasants, is only affirming itself, it was impossible to leave this weapon wholly in the hands of the enemy, for in such moments it is no less dangerous than bombs and machine-guns. That is why temporary extraordinary measures were taken to stem the torrent of filth and slander in which the yellow and green press would be only too glad to drown the recent victory of the people.

As soon as the new order becomes consolidated, all administrative pressure on the press will be terminated and it will be granted complete freedom within the bonds of legal responsibility, in keeping with a law that will be broadest and most progressive in this respect.

However, being aware that a restriction of the press, even at critical moments, is permissible only within the limits of what is absolutely necessary, the Council of People's Commissars resolves:

GENERAL PROVISIONS ON THE PRESS

1. Only those publications can be suppressed which (1) call for open resistance or insubordination to the Workers' and Peasants' Government; (2) sow sedition through demonstrably slanderous distortion of facts; (3) instigate actions of an obviously criminal, i.e. criminally punishable, nature.

2. Publications can be proscribed, temporarily or permanently, only by decision of the Council of People's Commissars.

3. The present ordinance is of a temporary nature and will be repealed by a special decree as soon as normal conditions of social life set in.

Chairman of the Council of People's Commissars
Vladimir Ulyanov (Lenin)

Source: Y. Akhapkin, *First Decrees of Soviet Power* (London: Lawrence and Wishart, 1970), 29–30. Used by permission of Lawrence and Wishart.

Declaration of the Rights of the Peoples of Russia (November 15, 1917)

This document is yet another attempt by the Bolsheviks to paint themselves as the free and "democratic" party interested in equality. Yet despite Stalin's arguments against the previous regimes, he himself would develop a system that used "persecution" and "provocation" as means to suppress any rival powers.

The October Revolution of workers and peasants began under the common banner of emancipation.

The peasants are emancipated from landowner rule, for there is no landed proprietorship any longer—it has been abolished. The soldiers and sailors are emancipated from the power of autocratic generals, for generals will henceforth be elected and removable. The workers are emancipated from the whims and tyranny of capitalists, for workers' control over factories and mills will henceforth be established. All that is living and viable is emancipated from the hated bondage.

There remain only the peoples of Russia, who have been and are suffering from oppression and arbitrary rule, whose emancipation should be started immediately, and whose liberation should be conducted resolutely and irrevocably.

In the epoch of tsarism the peoples of Russia were systematically incited against one another. The results of this policy are known: massacres and pogroms, on the one side, and slavery of the peoples, on the other.

There is no return to this infamous policy of incitement. From now on it is to be replaced by a policy of voluntary and sincere alliance of the peoples of Russia.

In the period of imperialism, after the February Revolution, which had given power to the Constitutional-Democrat bourgeoisie, the undisguised policy of incitement ceded place to the policy of cowardly distrust towards the peoples of Russia, the policy of petty excuses for persecution and provocation covered up with utterances about "freedom" and "equality" of the peoples. The results of this policy are known: increased national enmity, undermined mutual confidence.

This reprehensible policy of lie and distrust, petty persecution and provocation must be done away with. From now on it shall be replaced by an open and honest policy leading to complete mutual confidence of the peoples of Russia.

Only this confidence can lead to a sincere and firm alliance of the peoples of Russia.

Only thanks to this alliance can the workers and peasants of the peoples of Russia be welded into a single revolutionary force capable of holding out against any encroachments on the part of the imperialist-annexationist bourgeoisie.

Proceeding from these premises, the First Congress of Soviets in June of this year proclaimed the right of the peoples of Russia to free self-determination.

In October of this year the Second Congress of Soviets reaffirmed this inalienable right of the peoples of Russia more resolutely and definitely.

Carrying out the will of these Congresses, the Council of People's Commissars has resolved to base its activity in the matters of nationalities of Russia on the following principles:

1. EQUALITY AND SOVEREIGNTY OF THE PEOPLES OF RUSSIA.

2. THE RIGHT OF THE PEOPLES OF RUSSIA TO FREE SELF-DETERMINATION, UP TO SECESSION AND FORMATION OF AN INDEPENDENT STATE.

3. ABOLITION OF ALL AND ANY NATIONAL AND NATIONAL-RELIGIOUS PRIVILEGES AND RESTRICTIONS.

4. FREE DEVELOPMENT OF NA-
TIONAL MINORITIES AND ETHNIC
GROUPS INHABITING RUSSIA.

Concrete decrees stemming herefrom will
be worked out immediately after the establishment of the Commission for the Affairs
of Nationalities.

In the name of the Russian Republic
People's Commissar for Nationalities Affairs,
Joseph Dzhugashvili-Stalin

Chairman of the Council of People's
Commissars
V. Ulranov (Lenin)

Source: Y. Akhapkin, *First Decrees of Soviet Power*
(London: Lawrence and Wishart, 1970), 31–32.
Used by permission of Lawrence and Wishart.

Formation of the Red Army (January 28, 1918)

*As the Bolshevik Revolution ended and the Rus-
sian Civil War started, the Bolsheviks quickly
recognized the need for a military force to secure and hold the gains of the revolution. The
document below outlines how the Bolshevik
Party planned the new Red Army to be different
from the tsar's corrupt and flawed force. Note
the call for democracy and equality within the
force as a means to highlight the goals of the
Bolsheviks, but yet again these initial calls for
more democracy and equality were abandoned
as the Bolsheviks needed to build an effective
military as well as a viable state structure.*

January 28, 1918

The old army was an instrument of class oppression of the working people by the bourgeoisie. With the transition of power to the
working and exploited classes there has
arisen the need for a new army as the mainstay of Soviet power at present and the basis

for replacing the regular army by the arming
of the whole people in the near future, and as
a support for the coming socialist revolution
in Europe.

I

In view of the aforesaid, the Council of People's Commissars resolves to organize a new
army, to be called the Workers' and Peasants'
Red Army, on the following principles:

(1) The Workers' and Peasants' Red Army
is built up from the most conscious and organized elements of the working people.

(2) Access to its ranks is open to all citizens of the Russian Republic who have
attained the age of 18. Everyone who is prepared to devote his forces, his life to the defense of the gains of the October Revolution,
the power of the Soviets, and socialism can
join the Red Army. Joining the ranks of
the Red Army requires characteristics from
army committees or democratic public organizations standing on the platform of Soviet
power, Party or trade union organizations, or
at least two members of these organizations.
Joining by whole units calls for mutual guarantee and a signed vote.

II

(1) The Workers' and Peasants' Red Army
soldiers are fully maintained by the State
and receive, on top of that, 50 rubles monthly.

(2) invalid members of families of Red
Army soldiers who formerly were their de-
pendants are provided with everything necessary according to the local consumer quotas,
in keeping with the decisions of the local
bodies of Soviet power.

III

The supreme authority for the Workers' and
Peasants' Red Army is the Council of the

People's Commissar. Direct guidance and administration of the army is concentrated in the Commissariat of Military affairs and the special All-Russia Board attached to it.

Chairman of the Council of People's Commissars
V. Ulyanov (Lenin)

Source: Y. Akhapkin, *First Decrees of Soviet Power* (London: Lawrence and Wishart, 1970), 89–87. Used by permission of Lawrence and Wishart.

4 February 1918

To all, all, all

Soviet Troops entered Kiev on 29 January. The troops were under the direction of Yury Kotsyubinsky, Deputy to the People's Secretary for Military Affairs, Shakhari. The Kiev garrison with all its artillery has sided with Kotsyubinsky's troops and has declared that Kiev Rada of Vinnichenko and Porsh deposed. The General Secretariat at the Kiev Rada headed by Vinnichencko, abandoned by everyone, has gone into hiding. Odoevsky, who attempted to get together a compromise General Secretariat of Kharkov had been arrested. The Central Executive Committee of Soviets of the Ukraine together with its People's Secretariat in Kharkov has been proclaimed the supreme authority in the Ukraine. The following have been adopted:

Federal union with Russia and complete unity with the Council of People's Commissars in matters of internal and external policy. The Central Executive Committee of Soviets of the Ukraine and the People's Secretariat moved to Kiev on 3 February. The Army Radas of the South-Western and Romanian Fronts have disbanded themselves voluntarily. The representatives of both fronts have acknowledged the All-Ukrainian Central Executive Committee and the People's Secretariat as the sole authority in the Ukraine.

An All-Ukrainian Congress of Soviets of Workers', Soldiers' and Peasants' Deputies will meet shortly in Kiev.

All cities and guberniyas of the Ukraine without exception have stated that they agree to take part in it: Kharkov, Ekaterinoslav, Kiev, and Podoliya, Kherson guberniya and Poltava, Chernigov guberniya and the Donets Basin, Odessa, and Nikolaev, all coastal towns and the whole of the Black Sea Fleet, and the entire front and rear of the Ukraine.

The Congress is to be summoned and opened by the All-Ukrainian Central Executive Committee.

Orenburg has been occupied by Soviet troops finally.

Dutov, together with a handful of adherents, has gone into hiding. All government establishments in Orenburg have been occupied by Soviet troops. The Orenburg Soviet of Workers', Soldiers' and Peasants' and Cossacks' Deputies has been declared the local authority.

Simferopol has been occupied by Soviet troops. All authority on the peninsula is in the hands of the All-Crimean Soviet of Workers' Soldiers', Peasants'Deputies.

Chairman of the Council of People's Commissars
Vladimir Ulyanov (Lenin)

Source: J. M. Meijer, *The Trotsky Papers, 1917–1922,* Vol. 1 (The Hague: Mouton, 1964), 24–26. Reprinted by permission of Mouton via Copyright Clearance Center.

Compulsory Military Training (April 22, 1918)

Though recognizing the need to move away from militarism, the Bolsheviks rightfully acknowledged the need to build a Red Army as a means to hold the capitalists and bourgeoisie at bay. A second major point was the heavy reliance on the ultimate objectives, which were communism and the withering of the capitalist system. A third point to note is the emphasis on equality and democracy as advocated by the Bolsheviks, especially between women and men.

One of the main objects of socialism is to deliver mankind from the burden of militarism and from the barbarity of bloody clashes between nations. The goal of Socialism is universal disarmament, eternal peace, and fraternal cooperation of all peoples inhabiting the earth.

This goal will be achieved when power in all the strongest capitalist countries passes into the hands of the working class, which will wrest the means of production from the exploiters, turn them over to all working people for common use, and establish a Communist system as the unshakeable foundation of the solidarity of all mankind.

At the present time it is [in] Russia alone that state power belongs to the working class. In all the other countries the imperialist bourgeoisie is at the helm. Its policy is aimed at suppressing the communist revolution and enslaving all weak nations. The Russian Soviet Republic, surrounded on all sides by enemies, has to create its own powerful army to defend the country, while engaging in remaking its social system along communist lines.

The Workers' and Peasants' Government of the Republic deems it its immediate task to enlist all citizens in universal labor conscription and military service. This work is meeting with stubborn resistance on the part of the bourgeoisie, which refuses to part with its economic privileges and is trying, through conspiracies, uprising, and traitorous deals with foreign imperialists, to regain state power.

To arm the bourgeoisie would mean to generate constant strife within the army, thereby paralyzing its strength in the fight against external enemies. The parasitic and exploiter elements who do not want to assume the same duties and rights as others cannot be given access to arms. The Workers' and Peasants' Government will find ways of making the bourgeoisie share, in some form or other, the burden of defending the Republic, upon which the crimes of the propertied classes have brought unheard of trials and calamities. But in the immediate transitional period military training and arms will be given only to workers and to peasants who do not exploit the labors of others.

Citizens of 18 to 40 years of age who have undergone compulsory military training will be registered as subject to military service. At the first call of Workers' and Peasants' Government they will have to take up arms and join the ranks of the Red Army, which consists of the most devoted and selfless fighters for the freedom and independence of the Russian Soviet Republic and for the international socialist revolution.

1. Military training is compulsory for the citizens of the Russian Soviet Federative Republic of the following ages: (1) school age, whose youngest limit is determined by the People's Commissariat of Public Edcuation; (2) preparatory age, from 16 to 18 years, and (3) call-up age, from 18 to 40 years.

Female citizens are trained, with their consent, on an equal footing with males.

Note: Persons whose religious convictions do not allow the use of arms are trained only in those duties which do not involve the use of arms.

2. Training of persons of the preparatory and call-up ages is entrusted to the People's Commissariat for Military Affairs, and that of the school-age category to the People's Commissariat for Public Education, with the close cooperation of the Commissariat for Military Affairs.

3. Military training is compulsory for workers employed in factories, workshops, at agricultural estates and in villages, and peasants who do not exploit the labor of others.

4. In the provinces compulsory military training is organized by area, guberniya, uyezd, and volost military commissariats.

5. The trainees are in no way recompensed for the time spent in compulsory training; instruction shall be organized, as far as possible, in such a way so as not to divert the trainees from their normal permanent occupation.

6. Instruction shall be conducted continuously for eight weeks, at least 12 hours per week. The terms of training for special arms, and the procedure for refresher call-ups, will be determined in special regulations.

7. Persons who have been given training in the regular army can be excused from compulsory training after passing an appropriate test, with the issue of certificates that they have undergone a course of compulsory training.

8. Instruction shall be given by trained instructors in accordance with a program approved by the People's Commissariat for Military Affairs.

9. Persons who avoid compulsory training or neglect their duties stemming therefrom shall be called to account.

Chairman of the Central Executive Committee
Ya. Sverdlov

Source: Y. Akhapkin, *First Decrees of Soviet Power* (London: Lawrence and Wishart, 1970), 121–123. Used by permission of Lawrence and Wishart.

On the Rights and Duties of Soviets (January 6, 1918)

This is a fine example of the confirmation of the slogan "all power to the soviets." The Bolsheviks needed to make sure that the soviets were synchronized with the central party and could not be a venue for dissenters to launch a counterrevolution. Hence, despite previous calls for greater power to the soviets, the Bolshevik leadership again emphasized the need to use extralegal means to ensure the stability and vision of the regime by strictly defining the rights and duties of the soviets.

1. The Soviets of Workers', Soldiers', Peasants' and Farm Laborers' Deputies are the local organs (of power) and are completely independent in local matters but always act in accordance with the decrees and decisions of the central soviet power and of the larger bodies (uyezd, guberniya and oblast soviets) of which they form a part.

2. To soviets as well as to organs of power there fall the tasks of administration and service in every sphere of local life, administrative, economic, financial, cultural and educational.

3. In the field of administration, soviets must carry out all decrees and decisions of the central power, adopt measures to notify the population, to the greatest possible extent, of these decisions, issue obligatory decrees, carry out requisitions and confiscations, impose fines, suppress counter-revolutionary organs of the press, effect arrests and disband social organizations which propagate active opposition to or the overthrow of soviet power. Note: Soviets shall prepare a report for the central soviet power of all the measures taken by them and provide information on the most important events of local life.

4. Soviets shall elect from among their members an executive organ (executive committee, presidium) which shall be charged with putting into effect all its decisions and all its current administrative work.

Note:

(a) Military Revolutionary Committees as fighting organs, which came into being during the revolution, are disbanded.

(b) As a temporary measure, the appointment of commissars is permitted in those guberniyas and uyezds where the power of the soviet has not been sufficiently established or where soviet power is not fully recognized.

5. Soviets as organs of administration may grant credit from state resources for three months, on the presentation of detailed estimates.

The People's Commissariat of Internal Affairs

Source: U.S. Senate, *Brewing and Liquor Interests and German and Bolshevik Propaganda: Report and Hearings of the Subcommittee on the Judiciary, 66th Congress, 1st Session, Document 62,* Vol. 3 (Washington, DC: U.S. Government Printing Office, 1919), 1175–1176.

The Russian Civil War (1917–1922)

Fighting in Sviyazhsk (August 13, 1918)

As the Bolshevik Revolution ceded into the Russian Civil War, the Bolsheviks not only needed to manage the political aftermath of the revolution, but also had to fight against various counterrevolutionary forces for the future of Russia. In the document below, Leon Trotsky highlighted some of the advantages of the Red Army while also pointing out that there were weaknesses compared to the enemy the regime was fighting. Of special note is the care with which documents focusing on fighting spent little time talking about tactical or operational issues; instead, the Bolsheviks tended to focus on making sure that their propaganda highlighted the commitment and willingness of communists to fight for the new regime.

From: Sviyazhsk-Eastern Front Staff HQ

To: Moscow—Chairman of the Council of People's Commissars, Lenin

Stubborn fighting is in progress here. To date the numbers of those killed are to be counted in tens, those wounded in the hundreds. On our side we have a certain numerical preponderance in artillery. On his side the enemy is superior in organization and in the accuracy of his fire. The allegation that our men do not want to fight is a lie. Wherever there is a good or tolerably good commander and good commissars, the soldiers fight. The presence of workers who are Communists is most beneficial, there are many supremely devoted and courageous men among them. When the Commander wants to say that such and such a post is occupied by a reliable person, he says: I have got a Communist there. I am not going to attempt to predict what tomorrow may bring. But I have no doubt of victory.

Trotsky

Source: J. M. Meijer, *The Trotsky Papers, 1917–1922,* Vol. 1 (The Hague: Mouton, 1964), 79. Reprinted by permission of Mouton via Copyright Clearance Center.

Fighting at Kazan (August 21, 1918)

This document showcases the control and manipulation that the Bolsheviks used in internal memorandums. Frank and open discussion was not the hallmark of these events. Instead, the constant refrain that the Bolshevik forces would prevail, despite any number of obstacles, became a mantra for Vladimir Lenin and Leon Trotsky as they worked to solidify the gains of the Russian Revolution. The affirmation of the Soviet rules is interesting, as the Red Army tried to build itself and secure a foothold in Kazan and ensure that workers and peasants supported the Bolshevik cause. Despite the promise of amnesty, once the civil war ended, the Bolsheviks often negated their promises and exacted revenge on forces that the Bolsheviks coerced to join the regime.

The Struggle for Kazan

From: Moscow
To: Sviyazhsk-Trotsky

I am amazed and alarmed at the slowing down in the operations against Kazan; what is particularly bad is the report of your having the fullest possible opportunity of destroying the enemy with your artillery. One should not take pity on the city and put off matters any longer, as merciless annihilation is what is vital once it is established that Kazan is enclosed in an iron ring.

Lenin

The enemy's artillery is not weaker than ours.

Source: J. M. Meijer, *The Trotsky Papers, 1917–1922,* Vol. 1 (The Hague: Mouton, 1964), 90. Reprinted by permission of Mouton via Copyright Clearance Center.

Trotsky Insists on Stalin's Recall (October 4, 1918)

As the Bolshevik forces pushed for control of the Tsaritsyn front, the discussion between Leon Trotsky and Vladimir Lenin focused on the issue that Joseph Stalin was a hindrance to the operational situation on this front. Trotsky, on advice from commanders in the region, highly recommended that the best course of action for the Bolsheviks was to recall Stalin. By recalling Stalin, Trotsky and his field commanders believed that they could capitalize on the military situation in the region. However, the recall of Stalin was a very politically sensitive matter, as he proved to be a very capable organizer on the Southern Front of the fight. Though this matter may seem petty, it divided many Bolsheviks in their allegiance once the civil war ended.

From: Tambov
To: Moscow-Chairman of the Central Executive Committee.

I categorically insist on Stalin's recall. Things are going badly on the Tsaritsyn Front, despite a superabundance of military forces. Voroshilov is able to command a regiment, but not an army of fifty thousand men. None the less I will retain him as Commander of the Tenth Tsaritsyn Army on the condition that he places himself under the orders of the Commander of the Southern Front, Sytin. Right up to this day the Tsaritsyn people have failed to send even operational reports to Kozlov. I had required them to submit operational and intelligence reports twice daily. If this is not carried out tomorrow I shall commit Voroshilov and Minin for trial and announce this in an army order. So long as Stalin and Minin remain in Tsaritsyn, according to the constitution of the Military Revolutionary Council they merely enjoy the rights of members of the Military Revolutionary Council of the Tenth Army. For the purpose of launching an attack there remains only a short while before the autumn weather makes the roads impassable, when there will be no through road here either on foot or on horseback. Operations in strength are impossible without coordination of operations with Tsaritsyn. There is no time for diplomatic negotiations. Tsaritsyn must either obey or get out of the way. We have a colossal superiority in forces but total anarchy at the top. This can be put to rights within 24 hours given firm and resolute support [from] your end. In any event this is the only course of action that I can envisage.

Trotsky

Source: J. M. Meijer, *The Trotsky Papers, 1917–1922,* Vol. 1 (The Hague: Mouton, 1964), 135–137. Reprinted by permission of Mouton via Copyright Clearance Center.

Stalin Reports Victories at Tsaritsyn (October 23, 1918)

Juxtaposed against earlier documents and against the advice of Leon Trotsky, Joseph Stalin had officers and political operators who supported him. Below is an example of this support in a letter designed to counter the wishes of Trotsky to recall Stalin. In the course of the letter Iakov Sverdlov, a significant political organizer in the Bolshevik Party who had connections to Lenin, made a case for Stalin by arguing that he was a good party manager who was able to achieve the goals of the party while also adapting to the decisions and ideas pushed down from the government's leaders.

Stalin arrived today and brought news of three major victories of our troops in the vicinity of Tsaritsyn: one of them ten versts from Tsaritsyn, another the annihilation of four enemy regiments by the Steppe Army at Svetly Yar, which as it turns out, had been summoned up by the Tsaritsyn people, and the third near Muzga, where four enemy regiments were also annihilated.

Stalin has persuaded Voroshilov and Minin, whom he considers very valuable and irreplaceable workers, to stay on and accord full compliance to the orders from the center; the sole cause of their dissatisfaction, according to his words, is the extreme delay in the delivery of shells and small-arms ammunition, or their non-delivery, which is also having a fatal effect on the Caucasian army, two hundred thousand strong and in excellent fighting spirit.

Stalin would very much like to work on the Southern Front; he expresses great apprehension that people whose knowledge of this Front is poor may commit errors, of which he cites numerous examples. Stalin hopes that in the course of his work he will manage to convince people of the correctness of his approach, and he is not putting up any ultimatum about the removal of Sytin and Mekhonoshin but agrees to work jointly with them on the Revolutionary Council of the Southern Front and also expresses the wish to be a member of the Higher Military Council of the Republic.

In informing you, Lev Davydych, of all these statements of Stalin, I ask you to think them over and let me have a reply, firstly, as to whether you agree to talk matters over personally with Stalin, for which purposes he is ready to visit you, and, secondly, whether you consider it possible under given specific conditions to put aside former differences and arrange to work together as Stalin so much desires.

As far as I am concerned, my belief is that it is essential to make every effort towards arranging to work together with Stalin.

Sverdlov

Source: J. M. Meijer, *The Trotsky Papers, 1917–1922,* Vol. 1 (The Hague: Mouton, 1964), 159–161. Reprinted by permission of Mouton via Copyright Clearance Center.

Chronology

Date	Event
3/13/1881	Tsar Alexander II is assassinated, and his son succeeds him as Alexander III.
1883	The first Russian Marxist group forms in Switzerland and is named the Group for the Liberty of Labor.
2/14/1884	Counterreforms deprive universities and their faculties and students of their autonomy and impose more strict security policies on students.
3/14/1887	Lenin's older brother is arrested for his part in the conspiracy to assassinate Tsar Alexander III. He is later executed for his participation, and this was a radicalizing moment for Lenin.
11/1/1894	Tsar Alexander III dies, and his son succeeds him as Nicholas II.
1897	Lenin is exiled to Siberia for three years as a result of his political activities.
3/1/1898	Founding of the Social Democratic Party.
2/22/1899	Students at St. Petersburg Imperial University denounce the proclamation that prevented them from holding public festivals. Police harshly put down student demonstrations.
8/1/1899	Minister of Education Nikolay Bogolepov is assassinated by a student.
1/1/1902	Founding of the Socialist Revolutionary Party.
4/1/1902	Minister of the Interior D. S. Sipiagin is assassinated, and his murder motivates the tsar's government to radically expand police power in Russia.
8/1/1903	The Mensheviks split from the Social Democrat Party.
1904	The Zemstvo Union organizes medical brigades to support the war effort. Prince Lvov gets Tsar Nicholas II to agree to this. This marks the first time there is effective national organization of the zemstvos.

2/8/1904–11/5/1905	Russo-Japanese War.
7/28/1904	Minister of the Interior Vyacheslav von Plehve is assassinated.
9/30/1904	The Union of Liberation and Socialist Revolutionaries secretly meets in Paris to unite against the tsar's autocratic government.
11/6/1904–11/9/1904	The Zemstvo Congress meets in private residences in St. Petersburg and calls for a constitution for Russia. Although the meeting is sanctioned, the tsar rejects its recommendation for a constitution.
12/1/1904	Strikes in St. Petersburg begin that will grow into protests in January 1905.
1/22/1905	Tsar Nicholas II orders the violent suppression of protests in St. Petersburg led by Father George Gapon (Bloody Sunday), which begins the Russian Revolution of 1905. During this month, over 400,000 workers strike in protest of the violent repression of the protests.
2/17/1905	Grand Duke Sergei Alexandrovich is killed by a Socialist Revolutionary assassin. This occurs as the protests in reaction to Bloody Sunday continue to grow.
4/15/1905	The Second National Zemstvo Congress continues its calls for a meeting of a constitutional assembly.
5/27/1905	The Battle of Tsushima ends in defeat for Russia, with all Russian battleships sunk during the battle. This drives more calls for political liberalization.
6/27/1905–7/7/1905	Mutiny of the battleship *Potemkin*.
8/19/1905	The tsar proclaims the creation of the Duma. However, this does not satisfy the revolutionaries.
10/5/1905	In Moscow, printers go on strike. This will lead to the first general strike in Russia.
10/26/1905	First meeting of a soviet (elected governmental council) in St. Petersburg with a political agenda. The Bolsheviks are not present at the first meeting but do join at the third meeting two days later. This is the nucleus of future politically motivated soviets.
10/30/1905	Tsar Nicholas II signs the October Manifesto ending the 1905 revolution and establishing the Duma. This also leads to the establishment of the Octobrist Party and the Constitutional Democrat Party.
12/1/1906	Tsar Nicholas II disbands the Duma after it passes antigovernment legislation.
6/28/1914	Assassination of Franz Ferdinand of Austria-Hungary.
7/1/1914	Russia mobilizes for World War I.

8/1/1914	Germany declares war on Russia, beginning World War I.
8/7/1914	Zemstvos pledge their support for Russia in World War I, which will transform into the Union of Zemstvos and Towns.
11/1/1914	Russia declares war on the Ottoman Empire.
7/1/1915	Russia's great retreat begins. The Russian Army moves its forces back into Russian territory as its fortunes at the front take a turn for the worse.
	The Russian government forms the Central War Industries Committee to address the shortage of war matériel, such as rifles.
7/22/1915	Russian forces start to retreat from Poland and Galicia.
8/22/1915	The Kadets, Octobrists, and other similarly aligned political parties unite to create a political bloc to advocate for reforms.
9/18/1915	Tsar Nicholas II takes over command of the Russian Army. His advisers argue against this, as it will link him to any military problems that become politically problematic.
2/19/1916	The Duma begins meeting in Petrograd again.
6/1/1916	Russia begins the Brusilov Offensive.
7/3/1916	Tsar Nicholas II temporarily disbands the Duma on the advice of Grigory Rasputin and the tsarina.
10/1/1916	Tsar Nicholas II appoints Alexander Protopopov as interior minister.
12/17/1916	Rasputin is assassinated by Russian nobles.
1/22/1917	With a strike, 140,000 Russian workers commemorate Bloody Sunday.
2/1/1917	Strikes continue to grow in scale and will eventually involve most major urban areas.
2/27/1917	Last meeting of the State Duma.
3/9/1917	The February (March) Revolution will see about 200,000 workers strike in Petrograd. Government troops move in on March 11 to violently repress the uprisings.
	Tsar Nicholas II dissolves the Duma, and soldiers begin to refuse orders to suppress the revolts.
3/10/1917	Tsar Nicholas II permanently dissolves the Duma and mandates violent suppression of protests. Soldiers kill dozens of protesters, but the Duma ignores his command to dissolve.
3/11/1917	Soldiers mutiny and, after being ordered to shoot protestors, shoot their officers.
3/12/1917	The Duma and the Petrograd Soviet meet independently to determine how to handle the increasing instability.
3/14/1917	The Petrograd Soviet of Workers' and Soldiers' Deputies issues Order No. 1.

3/15/1917	Demonstrations in St. Petersburg lead to the abdication of Tsar Nicholas II. Last meeting of the State Duma. The Provisional Government forms. Tsar Nicholas II abdicates the throne for both himself and his son. The Provisional Government assumes power.
3/16/1917	Grand Duke Mikhail declines the throne unless there is popular support for his assuming the Romanov Crown. The Provisional Government issues a plan outlining its platform. Among the changes are expanded civil rights, election of a Constituent Assembly, and amnesty for political prisoners.
3/21/1917	The Provisional Government publishes a series of principles and goals. The demands of the war quickly overwhelm any possibility of further civil or legal reforms.
3/22/1917	The Bolsheviks place Tsar Nicholas II and his family under house arrest.
3/25/1917	Joseph Stalin arrives in St. Petersburg after his release from prison, where he was a political prisoner. The Provisional Government abolishes the death penalty in Russia.
3/27/1917	The Petrograd Soviet publishes the "Appeal to All Peoples of the World," which speaks against participation in World War I and advocates only a defense of Russia.
4/10/1917	The Provisional Government publishes its Declaration of War Aims, which reject the tsar's 1915 territorial claims.
4/16/1917	Lenin arrives in Petrograd from Switzerland with the help of German authorities.
4/17/1917	Lenin gives his April thesis speech, advocating all power to the soviets and an end to the war.
5/1/1917	Foreign Minister Pavel Miliukov causes a crisis for the Provisional Government when a leaked document captures his view that Russia is willing to continue the war and wants to increase its territory.
5/3/1917–5/4/1917	The April Days demonstrations showcase the frustration of the people with Miliukov's position on war aims.
5/17/1917	Leon Trotsky arrives in Russia after leaving the United States.
5/18/1917	The second Provisional Government, also known as the First Coalition Government, forms. Prince Lvov is both the president and the interior minister.
6/1/1917	The Provisional Government launches the Kerensky Offensive.
6/16/1917	The first All-Russia Congress of Workers and Soldiers Soviets opens.

7/1/17–7/11/17	Kerensky Offensive.
7/15/1917	Trotsky and his supporters join the Bolshevik Party.
7/16/17–7/20/17	Uprisings in Petrograd swell and will eventually unseat Prince Lvov and the second Provisional Government. Kerensky will assume leadership of the next government that will rule Russia until the Bolshevik Revolution in November 1917.
7/20/1917	The Provisional Government forces the arrest of Trotsky. Lenin flees to Finland.
7/21/1917	Alexander Kerensky replaces Prince Lvov as prime minister.
7/25/1917	At the request of Russian generals, the Provisional Government reinstitutes the death penalty for deserters and for those soldiers mutinying at the front.
8/1/1917	General Lavr Kornilov takes over command of the Western Front.
9/6/1917–9/13/1917	General Kornilov, who claims to be acting with the consent of the Provisional Government, announces his plans to take control of Petrograd from the socialists. This is known as the Kornilov Affair.
9/14/1917	Kerensky declares Russia a republic, forms a five-person Directory, and serves as the head of this politically weak body.
9/14/1917–9/17/1917	Over 700,000 railway workers strike across Russia. Several senior Bolshevik leaders are released from prison.
10/4/1917	The Provisional Government convenes a conference with all political parties in order to address the crisis. The Bolsheviks walk out of the conference, and this will lead to the October Revolution.
10/23/1917	The Petrograd Soviet creates the Military Revolutionary Committee to help fight the uprising that the Bolshevik Central Committee claimed was "inevitable." The Bolshevik Party and the Petrograd Soviet begin a conference, where they will vote to seize power. This is the beginning of the October Revolution, which will end with the Bolshevik takeover of Russia.
11/1/1917	Ukraine declares it independence. In elections for the third Constituent Assembly, Social Revolutionaries make up the largest bloc.
11/5/1917	The Provisional Government tries to shut down Bolshevik presses, leading to a confrontation with the Military Revolutionary Committee.
11/7/1917	Lenin declares that the Bolsheviks successfully took power of Russia and orders work to begin establishing the Soviet government.
11/7/1917	The Military Revolutionary Committee detains members of the Provisional Government in the Winter Palace but does not arrest Kerensky, who left St. Petersburg.

11/17/1917	Lenin announces the Decree on Land, which calls for the elimination of private ownership, and the Decree on Peace, which calls for an immediate cease-fire and an end to the war.
11/18/1917	Lenin forms the first Council of People's Commissars (Sovnarkom) and issues the decrees on peace and land.
12/6/1917	Finland declares its independence from Russia.
12/20/1917	The Bolshevik government creates the Cheka to hunt down political enemies.
1/5/1918	First and last meeting of the Constituent Assembly.
1/10/1918	Cossacks form the Republic of the Don as their own independent state.
1/12/1918	Latvia declares its independence but is still occupied by German forces.
1/18/1918	The Bolsheviks walk out of the Constituent Assembly, the body charged with writing the new Russian Constitution. The Bolsheviks had demanded that authority should be in the soviets, where they were the majority power, instead of in the assembly, where the Bolsheviks were a minority party. The next day they close down the assembly and do not meet again.
1/19/1918	Bolsheviks use troops to force opponents to leave the Constituent Assembly.
1/22/1918	Ukraine leaves Russia.
1/28/1918	The Finnish Civil War begins after Finland declares its independence from Russia.
2/1/1918	The Bolsheviks begin mass conscription in Moscow and Petrograd.
2/2/1918	The Bolsheviks separate the Orthodox Church from the state, and this encourages pillaging and destruction of churches throughout Russia.
2/9/1918	The Central Powers and Ukraine sign the Brest-Litvosk Treaty, ending World War I for Ukraine.
2/10/1918	The Red Army is created. Trotsky also states that Russia is out of World War I.
2/11/1918	Cossack leader Alexei Kaledin commits suicide, and Pytor Krasnov assumes leadership of the Cossacks.
2/13/1918	Russia switches to the Gregorian calendar.
2/16/1918	Lithuania declares its independence from Russia.
2/18/1918	The Germans invade Russia after Trotsky walks out of peace talks. The Red Army occupies Kiev and will maintain its position until March 3, 1918, when the Germans drive the army out.

2/24/1918	Estonia declares its independence from Russia.
3/3/1918	The Treaty of Brest-Litovsk is signed by the Bolsheviks, and the Social Revolutionaries leave the government in protest. During this month, the Bolshevik government allows the Czechoslovak Legion to withdraw from Russia, but it does not do so. The Bolsheviks change the party's name to the Russian Communist Party.
3/12/1918	The Bolsheviks move the capital from Petrograd to Moscow.
3/13/1918	Leon Trotsky assumes the position of war commissar and head of the Red Army.
4/5/1918	British and Japanese forces land at Vladivostok.
4/8/1918	The Germans take Kharkov and Rostov.
4/13/1918	Kornilov, commander of the White Army, is killed in the Battle of Yekaterinodar. Anton Denikin assumes command of the White Army.
4/22/1918	Transcaucasia is created when the Transcaucasus region forms a union independent of Russia. This union will last approximately a month and dissolve on May 26, 1918.
5/1/1918	The Czech Legion mutinies against the Bolsheviks and seizes Russian territory. The Germans take the city of Sevestapol.
5/29/1918	Trotsky orders the Czechoslovak Legion to hand over its weapons. They refuse and capture the Trans-Siberian Railway. This move gains the support of the United States.
6/11/1918	Committees of the Poor Peasantry form.
6/23/1918	British troops arrive in Murmansk to support White forces against the Red Army.
6/28/1918	War communism begins. This economic system will last until 1921.
7/1/1918	President Wilson approves the deployment of 5,000 U.S. troops to aid the White forces against the Bolsheviks. First Constitution of the Russian Soviet Federated Socialist Republic.
7/6/1918	The Socialist Revolutionary Party assassinates the German diplomat Wilhelm von Mirbach-Harff. In addition to the assassination attempt, there is an uprising by the Social Revolutionaries to overthrow the Bolsheviks. This fails and leads to the elimination of the party as a viable political opponent.
7/10/1918	The Fifth All-Russian Congress of Soviets adopts the 1918 constitution of the Russian Soviet Federated Socialist Republics.

7/17/1918	The Bolsheviks kill Tsar Nicholas II and his family to ensure that approaching White Army forces will not be able to capture the royal family.
7/25/1918	The Czech Legion captures the city of Yekaterinburg.
8/2/1918	British and French forces land at Archangel.
8/5/1918	White forces from the People's Army and the Czech Legion capture Kazan. This opens the door for a possible assault on Moscow.
8/8/1918	The siege of Tsaritsyn begins and will last until January 1920. During this siege, according to Soviet sources, Joseph Stalin's actions protect and save the city.
8/11/1918	More Japanese forces land at Vladivostok.
8/13/1918	The Battle of Sviyazhsk is a victory for Trotsky and his Red Army.
8/30/1918	Fanya Kaplan attempts to assassinate Lenin. Moisei Uritsky, the head of the Petrograd Cheka, is killed in revenge for the violence committed by the Cheka.
9/1/1918	U.S. troops arrive in Vladivostok.
9/2/1918	The Bolshevik government creates the Revolutionary Military Council, and the Red Terror campaign of violence and suppression begins.
9/4/1918	U.S. forces join British troops in the city of Murmansk to provide support to White forces.
9/5/1918–9/10/1918	In the Battle of Kazan, the Red Army defeats the Whites, who are allied with the Czechs.
9/6/1918	Colonel Vatsetis assumes the position of supreme commander in chief of the Red Army.
9/22/1918	The Second Battle of Tsaritsyn begins and will continue until October 15, 1918. It is a part of a broader struggle for the city that will make Joseph Stalin a hero of the Soviet Union.
10/31/1918	Obligatory labor is introduced in the Soviet Union.
11/18/1918	Alexander Kolchak launches a successful coup and assumes command of the White Army forces.
1/1/1919	Estonia forces out all Red Army forces. Mandatory requisitioning of grain begins, which leads to unrest in the rural areas as the Bolsheviks takes peasants' harvests without compensation or regard for their material needs. The Menshevik Party is allowed to publish a newspaper, and the Bolshevik government recognizes the party as a legitimate political party.
1/3/1919	The Red Army invades Latvia.

1/4/1919	Red Army forces capture the city of Riga.
1/15/1919	Central Russian peasants stage uprisings against the Bolshevik government.
1/18/1919	The Versailles Peace Conference begins. The United States, France, Britain, and other allied nations will determine the terms of peace. The Bolshevik government does not participate due to its separate peace negotiations with Germany.
1/24/1919	Grand Prince Pavel Alexandrovich and other relatives of the tsar are killed by the Bolsheviks.
2/1/1919	The Cheka closes the Menshevik newspaper after it publishes critical writings about the Bolsheviks.
2/3/1919	Reds capture Kiev.
3/1/1919	The third Comintern meets to plan how to export the socialist revolution to other countries.
	Ambassador William Bullitt goes to Moscow and receives a Bolshevik peace proposal. However, the Allies do not accept the offer. Allied nations subsequently offer aid to White forces such as those commanded by Denikin and Kolchak.
3/2/1919	The first meeting of the Congress of Communist International convenes at the Kremlin.
3/22/1919	Hungary establishes its Bolshevik government. Sandor Garbai serves as president, and Bela Kun serves as foreign minister. This will last until August 1919, when the Bolsheviks fall and the Kingdom of Hungary is established.
3/23/1919	The Politburo Central Committee of Moscow is founded.
4/8/1919	Bolsheviks establish a government in Ukraine after they push White forces out of the country.
4/16/1919	General von der Goltz, a German officer, launches a coup in Latvia.
5/18/1919	Soviets declare war against Romania.
5/20/1919	This is the date of the farthest advance west made by Kolchak's White Army forces.
5/22/1919	Red Army forces capture Ufa, sending Kolchak's forces into retreat.
6/1/1919	Finland declares war on the Soviet Union. During this month U.S. troops on the Polar Bear mission will leave Russia.
8/1/1919	British troops leave Russia.
8/18/1919	Denikin's forces take Odessa, and by the end of the month White forces will occupy most of Ukraine.
9/1/1919	During this month, Denikin will advance down the Volga toward Moscow.

10/8/1919	Allies mandate that the Germans leave Latvia.
10/13/1919	White general Yudenich's offensive on Petrograd fails, and the tide turns in the Bolsheviks' favor.
11/1/1919	Red Army successes push Yudenich's forces into Estonia.
11/14/1919	Yudenich disbands his army.
12/17/1919	Grigory Semenov overthrows Kolchak as leader of the White forces in Siberia.
12/31/1919	By the end of 1919, the Soviet government wins the civil war against the Whites. There will be some small engagements but no realistic threats to the new Soviet state.
1/1/1920	U.S. forces withdraw from Siberia.
1/4/1920	Kolchak is in the custody of Bolshevik forces.
2/7/1920	The Bolsheviks execute Kolchak.
2/27/1920	The United States rejects a peace offer from the Soviets.
3/27/1920	General Pytor Wrangel assumes command of Denikin's forces.
4/28/1920	The Red Army takes the city of Baku in Azerbaijan, which then becomes a Soviet republic.
8/1/1920	Bolshevik officials attempt to requisition grain from the city of Kamenka. Bolshevik quota levels are too high for the people to meet, and they riot. This uprising is known as the Tambov Uprising and marks the inception of the Green Army.
10/1/1920	The Black Army signs a peace treaty with the Bolsheviks.
3/1/1921	Sailors revolt in Kronstadt.
3/16/1921	The Anglo-Soviet Trade Agreement is signed.
3/21/1921	Lenin's New Economic Policy is formally published.
3/26/1922	Lenin has his first stroke.
12/30/1922	Formal establishment of the Soviet Union.
3/9/1923	Lenin has his second stroke, which removes him from politics.

Bibliography

Books

Acton, Edward. *Rethinking the Russian Revolution.* London: Edward Arnold, 1990.

Andrew, Christopher, and Vasili Mitrokhin. *The Sword and the Shield: The Mitrokhin Archive and the Secret History of the KGB.* New York: Basic Books, 1999.

Anonymous. *Felix Dzerzhinsky: A Biography.* Translated by Natalia Belskaya. Moscow: Progress, 1988.

Anweiler, Oskar. *The Soviets: The Russian Workers, Peasants, and Soldiers Councils, 1905–1921.* Translated by Ruth Hein. New York: Pantheon Books, 1974.

Ascher, Abraham. *The Revolution of 1905: Russia in Disarray.* Stanford, CA: Stanford University Press, 1988.

Ascher, Abraham. *The Russian Revolution: A Beginner's Guide.* London: Oneworld, 2014.

Ascher, Abraham. *The Mensheviks in the Russian Revolution.* Ithaca, NY: Cornell University Press, 1976.

Avrich, Paul, and Petr Alekseevich Kropotkin. *The Anarchists in the Russian Revolution.* Ithaca, NY: Cornell University Press, 1971.

Bemporad, Elissa. *Becoming Soviet Jews: The Bolshevik Experiment in Minsk.* Bloomington: Indiana University Press, 2013.

Brinkley, George A. *The Volunteer Army and Allied Intervention in South Russia, 1917–1921: A Study in the Politics and Diplomacy of the Russian Civil War.* Notre Dame: University of Notre Dame Press, 1966.

Brovkin, Vladimir N. *The Mensheviks after October: Socialist Oppostion and the Rise of the Bolshevik Dictatorship.* Ithaca, NY: Cornell University Press, 1987.

Bunyan, James, Harold Fisher, and Frank A. Golder. *The Bolshevik Revolution, 1917–1918.* Stanford, CA: Stanford University Press, 1934.

Burbank, Jane. *Intelligentsia and Revolution: Russian Views of Bolshevism, 1917–1922.* New York: Oxford University Press, 1986.

Burbank, Jane, Mark Von Hagen, and A. V. Remnev. *Russian Empire: Space, People, Power, 1700–1930.* Bloomington: Indiana University Press, 2002.

Burdzhalov, Eduard Nikolaevich. *Russia's Second Revolution: The February 1917 Uprising in Petrograd.* Edited by Donald J. Raleigh. Bloomington: Indiana University Press, 1987.

Bushkovitch, Paul. *A Concise History of Russia.* Cambridge: Cambridge University Press, 2011.

Bushnell, John. *Mutiny Amid Repression: Russian Soldiers in the Revolution of 1905–1906.* Bloomington: Indiana University Press, 1985.

Carley, Michael Jabara. *Revolution and Intervention: The French Government and the Russian Civil War.* Kingston: McGill-Queen's University Press, 1983.

Carr, E. H. *The Bolshevik Revolution, 1917–1923,* Vol. 1. New York: Norton, 1985.

Carr, E. H. *The Russian Revolution: From Lenin to Stalin.* New York: Free Press, 1979.

Chamberlin, William H. *The Russian Revolution,* Vol. 1, *1917–1918: From Overthrow of the Tsar to the Assumption of Power by the Bolsheviks.* Princeton, NJ: Princeton University Press, 2014.

Cherniaev, V. William Rosenberg, and Edward Acton. *Critical Companion to the Russian Revolution, 1914–1921.* Bloomington: Indiana University Press, 1997.

Cohen, Stephen F. *Bukharin and the Bolshevik Revolution: A Political Biography, 1888–1938.* Oxford: Oxford University Press, 1980.

Copp, John Walter. *The Role of Anarchists in the Russian Revolution and Civil War, 1917–1921: A Case Study in Conspiratorial Behavior During Revolution.* Ann Arbor, MI: UMI, 1994.

Daniels, Robert V. *Red October: The Bolshevik Revolution of 1917.* New York: Scrinber, 1967.

Denikin, Anton Ivanovich. *The White Army.* Gulf Breeze, FL: Academic Press, 1973.

Dukes, Paul. *October and the World: Perspectives on the Russian Revolution.* New York: St. Martin's, 1979.

Dune, Eduard M. *Notes of a Red Guard.* Translated and edited by Diane P. Koenker and S. A. Smith. Urbana: University of Illinois Press, 1993.

Ferro, Marc. *October, 1917: A Social History of the Russian Revolution.* London: Routledge, 1980.

Fitzpatrick, Shelia. *The Russian Revolution.* 3rd ed. New York: Oxford University Press, 2008.

Forsyth, James. *The Caucasus: A History.* New York: Cambridge University Press, 2013.

Frankel, Jonathan, Baruch Knei-Paz, and Edith Rogovin Frankel. *Revolution in Russia: Reassessments of 1917.* Cambridge: Cambridge University Press, 1991.

Galili y Garcia, Ziva. *The Menshevik Leaders in the Russian Revolution: Social Realities and Political Strategies.* Princeton, NJ: Princeton University Press, 1989.

Gatrell, Peter. *Russia's First World War: A Social and Economic History.* Harlow, UK: Pearson/Longman, 2005.

Geifman, Anna. *Russia under the Last Tsar: Opposition and Subversion, 1894–1917.* Hoboken, NJ: Wiley-Blackwell, 1999.

Getzler, Israel. *Nikolai Sukhanov: Chronicler of the Russian Revolution.* New York: Palgrave, 2002.

Golubev, A., and Charles Berman. *The Civil War of 1918–1920.* Washington, DC: U.S. Army War College, 1935.

Gordon, Alban Godwin. *Russian Civil War: A Sketch for History.* London: Cassell, 1937.

Halfin, Igal. *Intimate Enemies: Demonizing the Bolshevik Opposition, 1918–1928.* Pittsburgh: University of Pittsburgh Press, 2007.

Haupt, Georges, and Jean-Jacques Marie. *Makers of the Russian Revolution: Biographies of Bolshevik Leaders.* Ithaca, NY: Cornell University Press, 1974.

Heenan, Louise Erwin. *Russian Democracy's Fatal Blunder: The Summer Offensive of 1917.* New York: Praeger, 1987.

Hosking, Geoffrey A. *The Russian Constitutional Experiment: Government and Duma, 1907–1914.* Cambridge: Cambridge University Press, 1973.

Julicher, Peter. *Renegades, Rebels, and Rogues under the Tsars.* Jefferson, NC: McFarland, 2003.

Kaiser, Daniel H. *The Worker's Revolution in Russia, 1917: The View from Below.* Cambridge: Cambridge University Press, 1987.

Katkov, George. *Russia, 1917: The Kornilov Affair; Kerensky and the Breakup of the Russian Army.* London: Longman, 1980.

Keep, John J. H. *The Russian Revolution: A Study in Mass Mobilization.* New York: Norton, 1976.

Kettle, Michael. *The Allies and the Russian Collapse, March 1917–March 1918.* Minneapolis: University of Minnesota Press, 1981.

Khodarkovsky, Michael. *Bitter Choices: Loyalty and Betrayal in the Russian Conquest of the North Caucasus.* Ithaca, NY: Cornell University Press, 2011.

Kipp, Jacob, Robert Baumann, and David Schimmelpenninck van der Oye. *Reforming the Tsar's Army: Military Innovation in Imperial Russia from Peter the Great to the Revolution.* New York: Cambridge University Press, 2004.

Kowalski, Ronald I. *The Bolshevik Party in Conflict: The Left Communist Opposition of 1918*. Pittsburgh: University Press of Pittsburgh, 1991.

Leggett, George. *The Cheka: Lenin's Political Police*. New York: Oxford University Press, 1981.

Lincoln, W. Bruce. *In War's Dark Shadow: The Russians before the Great War*. DeKalb: Northern Illinois University Press, 2003.

Lincoln, W. Bruce. *The Romanovs: Autocrats of All the Russias*. New York: Doubleday, 1981.

Lincoln, W. Bruce. *Passage through Armageddon: The Russians in War and Revolution, 1914–1918*. Oxford: Oxford University Press, 1994.

Lincoln, W. Bruce. *Red Victory: A History of the Russian Civil War*. New York: Simon and Schuster, 1989.

Lockwood, David. *Cronies or Capitalists? The Russian Bourgeoisie and the Bourgeois Revolution from 1850 to 1917*. Cambridge, UK: Scholarly Publishing, 2009.

Luckett, Richard. *The White Generals: An Account of the White Movement and the Russian Civil War*. New York: Viking, 1971.

Malet, Michael. *Nestor Makhno in the Russian Civil War*. New York: Palgrave Macmillan, 1982.

Manning, Roberta Thompson. *The Crisis of the Old Order in Russia: Gentry and Government*. Princeton, NJ: Princeton University Press, 1982.

Marot, John Eric. *The October Revolution in Prospect and Retrospect: Interventions in Russian and Soviet History*. Boston: Brill, 2012.

Mawdsley, Evan. *The Russian Civil War*. Edinburgh, UK: Birlinn, 2000.

Mazour, Anatole Gregory. *The First Russian Revolution, 1825: The Decembrists Movement, Its Origins, Development, and Significance*. Berkeley: University of California Press, 1937.

McCauley, Martin. *Octobrist to Bolshevik: Imperial Russia, 1905–1917*. London: Edward Arnold, 1984.

McCauley, Martin. *The Russian Revolution and the Soviet State, 1917–1921: Documents*. New York: Barnes and Noble, 1975.

McMeekin, Sean. *The Russian Origins of the First World War*. Cambridge, MA: Belknap, 2011.

McNeal, Robert H. *Tsars and Cossacks, 1885–1914*. New York: St. Martin's, 1987.

Mel'gunov, Sergei Petrovich. *The Bolshevik Seizure of Power*. Santa Barbara: ABC-CLIO, 1972.

Moss, Kenneth B. *Jewish Renaissance in the Russian Revolution*. Cambridge, MA: Harvard University Press, 2009.

Patenaude, Bertrand M. *Trotsky: Downfall of a Revolutionary*. New York: HarperCollins, 2009.

Perrie, Maureen. *The Agrarian Policy of the Russian Socialist-Revolutionary Party from its Origins through the Revolution of 1905–1907*. New York: Cambridge University Press, 1976.

Peters, Victor. *Nestor Makhno*. Winnipeg: Echo Books, 1971.

Pinchuk, Ben-Cion. *Octobrists in the Third Duma, 1907–12*. Seattle: University of Washington Press, 1974.

Pipes, Richard. *A Concise History of the Russian Revolution*. New York: Knopf, 1996.

Pipes, Richard. *Russia under the Bolshevik Regime*. New York: Vintage Books, 1995.

Pipes, Richard. *Russia under the Old Regime*. New York: Scribner, 1974.

Price, Morgan Philips. *Dispatches from the Revolution: Russia, 1916–1918*. Edited by Tania Rose. Durham, NC: Duke University Press, 1997.

Radkey, Oliver H. *The Sickle and the Hammer: The Russian Socialist Revolutionaries in the Early Months of Soviet Rule*. New York: Columbia University Press, 1963.

Radkey, Oliver H. *The Unknown Civil War in Soviet Russia: A Study of the Green Movement in the Tambov Region, 1920–1921*. Palo Alto, CA: Hoover Institution Press, 1976.

Rawson, Donald C. *Russian Rights and the Revolution of 1905*. Cambridge: Cambridge University Press, 1995.

Riasanovsky, Nicholas. *A History of Russia*. 6th ed. Oxford: Oxford University Press, 2000.

Romanov, Olga Nikolaevna. *The Diary of Olga Romanov: Royal Witness to the Russian Revolution; With Excerpts from Family Letters and Memoirs of the Period.* Edited by Helen Azar. Yardley, UK: Westholme, 2013.

Rosenberg, William G. *Liberals in the Russian Revolution: The Constitutional Democratic Party, 1917–1921.* Princeton, NJ: Princeton University Press, 1974.

Rupp, Susan Z. "The Struggle in the East: The Anti-Bolshevik Opposition of 1918." Ann Arbor, MI: Dissertation, 1994.

Ruthchild, Rochelle Goldberg. *Equality and Revolution: Women's Rights in the Russian Empire, 1905–1917.* Pittsburgh: University Press of Pittsburgh, 2010.

Sablinsky, Walter. *The Road to Bloody Sunday: The Role of Father Gapon and the Petersburg Massacre of 1905.* Princeton, NJ: Princeton University Press, 1998.

Sanborn, Joshua A. *Drafting the Russian Nation: Military Conscription, Total War, and Mass Politics, 1905–1925.* DeKalb: Northern Illinois University Press, 2003.

Schild, Georg. *Between Ideology and Realpolitik: Woodrow Wilson and the Russian Revolution, 1917–1921.* Westport, CT: Greenwood, 1995.

Schwarz, Solomon M. *The Russian Revolution of 1905: The Workers' Movement and the Formation of Bolshevism and Menshevism.* Chicago: Chicago University Press, 1967.

Service, Robert. *The Bolshevik Party in Revolution: A Study in Organizational Change.* London: Palgrave Macmillan, 1979.

Service, Robert. *Comrades! A History of World Communism.* Cambridge, MA: Harvard University Press, 2007.

Service, Robert. *Lenin: A Biography.* Cambridge, MA: Belknap, 2000.

Service, Robert. *Lenin: A Political Life,* Vol. 1, *The Strengths of Contradictions.* Bloomington: Indiana University Press, 1985.

Service, Robert. *Lenin: A Political Life,* Vol. 2, *Worlds in Collision.* Bloomington: Indiana University Press, 1991.

Service, Robert. *Lenin: A Political Life,* Vol. 3, *The Iron Ring.* Bloomington: Indiana University Press, 1995.

Service, Robert. *The Russian Revolution, 1900–1917.* 4th ed. London: Palgrave Macmillan, 2009.

Service, Robert. *Spies and Commissars: Bolshevik Russia and the West.* London: Macmillan, 2011.

Shearer, David R., and Vladimir Khaustov. *Stalin and the Lubianka: A Documentary History of the Political Police and Security Organs in the Soviet Union, 1922–1953,* New Haven, CT: Yale University Press, 2015.

Shulgin, V. V. *The Years: Memoirs of a Member of the Russian Duma, 1906–1917.* New York: Hippocrene Books, 1990.

Sisson, Edgar Grant. *One Hundred Red Days, 25 November 1917–4 March 1918: A Personal Chronicle of the Bolshevik Revolution.* New Haven, CT: Yale University Press, 1931.

Smele, Jonathan D. *The Russian Civil Wars, 1916–1926: Ten Years That Shook the World.* New York: Oxford University Press, 2016.

Smele, Jonathan D. *The Russian Revolution and Civil War, 1917–1921: An Annotated Bibliography.* London: Continuum, 2003.

Smith, Scott B. *Captives of Revolution: The Socialist Revolutionaries and the Bolshevik Dictatorship, 1918–1923.* Pittsburgh: University of Pittsburgh Press, 2011.

Stavrou, Theofanis George. *Russia under the Last Tsar.* Minneapolis: University of Minnesota Press, 1969.

Strachan, Hew. *The First World War.* New York: Penguin Books, 2004.

Strakhovsky, Leonid Ivan. *Intervention at Archangel: The Story of Allied Intervention and Russian Counter-Revolution in North Russia, 1918–1920.* New York: H. Fertig, 1970.

Suny, Ronald G. *The Soviet Experiment: Russia, the USSR, and the Successor States.* New York: Oxford University Press, 1998.

Suny, Ronald, and Arthur Adams. *The Russian Revolution and Bolshevik Victory: Visions and Revisions.* Lexington, MA: D. C. Heath, 1990.

Taylor, Brian D. *Politics and the Russian Army: Civil-Military Relations, 1889–2000.* New York: Cambridge University Press, 2003.

Trotsky, Leon, and Max Eastman. *The History of the Russian Revolution.* New York: Simon and Schuster, 1932.

Tucker, C. Robert. *The Lenin Anthology.* New York: Norton, 1975.

Tucker, C. Robert. *The Soviet Political Mind.* New York: Norton, 1971.

Tucker, C. Robert. *Stalin as Revolutionary, 1879–1929: A Study in History and Personality.* New York: Norton, 1974.

Tucker, C. Robert. *Stalin in Power: The Revolution from Above, 1928–1941.* New York: Norton, 1992.

Ulam, Adam B. *The Bolsheviks: The Intellectual and Political History of the Triumph of Communism in Russia.* New York: Collier, 1968.

Unterberger, Betty Miller. *American Intervention in the Russian Civil War.* Lexington, MA: Heath, 1969.

Vasilev, Aleksiei Tikonovich. *The Ochrana: The Russian Secret Police.* New York: Lippincott, 1930.

Vatlin, Alexander, and Larisa Malashenko. *Piggy Foxy and the Sword of Revolution: Bolshevik Self-Protraits.* New Haven, CT: Yale University Press, 2006.

Verner, Andrew M. *The Crisis of Russian Autocracy: Nicholas II and the 1905 Revolution.* Princeton, NJ: Princeton University Press, 1990.

Wade, Rex A. *Documents of Soviet History,* Vol. 1, *The Triumph of Bolshevism, 1917–1919.* Gulf Breeze, FL: Academic International Press, 1991.

Wade, Rex A. *Red Guards and Workers' Militias in the Russian Revolution.* Stanford, CA: Stanford University Press, 1984.

Weinberg, Robert. *The Revolution of 1905 in Odessa: Blood on the Steps.* Bloomington: Indiana University Press, 1993.

Weinberg, Robert, and Laurie Bernstein. *Revolutionary Russia: A History in Documents.* New York: Oxford University Press, 2011.

Wildman, Allan K. *The End of the Russian Imperial Army.* Princeton, NJ: Princeton University Press, 1980.

Wood, Alan. *The Origins of the Russian Revolution, 1861–1917.* London: Routledge, 1993.

Yarmolinsky, Avrahm. *Road to Revolution: A Century of Russian Radicalism.* New York: Macmillan, 1959.

Articles

Arslanian, Artin H., and Robert L. Nichols, "Nationalism and the Russian Civil War: The Case of Volunteer Army-Armenian Relations, 1918–20." *Soviet Studies* 31(4) (1979): 559–573.

Avrich, Paul. "The Anarchists in the Russian Revolution." *Russian Review* 26(4) (1967): 341–350.

Avrich, Paul. "Russian Anarchists and the Civil War." *Russian Review* 27(3) (1968): 296–306.

Basil, John D. "Russia and the Bolshevik Revolution." *Russian Review* 27(1) (1968): 42–53.

Brainerd, Michael C. "The Octobrists and the Gentry in the Russian Social Crisis of 1913–14." *Russian Review* 38(2) (1979): 160–179.

Brovkin, Vladimir. "Workers' Unrest and the Bolsheviks' Response in 1919." *Slavic Review* 49(3) (1990): 350–373.

Brown, Stephen. "Communists and the Red Cavalry: The Political Education of the Konarmiia in the Russian Civil War, 1918–20." *Slavonic and East European Review* 73(1) (1995): 82–99.

Carr, E. H. "The Origin and Status of the Cheka." *Soviet Studies* 10(1) (1958): 1–11.

Chamberlin, William Henry. "The First Russian Revolution." *Russian Review* 26(1) (1967): 4–12.

Cole, G. D. H. "The Bolshevik Revolution." *Soviet Studies* 4(2) (1952): 139–151.

Edelman, Robert. "The Russian Nationalist Party and the Political Crisis of 1909." *Russian Review* 23(1) (1975): 22–54.

Figes, Orlando. "The Red Army and Mass Mobilization during the Russian Civil War 1918–1920." *Past & Present,* no. 129 (1990): 168–211.

Figes, Orlando. "The Russian Revolution of 1917 and Its Language in the Village." *Russian Review* 56(3) (1997): 323–345.

Garcia, Ziva Galiliy. "Workers, Industrialists, and Mensheviks: Labor Relations and the

Question of Power in the Early Stages of the Russian Revolution." *Russian Review* 44(3) (1985): 239–269.

Goldenweiser, Nicholas. "Antecedents of the Russian Revolution." *American Political Science Review* 11(2) (1917): 383–385.

Havelock, H. "The Cossacks in the Early Seventeenth Century." *English Historical Review* 13(50) (1898): 242–260.

Iswolsky, Helene. "The Russian Revolution Seen from Paris." *Russian Review* 26(2) (1967): 153–163.

Keep, J. L. H. "Russian Social-Democracy and the First State Duma." *Slavonic and East European Review* 34(82) (1955): 180–199.

Kerensky, Alexander. "Russia on the Eve of World War I." *Russian Review* 5(1) (1945): 10–30.

Landis, Erik. "Who Were the Greens? Rumor and Collective Identity in the Russian Civil War." *Russian Review* 69(1) (January 2010): 30–46.

Lazarski, Christopher. "White Propaganda Efforts in the South during the Russian Civil War, 1918–19 (The Alekseev-Denikin Period)." *Slavonic and East European Review* 70(4) (1992): 688–707.

Levin, Alfred. "The Russian Voter in the Elections to the Third Duma." *Slavic Review* 21(4) (1962): 660–677.

Loukianov, Mikhail. "Conservatives and 'Renewed Russia,' 1907–1914." *Slavic Review* 61(4) (2002): 762–786.

McDowell, Robert H. "Russian Revolution and Civil War in the Caucasus." *Russian Review* 27(4) (1968): 452–460.

O'Rourke, Shane. "The Don Cossacks during the 1905 Revolution: The Revolt of Ust-Medveditskaia Stanitsa." *Russian Review* 57(4) (1998): 583–598.

Pares, Bernard. "The Second Duma." *Slavonic Review* 2(4) (1923): 36–55.

Putnam, George. "P. B. Struve's View of the Russian Revolution of 1905." *Slavonic and East European Review* 45(105) (1967): 457–473.

Raun, Toivo U. "The Revolution of 1905 in the Baltic Provinces and Finland." *Slavic Review* 43(3) (1984): 453–467.

Rendle, Matthew. "Conservatism and Revolution: The All-Russian Union of Landowners, 1916–18." *Slavonic and East European Review* 84(3) (2006): 481–507.

Rendle, Matthew. "The Officer Corps, Professionalism, and Democracy in the Russian Revolution." *Historical Journal* 51(4) (2008): 921–942.

Richards, Michael, and Michael B. Share. "The Making and Remaking of the Russian Working Class, 1890–1917." *Journal of Social History* 21(4) (1988): 781–792.

Ryan, James. "'Revolution Is War': The Development of the Thought of V. I. Lenin on Violence, 1899–1907." *Slavonic and East European Review* 89(2) (2011): 248–273.

Sanders, Jonathan. "Lessons from the Periphery: Saratov, January 1905." *Slavic Review* 46(2) (1987): 229–244.

Seregny, Scott J. "A Different Type of Peasant Movement: The Peasant Unions in the Russian Revolution of 1905." *Slavic Review* 47(1) (1988): 51–67.

Shulgin, V. "The Months before the Russian Revolution." *Slavonic Review* 1(2) (1922): 380–390.

Smith, Jay C. "The Russian Third State Duma: An Analytical Profile." *Russian Review* 17(3) (1958): 201–210.

Stein, Sarah Abrevaya. "Faces of Protest: Yiddish Cartoons of the 1905 Revolution." *Slavic Review* 61(4) (2002): 732–761.

Suny, Ronald Grigor. "Toward a Social History of the October Revolution." *American Historical Review* 88(1) (1983): 31–52.

Suny, Ronald Grigor. "Violence and Class Consciousness in the Russian Working Class." *Slavic Review* 41(2) (1983): 436–442.

Thatcher, Ian D. "The St Petersburg/Petrograd Mezhraionka, 1913–1917: The Rise and Fall of a Russian Social Democratic Workers' Party Unity Faction." *The Slavonic and East European Review* 87(2) (2009): 284–321.

Tokmakoff, George. "P. A. Stolypin and the Second Duma." *Slavonic and East European Review* 50(118) (1972): 49–62.

Tschebotarioff, Gregory P., "The Cossacks and the Revolution of 1917." *Russian Review* 20(3) (1961): 206–216.

von Laue, T. H. "Count Witte and the Russian Revolution of 1905." *American Slavic and East European Review* 17(1) (1958): 25–46.

von Mohrenschildt, Dimitri. "The Early American Observers of the Russian Revolution, 1917–1921." *Russian Review* 3(1) (1943): 64–74.

Weinberg, Robert. "The Politicization of Labor in 1905: The Case of Odessa Salesclerks." *Slavic Review* 49(3) (1990): 427–445.

Zuckerman, Fredric S. "Political Police and Revolution: The Impact of the 1905 Revolution on the Tsarist Secret Police." *Journal of Contemporary History* 27(2) (1992): 279–300.

Editors and Contributors

Editors

Dr. Gates M. Brown
Assistant Professor of Military History
U.S. Army Command and General Staff
College

Dr. Sean N. Kalic
Professor of Military History
U.S. Army Command and General Staff
College

Contributors

John Beatty
Independent Scholar

Walter F. Bell
Independent Scholar

**Kevin S. Bemel, Rabbi, LCDR, CHC
USNR**
Director
Center for the Study of Everyday Life

Dr. Gates M. Brown
Assistant Professor of Military History
U.S. Army Command and General Staff
College

Dr. Dino E. Buenviaje
Visiting Assistant Professor
Riverside Community College District

Pamela L. Bunker
Senior Officer
Counter-OPFOR Corporation

Dr. J. David Cameron
Associate Professor of History
Southeast Missouri State
University

Dr. Charles M. Dobbs
Department of History
Iowa State University

Dr. Timothy C. Dowling
Associate Professor of History
Virginia Military Institute

Thomas Edsall
School of Journalism
Columbia University

David Elliott
Associate Professor of History
Santa Barbara City College

Dr. Arthur T. Frame
Professor of Operational Warfare
Department of Joint and Multinational
Operations
U.S. Army Command and General Staff
College

Dr. John C. Fredriksen
Independent Scholar

Dustin Garlitz
University of South Florida

John G. Hall
Independent Scholar

Dr. William Head
Historian
Warner Robins Air Logistics Center Office
of History
U.S. Air Force

Dr. Jonathan M. House
Professor of Military History
U.S. Army Command and General Staff
College

Dr. John M. Jennings
Department of History
U.S. Air Force Academy

Dr. Sean N. Kalic
Professor of Military History
U.S. Army Command and General Staff
College

Dr. Łukasz Kamieński
Associate Professor
Department of International and Political
Studies
Jagiellonian University in Krakow

Raymond D. Limbach, MA
Pritzker Military Museum and Library
American Military University

Andrew McCormick
Independent Scholar

Stephen McLaughlin
Independent Scholar

Joseph D. Montagna
Virginia Military Institute

Dr. Carolyn Neel
Assistant Professor of History
Arkansas Tech University

Steven J. Rauch
Command Historian
U.S. Army Signal Center at Fort
Gordon

Dr. Annette Richardson
University of Alberta

Dr. Margaret Sankey
Department of History
Minnesota State Moorhead

Dr. Claude R. Sasso
William Jewell College

Stephen T. Satkiewicz
Independent Scholar

Mark Schwartz
Communications Officer
George Mason University Libraries

Dr. Michael Share
Department of History
University of Hong Kong

Daniel Siegel
Independent Scholar

Colonel Robert J. Smith Jr.
Academic Instructor
Air Command and Staff College

Dr. Paul J. Springer
Professor, Comparative Military
Studies
Air Command and Staff College

Dr. Christopher H. Sterling
School of Media and Public Affairs
George Washington University

Dr. Eva-Maria Stolberg
Lecturer
Institute of Russian History

Dr. Yoneyuki Sugita
Professor of History
Osaka University, Japan

Dr. Pascal Trees
University of Bonn

Dr. Spencer C. Tucker
Senior Fellow
Military History, ABC-CLIO, Inc.

Dr. Andrew Jackson Waskey
Social Science Division
Dalton State College

Tim J. Watts
Content Development Librarian
Kansas State University

Dr. Hedley P. Willmott
Honorary Research Associate
Greenwich Maritime Institute

Dr. Tim Wilson
U.S. Nuclear Regulatory Commission

About the Editors

Sean N. Kalic, PhD, is a professor of military history in the Department of Military History at the U.S. Army Command and General Staff College, where he has taught since 2004. He specializes in Cold War history and the history of terrorism. Kalic's numerous contributions to major publications include "Post Cold War Conflicts" in *The Handbook of American Military and Diplomatic History, 1865 to the Present;* "Eisenhower" in *Generals of the Army: Marshall, MacArthur, Eisenhower, Arnold, Bradley;* "Terrorism in the Twenty-First Century: A New Era of Warfare" in *An International History of Terrorism: Western and Non-Western Experiences;* "Framing the Discourse: The Rhetoric on the War on Terrorism," in *Legacies of the Cold War;* and *US Presidents and the Militarization of Space, 1946–1967,* which was recognized by *CHOICE* as an Outstanding Academic Title in 2012. Kalic is the editor of *Thinking about War and Peace: Past, Present and Future.*

Gates M. Brown, PhD, is an assistant professor of military history at the U.S. Army Command and General Staff College at Fort Leavenworth, Kansas. His main research focus is the early Cold War period with a particular focus on U.S. nuclear and defense policy. Brown earned his doctorate from the University of Kansas. He served in the U.S. Army and deployed in support of Operation IRAQI FREEDOM.

Index

CPSIA information can be obtained
at www.ICGtesting.com
Printed in the USA
LVHW061928190421
684915LV00006B/204

9 781440 850929